DT 107.82 L53 1998 c. 2

The Society of the
MUSLIM BROTHERS
in Egypt

D1615747

To Merethe

The Society of the
MUSLIM BROTHERS
in Egypt

The Rise of
an Islamic
Mass Movement
1928–1942

Brynjar Lia
Foreword by Jamal al-Banna

THE SOCIETY OF THE MUSLIM BROTHERS IN EGYPT
THE RISE OF AN ISLAMIC MASS MOVEMENT 1928–1942

Ithaca Press is an imprint of Garnet Publishing Limited

Published by
Garnet Publishing Limited
8 Southern Court
South Street
Reading
RG1 4QS
UK

Copyright © Brynjar Lia 1998

All rights reserved.
No part of this book may be reproduced in any form or by
any electronic or mechanical means, including information
storage and retrieval systems, without permission in writing
from the publisher, except by a reviewer who may quote
brief passages in a review.

First Hardback Edition 1998
First Paperback Edition 2006

ISBN-13: 978-0-86372-314-8
ISBN-10: 0-86372-314-4

British Library Cataloguing-in-Publication Data
A catalogue record for this book is available from the British Library

Jacket design by Garnet Publishing
Typeset by Samantha Abley

Printed in Lebanon

Contents

Acknowledgements

This study is a product of two years of research in Cairo between 1993 and 1995, sponsored by the Norwegian Research Council and the Sasakawa Young Leader Fellowship Fund. I am grateful for their generous financial support. I would like to express my sincerest gratitude to Professor Ole Kristian Grimnes and Assistant Professor Bjørn Olav Utvik for their unfailing support and encouragement. I would also like to thank Professor Rauf Abbas who assisted me in Cairo and Professor Amira Sonbol of Georgetown University who chaired our panel on political memoirs at the British Society for Middle Eastern Studies Conference at Durham University in 1995. I am most grateful to my friend and colleague Abd al-Rahim Hallaj who assisted me during my research at the Egyptian National Archives in the spring of 1995. I also wish to extend my gratitude to Åge Røisli, Brit Røisli and James Whidden for their linguistic assistance. Finally, I am greatly indebted to Jamal al-Banna, a prominent Islamist writer and the brother of the late Hasan al-Banna, founder of the Society of the Muslim Brothers. His generous help and support and, not least, his unique recollections have been essential in carrying out this study.

Brynjar Lia

Abbreviations

IJMES	*International Journal of Middle East Studies*
JIM	*Jaridat al-Ikhwan al-Muslimin* (newspaper of the Muslim Brothers)
JIMY	*Jaridat al-Ikhwan al-Muslimin al-Yawmiyya* (daily newspaper of the Muslim Brothers)
MIA	Maktab al-Irshad al-'Amm (the highest executive body of the Muslim Brothers)
Mudh.	*Mudhakkirat al-da'wa wa al-da'iya* (memoirs of the call and the preacher, i.e. the memoirs of Hasan al-Banna)
SSME	Security Summary Middle East
YMMA	Young Men's Muslim Association

Note on Transliteration

No diacritical marks are used, though the letter ʻ*ayn* is represented by an opening quotation mark and the *hamza* by a closing quotation mark. Names and words which are familiar in English retain their English form; for example, Ismailia, Port Said, Cairo, Alexandria, Pasha and Effendi (not *Basha* and *Affandi*).

Foreword

I was very happy to meet Brynjar Lia because I discovered in him a serious researcher who perseveres in getting to the truth that is beyond common knowledge. Perhaps his steadfast pursuit of true knowledge was the reason why he was anxious to be in contact with me and to become familiar with the sources which I have at my disposal. I believe that the truth is the property of everyone, and that no one should keep it as a hidden treasure. I have therefore shared with him my feelings and thoughts in the course of five long meetings; I have answered his questions and have invited him to study many documents from the al-Banna family archive, documents which are either unpublished or no longer possible to acquire.

I think the work which Brynjar Lia has written about the Society of the Muslim Brothers between 1928 and 1942 distinguishes itself from other works in two respects. Firstly, it deals thoroughly with all that has been written so far about the movement (as can be seen from his list of references) and, more importantly, with new information the author has unearthed from private sources. This makes his study far more comprehensive and original than other works on the subject. Secondly, his work is characterized by strict impartiality as reflected in his conclusions which are clearly based on facts and events and not on preconceived ideas or prejudgements that have seriously tarnished many other books about the movement.

Although I believe that the present study will fill an important gap in our knowledge of the Society of the Muslim Brothers, I feel there is room for further research, particularly of the kind undertaken by Dr Lia. I hope that his future works will cast an ever-widening circle of light on a subject of great historical and contemporary importance.

Jamal al-Banna
Cairo, Egypt

Introduction

The renewed interest in Islamism has drawn much attention to the first modern Islamic mass movement, the Society of the Muslim Brothers (*Jam'iyyat al-Ikhwan al-Muslimun*), which was founded in Ismailia in Egypt in 1928 and emerged as a new force in Egyptian politics towards the end of the 1930s. Though the Society is usually considered the mother organization of all modern Islamist movements, the number of studies on the early history of the Muslim Brothers in Western languages has been surprisingly limited. It might well be that after Richard P. Mitchell's outstanding work, *The Society of the Muslim Brothers*, many scholars assumed that there was not much new to add to the early history of the Society. Since its publication in 1969, this book has been considered the definitive work on the Muslim Brothers. Mitchell spent several years in Egypt and regularly attended the meetings of the Muslim Brothers for over one and a half years in the early 1950s. Apart from being very well-informed through his personal contacts with prominent Brothers, he was also the first Western scholar to draw heavily upon Arabic primary sources.

Mitchell's study stated that at the outbreak of the Second World War the Muslim Brothers had developed from a local religious benevolent society into a significant political force:

> From these modest beginnings, which did not especially distinguish it from the many religious societies which throve in the capital, the Society of the Muslim Brothers grew, by the outbreak of the second world war, into one of the most important political contestants on the Egyptian scene. Its membership became so diversified as to be virtually representative of every group in the Egyptian society.[1]

However, this dramatic transformation of a peripheral Islamic welfare society into what became the largest political grass-roots movement in modern Egyptian history received only scant attention in Mitchell's study. Mitchell only allotted around 20 pages to the history of the Society of the Muslim Brothers prior to 1940, although this is universally accepted as its formative period.[2] The overwhelming part of Mitchell's study deals with the Muslim Brothers in the latter half of the 1940s and the

1950s. This gap in the historiography of the Muslim Brothers has been commented on by several scholars. Marius Deeb has pointed out: "Mitchell's analysis . . . lacks historical perspective, that is, it does not show the changes which took ·place since its [the Society of Muslim Brothers] foundation in the late 1920s to the late 1930s."[3]

This book will seek to describe and explain the rise of the Society from its founding in 1928 until the first repression of the movement in the autumn of 1941. As this is a broad topic, the following limitations will be imposed. First, while the Society's ideology will be analysed in order to understand its contribution to the rise of the movement and its appeal among segments of the Egyptian population, no attempt will be made to undertake a comprehensive analysis of all aspects of the Society's ideology. There are a number of reasons for this approach. A significant part of Hasan al-Banna's political and religious thinking, which subsequently came to be the Society's official ideology, was written and published in the 1940s and is thus outside our period of study. In other words, the Society's ideology was of a fairly rudimentary nature during most of the 1930s. A relatively limited emphasis on the importance of ideology in describing the rise of the Society can also be justified by the fact that there existed in this period a few Islamic associations, youth movements and a political party which appealed to the same groups as the Muslim Brothers, and propagated, at least in certain periods, a similar ideology. None of them, however, experienced an expansion comparable to that of the Muslim Brothers. While not denying the importance of ideology, it seems appropriate to look for characteristics and qualities other than just ideological particularities when searching for the reasons behind the Society's remarkable expansion in the 1930s. Another limitation made in this study is the relatively brief treatment of the socio-economic and cultural factors which created propitious conditions for the rise of the Muslim Brothers. Earlier studies have stressed factors like deteriorating socio-economic conditions, widening class differences, large-scale rural emigration to cities, unemployment among the rapidly growing educated middle class, the process of Westernization and secularization, the inertia of the religious establishment and the presence of a colonial power. While fully acknowledging the importance of all of these factors, this study will focus more on the actor than the structure in an attempt to fill the gap in previous studies which have failed to explain how the movement managed to exploit the favourable societal conditions in the 1930s for the building of a mass movement. Thus the emphasis will be on organization, internal structure, modes of action, methods of recruiting, reform programmes, ideological appeal and class interests of the members, rather than on the general societal setting.

Western and Egyptian Historiography on the Muslim Brothers

Apart from Mitchell's work, the existing literature on the Muslim Brothers in Western languages is confined to a few early works based on a much narrower range of sources than Mitchell's study. In addition, a number of smaller studies have explored certain aspects of the Society. The earliest Western work on the Muslim Brothers was a privately published book by J. Heyworth-Dunne dating from 1950. The author was a British convert to Islam who lived in Egypt for more than twenty years and produced several studies on Islamic associations for the British Embassy in Cairo. Besides being an eyewitness to the social and political environment that shaped the Muslim Brothers, he was heavily involved in some of the secret contacts between the British and the Brothers during the Second World War.[4] His book is characterized by many astute observations, and it fully acknowledges the social and economic crisis, and the political and religious vacuum that constituted the background for the emergence and success of the Muslim Brothers. While most of Heyworth-Dunne's work was primarily based on non-Arabic sources and his own experiences in the British Intelligence Service, the translation of Ishaq Musa Husayni's study published in 1956 filled an important gap by providing new empirical material from Arabic sources and added a new dimension by offering a perspective sympathetic to the Muslim Brothers.[5] When explaining the growth and expansion of the Society, Husayni suggested a number of internal factors, such as its tightly-knit organization and the charisma of their leader, Hasan al-Banna. He especially underlined the popular appeal of the Muslim Brothers' ideology, for instance Hasan al-Banna's ability to "compromise between socialism and religion". Furthermore, the Muslim Brothers' unwavering anti-imperialist stance and rejection of party politics were seen as important factors behind their success.[6]

A study from 1964 by an American researcher, Christina P. Harris, put heavy emphasis on the "stern anti-Westernism", "fanaticism" and "xenophobia" of the Society.[7] This was evidently the traditional view of the Muslim Brothers in the 1950s and 1960s. Acknowledged scholars like Manfred Halpern and Nadav Safran saw the rise of the Muslim Brothers as an expression of anti-Westernism and violent Muslim reactionism, strongly inspired by fascist leanings and bred by socio-economic stress.[8] This was also the common wisdom upon which Mitchell based his work, although he significantly modified the views of his mentors. In the 1960s, Islamism was essentially seen as a transitional phenomenon and a waning force. Mitchell wrote in his introduction: "Secular reform nationalism now in vogue in the Arab world will continue to operate to end the earlier appeal of this organization."[9] He was influenced by the orientalist traditions of H. A. R. Gibb who saw the Muslim Brothers as a force "gravitating towards the exclusivism and rigidity of the Hanbalite school". The Muslim Brothers, according to Gibb, represented the absolutist and totalitarian idea that "the mind and wills of men can [not only] be dominated by force, but that the truth can be demonstrated by the edge of the sword." This spirit of self-righteousness and intolerance, or in Mitchell's words "the sense of mission", precipitated violence. This "convulsive image of conservative radicalism . . . will probably remain the image of the Society of the Muslim Brothers", he concluded.[10]

Following Mitchell's study very little was published in Western languages about the history of the Muslim Brothers for more than a decade. It was not until the 1980s that a number of new studies on the early history of the movement appeared. For instance, the Brothers' active involvement in the Palestine Revolt in the late 1930s was examined,[11] and more light was shed on the composition of the Society's support base. There now appears to be a general consensus that the middle and lower echelons of the educated urban middle class formed the basis of the movement, not the workers, the peasants or the urban lumpenproletariat.[12] Hasan al-Banna's autobiography, which has so far been the only source on the birth of the Society, has been the subject of closer scrutiny in two studies.[13] The ideology of the Muslim Brothers in the pre-revolutionary period has received most attention, especially their conception of the West and of nationalism.[14] It seems clear that studies of the Society's ideology have dominated at the expense of works on its organizational structure, its social and political activities and its programmes for reform.

An attempt to examine the Society's organization in the 1930s was made by Deeb, but his brief study was seriously flawed by its lack of primary sources.[15] A number of studies have dealt with the Brothers indirectly, such as Ahmad 'Abdalla's work on the student movement in Egyptian politics, and Charles Tripp's Ph.D. thesis on Ali Mahir Pasha and the Palace between 1936 and 1942.[16] The Society's relationship with minorities and aspects of its social work have been briefly examined.[17] While these works fill some gaps in our knowledge of the Muslim Brothers, they nonetheless suffer from limitations, either because their main focus is not the Muslim Brothers, or because they have focused too narrowly on textual analysis of ideology. The Society's professed commitment to work, action and deeds, not to intellectual exercises, suggests that studies based solely on the Society's ideological tracts will fail to capture the essential nature of the movement. Only a broader study which includes the Society's political activities, organization and patterns of recruitment, will provide a thorough understanding of the factors behind the rise of the Society.

In contrast to Egyptian historiography, there has been little debate about the study of the Muslim Brothers in Western historiography. Although some of the views held by Egyptian leftist historians have been echoed in the writings of Western scholars, no general debate about the role of the Muslim Brothers in modern Egyptian history has taken place.[18] The output of literature on the Brothers in Western languages is small compared to the outpouring in Arabic. The publication of memoirs by Muslim Brother veterans has been prodigious ever since the late President Anwar Sadat's political liberalization in the mid-1970s and the veiled support given to moderate Islamists to balance the influence of leftist dissidents. These factors created a political climate in which the Brothers were no longer considered an anathema. Several dozen memoirs dealing with the movement have appeared. The most important of these is Mahmud Abd al-Halim's *The Muslim Brothers: Events that Created History*.[19] The author was an active member from the mid-1930s, and the first volume of his memoirs has been an important source of information for this study. Other sources worth mentioning are the memoirs of Abbas al-Sisi, Shaykh Ahmad Hasan al-Baquri, Umar al-Tilmisani and Muhammad Hamid Abu al-Nasr, all of whom became active members of the Muslim Brothers in the early or mid-1930s.[20] These and similar memoirs by veteran Brothers were written in response to the picture of the Society painted during the Nasser era when it was portrayed as a revolutionary terrorist organization attempting to violently overthrow the new regime in order to establish a reactionary state.

The Society's military wing, the notorious 'Special Section', has been the single most popular topic in the literature on the Egyptian Muslim Brothers. The memoirs of Mahmud al-Sabbagh, Ahmad Adil Kamal, Salah Shadi, Hasan Ashmawi, and Husayn Hammuda represent the Brothers' own accounts.[21] The main purpose of these memoirs was to refute allegations of blind violence and terrorism raised against the "Special Section". A comprehensive work by the Egyptian historian Abd al-Azim Ramadan, *The Muslim Brothers and the Secret Apparatus*, represents the traditional view of the present regime.[22] The discussion has been dominated by the question of whether the Muslim Brothers' military wing was engaged in terrorism against "patriotic Egyptians" or whether they were waging a war of liberation against "the foreign imperialists and their local lackeys". Although the answer to this question is of fundamental importance to the status and legitimacy of the movement today, the preoccupation with it has diverted attention away from many other and, at least for an historian, more important aspects of the Society. Unfortunately, the present political climate in Egypt does not encourage new and unorthodox approaches to the study of the Muslim Brothers. Academic studies on the Society have instead become ammunition to be used in the current confrontation between the government and the Islamists.[23]

A dominant theme in works on the Muslim Brothers by Egyptian leftist historians is the Society's relationship with the Palace, especially in the latter half of the 1930s and in the immediate postwar period. Egyptian politics in the late 1930s was characterized by an intensifying struggle between the largest political party, the Wafd Party, and the Palace. The strongman of Egyptian politics at that time, the Royal Councillor Ali Mahir Pasha, is said to have devised a strategy to use the Muslim Brothers to undermine the Wafd's popularity as the only political party with a mass following. By imbuing the young King Farouq with an "Islamic image", centred on the Caliphate title and the King's piety, the Royal Councillor hoped to protect the King's autocratic prerogatives against the democratically elected Wafdist government. In 1937, the Muslim Brothers made an oath of allegiance on the Qur'an to the King in front of Abdin Palace on the day of the King's coronation. The Society is also stated to have participated vigorously in the disturbances in late 1937 which toppled the Wafdists and brought a pro-Palace government to power. Thus, according to the Egyptian leftist historians Rif'at al-Sa'id and Tariq al-Bishri, the Muslim Brothers aligned themselves with the autocratic and "fascist forces" of the Palace, which aimed to destroy the "democratic forces" as represented by the Wafd Party.[24]

The Society's alleged alliance with the Palace and the reactionary forces is closely linked to another important theme in the Egyptian historiography on the Muslim Brothers: their alleged betrayal of the revolution. This was the official view of the Muslim Brothers held by the Nasser regime following its suppression of the Society in 1954. Among other things, it was alleged that the Muslim Brothers were staging a counter-revolution in alliance with the British. These ideas were adopted by prominent Egyptian historians, such as Tariq al-Bishri and Rif'at al-Sa'id from the leftist camp and Abd al-Azim Ramadan from the Wafd.[25] They were influenced by ideas from the leftist and communist movements after the Second World War which portrayed the Muslim Brothers as "fascists" aiming to destroy the nationalist movement and divert the anti-imperialist struggle by religious propaganda.[26] The Brothers' insistence on the application of Islamic laws and the politicization of religion was seen by these historians as a "manipulation of general discontent and perplexity by the propagation of simple solutions in a language which appealed to the people's religious sentiments".[27] According to them, the essential features of the political programme of the Muslim Brothers was vagueness, "obscurity" (*ghumud*) and the mixing of religious and political terms in such a way as to prevent a clear and rational analysis of the socio-economic contradictions and inequalities of Egyptian society.[28]

Against this background of scathing criticism of the Muslim Brothers by prominent Egyptian historians, it is astonishing to read the introduction to the second edition of Tariq al-Bishri's *The Political Movement in Egypt 1945–1952*, which has been viewed as a masterpiece of Egyptian history writing. Al-Bishri conceded in his new introduction that he had judged the Muslim Brothers unfairly by evaluating the Society not on its own terms but from the perspective of the leftist and communist movements in the 1940s. He stressed the need for a re-evaluation of the history of the Muslim Brothers. He argued that the Society's main objective was to struggle against the process of secularization and Westernization which cut Egypt off from her historical roots and accentuated class differences by separating the impoverished masses from a Westernized élite. The Muslim Brothers were the only political movement at that time to fully grasp the importance of fighting the cultural imperialism of the West, which was represented by Western education and the raising of a Westernized élite in the service of imperialism. Al-Bishri argued that his generation of historians erroneously equated secularization, nationalism and progress, thereby neglecting the struggle for ideological independence and the retention of Egypt's historical heritage as represented by Islam. The Western legal system introduced by the Capitulations and Mixed Courts was regarded by al-Bishri as unfit for Egyptian society, due to the chasm between Western law codes and Egyptian customs and values. Islamic laws could have met the Egyptian society's need for indigenous laws. However, al-Bishri argued that the Muslim Brothers' struggle against secularism could not justify their role in supporting the Palace-sponsored minority governments in the late 1930s and the 1940s. He concluded that both former and contemporary adversaries of the Muslim Brothers should reconsider their opposition to the Muslim Brothers. At the same time, he urged the Brothers to admit their past mistakes.[29] On the whole, al-Bishri's re-evaluation must be seen in connection with the numerous "defections" of leading Marxists and leftists to the Islamist camp in recent decades.[30] Leftists turning Islamists reflect a general disillusionment with the ideologies of socialism and secularism of the Nasserite era which failed to produce the desired progress.[31]

Apart from trying to reconcile the leftists and Islamists, al-Bishri's reappraisal of the role of the Muslim Brothers points to some fresh approaches. The Brothers' struggle against the process of secularization and Westernization must be seen in the context of the accentuating class differences in Egyptian society and the separation of the impoverished masses from a wealthy and Westernized élite. Al-Bishri identified the Muslim Brothers as "a popular political current" (*tayar siyasi sha'bi*), emphasizing the fact that more than any other contemporary political group, the Society could, by virtue of its mass following, claim to speak on behalf of a large section of the Egyptian people, especially the lower middle class.[32] Secondly, the Muslim Brothers' demand for the replacement of Western legal systems with Islamic laws might be seen as part of a programme for national and cultural liberation and for a modernity which was rooted in a native and authentic belief-system. In this sense the Muslim Brothers can be defined as an integral part of the national movement, instead of being considered its adversary.

The class perspective has been further elaborated by Hasan al-Banna's youngest brother, Jamal al-Banna, who is still a prominent Egyptian Islamist writer. In a recent study, *The Responsibility for the Failure of the Islamic State,* he identified the class composition of the Muslim Brothers as the most serious threat to the ruling aristocracy in pre-revolutionary Egypt. The Wafd Party claimed to speak on behalf of the masses, but only the upper classes and the wealthy dominant families were brought into the decision-making process in the party. The Muslim Brothers, by contrast, brought lower-class elements into leading positions in their organization:

> I think this was the Muslim Brothers' largest sin in the eyes of the Egyptian political community. The Brothers put carpenters, peasants, primary school teachers and minor functionaries in leading positions in political work and encouraged them to compete with Egypt's Pashas.[33]

Thus, the Society represented a truly popular force, not only because of its mass following but also because of the non-élite character of its leadership. These ideas have been important for this study.

The most detailed and thorough study of the Muslim Brothers' involvement in politics in the 1930s and 1940s can be found in Zakariyya Sulayman Bayumi's *The Muslim Brothers and the Islamic Associations in the Egyptian Political Life, 1928–1948.*[34] This is one of the few comprehensive and academic studies on the Muslim Brothers by Egyptian historians. It includes many critical reflections, especially on the autocratic leadership of Hasan al-Banna. Bayumi argues that the lack of democracy in the Society and Hasan al-Banna's autocratic leadership were serious flaws in the organization. As a result, the Society was weakened by numerous defections and crises. Bayumi partly accepted the criticism by leftist historians of "obscurity" and the lack of a well-defined political programme, and ascribed this to the Brothers' relationship with the Palace. This in combination with the general political circumstances of the time prevented the Muslim Brothers from developing "a modern applied theory for economic and social life, and a comprehensive educational programme". However, Bayumi underlined the importance of the Brothers' commitment to "the principle of totality of Islam". Their understanding of Islam enabled them to present interpretations compatible with the requirements of the time, and more important, to launch a "revolution against the passivity" of the official Islam of al-Azhar and the popular Islam of the Sufi orders. Bayumi placed much emphasis on the "moderateness" (*i'tidal*) of the Muslim Brothers, in contrast to the "extremist" secessionist group Muhammad's Youth (Shabab Muhammad) which broke from the Muslim Brothers in 1939-40. He further argued that the Muslim Brothers' condemnation of the party system of the pre-revolutionary era did not represent a total rejection of democracy as such. The demand for a one-party system was based on the need to establish a common front against imperialism.

While Bayumi was willing to accept the contention that the Muslim Brothers lacked a clear political programme and that this led to the charges of "obscurity", a young Muslim Brother sympathizer of the 1990s, Ibrahim Bayumi Ghanim, produced the first comprehensive study on Hasan al-Banna's political thinking with a view to refuting this assertion.[35] His analysis, *The Political Ideology of Imam Hasan al-Banna*, has been a valuable source of information to this study.[36] Ghanim deplored the lack of thorough studies on al-Banna's political thinking, illustrated by the fact that many researchers confined their study to *A Collection of Tracts by the Martyr Imam Hasan al-Banna*, which constitutes only a small part of al-Banna's production.[37] In his study, Ghanim drew upon the extensive writings of Hasan al-Banna published by the Muslim Brothers' press from 1933 to 1948. He discerned in al-Banna's writing a "complete Islamic alternative", characterized by its firmness in opposing the secularist and Western model adopted by the Egyptian élite.[38] He identified the political system as envisaged by al-Banna to be based on the unity of power without any division between the civil and religious powers, but still essentially different from the theocratic state of the European Middle Ages. Al-Banna accepted the constitutional and representative system as the political system closest to his vision of an Islamic state. However, he rejected the necessity of pluralism of parties. A political opposition was to be permitted within certain limits, but its role was to be different from that in the Western democratic system: it was to be limited to consultation and not to attainment of power unless the present regime forfeited its legitimacy. Finally, when an Islamic government had gained power in Egypt, it should expand its cooperation with other Muslim countries with a view to founding a 'League of Islamic Nations' which would subsequently appoint a Caliph, thereby re-establishing the Caliphate.[39]

Despite the bulk of Egyptian literature on the Muslim Brothers, the translation of Mitchell's work is used frequently as a reference in Egyptian as well as in Western historiography. Recalling what has been already stated above about Mitchell's superficial treatment of the early history of the Society, it is obvious that there is still a dearth of academic works on the Muslim Brothers. This is particularly pronounced in the early period of the Muslim Brothers' history and can be illustrated by the unfounded speculation about one of the most fundamental questions arising out of the early years of the Society: what caused the remarkable growth and expansion of the Society during the 1930s? Rif'at al-Sa'id, whose main objective apparently was to prove the Muslim Brothers' dependence on the Palace and Palace politicians, claimed that under Palace protection "during a year or two [1937–8] the number of branches of the Society doubled ten times".[40] Another Egyptian author noted that during the war years the Society's alliance with the Wafd Party facilitated the Society's greatest leap forward. From being a "traditional Islamic association . . . the Muslim Brothers grew under Wafdist protection into a political mass movement".[41] Gershoni, an Israeli historian who studied the Society's involvement in the Zionist–Arab conflict in Palestine, observed "an impressive increase in the number of branches" as a result of the Society's successful "exploitation of the pro-Palestine campaign as a material and ideological springboard for domestic expansion".[42] It appears to be a general tendency to reduce the rise of the Muslim Brothers to one or a few external factors. This trend has also been noticed in the literature on modern Islamism and on the exaggerated focus on Saudi oil money and financial support from abroad.[43] The continuous appeal of the ideas of the Muslim Brothers and their endurance despite recurring cycles of harsh repression strongly suggest that these and other external factors alone are insufficient to understand the rise of the Society.

Sources and New Theoretical Perspectives

Since Mitchell published his study in 1969, a wide range of new sources has been made available. These sources include the War Office and the Foreign Office files in the Public Record Office, and the 'Abdin files and security reports from the Egyptian National Archives (Dar al-Watha'iq). As has been shown above, there has also been a prodigious output of memoirs by Muslim Brother veterans in the 1970s and 1980s. The publication of two collections of Hasan al-Banna's personal letters written between 1926 and 1941 also supplies valuable new information. More important, a significant number of unpublished and hitherto unknown documents from the 1930s and early 1940s have been made available to me. These documents are internal publications which were distributed among the Muslim Brothers. They are of immeasurable value and give a unique insight into the internal life of the Society and shed new light on a number of crucial events in the Society's early history. Our main source is, however, the Society's newspaper from the 1930s. Its weekly reports of meetings, recruiting trips, ideological and religious articles, information to the members and so on, are the pillars of this study. All these sources combined have enabled the exploration of the characteristics of the Society in the 1930s in significantly more detail than previous studies.

Apart from the availability of new sources, new theoretical approaches to Islamism have been important for this study. Early studies on the Muslim Brothers had an almost unilateral focus on stern anti-Westernism, Muslim reactionism and rigid "Hanbalism" which were stated to breed violence and aggression.[44] Recent Western studies on Islamist movements have given more consideration to its modernizing and progressive aspects. Islamist associations have been described as a modern political force calling upon Islam to be the moral cement of societies which have suffered from centuries of misrule, corruption and oppressive regimes. Islamist movements have also been interpreted in the context of a struggle for cultural independence through reconnecting with an indigenous system of references.[45] Islamism has been studied in terms of the class interests of an educated middle class while its most radical manifestations have been seen as a way of expressing the resentment and antagonism felt by the poor and oppressed masses towards the well-to-do and more Westernized élite.[46] The traditional and often heard thesis that the increasing Westernization and secularization in Egypt in the first half of this century provoked a reactionary Muslim backlash, resulting in the emergence of Islamic fundamentalism in the form of the Muslim Brothers, has been successfully challenged. Eric Davis succinctly points out that such ideational models fail to explain why some Muslims are attracted to Islamic political movements while others are not, and he argues that the declining economic situation of young members of the educated middle class was an important factor behind Islamic activism.[47] However, as Ellis Goldberg has argued, the argument of socio-economic "pressure" makes less sense since members of radical Islamist groups were rarely recruited from the poorest and most dispossessed classes of society, nor were they social misfits economically alienated from society. Saad Eddin Ibrahim observed during his fieldwork among members of the radical Islamic groups of the 1970s, that they mostly came from stable and successful families, quite the opposite of the "alienated, marginal, anomic" individuals often presumed to be the basis for Islamist movements.[48] In addition, Goldberg suggests that the Islamic radicals "responded to the process of political centralization that enhanced the arbitrary political power of the political élite".[49] They were not "downwardly mobile, but the reverse", seeking to "find the concerted and methodical use of their talents rewarded".[50] The argument that the Islamists were a new, ambitious, self-conscious, upwardly mobile social group challenging the established political élite, supports the assertion that the rise of the first Islamist movement, the Muslim Brothers, represented a part of the rise of modern mass politics in Egypt. This took place during the 1930s and marked a watershed in modern Egyptian history. This decade saw the rise of the middle and working classes, diminishing the efficacy of traditional politics based on informal political patronage networks and clientalism, both in their limited élitist liberal form and in their more populist–nationalist Wafdist form. Other types of political organization were adopted by the rising classes,[51] and new mass parties emerged on the political scene in Egypt. The largest of these were the Muslim Brothers, representing a new political force based on ideological–political appeal and a mass organization.[52] All these new approaches have provided us with interesting ideas from which we have benefited greatly. I hope that our broad empirical study will provide a fresh approach to the debate on the rise of modern Islamism and contribute to a deeper understanding of Islamist movements in the Middle East.

NOTES

1 Richard Mitchell, *The Society of the Muslim Brothers* (London, Oxford University Press, 1969), p. 12.

2 *Ibid.*, pp. 9–27.

3 Marius Deeb, *Party Politics in Egypt: The Wafd and its Rivals 1919–1939* (London, Ithaca Press, 1979), p. 381. For a similar criticism, see Israel Gershoni, 'The Muslim Brothers and the Arab revolt in Palestine, 1936–1939', *Middle Eastern Studies*, vol. 22 (1986), pp. 367–8.

4 J. Heyworth-Dunne, *Religious and Political Trends in Modern Egypt* (privately published, 1950), pp. 38–9.

5 Ishaq Musa al-Husayni, *The Moslem Brethren: The Greatest of Modern Islamic Movements* (Beirut, Khayat's College Book Cooperative, 1956).

6 *Ibid.*, pp. 94–6.

7 Christina Phelps Harris, *Nationalism and Revolution in Egypt: The Role of the Muslim Brotherhood* (Stanford, CA, Hoover Institution Press, 1964), p. 172.

8 Nadav Safran, *Egypt in Search of a Political Community* (Cambridge, MA, Harvard University Press, 1961); Manfred Halpern, *The Politics of Social Change in the Middle East and North Africa* (Princeton, N.J., Princeton University Press, 1963).

9 Mitchell, *The Society of the Muslim Brothers*, p. xxiv.

10 *Ibid.*, pp. 320–31.

11 Abd al-Fattah El-Awaisi, 'The conceptual approach of the Egyptian Muslim Brothers towards the Palestine question, 1928–1949', *Journal of Islamic Studies*, vol. 2 (1991), pp. 225–44; James P. Jankowski, 'Egyptian responses to the Palestinian problem in the interwar period', *IJMES*, vol. 12 (1980), pp. 1–38; and Gershoni, 'The Muslim Brothers and the Arab revolt in Palestine', pp. 367–97. For the Muslim Brothers' participation in the Palestine War, see T. Mayer, 'The military force of Islam: the Society of Muslim Brethren and the Palestine question, 1945–1948' in E. Kedourie and S. G. Haim (eds.), *Zionism and Arabism in Palestine and Israel* (London, Frank Cass, 1982).

12 Eric Davis, 'Ideology, social classes and Islamic radicalism in modern Egypt' in S. Arjomand (ed.), *From Nationalism to Revolutionary Islam* (London and Albany, Macmillan and State University of New York Press, 1983). For the lack of support among Egyptian peasants, see Uri Kupferschmidt, 'The Muslim Brothers and the Egyptian village', *Asian and African Studies*, vol. 16 (1982), pp. 157–70.

For the Society's involvement in the Egyptian labour movement, see Joel Beinin and Zakariyya Lockman, *Workers on the Nile: Nationalism, Communism, Islam and the Egyptian Working Class 1882–1954* (London, I. B. Tauris, 1988); and Beinin, 'Islam, marxism and the Shubra al-Khayma textile workers: Muslim Brothers and Communists in the Egyptian trade union movement' and Ellis Goldberg, 'Muslim union politics in Egypt: two cases' both in E. Burke and I. Lapidus (eds.), *Islam, Politics and Social Movements* (Berkeley, CA, University of California Press, 1988).

13 Johannes J. G. Jansen, 'Hasan al-Banna's earliest pamphlet', *Die Welt des Islams*, vol. 32 (1992), pp. 254–8 and Brynjar Lia, 'Imposing on the past the order of the present: a critical analysis of Hasan al-Banna's autobiography: *Mudhakkirat al-da'wa wa al-da'iyah*' (paper presented at the British Society for Middle Eastern Studies (BRISMES) 1995 Annual Conference in Durham, UK).

14 Israel Gershoni, 'The emergence of pan-nationalism in Egypt: pan-Islamism and pan-Arabism in the 1930s', *Asian and African Studies*, vol. 16 (1982), pp. 59–94; Gershoni, 'Rejecting the West: the image of the West in the teaching of the Muslim Brothers 1928–1929' in Uriel Dann (ed.), *The Great Powers in the Middle East 1919–1939* (London, Holmes and Meier, 1988); Gershoni, 'Arabization of Islam: the Egyptian Salafiyya and the rise of Arabism in pre-revolutionary Egypt', *Asian and African Studies*, vol. 13 (1979), pp. 22–57; Zafar Ishaq Ansari, 'Contemporary Islam and nationalism: a case study of Egypt', *Die Welt des Islams*, vol. 7 (1961), pp. 3–38; Abdel Moneim Laban, 'Der Islamische Revivalismus – Ablauf der Bewegung der Moslem-Brüder', *Die Dritte Welt*, vol. 6, nos. 3–4 (1978); A. Z. al-Abdin, 'The political thought of Hasan al-Banna', *Hamdard Islamicus Pakistan*, vol. 11 (1988), pp. 55–70; Abd al-Monein Said Aly and Manfred Wenner, 'Modern Islamic reform movements: the Muslim Brotherhood in contemporary Egypt", *Middle East Journal*, vol. 36 (1982), pp. 336–61; Francis Bertier, 'L'Idéologie politique des Frères Musulmans', *Orient*, vol. 8 (1958), pp. 43–57; Ilysa Ade Bello, 'The Society of the Moslem Brethren. An ideological study', *al-Ittihad*, vol. 17 (1980), pp. 45–56; Sylvia Haim, 'The principles of Islamic government', *Die Welt des Islams*, vol. 5 (1958), pp. 245–53; Said Bensaid, 'Al-watan and al-umma in contemporary Arab use' in Ghassan Salamé (ed.), *The Foundation of the Arab State* (London, Croom Helm, 1987); and Ahmad S. Mousalli, 'Hasan al-Banna's Islamist discourse on constitutional rule and Islamist state', *Journal of Islamic Studies*, vol. 4 (1993), pp. 161–74.

15 Marius Deeb, *Party Politics in Egypt*, pp. 379–88.

16 Ahmad Abdalla, *The Student Movement and National Politics in Egypt* (London, Al-Saqi Books, 1985) and Charles Tripp, 'Ali Maher and Palace politics 1936–1942' (Ph.D. thesis, University of London, 1984).

17 Gudrun Krämer, *The Jews in Modern Egypt 1914–1952* (Seattle, University of Washington Press, 1989); Barbara L. Carter, *The Copts in Egyptian Politics 1919–1952* (London, Croom Helm, 1985); and Nancy Elizabeth Gallagher, *Egypt's Other Wars: Epidemics and the Politics of Public Health* (Cairo, AUC Press, 1993).

18 The views of Egyptian leftist historians like Rif'at al-Sa'id that the Muslim
    Brothers represented a kind of fascism have been adopted in a number of Western
    studies. See Maxime Rodinson, *Marxism and the Muslim World* (London, Zed
    Publications, 1979) and Halpern, *The Politics of Social Change in the Middle East
    and North Africa.*

19 Mahmud 'Abd al-Halim, *al-Ikhwan al-Muslimun: Ahdath sana'at al-tarikh. Ru'ya
    min al-dakhil* (Alexandria, Dar al-Da'wa, 1979).

20 'Abbas al-Sisi, *Fi qafilat al-Ikhwan al-Muslimin* (Alexandria, Dar al-Tiba'a wa
    al-Nashr wa al-Sawtiyyat, 1986); Ahmad Hasan al-Baquri, *Baqaya dhikriyat*
    (Cairo, Markaz al-Ahram, 1988); 'Umar al-Tilmisani, *Dhikriyat la mudhakkirat*
    (Cairo, Dar al-Tawzi' wa al-Nashr al-Islamiyya, 1985); and Muhammad Hamid
    Abu al-Nasr, *Haqiqat al-khilaf bayn al-Ikhwan al-Muslimin wa 'Abd al-Nasir*
    (Cairo, International Press, 1987). For other memoirs by Muslim Brother veterans,
    see Ahmad al-Bass, *al-Ikhwan al-Muslimun fi rif Misr* (Cairo, Dar al-Tawzi' wa
    al-Nashr al-Islamiyya, 1987); Ahmad al-Tahir Makki, 'Hasan al-Banna kama
    'ariftuhu: sura insaniyya ba'ida 'an al-siyasa', *al-Duha*, no. 115, 1405/1985,
    pp. 100–5; D. Mahmud 'Assaf, *Ma'a al-Imam al-Shahid Hasan al-Banna*
    (Cairo, Maktabat 'Ayn Shams, 1993); Sa'id Hawwa, *Hadhihi tajrubati wa hadhihi
    shahadati* (Beirut, Dar 'Ammar, 1988); Hasan Dawh, *Alam wa amal fi tariq
    al-Ikhwan al-Muslimin* (Cairo, Dar al-I'tisam, 1989); Farid 'Abd al-Khaliq,
    al-Ikhwan al-Muslimun fi mizan al-haqq (Cairo, Dar al-Sahwa, 1987); and 'Abd
    al-Mon'em 'Abd al-Ra'uf, *Arghamtu Faruq 'ala al-tanazul 'an al-'arsh: mudhakkirat
    'Abd al-Mon'em 'Abd al-Ra'uf* (Cairo, al-Zahra' lil-I'lam al-'Arabi, 1988).

21 Mahmud al-Sabbagh, *Haqiqat al-tanzim al-khass wa dawruhu fi da'wat al-Ikhwan
    al-Muslimin* (Cairo, Dar al-I'tisam, 1989); Ahmad Kamal 'Adil, *al-Nuqat fawq
    al-huruf: al-Ikhwan al-Muslimun wa al-Nizam al-Khass* (Cairo, al-Zahra' lil-I'lam
    al-'Arabi, 1986); Salah Shadi, *Safahat min al-tarikh: hassad al-'umr* (Kuwait City,
    Sharikat al-Shi'a', 1981); Hasan 'Ashmawi, *al-Ayyam al-hasima wa hassaduha: janib
    min qissat al-'asr* (Cairo, Dar al-Tawzi wa al-Nashr al-Islamiyya, 1991) and
    Hassad al-ayyam wa mudhakkirat harib: janib min qissat al-'asr (Cairo, Dar al-Fath,
    1992); and Husayn Muhammad Ahmad Hammuda, *Asrar harakat al-Dubbat
    al-Ahrar wa'l-Ikhwan al-Muslimun* (Cairo, al-Zahra' lil I'lam al-'Arabi, 1985).

22 'Abd al-'Azim Ramadan, *al-Ikhwan al-Muslimun wa al-tanzim al-sirri* (Cairo,
    Maktabat Madbuli, 1985).

23 Brynjar Lia, 'The use of history in Egyptian party politics', *Midtøsten Forum*,
    vol. 2 (1995), pp. 38–43.

24 Rif'at al-Sa'id, *Hasan al-Banna: mata, kayfa wa li-madha?* (Cairo, Maktabat
    Madbuli, 1977), pp. 106–7 and Tariq al-Bishri, *al-Haraka al-siyasiyya fi Misr
    1945–1952* (Cairo, Dar al-Tawzi' wa al-Nashr al-Islamiyya, 1972), pp. 46–8.

25 See Roel Meijer, 'Contemporary Egyptian historiography of the period 1936–
    1952: a study of its scientific character' (MA thesis, University of Amsterdam,
    1985), pp. 132–51.

26 See especially Muhammad Hasan Ahmad, *al-Ikhwan al-Muslimun fi'l-mizan* (Cairo,
    Matba'at al-Akha', n.d.) and Meijer, 'Contemporary Egyptian historiography of
    the period 1936–1952', pp. 132–4.

27 Meijer, 'Contemporary Egyptian historiography of the period 1936–1952', p. 137.

28 *Ibid.*, p. 134.

29 al-Bishri, *al-Haraka al-siyasiyya fi Misr.* For a summary, see Meijer, 'Contemporary Egyptian historiography of the period 1936–1952', pp. 145–51.

30 In addition to al-Bishri, names like 'Adil Husayn, Khalid Muhammad Khalid and Muhammad 'Ammara should be mentioned in this connection. Al-Bishri's gradual conversion to Islamism has been related to the fact that he was born and raised in a family of prominent religious scholars at the al-Azhar University. See Dr 'Abd al-Mon'em Ibrahim al-Jami'i, *Ittijahat al-kitaba al-tarikhiyya fi tarikh Misr al-hadith wa'l-mu'asir* (Cairo, 'Ein lil-Dirasat wa'l-Buhuth al-Insaniyya wa'l-Ijtima'iyya, 1975), p. 140.

31 There are, however, marked differences between the "cultural Islam" (*al-Islam al-hadari*) of Tariq al-Bishri, 'Adil Husayn, Jalal Amin and others and the contemporary Muslim Brothers. The formers' aim seems to be to integrate Islam into a nativist, nationalist or culturalist world-view where politics and economics have some corporatist characteristics. The Brothers, on the other hand, are much more politically vocal in their demand for an Islamic state and the application of *Shari'a*. See Nazih Ayubi, *Political Islam: Religion and Politics in the Arab World* (London, Routledge, 1991), p. 69.

32 al-Bishri, *al-Haraka al-siyasiyya fi Misr*, p. 23.

33 Jamal al-Banna, *Mas'uliyyat fashl al-dawla al-islamiyya fi'l-'asr al-hadith wa buhuth ukhra* (Cairo, Maktabat al-Islam, 1993), p. 47.

34 Zakariyya Sulayman Bayumi, *al-Ikhwan al-Muslimun wa'l-jama'at al-islamiyya fi'l-hayah al-siyasiyya al-Misriyya 1928–1948* (Cairo, Maktabat al-Wahba, 1978).

35 Ibrahim Bayumi Ghanim was arrested by the police in the spring of 1995 in one of the Mubarak regime's most sweeping crackdowns on moderate Islamists. Journalists who attended the subsequent military court case against the Muslim Brothers reported that Ghanim's academic work on Hasan al-Banna had been the reason for his arrest. Ghanim was acquitted after four months in detention.

36 Ibrahim Bayumi Ghanim, *al-Fikr al-siyasi lil-Imam Hasan al-Banna* (Cairo, Dar al-Tawzi' wa al-Nashr al-Islamiyya, 1992). See p. 33 for the question of "obscurity".

37 *Ibid.*, pp. 30–1.

38 *Ibid.*, p. 509.

39 *Ibid.*, pp. 509–13.

40 Rif'at al-Sa'id, *Hasan al-Banna: Mata, kayfa wa li-madha?*, p. 110.

41 Salah 'Isa, 'al-Ikhwan al-Muslimun: ma'sat al-madi wa mushkilat al-mustaqbal' (Introduction to the Arabic translation of Richard Mitchell's *The Society of the Muslim Brothers*) in *al-Ikhwan al-Muslimun*, p. 23.

42 Gershoni, 'The Muslim Brothers and the Arab revolt in Palestine', pp. 381–2.

43 Richard P. Mitchell, 'The Islamic movement: its current condition and future prospects' in Barbara Stowasser (ed.), *The Islamic Impulse* (London, Croom Helm, 1987).

44 A notable exception is the brief treatment of the Muslim Brothers in Wilfred Cantwell Smith, *Islam in Modern History* (Princeton, N.J., Princeton University Press, 1957), pp. 156–60.

45 Bjørn Olav Utvik, 'Islamism: digesting modernity the Islamic way'.

46 Ayubi, *Political Islam*, p. 221 and Jaques Waardenburg, 'Islam as a vehicle of protest' in Ernest Gellner (ed.), *Islamic Dilemmas: Reformers, Nationalists and Industrialization* (Berlin, Mouton, 1985).

47 Davis, 'Ideology, social class and Islamic radicalism in modern Egypt'.

48 Saad Eddin Ibrahim, 'Islamic militancy as a social movement: the case of two groups in Egypt' in Ali E. Hillal Dessouki (ed.), *Islamic Resurgence in the Arab World* (New York, Praeger, 1982).

49 Ellis Goldberg, 'Smashing idols and the state: the Protestant ethic and Egyptian Sunni radicalism', *Comparative Study of Society and History*, vol. 33 (1991), p. 21.

50 *Ibid.*, p. 34.

51 Roel Meijer, 'The quest for modernity: secular liberal and left-wing political thought in Egypt, 1945–1958' (Ph.D. thesis, University of Amsterdam, 1995), p. 24.

52 Sami Zubaida, *Islam, the People and the State: Essays on Political Ideas and Movements in the Middle East* (London, I. B. Tauris, 1993).

PART I

—

THE FORMATION OF A COMMUNITY
1928–1931

1

Hasan al-Banna and the Birth of the Society of the Muslim Brothers

---

O ye Muslims! This is the period of formation. Form
yourselves, and the nation will be created!

Hasan al-Banna

There are many accounts of the birth of the Society of the Muslim
Brothers (Jam'iyyat al-Ikhwan al-Muslimin) in Ismailia in the late
1920s.¹ Yet all accounts so far have been based almost exclusively
on Hasan al-Banna's autobiography, *The Memoirs of the Call and the
Preacher*,² which appeared first in instalments in the Muslim Brothers'
daily newspaper in the second half of 1947.³ These memoirs were
written partly in response to a serious internal crisis which threatened
the unity of the movement at that time and became the official history
of the foundation and early years of the Society. However, as a historical
source they must be used with caution.⁴

The lack of material on the early history of the Muslim Brothers
has been deplored by many historians. The new sources which have
been made available to me represent, therefore, a considerable step
forward. The two most important of these are a collection of Hasan
al-Banna's letters to his father, compiled by his younger brother Jamal,
and a pamphlet, written by one of the secessionists who left the Society
in 1932.⁵ This material provides for the first time critical alternatives to
Hasan al-Banna's autobiography and it sheds new light on the Society's
early history. The new sources support to some extent Hasan al-Banna's
version of the founding of the Muslim Brothers. Furthermore, they show
that Hasan al-Banna's father had connections in influential Islamic circles
in Cairo which were important during the early years of the Society.
They also reveal that Hasan al-Banna had novel and unconventional views
on religious matters and that these views brought him into conflict with

the religious élite in Ismailia. More importantly, the new material provides fresh information about the first internal crisis in the movement in 1931–2, and indicates that this crisis had more far-reaching consequences than has been assumed in earlier studies. Finally, the view previously put forward that Hasan al-Banna developed "emotional xenophobia" against foreigners or the Western civilization can be dismissed. Western ideas and influences were not anathema to the Society in this period.

As Hasan al-Banna, the founder and leader of the Muslim Brothers until his assassination in 1949, had an enormous impact on the Society, a review of his family background, his early life and education is necessary in order to understand some of the elements that shaped the movement. This chapter will trace the life history of Hasan al-Banna up to the founding of the Society of the Muslim Brothers in Ismailia and the establishment of its first institutions between 1928 and 1931.

Hasan al-Banna's Family and Early Influences

Hasan al-Banna (1906–49) was the elder son of Shaykh Ahmad Abd al-Rahman al-Banna al-Sa'ati (1881–1958), a local *ma'dhun, imam*[6] and mosque teacher in the provincial town of al-Mahmudiyya, in the district of Rashid. Shaykh Ahmad al-Banna was widely respected for his religious learning and piety, although he had had only a limited formal education in Islamic sciences. In his youth he had left his home village of Shimshira (in al-Gharbiyya province) to study at the Ibrahim Pasha Mosque in Alexandria, an important mosque school which later became the Religious Institute of Alexandria. The young Shaykh divided his time between his studies in the mosque and his apprenticeship in Hajj Muhammad Sultan's shop where he learnt how to repair watches. Due to Hajj Muhammad Sultan's extensive connections in Islamic circles, his shop was a meeting-place for prominent Islamic scholars. At that time, the ideas of the new Salafiyya movement were eagerly debated. The Salafiyya was an Islamic reform movement initiated by Shaykh Muhammad 'Abduh and Jamal al-Din al-Afghani, which advocated renewal and reinterpretation (*ijtihad*) by returning to the pristine Islam of the Prophet and the first generation of Muslims. In these Islamic circles Shaykh Ahmad al-Banna made valuable contacts. In the years that followed he edited and wrote several books on Islamic traditions in cooperation with other Islamic scholars. He soon embarked upon the ambitious project of classifying the voluminous compilation of traditions of Imam Ahmad ibn Hanbal al-Shaybani. His work came to be known as *musnad al-fath al-rabbani*.[7] This was an extremely laborious task which demanded much of his time. He was in touch with influential Islamic scholars not only in Egypt but also in countries like Syria, Hijaz and Yemen. Shaykh al-Urfi, a Syrian scholar from Deir al-Zur, the prominent Islamic centre in Syria, assisted Shaykh Ahmad al-Banna with the *musnad al-fath al-rabbani* during his stay in Cairo (Shaykh al-Urfi had been exiled from Syria by the French but was allowed to return in the early 1930s).[8] Shaykh al-Banna's acquaintances in the Islamic circles in Cairo proved to be valuable contacts for his son Hasan when he came to Cairo in 1923.

Neither Shaykh Ahmad al-Banna nor his wife belonged to the wealthy aristocracy which dominated the economic and political life of pre-revolutionary Egypt. However, they owned some landed property and Hasan al-Banna's mother was said to be from an affluent family.[9] Shaykh Ahmad al-Banna's closest associates in al-Mahmudiyya were the village chief (*'umda*), some local notables (*a'yan*) and well-to-do merchants, and an Islamic scholar (*'alim*), all of whom could be considered among the local élite in the village. The fact that he was appointed a *ma'dhun* and *imam* signified a certain social standing. Even at a young age he had the honour of giving the opening sermon (*khutba*) in a newly built mosque in al-Mahmudiyya. In addition to his property and the salary from his office, Shaykh Ahmad al-Banna owned a shop where he repaired watches and sold gramophones to supplement his income.[10] Although the social and economic standing of the family elevated them above the masses of destitute farmers, artisans and petty traders of the village community, economic concerns were very much a part of their daily life. They were undoubtedly affected by the economic crisis that afflicted the peasantry in the 1920s. Several of Hasan al-Banna's letters to his father in the 1920s deal with the plight of their land tenants and their inability to pay rent. When the family moved to Cairo in 1924 they often faced acute financial problems due to the rising cost of living in the capital.[11] Yet Hasan al-Banna's parents were determined that their children should be provided with a proper education even if economic hardship forced Hasan al-Banna's mother to sell her gold necklaces and bracelets to provide the necessary money for her son's higher education. After Hasan al-Banna assumed his first position as a primary school teacher in Ismailia in 1927, his salary became an essential part of the family's income. He also took care of some of his younger brothers and sisters whom the family could not provide for in Cairo.

The situation of Hasan al-Banna's family is an illustrative example of the changing social and economic environment in Egypt during the 1920s and 1930s. Not only did the family experience leaving the village community, where they had enjoyed social prestige and respect, they also faced economic hardship and uncertainty in the rapidly changing capital where religious learning and piety no longer guaranteed social standing. Shaykh Ahmad al-Banna belonged to the upper echelons of the merchant–artisan class (*ashab al-mihan*), among whom the virtues of religious piety and Islamic learning were highly cherished. This class included many Islamic scholars of little formal learning who devoted their lives to traditional Islamic sciences and eked out a living by practising some kind of craft or petty trade. Many members of this heterogeneous class had a hard time adjusting to new competition from large-scale international commerce and industry. Shaykh Ahmad al-Banna himself gave up his business partly due to new technology and competition in Cairo.

The family's social standing and its financial problems are hardly touched upon at all in Hasan al-Banna's memoirs. Instead, these focus primarily on spiritual and religious aspects of his early years. One of his father's closest associates, the village teacher Shaykh Muhammad Zahran, seems to have had an important influence on him. Shaykh Zahran was an Islamic scholar of considerable learning. The fact that he edited the Islamic journal *al-Is'ad* indicates a social and religious standing considerably above the ordinary Qur'an reciters and mosque school (*kuttab*) teachers in the village community. However, neither Shaykh Zahran nor Shaykh al-Banna had studied at the prestigious al-Azhar University in Cairo and had thus not obtained the *al-'Alamiyya* degree which was the formal certificate of Islamic scholars (*'ulama*).

Hasan al-Banna attended the mosque school of Shaykh Zahran until he was twelve years old. In his memoirs Hasan praised the virtues of his teacher, especially "the spiritual harmony and emotional association" that Shaykh Zahran was able to generate with his students. The young Hasan was allowed to use the Shaykh's library of religious literature and to listen to the discussions of Shaykh Zahran and his circles of Islamic scholars.[12] These influences of religious learning and piety were reinforced at home where his father taught him aspects of Islamic sciences and introduced him to his extensive library of Islamic literature.[13] Thus, Hasan al-Banna grew up in an environment where Islamic learning and piety were central values. Some accounts of Hasan al-Banna have focused on Ibn Hanbal's *musnad al-fath al-rabbani* which his father classified and have deduced that this influence of puritanical "Hanbalite fundamentalism" was the all-important influence in his early life.[14] Such conclusions seem unfounded. His father edited several studies on Islamic law schools other than the Hanbali school. What seems to be more characteristic of Hasan al-Banna's early years is his wish to obtain an education other than that offered by the religious establishment of al-Azhar University and its provincial institutes. When by the age of twelve Hasan had still not memorized the whole of the Qur'an, his father had wanted him to continue at the mosque school or with a Qur'an memorizer (*hafiz al-Qur'an*).[15] But Hasan opposed his father's wish and was enrolled in the middle school instead. Shaykh Ahmad al-Banna had wished to see at least one of his sons become an Azhar-educated *'alim*, a wish that was never realized. His elder son chose the Primary Teachers' Training School at Damanhur instead of the Religious Institute in Alexandria. He completed his education at Dar al-'Ulum, a teacher training school which was considered to be less traditional and conservative than al-Azhar University.[16] His choice of education indicates an urgent desire to avoid the traditionalism and seclusion which were hallmarks of the Islamic establishment at that time.

In the atmosphere of piety and respect for Islamic learning in which Hasan al-Banna grew up, we can single out two important elements which influenced him in his youth. The first was Sufism and the other the nationalist fervour following the Egyptian uprising against the British in 1919. In his memoirs he recalls that as a twelve-year-old boy he was attracted to the *dhikr* ceremony of the al-Hassafiyya Sufi order, in which he later became a fully initiated disciple (*murid*).[17] In the following years he regularly attended the weekly *hadra* of the order and joined them at the house of a local shaykh where books on Sufism were studied. He also paid frequent visits to the tombs of the "friends of God" (*al-awliya*) of the Hassafiyya order. His spiritual attachment to Sufism occupies a dominant part of the description of his youth. He says that the Hassafi brethren influenced him immensely and during his time at the Primary Teachers' Training School in Damanhur he "was completely engrossed in prayers and devotion to mysticism".[18] It seems clear that Hasan al-Banna developed a strong spiritual and emotional inclination during his exposure to Sufism. Some elements from Sufism, especially the emotional relations between the Shaykh and his young disciples, subsequently became central parts of Hasan al-Banna's leadership of the Society of the Muslim Brothers (see Chapter 3).

Hasan al-Banna recalls in his memoirs that he and his friends sometimes went too far in their religious practices. They were often teased by their fellow students because of their religious zeal. His eagerness to propagate Islam often overwhelmed him and on several occasions his insistence on a correct observance of Islam brought him into conflict with his teachers. At the Damanhur school and later at Dar al-'Ulum he objected to the school uniforms because they were not in accordance with what he perceived as Islamic clothing.[19] His religious zeal, manifest in his excessive Sufi practices and in his desire to enforce moral correctness, is said to have come in part from the surplus energy created by his early puberty. These tendencies were later tamed by marriage and the wisdom of an adult.[20] Hasan al-Banna's experience of religious zeal and passion in his youth must have been of great value to him at later stages in the Society's history. In the late 1930s and 1940s one of his most difficult tasks was to restrain and control young zealots among the Muslim Brothers. The fact that the Society avoided complete repression in these years was due in no small measure to al-Banna's ability to calm his most ardent followers. Religious zeal and passion frequently became an outlet for young men's sexual frustrations in the years of their puberty. "Teenage" was not a recognized stage of life and the exploration of the male–female relationship was largely prevented by segregated schools and a strict moral code.[21] At later stages in the history of the Muslim Brothers, al-Banna paid much attention to Scout movements and athletics, which aimed to divert the youth from bodily desires and to channel their energies into beneficial activities for the Islamic call.

A crucial influence on Hasan al-Banna during the years of his intense preoccupation with Sufism was the Egyptian revolution of 1919. It broke out when Hasan was thirteen years old. Demonstrations erupted throughout Egypt and several years of political activism, nationalistic fervour and occasional disorder followed. In his memoirs al-Banna clearly recollects the British troops in his home town. He described his role as one of the student activists leading demonstrations in Damanhur, composing nationalistic poetry and even negotiating with the police who tried to disperse the crowd of demonstrators.[22] To most young men of al-Banna's generation the revolution of 1919 had a profound symbolic value. The young politicians of the 1930s were eager to claim a role in these glorious days of national struggle, even if they had only been pupils in primary or secondary school.[23] Whatever extra colouring Hasan al-Banna might have added to his role in these events, it seems likely that the nationalistic fervour of these years must have pushed him towards an activist commitment to religion, differing from the purely academic efforts of his father. This is supported by the fact that he began to establish and participate in various Islamic reform societies at this time.[24] His activities in these societies reveal some influence from the agitation and activism of the early 1920s. Hasan al-Banna and his brother, Abd al-Rahman, reportedly printed pamphlets on a home-made printing press. These pamphlets were posted on the walls of mosques and coffee-houses. The experience from these reform societies was further developed when Hasan al-Banna and his friends founded a new reform society, the Hassafi Welfare Society (Jamiyyat al-Hassafiyya al-Khayriyya), which he later came to see as the precursor of the Muslim Brothers. Its twofold aim was to build the moral character of the people and check the missionary activities of three young women from the Christian Biblical Mission who "were preaching Christianity in the guise of nursing, teaching embroidery work and providing asylum to orphan children".[25] Thus, Hasan al-Banna's early influences did not encompass the traditional seclusion and other-worldliness that were usually attributed to Sufism.

From Islamic Circles in Cairo to a Primary School in Ismailia

When Hasan al-Banna moved to Cairo in 1923 to continue his studies at Dar al-'Ulum, his perspective of the state of religion in Egyptian society was dramatically broadened. During his four years of studies in Cairo (1923–7) he was exposed to influences of secularism and Westernization which had been unknown to him in "the peaceful Egyptian country-side".[26] His description of his encounter with the Cairo of the 1920s has frequently been used to illustrate how he and the Muslim Brothers experienced the combined effect of Westernization and modernism in Egypt in this era. He writes:

> A wave of dissolution which undermined all firm beliefs, was engulfing Egypt in the name of intellectual emancipation. This trend attacked the morals, deeds and virtues under the pretext of personal freedom. Nothing could stand against this powerful and tyrannical stream of disbelief and permissiveness that was sweeping our country . . . Mustafa Kamal had announced the abolition of the Caliphate and separated the state from religion in a country which was until recently the site of the Commander of the Faithful [Amir al-Mu'minin]. The Turkish government proceeded rashly and blindly in this direction in all spheres of life . . . [In Cairo] it was thought that the Egyptian University could never be a secular university unless it revolted against religion and waged war against all social traditions which derived from Islam. The University plunged headlong after the materialistic thought and culture entirely taken over from the West . . . The foundations were laid for the "Democratic Party" which died before it was born and had no programme except that it called for freedom and democracy in the meaning these words had at that time: dissolution and libertinism . . . I saw the social life of the beloved Egyptian people, oscillating between her dear and precious Islam which she had inherited, defended, lived with during fourteen centuries, and this severe Western invasion which was armed and equipped with all destructive influences of money, wealth, prestige, ostentation, power and means of propaganda.[27]

Despite his virulent attacks on freethinking and immorality in Cairo in his memoirs, al-Banna seems to have been much more attracted to Cairo than the above passage indicates. Cairo had much more to offer him than the backwardness of the countryside. In one of his letters to his father written during a brief stay with his relatives in the village of Sandiyun, Hasan al-Banna complains about the clamour, overcrowdedness and uncleanliness of the village and has a burning desire to return to Cairo. Similarly, when he was appointed to a primary school in Ismailia after his graduation, he protested violently, having no wish to leave the capital.[28] In his memoirs he describes his life in Cairo in these words:

... a wonderful mixture of different activities: participating in the
Sufi gatherings [*hadra*] at the Hassafi Shaykh's house or at the
residence of Ali Effendi Ghalib, visits to the bookshop of Muhibb
al-Din al-Khatib [Maktabat al-Salafiyya] and visits to the house of
Rashid Rida and his Islamic journal *al-Manar*. I also used to go to
the house of Shaykh al-Dajawi and to Farid Bey Wajdi. Sometimes
I would spend time in the library Dar al-Kutub and sometimes on
the mats in Shaykhun Mosque.[29]

Al-Khatib, Rida, al-Dajawi and Wajdi were all prominent members of
the religious élite in Cairo. Ali Effendi Ghalib was the successor of the
Hassafi Shaykh to whom Hasan al-Banna had sworn allegiance when he
became an initiated member of the order. Being an *effendi* and at the
same time a Sufi shaykh was quite unusual and Hasan recalls how they
used to call him "Our Master the Effendi" (*sayyiduna al-affandi*) for
fun.[30]

In this period Hasan al-Banna established valuable connections
in Islamic circles in Cairo. Among these was the Islamic Society for
Nobility of Islamic Morals (Jamiyyat Makarim al-Akhlaq al-Islamiyya),
in which he continued to participate after he moved to Ismailia in
1927. More importantly, he made valuable contacts in those circles
from which the prestigious Young Men's Muslim Association (Jamiyyat
al-Shubban al-Muslimin, hereafter referred to as the YMMA) was founded
in November 1927.[31] Despite its name, this association was headed
by older eminent personages who played a significant role in culture,
religion and politics in Egypt, such as Dr Abd al-Hamid Saʻid, Shaykh
Abd al-Aziz Jawish, Ahmad Taymur Pasha, Muhammad al-Khidr Husayn,
Muhammad Abd al-Latif Diraz and Muhibb al-Din al-Khatib.[32] The
association included a member of parliament who represented the
Nationalist Party (al-Hizb al-Watani). In fact, the YMMA was stated to
be "an alumni club" for the Nationalist Party. This party was fervently
anti-British and rejected negotiations with the British as long as British
troops remained on Egyptian soil.[33] This uncompromising stance was
later maintained by the Muslim Brothers. The YMMA received generous
support from members of the royal family, especially Prince Umar
Tusun. It enjoyed high prestige in Egypt and in the Arab world where
it spread rapidly. In these prominent circles a provincial student would
not be accepted without some sort of introduction. However, Hasan
al-Banna was much aided by some of his father's acquaintances, especially

Muhibb al-Din al-Khatib and Farid Wajdi Bey. The former was one of the most prominent personalities in Islamic circles in Cairo. In addition to becoming the Secretary-General of the YMMA, he edited a number of Islamic journals, the most important of which was *Majallat al-Fath* (the conquest). Farid Wajdi was a close friend of Hasan al-Banna's father and gave him much support.[34] His residence was a meeting-place for prominent Islamic scholars and personalities. The same can be said about the publishing house of Muhibb al-Din al-Khatib, al-Maktabat al-Salafiyya.[35] Consequently, the young Hasan al-Banna was given ample opportunity to expand his personal connections in Islamic circles. The fruits of this patronage became evident some time after his graduation. At the age of 23 he was given the honour of delivering a speech at the Islamic New Year's Eve celebration in the YMMA in Cairo. Furthermore, al-Banna was given generous space for his articles in *Majallat al-Fath*, and during 1928-9 more than 15 of his articles were published in this journal.[36] His patron's publishing house also printed his first official pamphlet in 1929.[37] Upon al-Banna's graduation, Muhibb al-Din al-Khatib warmly recommended his young protégé for an assignment at the Religious Institute in Mecca in 1928. Even the head of the YMMA, Dr Abd al-Hamid Sa'id, intervened in favour of Hasan al-Banna's candidature. (These efforts came to nothing, presumably because of the lack of diplomatic recognition between Egypt and Hijaz at that time.) Thus, one may safely conclude that Hasan al-Banna had managed to make valuable connections in the Islamic circles in Cairo during his four years at Dar al-'Ulum. The patronage which he enjoyed was sufficiently strong to provide him essential support for the leadership of the future Society of the Muslim Brothers.

In 1927, Hasan al-Banna was appointed to a primary school in Ismailia. This provincial town was situated in the heartland of the foreign-dominated Canal Zone where the British had huge military bases. In addition, the administration of the British and French-owned Suez Canal Company was situated partly in Ismailia. The presence of large foreign colonies inevitably came to dominate the social and cultural life of the town. Apart from the ubiquity of the British presence, the enormous class differences separating, on the one hand, the foreign residents and upper-class Egyptians and, on the other, the poor native Egyptians, appear to have contributed to al-Banna's keen awareness of the socio-economic injustice inherent in Egyptian society. In 1928, in one of his earliest speeches in the YMMA club in Cairo, al-Banna harshly criticized the upper class. He addressed "the upper class and the wealthy" by a long recitation from the Qur'an:

> Behold, ye are those invited to spend (of your substance) in the way of God: but among you are some that are niggardly. But any who are niggardly are so at the expense of their own souls. But God is free of all wants, and it is ye that are needy. If ye turn back (from the path), He will substitute in your stead another people; then they would not be like you.[38]

As will be seen later, Hasan al-Banna recruited many of his earliest followers from the lower classes of society and entrusted them with leading positions in his organization.

There is, however, less basis for the claim that al-Banna developed a "stern anti-Westernism" during his formative years in Cairo and Ismailia. His anti-Westernism has been greatly exaggerated in Western works on the Muslim Brothers. The historian C. P. Harris put it that Hasan al-Banna spent his four years in Cairo "kindling his hostility to Westernizing influences". When al-Banna moved to Ismailia, Harris claimed, his "already kindled intellectual hostility to Western influence then [in Ismailia] became crystallized into emotional xenophobia".[39] However, at this time al-Banna did not advocate the total rejection of Western influences, nor did he display xenophobic tendencies towards Westerners.[40] His main concern was the "blind emulation" of the West among educated Egyptians, which led to a rejection of Islam and Islamic culture. At the same time he took much pride in quoting a number of Western authorities to support his arguments about the necessity of religious education.[41] In his early writings in *Majallat al-Fath* and later in the 1930s in the earliest editions of his own newspaper, *Jaridat al-Ikhwan al-Muslimin* (the newspaper of the Muslim Brothers), references to the West are abundant. Al-Banna supported his arguments by using examples from Europe which he hoped Egyptians would emulate.[42] This image of the young Hasan al-Banna conforms with what is known about his lifestyle at this time. Contrary to the image of asceticism and simple living, which has generally become associated with the founder of the Muslim Brothers, al-Banna was an ambitious, chic and well-dressed young man in Ismailia. He cared much about his appearance and even adopted some of the customs of the more

[31]

Europeanized section of society in Ismailia. In the 1930s, however, when he began touring the impoverished Egyptian countryside for the sake of his "Islamic call" (*da'wa*), he adopted the asceticism and simplicity which became so legendary among his followers.[43]

In Ismailia, Hasan al-Banna contacted various Islamic reform societies, some of which he had been in touch with in Cairo. He began to deliver lectures to the educated youth who used to attend meetings in these societies.[44] Al-Banna's activities also included preaching and teaching in the local mosques twice a week. His lectures and evening classes must have attracted the attention of the community more than his social standing as a schoolteacher would imply. His prolific writing in Islamic journals, mainly in *Majallat al-Fath*, also enhanced his reputation. Hasan al-Banna quickly gained a reputation for his oratorical abilities, a gift he was eager to develop further. His eloquent speeches on various occasions brought him to the attention of the élite and he established close contacts with several of the influential notables (*a'yan*) of Ismailia, especially the wealthy contractor Shaykh Muhammad Husayn Zamalut and the judge at the Religious Court of Ismailia who provided him with both financial and moral support. However, in his memoirs al-Banna is anxious to portray his role among these notables and Islamic scholars merely as that of a mediator in religious disputes or that of a fearless prophet correcting his erring superiors. Although their financial support is mentioned, the credit for having established the Society is basically given to his poor and humble followers from the lower classes.[45] As will be discussed later, the movement's social basis was predominantly lower middle class. Although in the initial stages of the development of the Society the patronage of local élites was crucial, as time progressed any dependence on men of wealth and influence became anathema.

Novel Ideas versus Traditionalism

In his memoirs Hasan al-Banna recalls that soon after his arrival in Ismailia he embarked upon a campaign of preaching in coffee-shops (*qahawi*). This was an unusual way of bringing the word of God to the people. Coffee-shops were still a novel thing in those days and it was considered a "shame" (*'ayb*) for young people to spend time in them.[46]

This novel strategy had already been applied with some success by al-Banna and his friends in Cairo. It reflected their disillusionment with the Islamic establishment which did nothing to protect Islam. In his memoirs al-Banna describes at length how he had fearlessly addressed Cairo's leading Azhari dignitaries and blatantly denounced their lack of zeal for the Islamic cause. In contrast with their indifference and inertia, he eulogizes the piety of "the people" (al-sha'b) and their "faithful adherence to Islam" which he had witnessed during the time he spent preaching in coffee-shops.[47] Although al-Banna certainly exaggerated his role in Cairo's Islamic circles, his harsh criticism of the religious élite is reflected in his writings and corroborated by independent sources. In his very first article in *Majallat al-Fath* in 1928 he wrote:

> What catastrophe has befallen the souls of the reformers and the spirit of the leaders? What has carried away the ardour of the zealots? What calamity has made them prefer this life to the thereafter? What has made them . . . consider the way of struggle [sabil al-jihad] too rough and difficult?[48]

In Ismailia, his disillusionment with official Islam led al-Banna to conduct another preaching campaign in the coffee-shops. This was also motivated by the "religious disputes" of the Islamic scholars in the mosques in Ismailia.[49] His strong emphasis on his coffee-shop preaching is interesting in light of what we can term the "lay" or "populist" character of the Muslim Brothers. There are several references to coffee-shop preaching in the 1930s as well. For example, a brief survey of the Society's activities published in 1934 mentions that a number of its branches had committees for preaching and proselytizing in "gathering places which one would not expect to be a place for preaching, such as coffee-shops, clubs, wedding parties and funerals".[50] Nevertheless, in practical terms, it seems clear that the importance of the coffee-shop preaching campaigns must have been limited. When al-Banna began touring Egyptian villages and towns to spread "the Islamic call" (da'wa), he was careful to pray at the local mosque as the very first thing he did in the village. The mosques became one of the principal recruiting offices for the Muslim Brothers in the 1930s. The memoirs include a eulogy to the mosques, describing them as "the epitome of Islam", "the place for the fraternization of believers", and "the people's university".[51]

Thus, the coffee-shop campaigns should not be viewed as derogating the mosques but as reflecting the idea that the mosques were "not sufficient to bring the teaching of Islam to people". Obviously, al-Banna was searching for new and unconventional ways of bringing people back to God. As will be seen in the next chapter, an idea of a new kind of Islamic movement had already taken shape in his mind by the end of the 1920s. He intended to train groups of youth preachers and employ modern means of propaganda in order to disseminate the ideas of his society. In fact, al-Banna had more novel ideas than has usually been assumed. New evidence confirms that his views brought him into conflict with the religious élite in Ismailia. For instance, he advocated that the prayer at the Festival of the Breaking of the Fast (*salat 'id al-fitr*) should be performed in the desert instead of in the mosque. Although al-Banna maintained that this was an old practice of the Prophet, this proposal reportedly aroused a storm of protests from "the opportunists and exploiters of the Islamic call" who interpreted it as an "unlawful" innovation (*bid'a*) and "the suspension of the mosque". They claimed that he considered "the street better than the mosque [for offering prayers]!"[52] Similarly, his lectures during the annual celebration of the Prophet Muhammad's Midnight Journey (*'id al-isra' wa'l-mi'raj*) provoked similar reactions, when al-Banna had emphasized the spiritual character of the Prophet's miraculous journey in an attempt to win over sceptics. In so doing he exposed himself to the charge that he "denied that Muhammad's Midnight Journey was a miracle".[53] However, al-Banna was firmly supported in these matters by one of his patrons, the judge of the Religious Court.[54] Even so, the controversies must have heightened his awareness of the importance of avoiding conflicts with the local religious élite. He included a passage in his memoirs about this issue, although this could be seen as the laying down of guidelines to his propagandists in the 1940s rather than an accurate description of his relationship with the Islamic scholars in Ismailia:

> I adopted the attitude of regard and deep respect for the Islamic scholars. I was careful never to take the lead if one of them was present at a lecture or sermon. Whenever an Islamic scholar appeared during the course of my lecture, I withdrew myself and presented him to the people. My attitude created a good impression on the scholars and I won their appreciation.[55]

The disputes about the prayer at the *'id al-fitr* feast must have taught al-Banna valuable lessons on the potential danger of raising controversial religious issues. He often referred to the theological conflicts between the Islamic scholars in Ismailia as a warning of the detrimental effects of such disputes. In subsequent years, al-Banna made it a cardinal point to avoid theological controversies and he usually tolerated differences in minor religious issues.

The Founding of the Muslim Brothers

As mentioned earlier, the [Hassafi Welfare Society was the precursor] of the Society of Muslim Brothers. The roots of the Society can also be traced back to the time when Hasan al-Banna studied at Dar al-'Ulum. He reportedly invited a group of his friends and colleagues to participate in the founding of a society which was to train young people for preaching in mosques and, subsequently, in coffee-shops and clubs. This group of young devout Muslims reportedly "spread the Islamic call" in villages and towns to which they were appointed after graduation.[56] However, it is not clear from al-Banna's memoirs what shape this Society took in Cairo or to what extent it was linked to the Hassafi brethren. In fact, when his memoirs appeared for the first time in 1947 they incurred the displeasure of the partisans of al-Banna's friend and lifelong companion, Ahmad Effendi al-Sukkari. They claimed that the idea was originally conceived by al-Sukkari during his and al-Banna's common experience in the Hassafi order, and that the Society took a more definite shape in Cairo than Hasan al-Banna had suggested in his memoirs.[57] Al-Sukkari was the key personality in the 1947 crisis in the Society and there is little doubt that al-Banna's memoirs were written to a large extent in response to the challenge posed by him. Al-Banna's close contacts with the Hassafi Welfare Society, which was headed by al-Sukkari, strongly indicate that the idea of a new Islamic society must have been discussed. Furthermore, al-Sukkari also became the head of the local branch of the Muslim Brothers in al-Mahmudiyya. This branch appears to have been simply an extension of the Hassafi Welfare Society under the new name of the Muslim Brothers.

Wherever the idea was originally conceived, there is little doubt that Hasan al-Banna was the leading figure in Ismailia from the very beginning and that he very soon became the acknowledged leader for all branches of the Muslim Brothers. The report of the secessionists from 1932 does not question al-Banna's position as the leader and founder of the Society in Ismailia. It states: "We responded to his call to work solely for God and bring the Muslims together by the Holy Book and the Sunna and we pledged allegiance to him on that."[58] The report further states that Hasan al-Banna was considered the head of the other branches of the Society.[59] This version does not contradict al-Banna's memoirs apart from the fact that in the memoirs the initiative to found the movement was prompted not by al-Banna himself, but by six of those who had been influenced by his teaching and who came to him one day in March 1928 and said:[60]

> We know not the practical way to reach the glory of Islam and to serve the welfare of the Muslims. We are weary of this life of humiliation and captivity. Behold, we see that the Arabs and the Muslims have no status and no dignity. They are no more than mere hirelings belonging to the foreigners. We have nothing to offer except our blood, our lives, our faith, our honour and these few coins saved from our children's sustenance. We are unable to perceive the road to action as you perceive it, or to know the path to the service of the fatherland, the religion and the community as you know it. All that we desire now is to present to you all that we possess, to be acquitted by God of the responsibility, and for you to be responsible before Him for us and for what we must do.[61]

Impressed by their faith, al-Banna agreed to be their leader, and he told them: "Let us now swear to God to be soldiers for the call of Islam." He then named the society the Muslim Brothers (al-Ikhwan al-Muslimun). Al-Banna's version of the founding of the movement reveals some of those strong emotions which not only the Muslim Brothers but large sections of the younger generation in colonial Egypt tried to come to terms with: the feelings of being "no more than hirelings belonging to the foreigners" and having "no dignity and status". Al-Banna's version of the founding of the Society also sheds some light on his perception of the leadership of it. His followers entrusted the leadership to him because they were "unable to perceive the road to action" as he perceived it. In his memoirs al-Banna portrayed himself as a God-inspired leader, and success would only be granted by placing full confidence in him. New sources do confirm that the institution of an oath of allegiance (bay'a) to Hasan al-Banna was an integral part of the movement from the very beginning.[62] However, al-Banna's perception of authority was not universally accepted within the Society and as will be shown it became an important factor in precipitating the first serious conflict in the Society in 1932 (see Chapter 2).

It is not clear how the Society was organized during the first years after its foundation. It appears to have developed the external structure of an Islamic welfare society in the course of the first three years, but had at the same time "a strong touch of Sufism".[63] An important focus was the "moral upbringing" (tahdhib) of the members. Hasan al-Banna recollects in his memoirs how he and his followers rented a modest room in a local Qur'an school where the meetings of the Society were held. They started their own evening school, called the School of Moral Discipline (Madrasat al-Tahdhib), where they launched a programme of Islamic studies. This included Qur'an recitation and the memorization of Qur'anic verses and traditions with suitable commentaries. This was supplemented with lectures about the Islamic creeds and observances as well as Islamic history and the biographies of the Prophet Muhammad and the first generation of Muslims. Hasan al-Banna taught these subjects in a simplified way, with emphasis on practical and spiritual aspects. Those who had a talent for oratory were also taught poetry and prose and their skills were further developed by practical training in delivering lectures. Lastly, the members were taught how to implement the moral ethos of brotherhood, sacrifice and selflessness in their own lives. A strong attention to this kind of "Islamic education" (tarbiya islamiyya) can also be seen in al-Banna's writing and speeches in this period.[64] Indeed, the supreme objective of the Society was primarily defined in educational terms: "to raise a new generation of Muslims who will understand Islam correctly".[65] In light of the later development of the movement this characteristic appears to have been decisive. As will be seen in subsequent chapters, the Society's strength lay in its well-trained and zealous members as they became the vehicles for the rapid dissemination of its ideas to every town and village in Egypt.

From the very beginning a strong practical inclination was evident, especially in the way the members were trained. Hasan al-Banna was a primary school teacher and he obviously realized the pedagogical advantages of directing people's attention to practical rather than theoretical aspects of religion. He came to identify the Islamic associations, including his own, as the practical and active force of Islam, filling a gap between the spirituality of Sufism and the learning of al-Azhar:

> If God had wished so, and the scientific power [*quwa 'ilmiyya*] of al-Azhar had been combined with the spiritual power [*quwa ruhiyya*] of the Sufi orders and the practical power [*quwa 'amaliyya*] of the Islamic societies, then a unique and exceptional nation [*umma*] would have come into existence. This nation would have been a guide, not guided, a leader, not led![66]

In Ismailia, the "practical force" of the Muslim Brothers was coupled with spiritual and emotional elements of Islamic mysticism. The "strong touch of Sufism" which the Society was said to have in this period stemmed from al-Banna's belief that Sufism, in its pure form, represented an ideal educational programme for Muslims. The oath of allegiance (*bay'a*) was an important Sufi institution. The weekly meetings reportedly assumed the character of a Sufi congregation (*hadra*) with the chanting of Sufi hymns (*anashid*). On various occasions members wore green bands and ribbons carrying the Muslim creed. Processions were mounted in which some of the paraphernalia of Sufism was prominent.[67] As will be discussed in Chapter 3, al-Banna's leadership included many facets of Sufism. However, these influences became less pronounced throughout the course of the 1930s: the green banner and the Sufi hymns of the Muslim Brothers in Ismailia were abandoned and a new banner adopted (the legendary two crossed swords cradling a Qur'an), as well as a new official hymn. By the 1940s, leading members considered the Society to have totally rejected Sufism and "stiff dervishism".[68] This illustrates the profound transformation that the Society underwent in these years, where the modern features of the movement were reinforced at the expense of its traditional characteristics.

The social basis of the Society in Ismailia appears to have included both the educated middle class as well as lower-class elements, but it is not clear which group dominated the Society in this period. On one hand there are indications that civil servants were an influential part of the Society. (For example, proposals were raised about building a mosque in order to "root the organization more firmly in Ismailia society" since civil servants usually did not settle permanently as they were subject to frequent transfers.) On the other, the majority of those who are hailed as the first generation of Muslim Brothers in al-Banna's memoirs were mainly artisans, petty traders and drivers working for the Suez Canal Company. One of al-Banna's favourite stories, retold on numerous occasions, dealt with one of his humble followers who sold his bicycle, his only means of transportation, to provide money for the Society's mosque project.[69] Al-Banna further recalls how he amazed the General Inspector of Education who visited the School of Moral Discipline in 1931:

> The guest was wonder-struck by the tea party, especially when he was told that this speaker is a carpenter, this one is a gardener, the third speaker is an ironer, etc. He uttered: "This is the most peculiar and wonderful school I have ever seen".[70]

The visit is also recorded in one of Hasan al-Banna's letters to his father. He writes that the Inspector visited the mosque and the School of Moral Discipline and was very "impressed by what he saw of orderliness in the Society". Tea was served and the Brethren delivered speeches and poems (qasa'id) to greet the guest. The letter does not confirm that these speakers were gardeners or ironers, but other material shows that al-Banna appointed a carpenter to be his deputy in Ismailia and an ironer to be the head of the Society's school. He also refuted a claim made by leading members that these appointments would "weaken people's confidence in the Society" and would "convey an impression of insignificance and ignorance".[71] The appointment of a carpenter as deputy in Ismailia marked the beginning of a policy of admitting people of humbler backgrounds to important positions in the organization of the Muslim Brothers. Leading positions were generally occupied by persons from the lower echelons of the educated middle class and only very rarely from the upper classes. This policy gave the Society its popular and non-élitist character which it retained even after it had become an influential political force. As will be discussed later, this characteristic had the most far-reaching consequences for the Society's development.

The First Institutions

The propensity for practical work for the Islamic cause manifested itself when the Society embarked upon its first project of building a mosque. The building or rehabilitation of mosques was considered an uncontroversial cause and funds for such projects were forthcoming from the most respectable circles. In many ways, the successful completion of this project represented the actual foundation of the movement. The mosque project transformed the Society into a fully and formally registered Islamic welfare society with an administrative council, a general assembly, various committees and district branches. The collection of contributions for a mosque required a formal organization which enjoyed the confidence of potential donors. The support of two of Ismailia's wealthy contractors, Shaykh Muhammad Husayn Zamalut and Muhammad Effendi Sulayman, was crucial in this respect. The former donated £E500 to the mosque and became the treasurer of the mosque committee of the Muslim Brothers. His support to the Society "filled the minds of people with confidence and reassurance". Muhammad Effendi Sulayman donated the plot of land where the mosque was erected. The Society was then (in 1930) formally registered as an Islamic charitable society.

Hasan al-Banna's close friend, Shaykh Hamid Askariyya, also played an important role in rallying support for the project. He had been appointed "preacher of the Canal Zone" by the newly established Office of Preaching and Guidance at al-Azhar (Maktab al-Wa'dh wa'l-Irshad). As wa'idh was a religious position of significance in the provinces his support was important. However, Shaykh al-Askariyya was transferred to the town of Shubrakhit after some time, due to anonymous complaints to his superiors at the Office of Preaching and Guidance.[72] (His participation in the collection of contributions might have been incompatible with his position.)[73] Yet his transfer resulted in the establishment of a Muslim Brother branch in Shubrakhit in which a wealthy local notable played a role similar to that of Shaykh Zamalut in Ismailia.

The building of the mosque in Ismailia began in 1930 and was completed in one and a half years. A club as well as a school for 200 boys was built above the mosque. In September 1932, a school for girls was founded, the last addition to the Society's institutions in

Ismailia. The mosque required more funds than initially anticipated; in total it cost nearly £E2,000, a huge amount of money at that time. Hasan al-Banna made efforts to collect contributions from his followers, seeing the sacrifice of money as a test of their "sincerity and determination". These contributions amounted to only £E50 and more funds were needed. Apart from the generous contributions of Shaykh Zamalut and others, al-Banna also obtained a donation of £E500 paid in instalments from the Suez Canal Company, thus boosting the Society's finances.[74] The greater part of this donation came after the opening of the mosque in the spring of 1931 and enabled the Society to expand its school activities. Some of these funds were also used to subsidize Muslim Brother branches in other towns in the Canal Zone and in Cairo.[75] Al-Banna had probably taken the initiative to seek financial assistance from the Suez Canal Company although his memoirs claim the opposite. His version of the donation is heavily influenced by later anti-imperialist considerations.[76] The company was owned by French and British interests and it was seen as the embodiment of imperialist domination in Egypt. Indeed, ten years later, in 1941, the Muslim Brothers began calling for the nationalization of the Suez Canal.[77]

The British in Egypt were usually cautious not to stir up Muslim feelings, and the company's support of the building of mosques should be seen within this context. It seems clear that the donation of the funds from the company was not as controversial among the Muslim Brothers in 1930 as al-Banna's memoirs indicate. Several other contemporary sources also refer to the donation, but none of them mention the disputes which this grant reportedly provoked. In an article in *Majallat al-Fath* in 1931, Muhibb al-Din al-Khatib praised the efforts of "our brother and fighter for the cause of God, Hasan Ahmad al-Banna, who managed to persuade the Suez Canal Company to donate £E500 to a mosque".[78] The company's donation has sometimes been portrayed by Egyptian historians as the Muslim Brothers' "first link to the imperialists".[79] Such allegations are, however, politically motivated. There is no evidence to suggest that some kind of secret understanding existed between the British and the Muslim Brothers in Ismailia.[80]

The mosque project was in many ways a unique event in the early history of the Society. Although fund-raising for mosques and schools was an important activity in some branches, the movement as a whole never gave it the highest priority. There were several reasons for this. The mosque project in Ismailia had required substantial amounts of money and demonstrated the Society's financial dependence on local benefactors. This could easily render the Society vulnerable to the vagaries and capricious changes of small-town politics. Furthermore, it would severely restrict the Society's freedom of action. Most Islamic societies in the 1920s and 1930s were tied to their local financiers and easily became pawns in the hands of their patrons. Many Islamic societies were sponsored to oppose rival associations or to enhance the interests of the British, the Palace or other influential groups.[81] Protecting the financial independence of the Society became a major concern for Hasan al-Banna in the years to come. He advocated a policy of non-reliance on local authorities for financial aid to welfare projects and relied on benefactors who were not in a position to dominate the movement. The Brothers also displayed a remarkable ability to mobilize their own limited financial resources, giving the Society an independent source of income. There can be little doubt that the Society's professed non-alignment with the dominant political forces, underpinned by its relative financial independence, added much credibility to its ideological programme.

Besides the completion of the mosque in February 1931, several other events point to 1931 as an early watershed in the Society's history: in January Hasan al-Banna's first tract (of his *rasa'il*) to the members was printed;[82] an internal conflict erupted which had important consequences for the Society; and during March and April the Society received for the first time public attention in the press when the editor of *Majallat al-Fath*, Muhibb al-Din al-Khatib, wrote an article praising the achievements of the Muslim Brothers in Ismailia and their president, Hasan al-Banna. The heads of the local branches of the Society in Shubrakhit and al-Mahmudiyya, Shaykh Hamid al-Askariyya and Ahmad Effendi al-Sukkari respectively, were also mentioned.[83] In the following edition of *Majallat al-Fath*, al-Banna responded with an article in which he characterized the Society as "a not yet full-grown daughter" whose achievements he did not want to mention until "the traces of the Society could speak for themselves" and its "voice could be heard through its accomplishments". He respectfully stated that he was not entitled to the kind of public attention that *Majallat al-Fath* had drawn to him. "I have done less than a tenth of my duty", he wrote.[84] More significantly, in this article al-Banna presented himself for the first time as President of the Society of the Muslim Brothers.

Another important event in 1931 was the opening in July of a branch in Cairo. This came about as a result of the amalgamation of the Muslim Brothers and a small Islamic association established in Cairo by Hasan al-Banna's brother, Abd al-Rahman al-Sa'ati, and some of his associates. This branch was important in the sense that it provided the Society with an organizational presence in Cairo, thus bringing it closer to the Islamic circles which Hasan al-Banna had been anxious to cultivate. As Hasan al-Banna attached great importance to this Cairo branch he arranged for monthly subsidies to be made over from the Society's treasury in Ismailia to the new branch, thereby enabling its expansion. The transfer of funds was continued despite discontent among leading members in Ismailia.[85] In 1932, Hasan al-Banna began exploring the opportunities for a transfer to Cairo, finally obtaining a position at 'Abbas Primary School in the al-Sabtiyya quarter in Cairo in the autumn of that year. Thus, the opening of a Cairo branch served as a preliminary step to the transfer of both Hasan al-Banna and the Society's headquarters to Cairo later that year.

Prior to 1931, efforts had been made to establish new branches in the vicinity of Ismailia, but by 1931 there were still only three branches of any significance.[86] The branches established in Shubrakhit and al-Mahmudiyya had been founded by al-Banna's associates not by al-Banna himself. There are strong indications that in subsequent years these branches remained very much under the control of Ahmad al-Sukkari and were more loyal to him than to al-Banna.[87] When al-Banna wrote his memoirs in the late 1940s he considered the al-Mahmudiyya and the Shubrakhit branches to be "established without my style" and by people who were not among "the real Muslim Brothers".[88] He obviously had al-Sukkari – his principal rival in the 1946–7 conflict – in mind. Although there is no evidence of a conflict with al-Sukkari in the 1930s, al-Banna could perhaps not rely on subsidies from these branches for the founding of new ones in the Canal Zone. Thus, monthly subsidies from Ismailia were essential and in 1932 the controversies about these transfers and the election of a new leader in Ismailia precipitated the first internal crisis among the Muslim Brothers there. This will be examined in the following chapter.

NOTES

1 See Husayni, *The Moslem Brethren*, pp. 1–13; Harris, *Nationalism and Revolution in Egypt*, pp. 143–50; Mitchell, *The Society of the Muslim Brothers*, pp. 1–11; and Bayumi, *al-Ikhwan al-Muslimun wa'l-jama'at al-islamiyya fi'l-hayah al-siyasiyya al-misriyya*, pp. 73–85.

2 Hasan al-Banna, *Mudhakkirat al-da'wa wa al-da'iya* (Cairo, Dar al-Tawzi' wa al-Nashr al-Islamiyya, 1986, hereafter *Mudh.*). This edition will be used as a reference here. For a comparison with earlier editions, see Lia, 'Imposing on the past the order of the present', p. 1. It should be mentioned that Husayni and Mitchell also drew upon a few books written by Muslim Brothers in the late 1940s, especially the biography of Hasan al-Banna written by Ahmad Anis al-Hajjaji, *Ruh wa rayhan* (Cairo, Matba'at al-Wahba, 1946). Being a close friend of the Al Banna family from 1940 onwards, al-Hajjaji provides interesting information about Hasan al-Banna's father and the environment in which Hasan al-Banna grew up.

3 The daily newspaper of the Muslim Brothers was called *Jaridat al-Ikhwan al-Muslimin al-Yawmiyya* (*JIMY*) [the Muslim Brothers' daily newspaper]. A few pages of the memoirs had already been published in the Society's bi-monthly journal *Jaridat al-Ikhwan al-Muslimin* (*JIM*) on 19 September 1942. See *Mudh.*, p. 69–74 and al-Hajjaji, *Ruh wa rayhan*, pp. 118–22.

4 For more details, see Lia, 'Imposing on the past the order of the present'.

5 See Jamal al-Banna, *Khitabat Hasan al-Banna al-shabb ila abihi* [the young Hasan al-Banna's letters to his father] (Cairo, Dar al-Fikr al-Islami, 1990). The pamphlet is entitled *taqrir marfu' lil-ra'i al-'amm al-isma'ili mubayyin fihi a'mal ra'is Jam'iyyat al-Ikhwan al-Muslimin* [report submitted to the public opinion of Ismailia, explaining the actions of the president of the Muslim Brothers' Association] (Zaqaziq, al-Matba'a al-Haditha, 1932). It is dated 1932 and is signed by Mustafa Yusuf who had been the treasurer of the Society until he and seven other leading members resigned during the summer of 1932. Other sources which have been made available include *mudhakkira fi al-ta'lim al-dini* [memorandum on religious education] (Cairo, Matba'at al-Salafiyya, AH 1348/AD 1929). This was submitted by Hasan al-Banna, Ahmad al-Sukkari and Hamid al-'Askariyya to the King of Egypt, the princes, the Prime Minister and al-Azhar dignitaries amongst others in 1929. See also Muhammad Fathi 'Ali Shu'ayr, *Wasa'il al-i'lam al-matbu'a fi da'wat al-Ikhwan al-Muslimin* [the printed media in the Muslim Brothers' mission] (Jeddah, Dar al-Mujtama' lil-Nashr wa al-Tawzi', 1985), pp. 192–7, in which a complete list of Hasan al-Banna's publications and articles in the weekly *Majallat al-Fath* between 1928 and 1932 can be found. Jamal al-Banna, Hasan's youngest brother (b. 1920), spent a part of his childhood and early youth in Ismailia with Hasan. He also came to play an important role in the Muslim Brothers as head of the publishing house (from 1938) and editor of the

newspaper *Majallat al-Ta'aruf* (from 1940). His eyewitness accounts have made an important contribution to this study.

6 A *ma'dhun* was traditionally an official authorized by the Muslim judge, the *qadi*, to perform civil marriages and an imam leads the prayer in the mosque.

7 The compilation of Imam Ahmad ibn Hanbal contains nearly 30,000 traditions (*hadith*) organized according to the recounter (*rawi*). This rendered the compilation almost useless for anyone other than an expert. Shaykh Ahmad al-Banna classified the traditions according to subject-matter. His work was completed by his family after his death in 1958. It consisted of 24 volumes, all but 2 of which had been completed before his death.

8 Jamal al-Banna, *Khitabat Hasan al-Banna al-shabb ila abihi*, pp. 53–66.

9 Interview with Jamal al-Banna, spring 1995.

10 al-Hajjaji, *Ruh wa rayhan*, pp. 82–3.

11 Jamal al-Banna, *Khitabat Hasan al-Banna al-shabb ila abihi*, pp. 46–50.

12 *Mudh.*, pp. 13–15. Shaykh Zahran's mosque school was founded in 1915 when Hasan al-Banna was nine years old. When he was a student at Dar al-'Ulum, he sometimes deputized for Shaykh Zahran in the mosque school in al-Mahmudiyya. The Shaykh was given a permanent column in the Muslim Brothers' weekly newspaper when it appeared in 1933. See Jamal al-Banna, *Khitabat Hasan al-Banna al-shabb ila abihi*, p. 128.

13 'Abd al-Rahman Banna, 'Hasan al-Banna: zamil al-siba wa rafiq al-shabab' in Jabir Rizq (ed.), *al-Imam al-Shahid Hasan al-Banna bi-aqlam talamidhatihi wa mu'asirihi* [the martyr Imam Hasan al-Banna in the writings of his disciples and his contemporaries] (al-Mansura, Dar al-Wafa', 1985), pp. 67–8.

14 Harris, *Nationalism and Revolution in Egypt*, p. 143. See also Heyworth-Dunne, *Religious and Political Trends in Modern Egypt*, p. 16.

15 *Mudh.*, pp. 14–15. While al-Hajjaji's biography of Hasan al-Banna claims that he knew the Qur'an by heart at the age of nine, al-Banna recalls in his own memoirs that at the age of twelve he had still not completed the memorization of the Holy Book. Al-Hajjaji's account is probably an example of the exaggerations which are abundant in his highly emotional biography. See al-Hajjaji, *Ruh wa rayhan*, p. 94 and *Mudh.*, p. 15.

16 Dar al-'Ulum had been established in the latter half of the nineteenth century in an attempt to supplement the traditional religious education with some modern learning. It was essentially a higher teacher training school which specialized in Arabic and related subjects. However, compared to the newly established Fuad University in Cairo it was considered traditional.

17 Al-Hassafiyya was a suborder of al-Shadhiliyya. See *Mudh.*, p. 24. *Dhikr* is a Sufi ritual of remembrance. *Hadra* (lit. "presence") is a kind of Sufi gathering. For more details of both see the glossary and Michael Gilsenan, *Recognizing Islam: Religion and Society in the Middle East* (London, I. B. Tauris, 1992), p. 16.

18 *Mudh.*, p. 20 and p. 28.

19 *Mudh.*, pp. 31–2. See also Jamal al-Banna, *Khitabat Hasan al-Banna al-shabb ila abihi*, p. 97. The question of Islamic clothing seems to have been raised repeatedly

throughout the history of the Muslim Brothers. For example, in *Nahwa al-Nur* [towards the light], an open letter directed to the kings and the presidents of the Islamic world in 1937, Hasan al-Banna demanded, as a part of his cultural–religious Islamization programme, the consideration "of ways to arrive at a uniform mode of dress for the nation". More recently, Hasan al-Banna's son, Ahmad Sayf al-Islam al-Banna, presently a leading figure in the Egyptian Muslim Brothers, raised the issue of Islamic clothing in the Egyptian parliament in 1988, insisting on a uniform way of dressing at the universities as a preliminary step towards enforcing Islamic clothing for the whole country. See 'Madbu'at al-jalsa al-khamisa wa al-sab'in' (7 March 1988), reprinted in Muhammad 'Abd Allah al-Khatib, *al-Ikhwan al-Muslimun tahta qubbat al-barlaman* [the Muslim Brothers under the parliament's cupola] (Cairo, Dar al-Tawzi' wa al-Nashr al-Islamiyya, 1991), pp. 185–96.

20 Jamal al-Banna, *Khitabat Hasan al-Banna al-shabb ila abihi*, pp. 90–1.
21 Similarly, it has been argued that these and other aspects of the socio-psychological environment of Egyptian youth during the parliamentary period may have provided a personal prod to political involvement. See James P. Jankowski, *Egypt's Young Rebels: "Young Egypt" 1933–1952* (Stanford, CA, Hoover Institution Press, 1975), pp. 5–6.
22 *Mudh.*, pp. 32–4.
23 Jankowski, *Egypt's Young Rebels*, p. 7. Secondary school students were active in the demonstrations and riots that swept Egypt between 1919 and 1924. Accordingly, Hasan al-Banna's claim to have played a part in the "nationalist struggle" should not be dismissed out of hand despite the fact he was only thirteen in 1919.
24 *Mudh.*, p. 15 and p. 18. These reform societies were the Society of Moral Behaviour (Jam'iyyat al-Akhlaq al-Islamiyya) and the Society for the Prevention of the Forbidden (Jam'iyyat Man' al-Muharramat).
25 *Mudh.*, p. 25.
26 *Ibid.*, p. 53.
27 *Ibid.*, pp. 57–8.
28 Jamal al-Banna, *Khitabat Hasan al-Banna al-shabb ila abihi*, p. 98 and *Mudh.*, p. 98.
29 *Mudh.*, p. 67. Shaykh Yusuf al-Dajawi was a prominent Azharist and the founder of the Society of the Renaissance of Islam (Jam'iyyat Nahdat al-Islam).
30 *Mudh.*, p. 49. An *effendi* (pl. *effendia*) is a literate man (when referring to non-Westerners wearing Western clothes and the fez, *tarboosh*). In pre-revolutionary Egypt the *effendia* denoted civil servants and white-collar employees from the middle classes, educated at non-religious faculties and schools.
31 For more information on YMMA, see G. Kampffmeyer, 'Egypt and Western Asia' in H. A. R. Gibb (ed.), *Whither Islam* (London, Victor Gollancz, 1932), pp. 101–65; Husayni, *The Moslem Brethren*, pp. 1–8; Heyworth-Dunne, *Religious and Political Trends in Modern Egypt*, pp. 11–14; and 'Abd al-'Aziz Dawud, *al-Jam'iyyat al-islamiyya fi Misr wa dawruha fi nashr al-da'wa al-islamiyya* [the islamic associations in Egypt and their role in the islamic mission] (Cairo, al-Zahra' lil-I'lam al-'Arabi, 1992), pp. 199–225.

32 Kampffmeyer, 'Egypt and Western Asia', pp. 105–6. Dr 'Abd al-Hamid Sa'id was the first president of YMMA, Shaykh 'Abd al-'Aziz Jawish its vice-president, Ahmad Taymur Pasha its treasurer and Muhibb al-Din al-Khatib was appointed its general secretary. See Tariq al-Bishri, *al-Muslimun wa'l-aqbat fi itar al-jama'a al-wataniyya* [Muslims and Copts in the framework of national community] (Cairo, Dar al-Shuruq, 1988), pp. 466–7.

33 Arthur Goldschmidt, 'The National Party from spotlight to shadow', *Asian and African Studies*, vol. 16 (1982), pp. 11–30.

34 Farid Wajdi Bey had landed property in the same village as Hasan al-Banna's father. They used to cooperate in agricultural affairs as well as in Islamic learning. Interview with Jamal al-Banna, autumn 1995.

35 *Mudh.*, p. 59. The al-Maktaba al-Salafiyya was situated in the Bab al-Khalq quarter of Cairo. It published the Muslim Brothers' first newspaper until they acquired a printing press of their own. See *Mudh.*, p. 161.

36 For a survey of these articles and a reproduction of Hasan al-Banna's first article, see al-Shu'ayr, *Wasa'il al-i'lam al-matbu'a fi da'wat al-Ikhwan al-Muslimin*, pp. 192–3.

37 The pamphlet was called *Mudhakkira fi al-ta'lim al-dini* [memorandum about religious education] and is dated AH 1347/(1929) (unpublished).

38 Qur'an 37:38. Hasan al-Banna's speech was probably given at the YMMA club in 1928, and was reproduced in 'al-Da'wa ila Allah', *Majallat al-Fath*, no. 100, 1346/1928.

39 The idea that Hasan al-Banna was xenophobic and hostile to all Western influences has been advanced by C. P. Harris (see *Nationalism and Revolution in Egypt*, p. 148) and is echoed in several other studies.

40 His initiatives to secure a grant from a French director of the Suez Canal Company for a mosque in Ismailia illustrates this point.

41 See, for example, 'Hal nasir fi madarisina wara' al-gharb?', *Majallat al-Fath*, no. 165, 1348/1929, p. 8 and *Mudhakkira fi al-ta'lim al-dini*. For a discussion of Western influences on the Society's ideology, see Chapter 2.

42 For more details and examples, see Lia, 'Imposing on the past the order of the present', pp. 9–11.

43 Interview with Jamal al-Banna, spring 1995.

44 These Islamic reform societies were the Cooperative Society (Jam'iyyat al-Ta'awun), the Society for Prohibition of Liquor (Jam'iyyat Man' al-Musakkirat) and the Society of Nobility of Islamic Morals (Makarim al-Akhlaq al-Islamiyya). He also delivered lectures in the Workers' Club. See *Mudh.*, p. 80 and p. 98. See also Jamal al-Banna, *Khitabat Hasan al-Banna al-shabb ila abihi*, p. 118.

45 *Mudh.*, pp. 123–4. See also Lia, 'Imposing on the past the order of the present', pp. 14–15.

46 al-Sisi, *Fi qafilat al-Ikhwan al-Muslimin* [in the Muslim Brothers' caravan], p. 18.

47 *Mudh.*, pp. 60–1.

48 Hasan al-Banna, 'Da'wa ila Allah', *Majallat al-Fath*, no. 100, 1346/1928.

49 *Mudh.*, pp. 71–2.

50 *Hal nahnu qawm 'amaliyun?* [are we a practical people?], p. 16. For other references to their preaching in coffee-shops, see *JIM*, no. 28, 1352/1934; *JIM*, no. 41, 1354/1936, p. 23; and *JIM*, no. 4, 1356/1937, p. 16.

51 *Mudh.*, pp. 145–9. The passage is reportedly taken from the first sermon in the Society's mosque in Ismailia. .

52 *Mudh.*, pp. 122–3.

53 *Mudh.*, pp. 124–5.

54 Jamal al-Banna, *Khitabat Hasan al-Banna al-shabb ila abihi*, p. 109.

55 *Mudh.*, p. 77.

56 *Mudh.*, pp. 53–4. The following names are mentioned: Muhammad Madkur, Shaykh Hamid 'Askariyya (in Ismailia and Shubrakhit), Shaykh Ahmad 'Askariyya (in Cairo), Shaykh Ahmad 'Abd al-Hamid (in Cairo) and Ahmad Effendi al-Sukkari (in al-Mahmudiyya), all of whom came to play an important role in the Society.

57 Mitchell, *The Society of the Muslim Brothers*, p. 9.

58 *Taqrir marfu' lil-ra'i al-'amm al-isma'ili mubayyin fihi a'mal ra'is Jam'iyyat al-Ikhwan al-Muslimin*, p. 2.

59 *Ibid.*, p. 18. This is also collaborated by other sources. See *Majallat al-Fath*, no. 245, 1931, p. 3 and *Majallat al-Fath*, no. 310, 1932, p. 14.

60 For a discussion on the contradictions between the Islamic and Christian dates of the founding of the movement, see Mitchell, *The Society of the Muslim Brothers*, p. 8. There is no doubt that the Society was founded in March 1928 and not 1929. This is evident from Hasan al-Banna's memoirs as well as his earliest writing in *JIM*.

61 *Mudh.*, p. 83.

62 For the earliest oath of allegiance to Hasan al-Banna, see *Taqrir marfu' lil-ra'i al-'amm al-isma'ili mubayyin fihi a'mal ra'is Jam'iyyat al-Ikhwan al-Muslimin*, pp. 2–3.

63 Interview with Jamal al-Banna, spring 1995.

64 Hasan al-Banna, ''Anja' al-wasa'il fi tarbiyat al-nash' – tarbiya islamiyya khalisa' in Muhibb al-Din al-Khatib (ed.), *al-Muntaqa min muhadarat Jam'iyyat al-Shubban al-Muslimin*, vol. 2 (Cairo, al-Matba'a al-Salafiyya, AH 1349).

65 Article 1 in *Qanun Jam'iyyat al-Ikhwan al-Muslimin al-'Amm* [the general law of the Society of the Muslim Brothers] (Cairo, Matba'at al-Ikhwan al-Muslimin, 1934).

66 *Mudh.*, p. 28.

67 Interview with Jamal al-Banna, spring 1995.

68 Ahmad Anwar al-Jindi, *Qa'id al-da'wa: hayat rajul wa tarikh madrasa* [the leader of the islamic mission: a man's life and the history of a school] (Cairo, Dar al-Taba'a wa al-Nashr al-Islamiyya, 1946), p. 84.

69 *Mudh.*, pp. 91–2.

70 *Ibid.*, p. 101.

71 *Taqrir marfu' lil-ra'i al-'amm al-isma'ili mubayyin fihi a'mal ra'is Jam'iyyat al-Ikhwan al-Muslimin*, p. 11.

72 *Mudh.*, p. 93.
73 Hasan al-Banna mentions in his memoirs that the law prohibited the participation of government officials in fund-raising campaigns (*ibid.*, p. 98). Another reason might have been that Shaykh Hamid 'Askariyya was a co-author of the petition *Mudhakkira fi al-ta'lim al-dini*, a memorandum submitted to the King of Egypt, the princes, the Prime Minister, the dignitaries of al-Azhar and others in 1929. It may well be that submitting petitions of this kind was regarded as interference in politics.
74 *Mudh.*, pp. 104–5. See also Jamal al-Banna, *Khitabat Hasan al-Banna al-shabb ila abihi*, p. 126.
75 Jamal al-Banna, *Khitabat Hasan al-Banna al-shabb ila abihi*, p. 126; *Taqrir marfu' lil-ra'i al-'amm al-isma'ili mubayyin fihi a'mal ra'is Jam'iyyat al-Ikhwan al-Muslimin*, pp. 3–10; and *Mudh.*, p. 113.
76 *Mudh.*, pp. 104–5.
77 *al-Ikhwan al-Muslimun: al-mu'tamar al-dawri al-sadis* [the Muslim Brothers: the sixth intermittent conference] (unpublished).
78 Muhibb al-Din al-Khatib, 'Jam'iyyat al-Ikhwan al-Muslimin', *Majallat al-Fath*, no. 245, 1349/1931, p. 3.
79 See, for example, Rif'at Sa'id, *Safha min tarikh Jama'at al-Ikhwan al-Muslimin* [pages from the Muslim Brothers' history] (Cairo, Sharikat al-'Amal lil-Tiba'a wa al-Nashr, 1990), p. 90.
80 The Muslim Brothers are not listed among those Islamic organizations that the British subsidized. Other sources indicate that the first contacts between the British and the Muslim Brothers did not take place until 1941. See Heyworth-Dunne, *Religious and Political Trends in Modern Egypt*, pp. 38–9 and Mitchell, *The Society of the Muslim Brothers*, p. 28.
81 For the political use of Islamic associations by the Palace, the British and others, see FO 141/838, no. 15322, 12 March 1942.
82 *Mudh.*, p. 160.
83 *Majallat al-Fath*, no. 245, 1349/1931, p. 3.
84 *Majallat al-Fath*, no. 246, 1349/1931, p. 8.
85 *Taqrir marfu' lil-ra'i al-'amm al-isma'ili mubayyin fihi a'mal ra'is Jam'iyyat al-Ikhwan al-Muslimin*.
86 Muhibb al-Din al-Khatib's article from 1931 mentioned only three branches, established separately by Hasan al-Banna, Ahmad al-Sukkari and Hamid al-'Askariyya. There is no mention of the existence of branches in Suez, Port Said, Abu Suwayr and so on. See *Majallat al-Fath*, no. 245, 1349/1931, p. 3.
87 Lia, 'Imposing on the past the order of the present', p. 27. See also 'Abd al-Halim, *al-Ikhwan al-Muslimun: ahdath sana'at tarikh*, pp. 458–9.
88 *Mudh.*, p. 151.

[49]

PART II

—

FROM COMMUNITY TO MOVEMENT
1931–1936

2

To Make a Vision Come True

Verily, I can sense the first indications of success and I can
smell the perfume of victory from this renaissance in 'spiritual
guidance' which has spread to the souls of the youth and created
sincere propagandists [du'ah] among them.

Hasan al-Banna[1]
1928

The Society of the Muslim Brothers underwent profound changes
and expanded rapidly after its modest beginnings in Ismailia. The
following two chapters will trace the development and the growth of the
movement until 1936 when the outbreak of the Palestinian Revolt and
its repercussions in Egypt together with important organizational changes
inaugurated another era in the Society's history. More than any other
period of the Society's history, the pre-1936 period needs deeper study.
It has been generally assumed that the Society remained a traditional
Islamic welfare society until the latter half of the decade.[2] However, this
approach fails to address the factors underlying the remarkable expansion
that took place during this period, which transformed the Society from
a local welfare society consisting of three branches in 1931 into a potent
organization of more than a hundred branches in 1936, well-prepared to
take advantage of the new political developments in Egypt during the
Palestinian Revolt of 1936–9.

It will be argued that from very early on the Society revealed
significant differences from traditional Islamic welfare societies and that
these differences underlie the expansion of the Society. A vision of a
new kind of Islamic organization already existed in Hasan al-Banna's
mind in the late 1920s revolving around the ideas of youth preachers,
modern forms of propaganda and the avoidance of the "Islamic
officialdom" which was too submissive to temporal power. This vision
crystallized into a more concrete form after the first internal crisis in
1931-2, during which Hasan al-Banna's ideas and policies had been

questioned by the dissidents. In the years that followed, the Society developed the rudiments of a modern ideology and formulated several programmes for political, social, economic and religious reforms. It gave increasing attention to political affairs and defined Islam as a comprehensive concept which included politics despite the fact that interference in politics was strictly forbidden for Islamic welfare societies. At the same time the movement expanded dramatically by giving the highest priority to the recruitment of new adherents while streamlining the organization. The Society's organizational principles included promotion based on merit, the training of members and the attainment of financial independence. This was backed up by a practical commitment to Islamic causes, as demonstrated by its struggle to counter Christian missionary activities in Egypt as well as its social and educational work. Another important catalyst was the charisma and oratorical qualities of its leader which undoubtedly attracted people to its ranks. Hasan al-Banna's newly adopted austere lifestyle as well as his openness to traditional Sufism strengthened the Society's image as a non-élite and popular movement opposed to the ruling establishment of wealthy landowners and the urban aristocracy. It is also important to bear in mind that the Muslim Brothers operated in the traditional setting of an Islamic welfare society which enabled them to benefit from the extensive network of contacts and opportunities provided through mosques, mosque preachers, the celebration of Muslim feasts and through other Islamic welfare societies. Hasan al-Banna undertook frequent round trips to strengthen these local networks, while at the same time monitoring the implementation of organizational changes in the Society's branches. Like most other political and religious associations in Egypt the Muslim Brothers also attempted to obtain the patronage of sympathetic politicians and dignitaries, but the results of these efforts were still at this point comparatively limited. The Brothers did succeed, however, in establishing fruitful relations with Hijazi dignitaries who were confidants of the Saudi King and their support appears to have been of some importance from the mid-1930s.

A Vision of a New Islamic Movement

Pre-revolutionary Egypt had an active and flourishing civil society, encompassing a wide range of Islamic welfare societies which offered various kinds of religious and social services not only to its members but also to the population at large.[3] Existing surveys have broadly categorized the Islamic societies in Egypt as politico-religious, religious, social, cooperative, vocational and charitable. Most of these societies had a limited scope and were aimed at specific vocational and social groups. Many Islamic associations concentrated their resources on the cause for which the association had been founded, like the Society for the Rehabilitation of Mosques, the Society for the Prevention of Liquor and the Society for the Memorization of the Holy Qur'an. There were, however, Islamic associations which involved themselves in politics, at least indirectly, by taking up various Islamic causes, such as the oppressive colonial policies against Muslims in Morocco and Libya, or by voicing their concerns about Egyptian educational policies and the declining status of religion in Egyptian schools. The Young Men's Muslim Association (YMMA) was the most prominent among these associations and Hasan al-Banna had been an active YMMA member since its foundation in 1927.

However, there were a number of reasons why the YMMA did not satisfy the young Hasan al-Banna. Neither Mitchell's work nor works by other historians have clarified this point. Heyworth-Dunne, for example, has suggested that the YMMA's political connections to the Nationalist Party (al-Hizb al-Watani), and therefore to the political establishment, might have discouraged al-Banna who thought of his own movement as "broader and more deeply rooted" than the YMMA.[4] Yet new evidence sheds further light on this issue. In fact, a fundamental reason behind al-Banna's decision to leave the YMMA in order to found a new Islamic society appears to be his profound dissatisfaction with the YMMA's commitment, or rather lack of it, to Islamic education. In his eyes the YMMA was not facing up to the biggest threat to Islam, namely the educated youths' excessive fascination and infatuation with Western culture and habits. This led to a disparaging attitude to Islam and a blind imitation of the West. Educated youths were not only negligent in performing religious duties but also ignored the study of Islamic history and traditions and considered, as al-Banna wrote in 1929, "the study of this glorious history as backwardness and inertia [ta'akhkhur wa jumud]".[5] The mission of bringing the young back to Islam was not taken seriously by either the Islamic scholars or the Islamic societies. This is not to say that Hasan al-Banna opposed the intellectual efforts of the Islamic reformers. Indeed, in the late 1930s he took great pride in resuming the publication of the renowned Islamic journal *al-Manar*, which the famous Islamic thinker Rashid Rida had been editing until his death in 1935. Nevertheless, al-Banna believed that the intellectual efforts of Islamic reformers were confined to academic works, and the Islamic societies where their ideas were discussed remained secluded from the people. As a result, their message had little or no impact on the educated youth of Egypt whose number was sharply increasing in this period. In the early 1930s Hasan al-Banna wrote:

> [Despite] the present renaissance in literature, sciences and education . . . the religious sciences have not managed to attract a single bit of this renewal . . . We have had minimal benefit of the religious sciences because these books are written in a way that does not correspond to modern methods of studying.

He further claimed that religious literature remained highly inaccessible to young people:

> If a young man with a modern education asks you for a book that briefly and convincingly summarizes the Islamic creeds or the rituals of worship in a way that fits his mind, there is not a single book to recommend![6]

Hasan al-Banna held that Islam could become an attractive ideology to young Egyptians if one raised a group of young dedicated preachers, employed the most modern forms of education and avoided the Islamic establishment with its close ties to the political authorities. These youths would then form the kernel of a new Islamic society which presented Islam in a new fashion by using modern forms of mass media and propaganda.

Hasan al-Banna was disenchanted by the lack of zeal for the Islamic cause among the members of the YMMA, a dissatisfaction he openly expressed. In one of his earliest lectures in the YMMA club in Cairo, he reminded the audience that the YMMA's professed aim was to "form a generation of virtuous Muslim youth". He felt obliged to add that the YMMA had not achieved this aim to "the desirable degree".[7] Thereupon, he outlined a detailed programme for the education of young men in the spirit of Islam, including educational reform, the establishment of a private Islamic school system independent of the government system as well as rules on how to create a virtuous Islamic home and environment. Only when these steps had been taken and the members had been thoroughly prepared and inculcated with the Islamic spirit, could the Islamic message (da'wa) be communicated to others. Hasan al-Banna also made an interesting reference to the Jesuit orders who, in his opinion, had been "extremely successful" in disseminating their message. The Jesuits had achieved this by:

> reforming the education, and establishing their own schools at all levels for the various classes of society. They detached themselves from the system of education and withdrew from the administrative and technical structure [of the state]. They were thus forced to give special training to their own teachers who served at their schools. This special training produced the results which the Jesuit orders wanted.[8]

Hasan al-Banna also referred to the short-lived School of Preaching and Guidance (Dar al-Da'wa wa'l-Irshad), established by Rashid Rida in 1912, which aimed to produce teachers and propagandists (du'ah) who performed their activities "independently of the government and formal restrictions".[9] Although it is impossible to exactly determine from the available sources what kind of new Islamic movement Hasan al-Banna had in mind, it seems obvious that his vision involved the following points: the training of young dedicated preachers; the application of the most modern forms of propaganda, education and organization; an avoidance of the Islamic establishment; and finally, a strong interest in political and national issues.[10] These elements became cornerstones in the successful development of the Muslim Brothers.

Contrary to Hasan al-Banna's vision, the prestigious YMMA – Egypt's largest Islamic association in the early 1930s – never undertook systematic ideological training of its members with a view to producing dedicated propagandists. A recent Egyptian study noted that the YMMA "failed to produce a specific ideological identity among their members and it became merely a social club practising various activities".[11] Perhaps as a consequence of their heavy emphasis on ideological education, the Muslim Brothers soon became more politicized than the other Islamic societies. This became more visible in the latter part of the 1930s, but even the earliest ideological tracts of Hasan al-Banna had an unmistakably political or politico-religious character. He began to define politics as an integral part of Islam and gave the youth a free rein by launching campaigns for Islamic causes which had clear political and anti-imperialistic implications. Conversely, the leadership of the YMMA discouraged politicized and strongly anti-imperialistic propaganda at its meetings, and asked the rank and file to "avoid the suspicion of interfering with politics".[12] The YMMA's more restrained and cautious position probably stemmed from the fact that contrary to its name it was headed by old, distinguished men, some of whom were Members of Parliament and belonged to the ruling élite. Thus, they were unlikely to participate too overtly in the political activism and demonstrations that swept the country in the late 1930s.[13] Yet this was unpopular amongst Egyptian youth, and young YMMA members sometimes complained that the organization was dominated by an old élite. As has been noted by the distinguished Egyptian historian Tariq al-Bishri, the YMMA came to reflect a "reform spirit and a distance from politics under the influence of the old generation who presided in the Society". When the Society was pushed forward to "the brink of politics", this was entirely due to "pressure from the youth". However, the old guard halted the movement towards politicization, and prevented the Society from direct political involvement.[14] The YMMA appears to have recruited most of its members from the upper middle classes and included people of significant religious and social standing, and it became closely associated with members of the royal family and the ruling establishment from whom it received substantial annual contributions.[15] In the late 1930s the YMMA's dependence upon government subsidies increasingly constrained its activities. All these factors must have left it ill-equipped to serve the interests of the rapidly growing and politicized sections of the educated middle classes.

The YMMA may also have alienated many potential members by not adhering strictly to the tenets of Islam as understood by many Muslims. For example, the weekly lotteries it organized in the 1930s to raise funds were seen by many as unlawful gambling. In addition, their views on modern art and entertainment were also frowned upon.[16] The YMMA was also criticized for not taking a firm stand against the missionary schools; it merely confined itself to advising its members not to send their children to them before they had been given "the force of the Islamic faith".[17] As will be discussed below, the Muslim Brothers differed from the YMMA on these points, and to young educated middle-class Muslims the Muslim Brothers must have appeared a more attractive choice than the YMMA.

As for purely religious societies, they suffered from a number of weaknesses which might have given the Muslim Brothers a relative advantage. Most of them were said to suffer from limited resources and a lack of dedicated members, and their performances were thus weak. The Society of Nobility of Islamic Morals (Jam'iyyat Makarim al-Akhlaq al-Islamiyya), in which Hasan al-Banna had been an active member, was criticized for being limited in aims and methods.[18] One of the most flourishing Islamic societies, the Society of Religious Legality (al-Jam'iyya al-Shar'iyya), shared some of the Muslim Brothers' features: it established welfare institutions for its members and endeavoured to educate them to become missionaries for the organization. This society was a devout adherent of the Salafiyya tradition, the tradition represented by the "Great Ancestors" – the Prophet and the first generation of Muslims. Originally a religious reform movement initiated by Muhammad 'Abduh in Egypt at the turn of the century, advocating religious renewal and reinterpretation by returning to the pristine Islam, Salafiyya became increasingly associated with religious rigidity and a hatred of Sufism and popular Islam. The zealous members of the Society of Religious Legality did much to promote this image in their harsh condemnation of deviations from the pure *Sunna* of the Prophet. One observer commented that "they fought innovations and forbidden actions [*bid'a wa munkarat*] with unrelenting fervour", with the result that their reputation "was at times tarnished by their crudeness, insults and derogatory remarks".[19] Moreover, their struggle against unlawful practices was often seen as a diversion of the struggle against the real enemies of Islam: Zionism and imperialism. A Muslim Brother recalls in his memoirs that even at the height of the Palestinian Revolt, preachers belonging to the Society of Religious Legality were mainly preoccupied with ritualistic particularities, for instance that "reciting the Sura of the Cave [*Surat al-Kahf*] on a Friday . . . and praying without sandals was blasphemy [*kufr*]".[20] Although Hasan al-Banna displayed considerable interest in this group and attempted to attract some of its members to his following, he differed fundamentally from them. He had a profound belief in the piety of the masses, perhaps stemming from his own experience in a Sufi order, and he did not hesitate to criticize those who undermined people's attachment to religion with violent and excessive attacks on old religious practices. He called for wisdom and reason when dealing with the religious traditions of the masses.[21] Evidence that his views clashed with the orthodox views of the Salafiyya adherents can be found in an interesting discussion about Sufi rituals (*dhikr*) in the Society's newspaper in 1933, in which al-Banna was asked how he could accept *dhikr* as lawful in Islam, even with the stipulations that it must take place in a mosque, that the pronunciation must be correct and so on. Al-Banna answered by questioning anyone's right to condemn *dhikr* as "unlawful innovation" (*bid'a*), maintaining that there was a vast difference between a true reformer and people who commit *bid'a*. Moreover, he argued that what was defined as *bid'a* changes throughout history.[22] As al-Banna drew upon traditions from Sufism in shaping his movement, he avoided the extreme dichotomy between rigid religious orthodoxy and unlawful Sufi deviations which characterized the preaching of some of the other Islamic societies, in particular those labelled the Salafiyya societies.[23] One may thus conclude that the Muslim Brothers differed from other existing Islamic welfare societies in the 1930s. The transformation of the Society of the Muslim Brothers into a mass movement was not an accidental development which took place within an ordinary Islamic welfare society. It was linked to al-Banna's visions and priorities which were visible at the very onset of the movement in the late 1920s, and which shaped a new movement inspired by modern principles of education, organization and ideology, while at the same time keeping well inside the existing traditions and religious culture, thereby bridging the gap between tradition and modernity in the rapidly changing Egyptian society.

The First Crisis and its Consequences

In 1931, shortly after the Society's mosque in Ismailia had been completed, a serious internal crisis erupted. This crisis accentuated the differences between Hasan al-Banna's visions and priorities on the one hand, and prevalent views of how a local Islamic welfare society should function on the other. In the course of the conflict al-Banna was confronted with some of the practical and more mundane problems that the realization of his visions entailed and in its aftermath the formula for the further development of the Society took a more concrete shape.

All historians dealing with the first internal crisis among the Muslim Brothers in Ismailia have relied solely on Hasan al-Banna's memoirs, obviously being unaware of the existence of a pamphlet which although signed and distributed in 1932 in the name of one of the secessionists, Mustafa Yusuf, a former treasurer and prominent member of the Society's Administrative Council, was clearly the work of all of the eight secessionists.[24] Published at the time of the crisis (July–August 1932), Mustafa Yusuf's pamphlet must be regarded as a more accurate historical source than al-Banna's memoirs, which were written some fifteen years later. The following is a brief summary of both versions of how the crisis developed.

Mustafa Yusuf's pamphlet states that the conflict was sparked by the decision of the Administrative Council, taken during Hasan al-Banna's absence, to set the wages of the prayer leader (*imam*) and handyman (*farrash*) of the Society's mosque at 90 piastres and £E1.50 a month, respectively (as a comparison, a newly graduated schoolteacher earned around £E15). These meagre remunerations were not to al-Banna's liking and as a result he suspended the meetings of the Administrative Council for a period of six months. During this time he doubled the wages of the prayer leader and the handyman and convened "fictitious meetings" of the council where absent members were registered among the attendees. He then made further "encroachments upon the rights of the Administrative Council" by dealing with the affairs of the Society as he wished, causing "chaos" especially in financial matters. He dispatched £E2.50 to an "alleged" Cairo branch, which no one in the Society had heard of. He also sent £E1.50 and various items of property to the Port Said branch with neither the knowledge nor the consent of the council. Furthermore, financial mismanagement and inaccuracies in the bookkeeping were said to have caused a considerable loss of money. However, the conflict subsided when al-Banna finally reconvened the Administrative Council and established a finance committee. Knowing that none of the irregularities had been recorded anywhere, the secessionists accepted al-Banna's plea for renewed confidence.

The respite was not to last long. Controversies over the election of a deputy who was to have al-Banna's powers and fill his position when he was absent, caused the conflict to flare up once again. Mustafa Yusuf's faction objected to this and argued that there was no "appropriate candidate" for this position. But al-Banna insisted on the election of such a deputy and reportedly took measures to ensure that his choice of candidate, Ali al-Jadawi, won the elections in the General Assembly. The secessionists held that the election of al-Jadawi would be detrimental to the Society as his low social position and lack of formal education would "weaken people's confidence" in it and would "convey an impression of insignificance and ignorance".

The Administrative Council, in which the rival faction occupied leading positions, acted promptly. Two days after Ali al-Jadawi's election, it demanded access to the accounts and records of the Society to bring order to the "chaotic financial situation". This demand was not met by al-Banna who reportedly grew "stubborn and pigheaded". The treasurer (Mustafa Yusuf) then refused to grant money on al-Banna's request and announced that funds would only be used with the consent of the president of the Committee of Finance, which the secessionists controlled. Several meetings followed and insults were exchanged during the heightened disputes over the control of the treasury. Hasan al-Banna insisted on a monthly grant of £E2 to the Cairo branch, and threatened to resign if his request was not met. The pamphlet states: "The majority of the members were not aware of the gravity of the financial situation and feared the threats and anger of the President [Hasan al-Banna] and they agreed to grant the amount." The secessionists made attempts to save the Society from a "financial catastrophe" by calling upon the leaders of the other branches and Hasan al-Banna's father to mediate in the conflict, but these came to nothing. Finally, they presented Hasan al-Banna with an ultimatum: either he had to assume personal responsibility for the Society's entire debt or he had to convene the General Assembly in order to elect a responsible committee to administer the debt. Al-Banna chose the former. As a result, the vice-president, secretary, and treasurer along with five other members resigned.

Their resignation did not end the conflict. A campaign of "espionage" was waged against them by al-Banna's supporters, and the headmaster and several others at the Society's school were said to have been fired due to their contacts with the secessionists. To replace them al-Banna employed unqualified people as teachers, including two of his younger brothers who were still students, and a nearly illiterate ironer as the new headmaster. The secessionists decided to publish a pamphlet about mismanagement in the Society under al-Banna's leadership in order to clear themselves of responsibility and to refute malicious rumours that the Muslim Brothers had spread about them. An additional motive was to protest against what they described as al-Banna's "autocratic leadership" and his "disregard for the Islamic principle of consultation [*shura*]".

The version of the 1931–2 crisis in Hasan al-Banna's memoirs forms part of a larger context in which his image as a carrier of a divine mission is central. His memoirs projected this image in a variety of ways, perhaps most importantly by describing various plots and conspiracies that people had hatched against the movement. The fact that vicious people wished the destruction of the Society was seen as a confirmation of the divine character of al-Banna's mission.[25] The various "plots" described in his memoirs have caused some confusion amongst historians. This especially concerns the accusations of "secret activities" and the investigation case against al-Banna which had been ordered by the Minister of Education at the request of the Prime Minister, Sidqi Pasha.[26] Yet, as I have shown elsewhere, the memoirs most probably contain a number of fictionalized or allegorical stories which are related to the difficult political situation faced by the Muslim Brothers in the second half of the 1940s. These stories served to ridicule the political propaganda against the Society at that time, and have little or no connection to the events of the early 1930s.

Hasan al-Banna's version of the crisis is permeated by the dichotomy between "forces of truth" and "forces of evil" [*quwa al-haqq* and *quwa al-batil*].[27] He described at length the generally disrupting effects of money and prestige. The Muslim Brothers in Ismailia were "an unadulterated and uncorrupted example of love, spiritual amalgamation and purity". "Alien elements" entered into this ideal community when some new officials were appointed at the Society's school. Though they "had diplomas of higher learning and formally recognized qualifications, they lacked the spiritual qualities and moral education to carry out the programme of the Islamic mission [*da'wa*]". These persons, especially an unnamed shaykh, began to strive after the money which they believed the Society possessed as well as the leading positions in the organization. The first conspiracy unfolded some time after the unanimous election by the General Assembly of Ali al-Jadawi as Hasan al-Banna's deputy in Ismailia. Some of the members had suggested that al-Jadawi should give up his carpenter's workshop in order to devote his full attention to the mosque for which he would receive a small salary (£E3 a month) from the Society. This was also unanimously accepted. However, the shaykh who aspired to become the new leader in Ismailia could not stand the idea of being passed over in favour of a carpenter. As a result, he initiated a whispering campaign claiming that al-Banna had treated him unfairly and did not acknowledge his sacrifices for the Islamic mission. He further maintained that the meeting of the General Assembly which had elected Ali al-Jadawi had been unconstitutional since it had been convened at very short notice. The shaykh also complained about the salary received by the new deputy; such money should not be wasted when the Society owed more than £E350, while he had offered to perform the duties at the mosque for free.

Hasan al-Banna writes in his memoirs that he did not want to be too harsh on the shaykh and his friends and he generously agreed to convene the General Assembly once more. The subsequent election was a landslide victory for al-Banna's candidate, with 500 votes being cast against the 4 of the shaykh's faction. But the whispering campaign continued, causing some people to halt their subsidies to the Society. Al-Banna then summoned the creditors and personally assumed responsibility for the Society's total debt of £E350 by offering to pay it back in eight monthly instalments. This heroic act of selflessness and sacrifice came as a complete surprise to the dissidents. They began to make "lame excuses" and one of them, the treasurer Mustafa Yusuf, had no choice but to hand over the treasury to al-Banna's supporters.[28] When the news spread that al-Banna had taken the whole burden of the debt upon his shoulders, the Brothers' benefactor and supporter, Shaykh Muhammad Zamalut, summoned the dignitaries of Ismailia to a meeting where sufficient donations were made to cover the entire debt.

However, according to Hasan al-Banna's memoirs, the crisis did not end with the settlement of the debt. The secessionists brought a case to the prosecuting authority based on charges that al-Banna was sending money primarily donated to the Society in Ismailia to his brother in Cairo and to the branches in Port Said and Abu Suwayr, thus squandering the Society's funds. But al-Banna was cleared of all charges and Shaykh Hamid Askariyya, an old dignitary and the head of the Muslim Brothers in Shubrakhit, arrived in Ismailia to "bring these strong-headed youths back to the ranks of the community". However, he concluded that as the secessionists no longer perceived "the loftiness of the Islamic mission" and had "lost the sense of obedience to the leadership", they could do "no good to the Muslim Brothers". Thus, al-Banna considered the option of convening the General Assembly in order to expel his opponents, but they took the initiative themselves and resigned. They did, however, continue to "conspire" by levelling charges against the Brothers in anonymous letters to the Ministry of Education and the police. These "machinations" also included an attempt to defame the Society through the publication of a pamphlet (Mustafa Yusuf's pamphlet), which contained "lies" about the Muslim Brothers. The conflict came to an end when al-Banna disclosed the identity of the shaykh whom he considered the mastermind behind these "evil plots" and dismissed him from the Society's school.[29]

However, al-Banna's victory over his opponents in the 1931–2 crisis was not complete. There are indications that tension remained in the Ismailia branch until 1933, and perhaps even longer. The reconciliation reached in July 1932 was only temporary.[30] After al-Banna's transfer to Cairo, one of the secessionists wrote to the head of the school to which he had been transferred, attempting to discredit him. When this became known, some of "the zealous youths from the town [Ismailia]" ambushed the man and beat him "so he could hardly walk". They were all taken to court, but were subsequently acquitted. Although sources are scarce on this point, this incident must have aggravated the relationship between al-Banna and the secessionists who seem to have had some influence in Ismailia. When the Ismailia branch hosted the First General Conference of the Muslim Brothers in May 1933, the first summary of the Conference was only a short note, stating that the "representatives of the branches met in the Society's club in Ismailia despite the fact that the crisis has deepened and occupies everyone's mind".[31] It is symptomatic of the strained relationship between elements in Ismailia and Hasan al-Banna that the Ismailia branch, despite its size and importance, was not represented in the new supreme executive organ, Maktab al-Irshad al-'Amm (MIA), established at the Conference.

In comparing the two versions of the crisis, it is obvious that they differ on a number of details as well as on the underlying reasons for the crisis. The memoirs are undoubtedly biased on certain points. First of all, al-Banna's financial policy and his reluctance to cooperate with the Administrative Council were more important factors in the crisis than his memoirs indicate. The struggle for the control of the Society's treasury was a central element in the conflict, and not only the disagreement about the new deputy. In this context, al-Banna's nonchalant attitude towards formal procedures and rules probably exacerbated the crisis. Secondly, al-Banna's own role and the relationship between him and the members were somewhat embellished. He was seen as "intransigent and pigheaded" by some of the members and the crisis was aggravated by his unwillingness to compromise. This attitude is illustrated by the suspension of the Administrative Council and his threats to resign unless his will was obeyed.

On the other hand, Mustafa Yusuf's pamphlet also had a certain bias. The allegation that the branch in Cairo was unknown to members in Ismailia seems to be unfounded. The amalgamation of the Society of Islamic Civilization (Jam'iyyat al-Hadara al-Islamiyya) in Cairo and the Muslim Brothers was officially announced (in *Majallat al-Fath*) in July 1931. It is also clear that the secessionists began to demand a closer scrutiny of the Society's finances only after al-Banna arranged for the election of a deputy outside their circle. It seems likely that the secessionists found it easier to decry financial mismanagement than voicing their grievances against a deputy who had been elected by the General Assembly. Their disapproval of the new deputy might have been a more important reason for their secession than they indicated in the pamphlet.

Both versions do confirm, however, that the low social status of Ali al-Jadawi, the transfers of funds to new branches and Hasan al-Banna's leadership were central elements in the conflict. If one attempts to analyse this first internal crisis of the Society, it seems clear that it was essentially a clash between al-Banna's vision and the traditional perception of what an Islamic welfare society should be. Although personal rivalry undoubtedly played a part, fundamental differences in the perception of the Society's future role were at the core of the conflict. Judging by their pamphlet, Mustafa Yusuf's faction obviously perceived the Muslim Brothers as an ordinary Islamic welfare society consisting of a welfare project (the mosque and school), an administrative council, a committee of finance or a treasury and a general assembly constituted through laws and statutes. The Society should enjoy the confidence of local benefactors and conservative notables. Open and orderly finances, strict adherence to the Society's statutes and a president who enjoyed a

[66]

high social standing were seen as a guarantee for stability and success. The objective of the Society, in Mustafa Yusuf's view, was the welfare of the Ismailia community of Muslims and the provision of moral education through a school of qualified teachers and a mosque. These institutions were the main pillars of the Society and should be given the highest priority.

This traditionalist perspective was in most aspects utterly incompatible with Hasan al-Banna's vision, and there is much evidence to show that the 1931–2 crisis and its repercussions urged al-Banna to create a new formula which more explicitly distinguished the Muslim Brothers from traditional Islamic welfare societies. This is clearly reflected in his earliest writing in the Society's weekly newspaper. In 1933 he wrote that the Muslim Brothers were to pursue a course different from that of other Islamic welfare societies. These associations, he stated, worked for "the diffusion of Islamic culture, the eradication of illiteracy, the founding of schools and mosques". However, in al-Banna's opinion this was not enough:

> A renascent nation . . . needs another kind of solution to its problems and another kind of endeavour to reach the desired goal. The solution is the education and moulding of the souls of the nation in order to create a strong moral immunity, firm and superior principles and a strong and steadfast ideology. This is the best and fastest way to achieve the nation's goals and aspirations, and it is therefore our aim and the reason for our existence. It goes beyond the mere founding of schools, factories and institutions, it is the "founding" of souls [insha' al-nufus].[32]

This passage reveals one of the Brothers' most characteristic features in the 1930s: a strong ideological consciousness centred on political and national aims in the sense that the education of souls was seen as a step towards the achievement of "the nation's goals and aspirations".

The end of the crisis marked the beginning of the Society's involvement in political issues. In his writing prior to 1932, Hasan al-Banna had displayed an unmistakably political inclination by maintaining that the duty of the "Islamic mission" first and foremost fell upon the government, and secondly upon parliament because of its legislative powers. The rich and wealthy were "the third class who were capable of reform". Finally, the duty of Islamic reform fell upon the

Islamic scholars and students. However, the government was primarily responsible for carrying out reforms, in compliance with the Prophetic saying: "Verily, God will not permit for the Sultan what is prohibited in the Qur'an." Hence, on this basis al-Banna began to raise issues such as educational reform, the prohibition of prostitution, nightclubs, alcohol and gambling, and opposition to Christian missionaries. With his two confidants, Ahmad al-Sukkari and Shaykh Hamid al-Askariyya, al-Banna had published a pamphlet in the spring of 1929 expressing deep concern about the declining status of religion in Egyptian schools.[33] Al-Banna had also personally submitted a similar memorandum to the Ministry of Education and al-Azhar in December 1930.[34] However, prior to the resolution of the crisis, al-Banna had not signed any of his politico-religious articles as the leader of the Muslim Brothers. But following the crisis this changed, and in July 1932 al-Banna formed a committee among the Muslim Brothers in Ismailia to draft a memorandum to the Minister of the Interior, suggesting the necessary steps to be taken in order to abolish legal prostitution.[35] The memorandum was followed by two open letters to the Minister, reminding him of the detrimental effects of legal prostitution and urging him to take action.[36] Such activities might have been interpreted as an expression of religious sentiments, not "interference in politics" (*tadakhkhul fi al-siyasa*), which was strictly forbidden to Islamic associations. All Islamic organizations at this time usually had general laws, including one or several paragraphs which explicitly stipulated the association's non-involvement in political affairs. As far as is known, this was included in the earliest laws of the Muslim Brothers drafted around 1930. Even as late as December 1937 one of the Society's members from Upper Egypt maintained that the General Law of the Society of the Muslim Brothers (*Qanun Jam'iyyat al-Ikhwan al-Muslimin al-'Amm*) forbade political involvement.[37] However, when al-Banna revised these statutes in the spring of 1934 the paragraph dealing with the issue of non-involvement in politics was dropped. At the same time accusations were reportedly levelled against the Muslim Brothers that they were a political group with a political mission.[38] To this al-Banna responded:

> We summon you to Islam, the teachings of Islam, the laws of Islam and the guidance of Islam, and if this smacks of "politics" in your eyes, then it is our policy. And if the one summoning you to these

principles is a "politician", then we are the most respectable of men, God be praised, in politics . . . Islam does have a policy embracing the happiness of this world.[39]

The Society did not officially announce its intentions to take up political issues and deal openly with politics until 1938 – even then the Muslim Brothers made it one of their cardinal virtues to avoid party politics (al-hizbiyya). Nevertheless, as will be seen, their programme and ideology had strong political implications and, judging by the memoirs of several of those who joined the Society in the 1930s, it seems evident that the Muslim Brothers' ardent interest in current affairs and politics strongly appealed to the youth of Egypt.[40]

Apart from the strong interest in politico-religious issues, a number of the Society's other characteristic features became more discernible after the 1931–2 crisis. First of all, there are indications that the Society became more of a charismatic community and less of a bureaucratic welfare organization. In the years following the crisis, al-Banna repeatedly stressed that the internal life of the Society should not only be guided by formal procedures but also by its spiritual mission; he maintained that the Society was not "a system of external regulations" (nizam mazhari) nor an "administrative idea" (fikra idariyya).[41] "Administrative titles", he wrote less than two years later, "will not produce the true faith."[42] The Society, in his eyes, was a principle, a doctrine and a conviction. It aimed at "the purification of souls and moral rectification".[43] According to al-Banna, the Society's financial situation depended primarily on the fulfilment of its spiritual mission, because only proper spiritual education, not the pedantry about statutes and formalities, would "produce the will to sacrifice". In the aftermath of the crisis, al-Banna came to see the successful settling of the Society's debt in Ismailia as an outstanding example of the importance of

> educating the souls and imbuing them with love for the Islamic cause . . . When this love becomes sufficiently strong, it generates the will to sacrifice . . . and makes the members contribute whenever necessary to make the projects of the Muslim Brothers successful . . . This aspect is perhaps the Society's most remarkable quality.[44]

The increased emphasis on charisma also extended to those occupying leading positions in the Society; spiritual qualities were deemed essential and not higher formal education or social standing which, on the contrary, tended to "corrupt souls". The position and status of the individual member should be determined exclusively on the basis of his devotion to the cause. An important consequence of this was that leading positions in the Society did not become the preserve of local dignitaries or influential families, but remained open for people from the middle and lower classes of society. As will be discussed in Chapter 6, this principle became firmly embedded in the organizational structure in the years to come.

Another and equally important result of the crisis was the victory of national (or even international) ambitions over the local focus of the Society. To al-Banna, the Muslim Brothers of Ismailia were only a part of a larger community of believers, and the Islamic mission knew no boundaries. Hence, the dissemination of the Society's ideas, not the provision of welfare, should be given the highest priority. From this perspective the sponsoring of embryonic branches elsewhere was of fundamental importance. Hasan al-Banna not only wished to subsidize and strengthen the Cairo branch as a preliminary step to his own transfer to Cairo, but he also insisted that monthly grants be provided for the Port Said and Abu Suwayr branches in the Canal Zone. The headquarters in Cairo reportedly received subsidies from the Canal Zone branches at least until the mid-1930s, and there is little doubt that the policy of subsidizing developing branches – a policy that was pursued persistently at later stages as well – greatly facilitated the spread of the Society.

Finally, the Society's first internal conflict appears to have strengthened the authoritarian and centralized character of the movement. Hasan al-Banna believed that the Society could never be successful unless it commanded the total confidence and obedience of its members, and all demands for "consultation" (*shura*) and the diffusion of authority were rejected as nit-picking criticism and a lack of understanding of the Society's supreme mission. Hasan al-Banna soon came to display considerable scepticism towards the usefulness of democratic elections in the Society:

> I have never ever seen a single election as a result of which the most qualified workers have been chosen. I have never seen an election that has left anything but a negative influence in the souls. They

[the elections] always provoke a stream of invective and abuses from those who were not elected.[45]

The General Law, drafted by al-Banna in 1934, stipulated the highly centralized control of the Society, investing extensive powers in an executive body whose members were chosen directly by al-Banna himself. There can be little doubt that the 1931–2 crisis – in the course of which al-Banna's opponents had tried to exploit the existing legal structure of the Society to their own advantage – provided the impetus for the new laws to be drafted while the repercussions of the crisis were still noticeable. These experiences had, in al-Banna's opinion, severely undermined the virtues of a democratic structure.[46] It appears that he also responded to the crisis by making determined efforts to define a set of rules or guiding principles for the conduct of discussions in the Society so as to avoid personal conflicts and animosity:

> I wish that our discussion should be based on these premises . . . we must allow our brother to complete his arguments without interruption. Trivialities and minor details should be avoided. Everybody must base their arguments on evidence and not be content with destroying the arguments of his brother.[47]

These rules were included in the General Law of the Society. In addition, committees were formed at the headquarters and in the branches to mediate when disputes arose, and the secretaries at local conferences were instructed to report disputes and conflicts in the branches to the conference so that these could be solved by mediation. Although these measures were not sufficient to avoid controversies and crises in the years to come, they implied a preparedness to deal openly with contentious issues.

In sum, the 1931–2 crisis accentuated the conflict between the traditional perception of the role of Islamic welfare societies and Hasan al-Banna's vision. Viewed from a longer-term perspective, the victory of his vision during the crisis was of fundamental importance. This is a somewhat different position from the traditionally accepted view that al-Banna's dominant position and autocratic leadership were detrimental to the Society in the long run and caused numerous secessions which weakened the Society.[48] While this might well be true for the late 1940s when al-Banna dismissed his two closest civilian leaders, precipitating a serious leadership crisis which led to the ascendancy of the notorious military wing, al-Banna's obstinate insistence during 1931–2 that his plans for the Society should be followed meant that the Muslim Brothers did not remain a local and peripheral Islamic welfare society. Instead, the Brothers were set on a course which in less than a decade made them the largest Islamic association in Egypt.[49]

The Development of an Islamic Ideology

During the 1930s Hasan al-Banna formulated an important part of the Society's ideology through a series of tracts printed in the Society's newspaper and internal publications.[50] As has been noted, his writing marked a watershed in modern Islamic discourse by making "the successful transition [of Islam] into an ideology", thus providing an "ideological map of 'what is' in society and a 'report' of how it is working". This "elaborate code" enabled the Muslim Brothers to analyse the world and create a solidarity that extended beyond the boundaries of family and locality.[51] The creation of an ideological framework for the Society was undoubtedly one of the most fundamental changes during the 1930s; it laid the basis for the formulation of comprehensive reform programmes, involving the political, economic, social, cultural and religious spheres, which in turn greatly enhanced the Society's appeal. The Society's political thinking was still rudimentary throughout the 1930s and attention here will be focused merely on the most salient features of the Society's Islamic ideology during the 1930s as a part of an overall analysis of the rise of the Muslim Brothers in this period.

A characteristic feature of the Society's writings in the 1930s was its professed commitment to action and work – not words and idle talk – preferring deed to idea. One Muslim Brother expressed this as follows: "There is no redemption in writing articles which some write and others read. There is no redemption in lectures . . . The only salvation is through productive work and rapid action."[52] This attitude could be found among several of the new political forces which appeared in Egypt in the 1930s, especially the Young Egypt Party (Misr al-Fatah), and it reflected the general disillusionment with the political establishment which failed to achieve the two main political objectives in Egypt:

liberation from imperialism and economic progress. The 1930s were the time "of youthful disenchantment with the professional politicians",[53] and it was within this political context that al-Banna produced his earliest tracts which formulated a new political ideology based on Islam.

Despite the immense influence of the political situation, most analysis of the Society's ideology tends to focus unilaterally on the cultural–religious context by advancing a modernist–traditionalist dichotomy, in which the Muslim Brothers are portrayed as staunch defenders of an embattled identity in the face of the onslaught of modernism. While earlier Islamic reformers, in particular Muhammad 'Abduh, attempted to expand the scope of rationalism within Islam at the end of the nineteenth century, the Muslim Brothers reversed this trend by developing a "neo-traditionalism within the confines of the conservative discourse of authenticity, which tried to keep the society closed to the expansion of modernism". Although it is conceded that the Society applied "instrumental rationalism" by developing an efficient organization, their discourse was marked by self-defensiveness and a lack of rationalism which prevented a clear analysis of society.[54] The process of modernization and its cultural–religious by-products are, however, more complex than most analysis of the Muslim Brothers' ideology has recognized. In the Egyptian monarchical period, the would-be spokesmen of liberalism, rationalism and modernism in fact belonged mostly to a feudal landed aristocracy, and their counterparts in the communist movement were recruited largely from among their sons and other rebellious and adventurous upper-class youths. As a further indication of the fundamental contradictions of Egyptian political life, one of the largest labour movements was organized and led by a member of the royal family. Thus, any textual analysis of discourse which ignores these political and social realities can be very deceiving.

There is little doubt that the earliest attempts by the Society to formulate a comprehensive ideology were riddled with many short-comings, a glaring naivety and simplistic generalizations, giving rise to accusations of "obscurity" (*ghumud*) among Egyptian critics of the Muslim Brothers.[55] However, this criticism does not help us much in understanding why the Muslim Brothers' ideas had such an appeal among certain sections of the Egyptian population in this period. It can be argued that the importance of their ideology lies not so much in its intellectual perfection or lack thereof, but in the fact that the spokesmen of this ideology were the educated youth of the middle or lower middle classes – not the religious or political establishment. New evidence shows clearly that young men formed the core of Hasan al-Banna's following in the 1930s, and that the overwhelming majority of the active members were in their early twenties.[56] They represented a new and popular voice, challenging the ruling élite and questioning their monopoly of power. By developing an alternative ideology based on their interpretation of Islam and calling upon the government to acquiesce to it, the Brothers essentially demanded the right to political participation in a society where this was still the preserve of a small élite (see Chapter 7). This factor undoubtedly contributed to the appeal of the Muslim Brothers to middle-class young men.

Another essential factor was that a large number of the Muslim Brothers' recruits were first-generation immigrants to an urban environment in addition to being the first in their families to obtain a middle or higher education in the new non-religious educational institutes in Egypt. Thus, they experienced the enormous differences in culture, traditions and religious practice between their own traditional–rural background and the modernist–intellectual environment at the university at Cairo as well as other higher educational institutes. The appeal of the Muslim Brothers' ideology was closely connected to the way it addressed the cultural conflict between modernism and religious traditionalism which haunted Egyptian society. Their ideology served in many ways as a bridge between the traditional and modernist camps by its insistence on Islam as its only ideological tenet, but incorporating at the same time many aspects of modern ideologies and thinking. A main focus for the Muslim Brothers was how societal development could be based on Islam, reflecting very much an "applied Islam" as opposed to the religious scriptualism of Islamic officialdom. This ability to relate religion to mundane political and economic problems undoubtedly accounted for the Society's appeal among a younger generation raised in a traditional religious environment, but at the same time disenchanted by the conservatism and seclusion of the religious élite.

In the previous chapter we have already seen how Hasan al-Banna described his encounter with the modernist and Westernizing trends in Cairo in the 1920s. In the first half of the 1930s he made several attempts to diagnose this "societal crisis" of modernity and tradition. He asserted that Egypt and the Islamic world had undergone a dramatic period of transition, but lacked a foundation which could define and direct the course of societal development.[57] According to al-Banna, the social systems in Egypt, including education, family, traditions, ways of behaviour, culture, science and economy, were contradictory – oscillated between a "stern religiosity and a frivolous permissiveness". There existed a profound intellectual and cultural confusion, ranging from rigorous conservatism to shameless moral dissolution. He also saw the economic system's disarray as part of this general confusion: the destructive economic system had created a debt crisis which threatened to "annihilate everything merchants, farmers and property owners had inherited by transferring it to foreigners"; furthermore an attitude of "arrogance and contempt among responsible authorities towards the dispossessed" exacerbated the economic crisis. Al-Banna held that the reformers had been concerned exclusively with the achievement of political reform (i.e. independence from Britain) and ignored the need for a comprehensive programme of reform. He maintained that if the nation wished to bring about a "harmonious renaissance" such a programme, encompassing all aspects of life, was necessary. He then presented a tentative solution to this crisis in the form of "a general societal customary law" (*'urf ijtima'i 'amm*) which united the nation and provided a basis for general reforms. "If the Muslims searched," he wrote, "this basis might be found in the Qur'an." Hence, it followed that only by defining a formula for development could the desired progress be achieved. As has been noted by Cantwell Smith, the Muslim Brothers represented "a determination . . . to get back to a basis for society of accepted moral standards and integrated vision, and to go forward to a programme of active implementation of popular goals." Through this they sought to "transform Islam . . . into an operative force actively at work on modern problems".[58] Thus, the desired national and religious renaissance or renewal (*nahda*) could be brought about, not by confining religion to the private sphere as had been done during the European Renaissance, but on the contrary by defining a new and broader understanding of Islam. This understanding of Islam became the very core of the Society's ideology:

> Our mission is one described most comprehensively by the term "Islamic", though this word has a meaning broader than the narrow

definition understood by people generally. We believe that Islam is an all-embracing concept which regulates every aspect of life, adjudicating on every one of its concerns and prescribing for it a solid and rigorous order.[59]

A Western reader would perhaps automatically dismiss this as a naive belief in the divine power of the Qur'anic texts to transcend nearly fourteen centuries of human development. It must, however, be seen as a commitment to develop an all-embracing ideology based on Islam, not as a xenophobic rejection of the modern world. Such a commitment to renewal and modern interpretations can be found in Hasan al-Banna's earliest writings. In his very first article in the Society's newspaper in 1933 he deplored at length the lack of renewal in religious sciences. Not only were the ways of writing and presenting religious studies out of date and "of little use"; there was also a glaring gap in religious literature about most aspects of modern life. "It is our duty", al-Banna stated, "to endeavour to deal with these novel aspects in our era in light of the basis that our predecessors have laid down."[60] The Muslim Brothers' views were "solely based on our understanding of the Book of God and the biographies of the first Muslims".[61] Implicitly, al-Banna rejected the need to follow rigidly the enormous body of Islamic thinking and traditions from the Middle Ages. Instead, he stressed that interpretations of the meanings of the Glorious Qur'an must be linked "scientifically, socially and morally" to aspects of modern life, and "modern theories and ways of thinking" should be employed to face the challenge of the new scepticism about Islamic dogmas.[62] He particularly stressed that although their mission was to develop an all-encompassing concept, "it does not turn its back on the beneficial aspects of any other mission, without familiarizing itself with them and recommending them."[63] This was the fundamental principle that enabled al-Banna and his followers to adopt and incorporate a wide range of aspects from modern ideologies and thoughts from both East and West.

It has become commonplace to assume that the Society's ideology represented a kind of stern anti-Westernism or a total rejection of the Western civilization. A recent study, for example, emphasized the "method of contrasts" used in the Muslim Brothers' propaganda: "Only by demonizing the essence of the West, by formulating it in Satanic terms, would it be possible to emphasize the eternal and humanistic message of Islam, and to create for it a completely positive image."[64] True, there was a strong ambiguity and, at times, an outright hostility among the Muslim Brothers towards Western civilization because the West was conceived of as encroaching upon and assaulting the Islamic world from outside and within, not only by sheer military, economic and political dominance but also by undermining its cultural traditions and religion. Nevertheless, the conclusion that the Society's ideology represented an overall rejection of all aspects of Western civilization is unfounded. The frequent anti-Western outbursts must be seen as a part of the Brothers' struggle to fight what they saw as excessive and unqualified fascination with all aspects of Western culture among their fellow Muslims, resulting in an ingrained inferiority complex (*'uqdat al-khawaja*) with regard to their own culture and traditions.[65] The Brothers' ambiguous attitude to Western civilization is best illustrated by their occasional unwillingness to admit that they adopted or were inspired by aspects of Western civilization. They were often at pains to demonstrate that a number of the "so-called Western principles" had been developed by the Muslims long before the Europeans even knew them, and existed in a more perfect and sublime form in Islam than in Western thinking. One Brother claimed that the principles of the French Revolution were actually "stolen" from Islam; another stated that democracy was an Islamic principle which the West for some time had tried to apply, but the rise of Fascism demonstrated that the West had failed to implement this Islamic principle.[66]

Evidence that the Muslim Brothers did not espouse a blind xenophobia to everything Western can be found in the numerous references to Western authorities in their press. One of the most popular articles in the Society's newspaper was a serial called 'Islam in the West' (*al-Islam fi'l-gharb*), which was based on translations of works by Italian orientalists on Islam.[67] A number of Brothers had studied in Great Britain and France, and one of them had become acquainted with a French orientalist in Paris who wrote a few comments to the Society's ideological ABC, a tract called *'Aqidatuna* (our doctrine). His positive and laudable remarks received wide coverage in the Society's magazine and were later reproduced in al-Banna's memoirs. There are many other examples to show that references to Western sources did not become anathema to the Society. In fact, the situation was quite the reverse. For example, in one of al-Banna's theological treatises, *al-'Aqa'id* (dogmas), he quoted extensively from René Descartes, Isaac Newton and Herbert Spencer amongst others to underpin his arguments about the existence of God. The Brothers also frequently referred to European manifestations of religiosity and other indications that religion was on the rise in Europe in order to support their arguments for a larger role for religion in Egyptian society.[68]

There cannot be any doubt that the Brothers adopted a wide range of influences from the West. This was sometimes done by stating that these ideas or innovations were not contrary to the tenets of Islam, or that these had already existed in Islam before the West developed them. This selective and pragmatic approach is particularly evident in a passage from al-Banna's articles on educational policies in the mid-1930s in which he stated: "The teaching of foreign languages is a vital element in education, particularly in the present circumstances . . . We need to drink from the springs of foreign culture to extract what is indispensable for our renaissance." Nevertheless, being an Arabic teacher he naturally became incensed by the proposed educational reforms which allotted only six hours to Arabic and fourteen to foreign languages. He also displayed a profound interest in Western innovations which could benefit his organization. In 1939 he proposed to send a number of his journalists to the American University in Cairo for training in modern journalism, as he considered the press to be "the strongest weapon of propaganda". At the same time he proposed to send another group of his cadres to the School of Social Service, a Western school. As proof of his conscious pragmatism in this field, al-Banna stated that this school had allegedly been established to "serve the missionaries and imperialists" in Egypt. Nonetheless, he maintained:

> Whatever the case, there is no doubt that its scientific and practical programme will greatly facilitate the training [of the Brothers] in social welfare works. There is no doubt that this will open doors to our efforts to penetrate Egyptian society.[69]

Thus, the Brothers did not reject all aspects of the West, but were keen to adopt those which they thought would strengthen and modernize their organization. This conscious pragmatism was the fundamental distinction between the Society and doctrinaire religious groups, such as the Society for Religious Legality. This openness to Western innovations, sciences and knowledge accounted for the modern features of the Muslim Brothers and their appeal to Egyptian youth.

Another example of European influences on the Society's ideology is its conception of nationalism, which occupied a central position in Hasan al-Banna's earliest ideological tracts. His treatment of nationalism reveals an openness to contemporary European political thought, while at the same time attempting to define an Islamic version or formula in order to make his nationalism distinct. As has been noted in two recent studies by Said Bensaid and Ali Qumlil, al-Banna used modern notions such as constitution, law and national sovereignty as well as "the notion of *watan* [geographical homeland] in the same sense in which it is used by modern Arab political thinkers", but he tried to "translate them Islamically".[70] The Islamist attitude represented by al-Banna was marked by "an openness and even a willingness to borrow from the Occident".[71]

As the Society's ideology was targeted at Egyptian youth, it was no coincidence that nationalism was emphasized heavily in al-Banna's early writing. He was particularly anxious to stress that the Muslim Brothers were the "most fervent and zealous of all nationalists" as their nationalism was ordained by God.[72] Although he stressed that Muslims had the deepest love for their *watan*, he and his followers lost no opportunity to condemn thinkers, such as Taha Husayn and Salama Musa, who advocated secular Egyptian nationalism. Islam, according to al-Banna, rejected narrow geographical nationalism. The nation of Islam, the *umma*, was linked together by bonds of creed and of brotherhood, which extended far beyond the geographical borders of Egypt.[73] The Qur'anic verse "The believers are none other than brothers" was often quoted to support this argument.[74] In early 1934, in an editorial entitled "Qawmiyyat al-Islam" (nationalism of Islam), al-Banna defined the Islamic fatherland thus:

> Every piece of land where the banner of Islam has been hoisted is the fatherland of the Muslims . . . It is a duty encumbent on every Muslim to struggle towards the aim of making every people Muslim and the whole world Islamic, so that the banner of Islam can flutter over the earth and the call of the Muezzin can resound in all the corners of the world: God is greatest! This is not parochialism, nor is it racial arrogance or usurpation of land.[75]

These ideas were further developed in 1935 in a series of editorials by Hasan al-Banna called "Da'watuna" (our mission). A hierarchy of loyalties was defined, reconciling the potential conflict between Egyptian patriotism, Arabism and Islamic unity. In al-Banna's writing the three allegiances were seen as interacting and reinforcing each other. The liberation of Egypt and the establishment of an Islamic order in Egypt was the first step. Secondly, the struggle for Arab unity was essential since it was a prerequisite for achieving Islamic unity.[76] The revival of the Islamic Caliphate (which had been abolished by the Turkish leader Kamal Atatürk in 1924) was sometimes described as the final aim, though the ultimate goal was the universal brotherhood of mankind and the global hegemony of the Islamic nation.

At times the Muslim Brothers espoused varying degrees of expansionism and irredentism, especially in the late 1930s when this kind of nationalism was fashionable in Europe and amongst Egyptian youth. Quoting the Qur'anic verse "And fight them till sedition is no more, and the faith is God's",[77] the Muslim Brothers urged their fellow Muslims to restore the bygone greatness of Islam and to re-establish an Islamic empire. Sometimes they even called for the restoration of "former Islamic colonies" in Andalus (Spain), southern Italy, Sicily, the Balkans and the Mediterranean islands.[78] These and similar statements have earned the Muslim Brothers labels such as "neo-Islamic totalitarian" and "fascist".[79] However, al-Banna was anxious to distance himself from the aggressive chauvinism and racism that flourished in several countries in the 1930s, and rejected racial theories as utterly incompatible with Islam.[80] In fact, the Muslim Brothers used to make fun of the Young Egypt Party (Misr al-Fatah) which they saw as trying to imitate the German Nazis.[81] Although they did admire certain aspects of "the new regimes" in Germany and Italy, they mostly criticized and condemned Fascism and Nazism in their press, especially Fascist Italy because of its brutal colonialism in Libya. When they did express admiration of certain aspects of Nazism or Fascism, it was usually in the context of demonstrating that the Europeans had implemented some of "the principles of Islam", such as a modest dress code, encouragement of early marriage, a strong patriotism and a military *jihad* spirit.

The Muslim Brothers propagated their Islamic nationalism at a time when secular Egyptian nationalism was retreating and losing ground to pan-Arab and pan-Islamic nationalistic sentiments.[82] This undoubtedly added momentum to the Society's ideological appeal, but the essential factor behind its growing popularity appears to have been that this brand of nationalism became a powerful vehicle for anti-imperialistic propaganda against British colonialism not only in Egypt but in the Islamic world as a whole. This point will be further elaborated in Chapter 8 on the Society's campaign for the Palestinian Arabs from the mid-1930s, a campaign which drew its strength from growing anti-imperialistic and pan-Islamic sentiments in Egypt. However, even before the eruption of the Palestine Revolt in 1936, the Muslim Brothers had already adopted a strong anti-imperialistic stance. In al-Banna's earliest tracts this was less explicitly expressed than at the Society's meetings, and he often resorted to religious rhetoric or obvious analogies. For example, when describing the path which a nation had to tread in order to achieve prosperity and glory, he wrote:

> We have now before us a proud tyrant who enslaves God's worshippers, despising them as weaklings and using them as servitors, attendants, slaves and chattels, while on the other hand we have a noble and glorious people enslaved by this overbearing despot.[83]

It seems clear that the political and anti-imperialistic propaganda was less pronounced in the Society's press in the first half of the 1930s than at their meetings. At this time al-Banna was still careful to avoid attracting the attention of the Political Police for disseminating subversive propaganda. A confrontation would have been fatal to the Society at this stage, especially during the repressive regime of Prime Minister Isma'il Sidqi Pasha between 1930 and 1933. However, at the Society's meetings it appears that freer reins were given to political propaganda. The first known British intelligence reports on the Muslim Brothers, which date back to April and May 1936, show that the speeches at the Society's meetings were strongly anti-imperialistic. The reports state that at such meetings the audience was encouraged to shout "Down with imperialism!" in chorus, and one of the fundamental aims of the Society was stated to be "to purge all Islamic countries of the presence and control of Europeans".[84]

Social justice gradually became a more and more important theme in the Society's ideology. Careful reading of al-Banna's earliest tracts reveals that already at this stage one could find criticism of social inequality and verbal attacks on the Egyptian upper class. For example, when he expounded the virtues of the first generations of Muslims, he repeatedly stressed the egalitarianism and asceticism that existed among them, and added:

> Have the Muslims today understood the Book of their Lord in this fashion . . . or are these prisoners of lust and slaves of their cravings and greed, whose sole interest is a delicate mouthful, a fast car, a handsome suit . . . a false front and an empty title?[85]

This veiled criticism of the wealthy aristocracy became far more pronounced in the late 1930s, and in 1939 the upper class was defined as "the arch-enemies of this Islamic call".[86] This kind of rhetoric raised concerns among the authorities that the Muslim Brothers would call for a social revolution, as had their rival the Young Egypt Party (see Chapter 8). At the same time a strong commitment to social justice and the narrowing of the gap between the classes became thoroughly embedded in the Muslim Brothers' programme.[87]

Another central theme in the Society's ideology was Islamic unity, not only political unity through the pan-Islamic vision of a re-established Caliphate but also a desire for greater religious and theological unity in Islam. In this context al-Banna particularly emphasized the importance of avoiding destructive disputes about controversial issues in Islam, and he seriously questioned the utility of legal schools in Islam, seeing them as causing "confusion" and "ignorance among the masses about the legal rules of the Islamic rituals".[88] Theological wrangling was, in al-Banna's opinion, "the minefield in the building of communities".[89] Thus, the avoidance of theological disputes became a fundamental part of the ideology of the Muslim Brothers. Al-Banna stressed this point on numerous occasions and defined it as one of the five essential characteristics of the Society's message. The desire for greater Islamic unity manifested itself in the attempts to bridge or at least lessen the traditional Salafi–Sufi divide as has been referred to above. When the Society became the most dominant Islamic society in Egypt in the 1940s, it also embarked upon a campaign for a *rapprochement* between Shi'a and Sunni Islam.[90]

An underlying theme in all of Hasan al-Banna's writings was that the Islamic world could never expect to rise out of its backwardness and its submission to Western colonialism unless it revolted against the submissiveness itself. He held that "today's Muslims" reflected a distorted picture of Islam:

> Those who do not know the principles of Islam and look at the behaviour and conditions of its people, will believe that Islam is a religion of lowliness and apathy, weakness and resignation, and that Islam contradicts national glory.[91]

The Brothers spent a lot of time and energy explaining to their fellow Muslims the utter humiliation and disgrace that the Islamic world had been forced to endure, and they exhorted them to wake up and divest themselves of their apathy and inaction. This was done by comparing the disgraceful and degrading situation of "today's Muslims" with the glorious days of the first generation of Muslims, whose triumphant conquest of the vast Islamic empire and other remarkable achievements were incessantly retold at the Brothers' meetings and in their press. The Qur'anic verse "You are the best nation which has been brought forth to mankind" was frequently quoted to raise the spirits of their fellow Muslims.[92] The Brothers also quoted the Qur'anic verse from the Sura of Thunder, "Verily never will God change the condition of a people until they change it themselves (with their own souls)",[93] as a basis for their revolt against fatalism, ingrained passivity and apathy which prevented Muslims from taking charge of their destiny.

A consequence of this view was that the Muslim Brothers attached far greater importance to the Islamic duty of struggle (*jihad*) than was the tradition in Islamic circles at that time, and they made *jihad* one of the essential pillars in their ideology.[94] As has been noted in a recent Egyptian study, *jihad* in the vocabulary of the Brothers was not only a duty to wage war against the occupying colonial power, although a growing militancy certainly influenced the Society especially among the young and more radical members, but was also a pledge to eradicate the deeply ingrained resignation of the souls and minds of their co-religionists and remove their inferiority complexes. *Jihad* became a keyword denoting all self-initiated productive work or activities aimed at bettering the conditions of the Islamic community. Furthermore, *jihad* also implied a solemn avowal to fearlessly reproach and correct unjust rulers by demanding justice and reform, thereby abandoning the traditional political quietism which characterized other contemporary Islamic groups. The tradition of Abu Sa'id al-Khidri, "The greatest struggle [*jihad*] is to utter a word of truth in the presence of a tyrannical ruler", became one of the guiding principles of the Brothers, and indeed it still is.[95] It was in this spirit that they began from the mid-1930s to submit their frequent petitions, reform proposals and letters of protest to the government, proposing, and later demanding, policy changes and reforms.

The enormous importance which the Brothers attached to the concept of *jihad* also influenced the way they viewed their fellow Muslims. Hasan al-Banna often described the Muslim masses as a dormant force which had to be activated by the Muslim Brothers, and he defined the essential difference between a Muslim Brother and other Muslims in this way: "Among them it [Islam] is an anaesthetized faith, dormant within their souls . . . according to whose dictates they do not wish to act; whereas it is burning, blazing, intense faith fully awakened in the souls of the Brothers."[96]

The first stage of al-Banna's programme was to create "a mighty spiritual strength" among his followers and fellow Muslims which would manifest itself in "a strong will which no weakness can penetrate; a steady loyalty . . . a noble spirit of self-sacrifice, unaffected by greed or avarice and a knowledge of the principle". He acknowledged that the lack of "material strength in form of money and equipment, and the instruments of war and combat" prevented Egyptians as well as other Eastern peoples from "rising up and defeating the nations which have stolen its rights and oppressed its people". However, "spiritual strength" was even more important and necessary. Al-Banna argued, "If the East believed in its right, wrought changes in itself, concerned itself with the strength of spirit . . . the means of achieving material strength would come to it from any or every direction."[97] The strength of al-Banna's programme was its focus on mentality. Only after having convinced his followers about their ability to produce lasting changes despite their lack of material resources did he direct their attention towards productive work and practical efforts. This turned out to be a successful formula for building a grass-roots movement. Al-Banna had been working to this strategy since he gathered his first followers in Ismailia. This was his first experience of developing human resources in the service of the movement, and as we will see in subsequent chapters, the ability to train, educate and utilize available human resources became one of the secrets of the Society's remarkable success.

It is evident from al-Banna's writing that he considered his own movement as the only Muslim group who had fully grasped the true meaning of Islam. Despite the commitment the Muslim Brothers professed to have made to Muslim unity, they saw themselves as a distinct group separated from the Muslim masses, or sometimes as an avant-garde elevated above them, whose mission was to awaken other Muslims from their lethargy and to summon people to accept their understanding of Islam. As the Society undoubtedly nurtured a strong sense of mission among its members, Mitchell claimed that this sense of religious power generated "a self-righteous and intolerant arrogance which opened an unbridgeable gap between the Society and its fellow citizens", resulting in "a violence inspired by a social and religious exclusiveness".[98] This conclusion was obviously influenced by the wave of postwar violence in which the Society's military wing was involved. However, a number of other radical groups participated in this surge of disturbances and violence, stemming from the continued colonial domination as well as the general political and socio-economic impasse which characterized the postwar monarchical Egypt. It seems unlikely, however, that the Society's involvement in political violence in these extraordinary circumstances was rooted mainly in its "social and religious exclusiveness" and "its self-righteous and intolerant arrogance" as Mitchell suggested, especially since the Society had not been involved in violence since its inception in 1928 until the late 1940s, and when it was finally used it was condemned by the leadership. True, a religious exclusiveness which bred violent acts found expression in some of the young radicals in the Society in the late 1930s (for example, their attempts to enforce veiling among Cairo's women by smearing the clothes of unveiled women with mud). These extremists were, however, expelled from the Society because of their erratic radicalism,[99] and this expulsion firmly established the principle that the Society's message should be spread by persuasion not by force. This principle had been enshrined in Article 7 of the 1934 General Law which instructed the members to always apply "friendliness and gentleness" in their missionary activities, and to avoid by all means "bluntness, crudeness and abuses in words or by hints". There is no evidence to suggest that the Society's preaching and its message in general created "an unbridgeable gap" between them and their fellow citizens during the 1930s. To the contrary, the ideas preached by the Muslim Brothers were popular and were welcomed by a substantial section of the population, especially their vision of a just economic and social order regulated by principles of Islamic brotherhood and mutual social responsibility. As has been noted by Joel Beinin, this vision "corresponded with a widely shared, if imprecisely articulated, popular and traditional definition of social justice in Egypt".[100]

In conclusion, the Muslim Brothers became the mouthpiece of educated middle-class youth during the 1930s, by offering an ideology which eased the difficult transition for rural youth raised in a traditional environment and confronted by the modern age in the new urban setting of their educational institutes. The ideological framework of the Society, albeit still rudimentary throughout the 1930s, was rooted in a new understanding of Islam as an all-encompassing concept on which a comprehensive ideology could be based, including a search for renewal and novel interpretations which would make Islam relevant to modern Muslims. As a result, the Muslim Brothers' thinking was at this stage marked by an openness and a willingness to borrow from the West that which could strengthen the movement. Important elements in the Society's ideology included a strong pan-Islamic nationalism and anti-imperialism, a rejection of political quietism, a strong emphasis on Islamic unity, both political and theological, a call for mobilizing the dormant Muslim masses and a growing commitment to social justice.

NOTES

1 Hasan al-Banna, 'al-Da'wa ila Allah', *Majallat al-Fath*, no. 100, 1346/1928.
2 Mitchell, *The Society of the Muslim Brothers*, pp. 12–13.
3 Unfortunately no comprehensive study covers the wide range of Islamic societies in Egypt during this period. Only a number of smaller studies are available. See, for example, Dawud, *al-Jam'iyyat al-islamiyya fi Misr wa dawruha fi nashr al-da'wa al-islamiyya*; Kampffmeyer, 'Egypt and Western Asia'; Heyworth-Dunne, *Religious and Political Trends in Modern Egypt*; Bayumi, *al-Ikhwan al-Muslimun wa'l-jama'at al-islamiyya fi'l-haya al-siyasiyya al-misriyya*, pp. 54–72.
4 al-Husayni, *The Moslem Brethren*, p. 10.
5 *Majallat al-Fath*, no. 151, 1348/1929, pp. 5–7.
6 *JIM*, no. 1, 1352/1933, p. 3.
7 Hasan al-Banna, 'Anja' al-wasa'il fi tarbiyat al-nash' – tarbiya islamiyya khalisa', p. 227.

8 *Ibid.*, p. 229.

9 *Ibid.*, p. 230. The idea of a school for Islamic missionaries and preachers was originally conceived by Muhammad 'Abduh, but only one of his disciples, Rashid Rida, managed to realize this. The school, established 1n 1912, only lasted until the outbreak of the First World War. Its educational programme strictly forbade political activities or political involvement for both students and teachers. See Hourani, *Arabic Thought in the Liberal Age 1798–1939*, p. 227.

10 See, for example, Hasan al-Banna's pamphlet criticizing the government's educational policies in 1929 and his articles in *Majallat al-Fath* (1928–32) protesting against the government's policy on prostitution, gambling, missionary schools and so on.

11 Dawud, *al-Jam'iyyat al-islamiyya fi Misr wa dawruha fi nashr al-da'wa al-islamiyya*, pp. 192–3 and p. 222.

12 Kampffmeyer, 'Egypt and Western Asia', pp. 131–2.

13 Jankowski, 'Egyptian responses to the Palestinian problem in the interwar period', p. 14.

14 Tariq al-Bishri, *al-Muslimun wa'l-aqbat fi itar al-jama'a al-wataniyya*, p. 471.

15 Kampffmeyer, 'Egypt and Western Asia', p. 132. See also Khalil Na'im, *Tarikh Jam'iyyat Muqawamat al-Tansir al-Misriyya 1933–1937* (Cairo, Kitab al-Mukhtar, 1987), p. 20.

16 *Majallat al-Fath*, no. 566, 1356/1937, p. 12.

17 Kampffmeyer, 'Egypt and Western Asia', p. 111. See also Dawud, *al-Jam'iyyat al-islamiyya fi Misr wa dawruha fi nashr al-da'wa al-islamiyya*, p. 223.

18 *Majallat al-Fath*, no. 566, 1356/1937, pp. 12–13.

19 Ahmad al-Rifa'i al-Liban, 'al-Jam'iyyat al-islamiyya', *Majallat al-Fath*, no. 566, 1356/1937, pp. 12-13. For more information about the Society of Religious Legality, see Heyworth-Dunne, *Religious and Political Trends in Modern Egypt*, pp. 29–30 and Dawud, *al-Jam'iyyat al-islamiyya fi Misr wa dawruha fi nashr al-da'wa al-islamiyya*, pp. 123–73.

20 'Abd al-Halim, *al-Ikhwan al-Muslimun: Ahdath sana'at tarikh*, pp. 140–1.

21 Hasan al-Banna, 'Fatawi al-Jaridah', *JIM*, no. 20, 1352/1933.

22 Hasan al-Banna, 'al-Qism al-dini', *JIM*, no. 13, 1352/1933.

23 For the influence of Sufism on the Society, see Chapter 3. For a good account of the Islamic Salafiyya societies, see Dawud, *al-Jam'iyyat al-islamiyya fi Misr wa dawruha fi nashr al-da'wa al-islamiyya*.

24 This pamphlet, entitled *Taqrir marfu' lil-ra'i al-'amm al-isma'ili mubayyin fihi a'mal ra'is Jam'iyyat al-Ikhwan al-Muslimin*, is signed by Mustafa Yusuf. However, Hasan al-Banna's memoirs confirm that it was written by the entire group. Although al-Banna managed to dissuade them from publishing it, Mustafa Yusuf refused the compromise. See *Mudh.*, pp. 138–9. The following section is based upon this pamphlet.

25 Lia, 'Imposing on the past the order of the present'.

26 Mitchell, *The Society of the Muslim Brothers*, pp. 9–11.

27 Some historians belonging to the Islamic current trend see the struggle between the "forces of truth" and the "forces of evil" as the greatest cause (*al-qadiya al-kubra*) in history, and claim that if historians "are unaware of this cosmic struggle they can never produce useful studies". See Ibrahim Ghanim, 'Munaqasha' [debate] in Ahmad 'Abd Allah (ed.), *Tarikh Misr bayn al-manhaj al-'ilmi and al-sira' al-hizbi* (Cairo, Dar Shuhdi lil-Nashr, 1988), p. 390.

28 Neither Mustafa Yusuf nor the other dissidents are mentioned by name in the description of the dispute. Hasan al-Banna apparently made it a cardinal rule not to mention his opponents by name in his memoirs.

29 This section is based on Hasan al-Banna's version of the crisis in *Mudh.*, pp. 129–43.

30 Jamal al-Banna, *Khitabat Hasan al-Banna al-shabb ila abihi*, p. 128.

31 *JIM*, no. 2, 1352/1933.

32 Hasan al-Banna, 'Aghrad al-Ikhwan al-Muslimin', *JIM*, no. 7, 1352/1933.

33 *Mudhakkira fi al-ta'lim al-dini*.

34 *Majallat al-Fath*, no. 234, 1349/1931, pp. 12–15.

35 *Majallat al-Fath*, no. 300, 1351/1932, pp. 12–13.

36 *Majallat al-Fath*, no. 304, 1351/1932, pp. 11–13 and *Majallat al-Fath*, no. 314, 1351/1932, p. 15.

37 Muhammad Muhammad 'Abd al-Zahir (the representative of the Muslim Brothers in Qina), 'Bayan haqiqa', *JIM*, no. 27, 1937.

38 'Ila ayi shay' nad'u al-nas?' [To what call do we invite people?], a series of editorials by Hasan al-Banna in *JIM*, beginning April 1934. A translation can be found in Charles Wendell, *Five Tracts of Hasan al-Banna* (Berkeley, CA, University of California Press, 1978), pp. 74–5.

39 *Ibid.*, p. 75.

40 See, for example, 'Abd al-Halim, *al-Ikhwan al-Muslimun: ahdath sana'at tarikh*, p. 45.

41 *JIM*, no. 1, 1355/1936, editorial.

42 Article 4 of the General Law of the Society of the Muslim Brothers (1934), p. 5.

43 *JIM*, no. 1, 1355/1936, editorial.

44 *JIM*, no. 4, 1356/1937, p. 16. See also *Mudh.*, p. 113.

45 *Taqrir ijmali khass* (unpublished), p. 27. See also *Mudh.*, p. 133.

46 *Mudh.*, p. 133.

47 *JIM*, no. 41, 1353/1935. See also *Mudh.*, p. 208.

48 Bayumi, *al-Ikhwan al-Muslimun wa'l-jama'at al-islamiyya fi'l-hayah al-siyasiyya al-misriyya*, p. 322.

49 It seems clear that by the second half of the 1930s the Muslim Brothers had become the largest Islamic movement in Egypt. It also became one of the largest contenders for the support of youth – surpassing the Young Egypt Party. See *Majallat al-Fath*, no. 566, 1356/1937, pp. 12–13; Ahmad Husayn, 'Nahnu wa'l-jam'iyyat al-diniyya', *Jaridat Misr al-Fatah*, no. 77, 1938, pp. 3–5; and Heyworth-Dunne, *Religious and Political Trends in Modern Egypt*, pp. 29–31.

50 A number of these tracts have been collected and translated by Charles Wendell in his book, *Five Tracts of Hasan al-Banna*. The availability of these tracts in English has undoubtedly contributed to the relatively large number of studies focusing in particular on the Muslim Brothers' political and religious thinking.
51 Meijer, 'The quest for modernity', pp. 33–4. See also Ernest Gellner, *Postmodernism, Reason and Religion* (London, Routledge, 1992), pp. 17–21.
52 *JIM*, no. 39, 1353/1935, editorial. A preference for "deed" over "idea" has also been observed by Mitchell. See *The Society of the Muslim Brothers*, p. 326.
53 Abdalla, *The Student Movement and National Politics in Egypt*, p. 42.
54 Meijer, 'The quest for modernity', pp. 33–6. See also Eric Davis, 'The concept of revival and the study of Islam and politics' in Barbara Stowasser (ed.), *The Islamic Impulse* (London, Croom Helm, 1987) and Ellis Goldberg, 'Bases of traditional reaction: a look at the Muslim Brothers', *Mediterranean Peoples*, vol. 14 (1981), pp. 79–96.
55 Most Egyptian historians from the Wafdist or leftist camp have pointed out the "obscurity" of the Muslim Brothers' ideology as its most characteristic feature. Some even argue that this "obscurity" was consciously manufactured in order to conceal the Muslim Brothers' true intentions from the masses. For a good summary, see Meijer, 'Contemporary Egyptian historiography of the period 1936–1952', pp. 132–51.
56 This observation is based on more than a hundred photographs of individual members printed in the Society's newspaper in 1935–6. This is also confirmed by other sources, such as *al-Nadhir*, no. 26, 1357/1938, editorial; and early British intelligence reports, 'Pan-Islamic Arab Movement', Lampson to FO, no. E3153, 8 April 1936, FO 371/19980 and 'Pan-Islamic Arab Movement', Lampson to FO, no. E2120, 28 May 1936, FO 371/19980.
57 Hasan al-Banna, 'Nahiya wahida la yakfi!', *JIM*, no. 30, 1353/1934, editorial.
58 Cantwell Smith, *Islam in the Modern History*, p. 156.
59 Wendell (tr.), *Five Tracts of Hasan al-Banna*, p. 46.
60 Hasan al-Banna, 'Kayf aktub al-qism al-dini', *JIM*, no. 1, 1352/1933.
61 Wendell (tr.), *Five Tracts of Hasan al-Banna*, p. 47.
62 Hasan al-Banna, 'Kayf aktub al-qism al-dini', *JIM*, no. 1, 1352/1933.
63 Wendell (tr.), *Five Tracts of Hasan al-Banna*, p. 47.
64 Gershoni, 'Rejecting the West'.
65 Dr Yunan Labib Rizq, a prominent Egyptian historian, held that the Egyptian inferiority complex was one of the most important features characterizing the Egyptians' attitude towards the West. Lecture by Dr Rizq, the American University in Cairo, spring 1994.
66 *JIM*, no. 35, 1354/1935, p. 9 and *JIM*, no. 24, 1356/1937, pp. 4–5 respectively.
67 This serial became so popular that the Society found it worthwhile to compile the articles and publish them in a book. See Mahmud Hamdi al-Jarisi, 'al-Islam fi'l-gharb: nur wa zalam', *JIM*, no. 32, 1354/1935, p. 27 and Mahmud Hamdi

al-Jarisi, *al-Islam yata'adda al-madhahib wa al-diyan* (Cairo, Dar al-Turath al-'Arabi, 1976), pp. 6–7.

68 See, for example, Hasan al-Banna, 'Ma'a hadha yaqulun Uruba la diniyya?' [despite this they say that Europe is not religious?], *JIM*, no. 12, 1352/1933 and 'Arba'a kana'is fi maqarr al-jaysh al-britani fi'l-Hunaydi', *JIM*, no. 33, 1356/1938, p. 20. For other examples, see *JIM*, no. 9, 1352/1933; *JIM*, no. 17, 1352/1933; and *JIM*, no. 12, 1354/1935.

69 *Taqrir ijmali khass*, pp. 12–13.

70 Ali Qumlil, *Fundamentalist Movements and Nationalist State*, p. 136; see also Bensaid, 'Al-watan and al-umma in contemporary Arab use', pp. 170–1.

71 *Ibid.*, p. 170.

72 Hasan al-Banna, *Ila al-shabab wa ila al-talaba khassatan* (Alexandria, Dar al-Da'wa lil-Tiba'a wa al-Nashr wa al-Tawzi', n.d.), pp. 16–17.

73 Hasan al-Banna, 'La al-qawmiyya wa la al-'alamiyya bal al-ikhwa al-islamiyya', *JIM*, no. 8, 1352/1933, editorial. For an analysis of the Muslim Brothers' definition of the Islamic nation or *umma*, see El-Awaisi, 'The conceptual approach of the Egyptian Muslim Brothers towards the Palestine question', pp. 227–32 and Bensaid, 'Al-watan and al-umma in contemporary Arab use', pp. 169–71.

74 Qur'an, 49:10. The Society's newspaper usually carried this verse on the front page throughout the 1930s.

75 *JIM*, no. 29, 1352/1934, editorial.

76 For the role of the Muslim Brothers in promoting Arab nationalism, see Gershoni, 'Arabization of Islam', pp. 22–57.

77 Qur'an, 2:193.

78 See *al-Nadhir*, no. 21, 1357/1938; *al-Nadhir*, no. 8, 1357/1938, p. 17; and *JIM*, no. 10, 1354/1935, p. 32.

79 Halpern, *The Politics of Social Change in the Middle East and North Africa*, pp. 135–6. See also Tareq and Jacqueline Ismael, *Government and Politics in Islam* (London, Frances Pinter, 1985), p. 77.

80 *JIM*, no. 47, 1356/1937, editorial. For racial and anti-Jewish sentiments in Egypt in this period, see Krämer, *The Jews in Modern Egypt*.

81 *JIM*, no. 8, 1355/1936, p. 12.

82 A number of studies have dealt with the upsurge of pan-Islamism and pan-Arabism in the 1930s. See, for example, Gershoni, 'The emergence of pan-nationalism in Egypt', pp. 59–94 and 'Arabization of Islam', pp. 22–57. See also Ernest Dawn, 'The formation of pan-Arab ideology in the interwar years', *IJMES*, vol. 20 (1988), pp. 67–91.

83 Wendell (tr.), *Five Tracts of Hasan al-Banna*, p. 98.

84 See 'Pan-Islamic Arab Movement', Lampson to FO, no. E2120, 8 April 1936, FO 371/19980 and 'Pan-Islamic Arab Movement', Lampson to FO, no. E31530, 28 May 1936, FO 371/19980.

85 Wendell (tr.), *Five Tracts of Hasan al-Banna*, p. 72.

86 *al-Nadhir*, no. 10, 1358/1939, editorial.

87 See *al-Minhaj: bayanat khassa* (unpublished), pp. 25–7.

88 Hasan al-Banna, 'Kayf aktub al-qism al-dini', *JIM*, no. 1, 1352/1933.

89 *JIM*, no. 6, 1355/1936, p. 7.

90 Interview with Jamal al-Banna, spring 1995.

91 *JIM*, no. 29, 1352/1934, editorial.

92 Qur'an, 3:110.

93 Qur'an, 13:11.

94 See 'On Jihad' in *Five Tracts of Hasan al-Banna*. This tract was written in the latter part of the 1930s and became a required part of the Muslim Brothers' curriculum. See also Chapter 6.

95 For information on the contemporary Muslim Brothers, see Sana Abed Kotob, 'The accommodationists speak: goals and strategies of the Muslim Brotherhood of Egypt', *IJMES*, vol. 27 (1995), p. 332.

96 Wendell (tr.), *Five Tracts of Hasan al-Banna*, p. 44.

97 *Ibid.*, p. 86.

98 Mitchell, *The Society of the Muslim Brothers*, pp. 319–31.

99 These radicals formed a secessionist group, Muhammad's Youth, in 1939–40. See Chapter 8.

100 Beinin, 'Islam, Marxism and the Shubra al-Khayma textile workers', p. 219.

3

Charismatic Leadership, Organization and Social Works

Our programme includes the present and the future. We
will work to realize our objectives by building, not destroying.
We prefer to work quietly and unobtrusively, inspired by God.
We do not strive after publicity and fame.

Hasan al-Banna[1]
1934

Expansion and the Emergence of a Modern Organizational Structure

The number of branches and members of the Society of the Muslim
Brothers rose dramatically in the first half of the 1930s.[2] During
this period the activities of the Society became more diversified and
a number of new committees and organizational bodies came into
existence.[3] Qualitative improvements were made in the organizational
structure, and training programmes for members were introduced which
emphasized qualities such as struggle, obedience and sacrifice for the
cause. The rudiments of a class of cadres emerged in the organization
and at the same time much attention was given to the recruitment of
new adherents. An important contribution to our knowledge of these
organizational developments is the General Law of the Society of the
Muslim Brothers (Qanun Jam'iyyat al-Ikhwan al-Muslimin al-'Amm),
drafted by Hasan al-Banna in 1934 and adopted without major
amendment at the Third Conference in March 1935.[4] Although this
document exists in numerous reprints, it has not come to the attention
of historians. Together with a number of other sources, it gives us a new
insight into the internal organization and activities of the Society at this
early stage.

At the time of the First General Conference of the Muslim Brothers (convened in Ismailia in June 1933), the Society was reported to have fifteen branches. Apart from the branch in Cairo and the five in the Canal Zone, the branches were scattered throughout the Delta region.[5] Three months later, following one of Hasan al-Banna's tours, seven new branches were founded in the region of al-Bahr al-Saghir in the north-eastern part of the Delta, increasing the total number of branches in this area to ten.[6] This expansion made al-Bahr al-Saghir an important stronghold of the Muslim Brothers. Until then, the nearby Canal Zone had been the only region of importance. From December 1933 the branches in al-Bahr al-Saghir began to organize their own regional conferences in which high-standing local dignitaries participated. In subsequent years regional conferences were held more or less on a monthly basis in this area and several of these branches established welfare institutions.[7]

In the latter half of 1933 some 20 branches were founded. These included another branch in the Canal Zone and several branches in the Delta provinces of al-Qalyubiyya and al-Sharqiyya. Apparently, the first branches in Upper Egypt were also founded at this time.[8] In addition, departments were reportedly established at the university in Cairo and other higher educational institutions, indicating the beginning of the Society's recruitment of students.[9] During the spring of 1934 the Society's presence in Cairo expanded from a small office in Hasan al-Banna's home to new, albeit modest, headquarters and 5 branches.[10] The Second Conference in January 1934 was attended by 76 delegates from 24 branches. In addition to these, the Society had another 8 branches which were unable to send a delegate to the conference. At this time some of the branches were referred to as "districts" (dawa'ir), denoting a group of small branches, so the number of actual organizational units might have been even higher.[11] Despite this progress, Hasan al-Banna stated in his opening speech to the Conference that the Muslim Brothers were still only "a handful of men" and no time could be wasted if the lofty goals of the Society were to be realized.[12] Half a year later he announced that the "idea of the Muslim Brothers had spread to more than 50 villages and towns in Egypt".[13] Although a number of these branches were still merely based upon a small group of people who had established contact with the headquarters, the Society's growth from the modest number of 15 branches just a year before was nonetheless impressive.

Reports of the opening of new branches during the subsequent two years (April 1934–April 1936) are less plentiful. The most reliable source – the annual report of the General Guidance Council – stated that 20 new branches had been established during AH 1353 (April 1934 –April 1935).[14] During the next year the Society's newspaper published reports of another 12 newly formed branches. However, it is evident that reports of the opening of new branches often failed to reach the Society's newspaper as local members did not send sufficient information to the Society's headquarters.[15] If we assume that the number of new branches founded during AH 1354 (April 1935–March 1936) is higher than the 12 reported, the number of branches had reached at least a total of 100 by the spring of 1936. This assumption is supported by an article in the Society's newspaper in July 1936 which estimated the number of branches to be 150.[16] The available sources indicate that during 1934 and 1936 the Society made significant progress outside its strongholds in the Canal Zone and al-Bahr al-Saghir. Some 5 new branches were reportedly established in Cairo and approximately 10 in al-Qalyubiyya province, just to the north of Cairo.[17] The relative importance of this region increased throughout the period. It was also enhanced by the organization of regional conferences which local dignitaries attended as guests of honour.[18] The Society also gained a foothold in al-Mansura, the provincial capital of al-Daqahliyya, as well as in a number of important towns in Upper Egypt.[19] Finally, the first branches in Alexandria and its hinterland were also founded. The progress was also reflected in the acquisition of new headquarters in al-Sayyida Zaynab, a lower- to middle-class district in Cairo, in October 1935.

In 1936 it was evident that the Society had expanded considerably from its modest beginning in Ismailia some years before. The increase in the number of branches was accompanied by a significant influx of new adherents. Although it is difficult to put an exact figure on the number of members as sources are scarce and unreliable on this point, the Society was sufficiently large to attract the attention of the British Intelligence Service in April 1936, whose informer stated, "the total membership in Egypt is believed to be about 800".[20] One of the Society's meetings included some 200 people, most of whom were university and Azhar students, he reported.[21] These estimates, particularly the total number, appear to be too low. However, as will be discussed below, the Society had several degrees of membership and 800 might have been the number of "workers" ('amilun). Reports in the Society's press stated that in one year, in 1935, the number of members had increased by several thousand.[22] Their celebration of the Muslim Feast 'id al-isra' wa'l-mi'raj in Cairo in that year was reportedly attended by "tens of hundreds".[23] In February 1936, meetings with Hasan al-Banna during his visits to the provincial towns of al-Mansura and Tukh attracted 300 and 500 people respectively, according to the Society's estimates.[24] With anywhere between 100 and 150 branches in 1936, the Society is likely to have had several thousand members and sympathizers. A survey of Islamic associations published in *Majallat al-Fath* in 1937 reported that the Muslim Brothers had more than 20,000 registered members. However, the surveyor, an YMMA sympathizer, doubted whether all of these had really embraced the Society's principles and worked for its cause'.[25]

From 1933 the Society began to develop a tighter and more hierarchical organization. After the transfer of the headquarters to Cairo in the autumn of 1932, annual conferences were convened consisting of representatives from the branches.[26] The First Conference in Ismailia in 1933 led to the creation of the General Guidance Bureau (Maktab al-Irshad al-'Amm, hereafter MIA), which became and remains today the Society's central decision-making body. The first MIA consisted of two distinguished Azharite teachers from Cairo, four prominent heads of local branches as "associated members" and four of the leading members of the Cairo branch, including Hasan al-Banna's brother. At the Second Conference in Port Said in January 1934, Hasan al-Banna initiated steps to secure a tighter organization of the members.[27] The local representatives were instructed to register all new members and make them take a special written oath of allegiance (bay'a). Various measures were taken to strengthen the finances of the MIA.[28] Administratively, the MIA was reinforced by the addition of four new permanent members and an associate member, increasing its total number of members to fifteen. Attempts were also made to strengthen the spiritual unity of the Society by various means. Firstly, Hasan al-Banna was given the mandate to formulate a more detailed set of general principles which was to be studied and memorized by the members in the branches. Secondly, the members were instructed to invigorate the bonds of fraternity through correspondence, monthly reports and mutual visits. Thirdly, the MIA was to appoint a preacher (*wa'iz*) to be responsible for the religious guidance of the Society's members. Finally, steps were taken to introduce a training programme for the members at the headquarters in Cairo.

In 1933, the weekly newspaper of the Muslim Brothers (*Jaridat al-Ikhwan al-Muslimin*) was launched with the unstinting support of Muhibb al-Din al-Khatib, Hasan al-Banna's patron, and Shaykh Jawhari Tantawi, a retired Dar al-Ulum teacher and a distinguished figure in Islamic circles.[29] Prior to 1933, occasional pamphlets and leaflets had been printed to propagate the principles and laws of the Society. However, the acquisition of a newspaper was a major achievement, and great efforts were made to increase its circulation.[30] Despite its shortcomings and limited readership,[31] it nevertheless became an important instrument in spreading the ideas of the Muslim Brothers and in directing information to the branches.[32]

The newspaper folded in January 1938 after a conflict between Hasan al-Banna and Muhammad al-Shafi'i, the then editor-in-chief. Soon a new newspaper, *al-Nadhir* (the harbinger), was set up to serve as the mouthpiece of the movement, and in the following year al-Banna acquired a licence to restart *al-Manar* (the lighthouse), the prestigious Islamic journal of Rashid Rida. Although both publications were shut down on government orders in October 1939, they were allowed to reopen a few months later. *Al-Nadhir* subsequently became the mouthpiece of a secessionist group, Muhammad's Youth, whereas *al-Manar* was regained by the Muslim Brothers. In February 1940 the Society also acquired the journal *Majallat al-Ta'aruf*, which was followed by two other journals, *al-Nidal* and *al-Shu'a'*. Due to increasing government restrictions each of these only lasted until October 1941 when the Egyptian government, acting under strong British pressure, again shut down all of the Muslim Brothers' publications.[33]

The acquisition of the newspaper in 1933 raised the issue of the need for a printing press, and this became the next major project for the Society. The Second Conference in 1934 passed a decision to establish a small joint-stock company to finance a publishing company, including a printing press. The project was a major financial task for the Society, and it was stated to have drained a large part of the MIA's resources in 1935.[34] Only members were allowed to buy shares in the joint-stock company,[35] and the realization of the project is tangible proof of the Society's self-reliance and financial independence. A survey of the list of contributors reveals that the largest donation was £E20 out of the total sum of £E300. In fact, most contributions were less than £E1. This is illustrative of the Society's determined efforts to avoid dependence on patrons and wealthy dignitaries. The fund-raising for the publishing company became the first of a long series of internal campaigns to generate funds in which the members themselves bought shares and thus became the owners of the Society's institutions. As we have seen above, the Society's mother organization, the YMMA, was dependent on government subsidies and contributions from the Palace to finance many of its activities. By contrast, Hasan al-Banna always emphasized the Muslim Brothers' financial independence and self-reliance, and he frequently ascribed the Society's progress to the fact that it did not receive financial support from the government.[36] It seems likely that this strengthened the Society's image as a truly independent movement, resolutely refusing to fall under the influence of an aristocratic leadership.

The organizational structure of the Society took a more concrete form from the mid-1930s. The policies of strengthening the central authority of the organization as outlined at the Second Conference, particularly with regard to the MIA, were pursued during the subsequent years. The General Law, amended in 1934 and adopted by the Third Conference in 1935, recognized the supreme authority of Hasan al-Banna and conferred on him the title of General Guide (al-Murshid al-'Amm). Article 10 reads:

> The MIA is the general executive body of the Muslim Brothers. It consists of the General Guide who is the head of all organizational bodies of the Society. He also represents its ideas and ideology. Additionally, the MIA consists of a number of members whom the General Guide selects to assist him. The MIA's headquarters is where the General Guide is.

The mandates of the MIA included the right to appoint deputies to supervise the implementation of its decisions in the branches:

> The MIA has the right to appoint a deputy who will represent the MIA in [all lower organizational levels] . . . This deputy will have the right to attend local meetings and participate in the discussion without the right to vote. If he finds that some of the decisions will violate the prerogatives of the MIA, he has the right to veto, especially after having consulted the MIA.[37]

The MIA could also appoint deputies to liaise between each of the administrative areas (*al-manatiq*) and the MIA, and had a decisive role in selecting representatives to the General Conference, which was the highest legislative authority in the Society.[38] The MIA was further given the right to grant honorary titles to members at its own discretion, and was to directly supervise the training of the most dedicated members, the "activists" (*mujahidun*).[39]

The policy of strengthening the MIA's finances was continued and it was given the right to collect a piastre from every member during Ramadan and on the Prophet's Birthday.[40] It appears that this policy was met with recalcitrance by members in some branches who disliked the idea of sending even part of their scarce funds to the Cairo branches.[41] This problem was solved to some extent when the MIA was detached from the administration of the Cairo branches and became a separate entity in December 1936, and a new fund-raising campaign was launched to provide the MIA with financial resources.[42] Meanwhile, Hasan al-Banna reassured his followers that the bonds between the MIA and the district branches were "purely spiritual and fraternal", and, as a result, financial transfers from the branches to the MIA were made voluntary not mandatory.[43] In so far as the membership fees provided the Society's main source of income, the MIA was in effect at the mercy of effective provincial administration for the income necessary for its work. Throughout the history of the Society the inefficient functioning of the financial system continued to bring complaints from the MIA that its work was cramped by the excessive use of funds on the lower levels of the organization which automatically cut the amount forwarded to the upper level.[44]

The administration of the Society in the 1930s was divided into four levels: the headquarters in Cairo, the "areas" (*manatiq*, 12 in 1935 and 20 in 1940), the "districts" (*al-dawa'ir*, 89 in 1937) and finally the "branches" (*al-shu'ab*), although the distinction between the two lower levels was often blurred.[45] The basic administrative unit of the Society at this time was theoretically the district (*da'ira*).[46] However, in practice, the branches appear to have remained the essential administrative unit locally. The district seems to have originated when some of the older branches, like Shubrakhit and al-Manzala, founded nuclei of branches in their neighbouring villages.[47] In the latter part of the 1930s a district usually included anything between one and five branches, dependent on local conditions. Very few districts had more than ten branches. The districts corresponded roughly to the *marakiz* which were the local administrative centres in Egypt at that time. It appears that the formation of districts was a response to the expansion of branches in towns and villages where the administrative apparatus coordinating the activities was inadequate. By connecting several neighbouring branches Hasan al-Banna hoped to create viable and effective administrative units.

The administrative body of the district was called the Central Consultative Council (Majlis al-Shura al-Markazi), which was given a large degree of freedom in organizing the district. It consisted of a representative (*na'ib*), a vice-representative (*wakil*), a secretary, a treasurer and a number of members. In theory, the council also included a number of committees, propagating one or several of the Society's causes, such as the campaign for the pilgrimage to the Holy Places of Mecca and Medina (*hajj*) and alms-giving (*zakah*) in 1935, for educational reform in 1935–6 and the Palestinian cause in 1936–9. The Central Consultative Council was also instructed to form Muslim Sister Groups and Rover Scout units, and to elect an "honorific organizational body for the Society, consisting of distinguished members with high social standing".[48] The formation of honorific committees was not confined to the district level. Article 10 in the General Law stipulated that the MIA also had the right to form an honorific committee consisting of people whose contacts would "bring the Society benefits".[49] The background for these committees was the belief that the expansion of the Society would be greatly facilitated if the Muslim Brothers gained the support of dignitaries who wielded influence and patronage. As will be discussed in the next chapter, these measures were part of a general policy outlined by the Society in the latter part of the 1930s, which aimed to regulate the Society's attitude towards patronage and informal contacts in influential circles and to forestall any financial or political dependence on members of the ruling élite.

The area, which in theory was the administrative level between the district and the MIA, played only a minor role prior to 1936. Article 13 of the General Law stipulated that an area conference, consisting of the district representatives (*nuwwab*) in the area, was to be convened every month and a permanent secretary was to be appointed to liaise between the MIA and the districts of each area. The idea of area conferences had originated in al-Bahr al-Saghir in the north-eastern Delta where monthly area conferences were convened from 1933.[50] A group of local dignitaries had been the main force behind the expansion of branches in al-Bahr al-Saghir from the early 1930s. The rapid growth of the Society in this area and the various welfare activities undertaken by the branches made it a model to be emulated by other areas. After the Third Conference, efforts were made to convene similar conferences elsewhere. However, apart from an area conference in Shibin al-Qanatir (to the north of Cairo), holding such conferences seems to have existed merely as a paper decision until the second half of the 1930s.[51]

An important instrument in building the organization were the educational programmes for the members, which were designed to create a class of dedicated cadres. An early example of the educational efforts of the Society can be found in the Excursion Groups (Firaq al-Rahalat), which were a kind of Islamic Scouts. They had been established in the early 1930s in Ismailia, and Hasan al-Banna himself had trained the first groups. According to his memoirs, the idea of Scout groups was linked to the Islamic concept of *jihad*.[52] The idea was also said to derive from the Prophetic tradition: "The strong believer is better and more loved by God than the weak believer."[53] The name Excursion Groups vanished some time in the mid-1930s and was replaced by Rover Scouts (Jawwala).[54] The Rover units had their own organizational hierarchy. They were formed by the local branches and cooperated closely with them. However, by the time of the Third Conference in 1935 it appears that only the branches of Ismailia, Port Said, Suez, Abu Suwayr and Cairo had organized Rover units.[55] A photograph from late 1935 shows 80–90 Rovers gathered around Hasan al-Banna during one of his visits to Ismailia, the stronghold of the Rover Scouts, indicating that the total number of Rovers was no more than a few hundred.[56] As a result, major efforts were directed towards expanding the Rover units, and all main branches were required to form units consisting of members between the ages of 20 and 30, although younger and older members could join if the leadership regarded them as qualified. Mukhtar Effendi Isma'il was appointed as general instructor for the Rovers. He was given the opportunity through his more or less weekly column in the Society's newspaper to elaborate on the practical and theoretical aspects of the Rovers.[57] The aim was stated to be to "raise the Islamic sports spirit in the souls of the youth" and to accustom them "to obedience and order". Furthermore, the Rovers were designed to familiarize the young with "a life of roughness and asceticism" and to create "true manliness" and "dignity" in their souls. The Rover units were also stated to be an instrument for "public service and the general welfare" and would be "assigned the duties of maintaining order at the Muslim Brothers' meeting and parades". Finally, an essential part of the Rover Scouts' activities was to "embark on tours, reviving thereby the Islamic tradition of mutual visits [*sunnat al-tazawur*]".[58] These frequent tours and visits to other branches were a fundamental factor in moulding a strong sense of community and group cohesion within the Society.

The tradition of mutual visits was not confined to the Rover Scouts, but became the starting-point for a general policy to encourage the branches to strengthen bonds of fraternity. Endeavours to make mutual visits on a regular basis seem to have met with some success in the mid-1930s.[59] In this spirit, farewell parties were organized whenever civil servants belonging to the Muslim Brothers were subjected to transfers. Parties were also held at the end of the academic year for students who had some affiliation to the Brothers. In addition, the branches were instructed to organize an "acquaintance day" (*yawm al-ta'aruf*) once a month. It was supposed to be a party "in which simplicity should prevail", and members who were prevented from attending the Society's regular meetings were invited as special guests.[60] Measures of this kind undoubtedly accounted for a great deal of the internal cohesion that characterized the Society.

The General Law also stipulated that the fundamental aim of the Society was "to raise a generation of Muslims who would understand Islam correctly and act according to its teachings".[61] Consequently, all organizational bodies were given detailed instructions on how to educate and train their members.[62] This stemmed from Hasan al-Banna's belief that only a comprehensive spiritual and ideological education and training programme would produce a class of propagandists or missionaries (*du'ah*) who could spread the Society's ideas, thereby expanding the organization.

When addressing the Third Conference in 1935, Hasan al-Banna once again underlined that what gathered this congregation was not "kinship, relationship by marriage, family ties or alliances, nor are material interest or worldly benefits involved. Only the love for God, the service of Him and the Islamic mission have brought us together."[63] Such statements were a part of al-Banna's religious rhetoric, reflecting his vision of a new Islamic movement which transcended all barriers of kinship and social status. However, as will be discussed, consistent and successful attempts were made to implement this vision in the basic structure of the Society's organization during the 1930s. This was reflected in the General Law, which included a three-page list of religious, moral and social duties to be fulfilled by the individual members. The fulfilment of these duties was stated to be:

> the measure of the member's faith in the [Society's] idea. It measures his observance, his devotion and zealotry for the ideology of the Society. His position and status [*manzalatuhu*] in the community will be on the basis of this [i.e. of his fulfilment of these duties] and on this basis the Muslim Brothers will be divided into "assistant" [*musa'id*], "associate" [*muntasib*], "worker" [*'amil*] and "activist" [*mujahid*].[64]

The ideological training included theoretical and practical aspects. At the heart of the programme was the memorization of *'Aqitatuna* (our doctrine), a one-page tract consisting of ten articles, neatly summarizing the ideology of the Society and the duties of the individual members. Members of higher ranks, the "workers" and "activists", were also required to study a set of commentaries to *'Aqidatuna* and memorize a number of Prophetic traditions. The required reading also included a number of booklets, printed and distributed by the MIA. The degree of participation in the Society's activities was dependent on the membership rank. For instance, an "associate" member was only obliged to attend weekly and annual meetings. The "workers" and "activists" were required to join Qur'anic study groups organized by the Society. In addition, they were obliged to join one of the Society's Rover Scout groups. The practical part of the training aimed to mould the

"Islamic personality" of the members. The members were to make personal efforts to implement the laws of Islam in their daily life and in their homes. "Workers" and "activists" were also required always to speak classical Arabic (*fus-ha*), not the usual Egyptian colloquial. The "activists" were to abstain from all kinds of ephemeral pleasures, and idle talk and joking was to be avoided. "Seriousness . . . must always be a part of our Islamic mission", a leading member stated.[65] Failure to fulfil some of the prescribed duties, such as saving money for the pilgrimage (*hajj*) or alms-giving (*zakah*), automatically relegated "workers" and "activists" to a lower rank.[66] The expected financial contribution was to a large extent dependent on the rank and the financial situation of the individual member. Officially, the membership fee was not obligatory at all and poor members were exempted from membership fees.[67] This facilitated the recruitment of adherents from the lower classes while at the same time underlining the non-élite character of the Society.

The chances of promotion and the privileges specified for each rank must have been important encouragements for young ambitious members. Additional incentives were provided by the granting of honorific titles, special training programmes at the headquarters and other privileges to particularly dedicated members. Finally, members having qualified themselves for higher ranks received much attention at district conferences and meetings, where the promotions were marked by formal and solemn ceremonies (see Chapter 6). By defining a wide range of duties and responsibilities and making status directly dependent on the fulfilment of duties, the Society had de facto created a ranking system based on merit not on social standing and patronage. In the Egyptian society of the 1930s this was a very untraditional and revolutionary feature. There can be little doubt that this organizational principle accounted for the Society's remarkable ability to produce dedicated cadres.

Obedience to superiors was a crucial virtue in the Society. All members were required to take an oath of allegiance (*bay'a*) to Hasan al-Banna, representatives of the branches or to others who had this mandate. In the 1940s the oath of allegiance provoked a number of controversies, with critics considering it a kind of personal worship of Hasan al-Banna.[68] In recent years this issue has been raised repeatedly, and the Brothers and their critics disagree over whether the oath represented a form of blind obedience and veneration of al-Banna or whether it was essentially to God and represented a pledge to work for the sake of His call.[69] A study of Article 6 of the General Law, where the wording of the oath is given, shows that the oath taken by ordinary members in the 1930s was basically a commitment to the principles of the Society, and not a pledge of unquestioning obedience to its leadership. The oath read:

> Do you pledge to uphold the principles of the Society and work for the realization of its aims and adhere firmly to the moral of Islam and preserve the dignity of the Society, so let God be my witness. [Requiring the response "I do".] Then I accept you on behalf of myself and the Muslim Brothers as one of our brothers in God and I enjoin on you patience and truthfulness and may God forgive me and you. [The response being "I do. I have accepted this and will be your brother."][70]

However, the degree of obedience depended on the membership rank, apparently exempting the "associates" but demanding "activists" "to obey the MIA's call at any time or place".[71] At the Third Conference in 1935 it was reported that the delegates "swore complete confidence and absolute obedience [al-sama' wa al-ta'a] to the General Guide in what one likes or dislikes to do [fi mansha' wa'l-makrah]".[72] Despite this, there were restrictions on the degree of obedience. Article 15 of the General Law stipulated: "The General Guide should be dismissed by the General Consultative Council if it is proved that he has brought the Society on a course that contradicts the fundamentals of Islam and its basic laws."

The importance of obedience in the Society can also be seen from the sanctions that could be imposed on those who neglected their duties. The need to impose penalties on members who violated the principles of the Society was repeatedly emphasized. From 1935 onwards a pamphlet entitled Risalat al-Ta'a (duty of obedience) was distributed, which stressed the virtues of obedience and the fatal consequences of insubordination.[73] However, the heavy emphasis on obedience did not prevent members from openly expressing their differences with the policies of Hasan al-Banna,[74] and, as will be discussed, the frequent calls for obedience to the leadership indicate a restive membership, difficult to control, rather than an organization permeated by blind obedience. The crucial importance of obedience was demonstrated in the late 1930s and during the Second World War when the Society's most radical members threatened to bring repressive police measures upon the movement. There can be little doubt that the Society's ability to restrain its unruly members was an essential asset during these years.

It is hard to evaluate the extent to which the ideological training of the members was carried out in the various branches and districts, but it appears that by the mid-1930s the programme had already begun to "mould the souls" of the members. A member who joined the Society in early 1936 wrote that the Muslim Brothers in Cairo at that time had an outlook of seriousness "as if they carried the responsibility of the whole nation on their shoulders, even if they were still only students".[75] Observations made by agents of the Political Police who attended a meeting of the Muslim Brothers in 1936 attest to the strong ideological commitment as well as youthful zealotry among the Society's members:

> They are all devout young men who make their prayers punctually and who adhere to the tenets of their religion to the point of fanaticism. Some of them deliver speeches in which they urge those present to lament the bygone days of the Arabs and to do their best to chase out imperialists (Cheers of "Down with imperialism"). In the course of these speeches reference was made to certain Koranic verses and Prophetic sayings dealing with martyrdom and self-sacrifice for the sake of God and Country . . . I consider that the "Moslem Brethren Society" will in the course of time be in a position to produce a reckless and heedless generation who will not abstain from selling their lives cheap and whose best wish would be to die as martyrs for the sake of God and their country. It is a custom of the members of this society not to applaud speakers, but to shout in chorus: "God is great! Praise be to God!"[76]

It is likely that some parts of the Society's training programme were not followed very strictly in the provinces where conservative local dignitaries were influential. However, as will be discussed in Chapter 6, new ways of training, such as summer camps and special training courses for propagandists, were introduced in the late 1930s. The intense political campaigning and pamphleteering for the Palestinians between 1936 and 1939 also provided new opportunities for struggle and sacrifice which gave fresh impetus to the ideological training programme drawn up by Hasan al-Banna in the mid-1930s.

There was a close relationship between the training of members and the recruitment of new adherents. The training within the Society aimed at preparing them for missionary efforts in the service of the Society. The members were obliged to "spread the principles [of the Society] in all their social spheres and devote themselves completely to this task . . . whatever unpleasant situations that may entail".[77] In particular, they were instructed to spread the Islamic mission (*da'wa*) among their colleagues, family and relatives. Hasan al-Banna was determined to avoid the excesses of some of the Islamic Salafiyya societies and instructed his followers to apply "friendliness and gentleness". Article 7 of the General Law stated: "Bluntness, crudeness and abuses in words or by hints must be avoided at all cost. He [the member] should bear offences, insults and attacks that might come with magnanimity and forbearance." It appears that the Society at this stage recruited many of its new adherents through the members' personal contacts. Testimonies by people who were recruited in the 1930s show that personal efforts by individual members were decisive in making them join the Society.[78]

The Muslim Brothers sought to facilitate "the spread of the Islamic mission", i.e. to expand the Society, in a number of ways. For example, at the Third Conference in 1935 a fund for the Islamic mission (Sanduq al-Da'wa) was established in order to cover the expenditures of members who devoted themselves to preaching and proselytizing.[79] Similar measures were taken at lower levels in the organization,[80] and the branches were instructed to arrange local conferences in their districts and "point out to the secretary those persons in the neighbouring villages in whom they have noticed love for Muslim Brothers' ideas".[81] In some areas volunteers from the Muslim Brothers toured villages on Fridays and looked for people who performed their religious duties, and these were invited to form the nucleus of a new branch.[82] Those branches which managed to spread the Society to new areas received much attention and praise.[83] Some years later the branches were classified, not unlike the membership ranks, as "worker" (*'amila*), "activist" (*mujahida*) and "chosen" (*mukhtara*) according to their performance in establishing new branches.[84]

People who were willing to assume the task of forming a branch were given a large degree of organizational freedom, at least in the initial stages.[85] The Society stressed that forming a branch was very easy. There were no requirements except for a desire to serve the cause of Islam. Duties were imposed only after the members had been thoroughly acquainted with the Society's ideas and trained to "carry the burden of the Islamic mission".[86] The Society presented itself as a spiritual community asking primarily for "spiritual participation" rather than money, or in Hasan al-Banna's words: "Although money is a basis for projects, the Muslim Brothers are first and foremost preoccupied with the education of souls."[87] The voluntary membership fees and the policy of subsidizing embryonic branches reflected this attitude. Hasan al-Banna recalled in his memoirs:

> When the membership fees were insufficient to cover the expenses of the clubhouse [of the Muslim Brothers in Suez], then the Brothers had a fixed rule never to ask people for money unless they already were firm believers in the Islamic mission and realized what these seeds of sacrifice one day would bring. The Brothers were studying their hearts, not delving in their pockets.[88]

At the same time, the Society also attempted to relieve the economic problems of their members by instituting a kind of cooperative fund or a rudimentary form of social insurance. This cooperative attitude inspired efforts to revive the Islamic duty of alms-giving (*zakah*), which undoubtedly appealed to poor students and people from less well-to-do families.

The Muslim Brothers were pragmatic in religious issues when they recruited new members. They did not demand an immediate conversion to a strict moral and religious correctness. A passage from Hasan al-Banna's memoirs illustrates this point:

> He always said to me: "Listen, never refrain from admitting in your organization people who are negligent in some of their pious deeds and not regular in their prayers, as long as they are God-fearing, obedient and respect the system. Such people will very soon repent and improve. The Islamic call is like a hospital where patients come for treatment. Never close the door in their face. If you can attract them by any means, do it! This is the prime mission of the Islamic call!"[89]

The attention given to the recruitment of new adherents, the ideological education of the members, organizational strength, promotion based on merit and financial self-reliance were essential for the further growth of the Society. These features distinguished the Muslim Brothers from conservative Islamic welfare societies and laid the foundation for a popular mass movement.

The Development of the Society's Social and Charitable Work

In the summer of 1935 Hasan al-Banna returned to Cairo after his two-month journey through the Egyptian countryside. Deeply impressed by his experiences, he wrote a series of articles, filled with scathing criticism of the government's indifference to the inequality he witnessed in the countryside.[90]

> Nobody can escape noticing the vast chasm between the comfortable, exciting and boisterous city life of luxury, entertainment and pleasure, and the life of the countryside where people have sunk into the deepest misery. It is as if the manifestation of city life forces itself upon those who rule this country. These men have forgotten that the dispossessed who starve to death and succumb in their wretchedness are the material support for Egypt and the pillars of her wealth and welfare. Where are the eyes of our pampered Ministers and Senior Civil Officials? Why don't they spend some of their holidays in the countryside . . . instead of enjoying their vacations in frivolous amusement places? They know better than anyone that what they are enjoying is the sweat of deprived peasants . . . O ye Ministers and Senior Officials! These miserable peasants are sons of Egypt . . . For these subjugated and wretched of the earth God will summon you to a difficult and scrupulous account![91]

These articles reflect the increasing importance of social justice in the Society's ideology, a development which can be traced back to al-Banna's experiences in Ismailia. Consequently, an important part of the Society's activities in the 1930s concerned social and charitable work. As early as 1934 the Society was stated to have a "benevolent project or welfare institution" in almost all of its 50 branches.[92] Since many branches were still being established in the first half of the 1930s, only a minority of the Society's branches had managed to found their own charitable institutions. The social work in most branches was mainly confined to various kinds of small-scale social and educational work rather than welfare institutions.

Since its modest beginning in Ismailia in 1928, the Society had erected and repaired a number of mosques and places of prayer (*musalla*). Two schools had been established in Ismailia and Qur'an schools had been established in a number of branches.[93] In pre-revolutionary Egypt around 80 per cent of the population was illiterate and the Qur'an schools were a cornerstone in the educational system, teaching children reading and writing. Small enterprises, like workshops, carpet and embroidery factories, had also been founded in some of the branches.[94] These were closely linked to the schools which the Society had founded and offered opportunities for pupils who were incapable of completing their education.

In the first half of the 1930s the Muslim Brothers put more of their energies and resources into conducting social work among the poor and destitute than in founding charitable institutions. This could be explained by the nature of the Society's ideology which stressed that the "education of the souls" was its primary goal. There were also obvious economic reasons to avoid exhausting all the Society's resources on expensive charitable projects. However, this did not prevent the Society from undertaking some charitable work, especially in developing projects based around alms-giving or *zakah*, which was a prescribed Islamic duty.[95] These projects enabled the Muslim Brothers to raise funds among their co-religionists without having to delve too deeply into the scarce financial resources of their treasury. A successful *zakah* project in the village of Birimbal al-Qadima in the Delta province of al-Daqahliyya was used as a model for a general campaign to expand the collection of *zakah* to all branches because it generated no conflict or disputes and proceeded in an orderly fashion. Most importantly, the Brothers themselves played an important role in it and promoted themselves through organizing it. "Sincerity and orderliness" were stated to be the causes of the success in Birimbal al-Qadima.[96] Equally important was the support from the village dignitaries and the propaganda for *zakah* in mosques. Prior to the Third Conference in 1935 a committee drafted a set of detailed procedures regulating the collection and use of *zakah*, which aimed to ensure the just redistribution of funds and to avoid the disputes which were stated to occur often when *zakah* was collected. Thereupon, the Society's branches were instructed to form *zakah* committees to perform this duty according to the General Law. A deputy from the headquarters in Cairo toured the branches to supervise the implementation of the *zakah* projects.[97] This campaign was one of the Society's most important causes in the mid-1930s.

The founding of benevolent institutions under the auspices of the Society was stepped up significantly from the mid-1930s as the branches became more firmly established. In 1933, the Society had founded their own pharmacy in Rode al-Faraj in Cairo.[98] This was the beginning of an impressive increase in the Society's health care provision not only for its own members but also for the general public. In 1935 some branches were trying to establish hospitals and an ambulance service.[99] Such projects were aided by the fact that the Society had by then attracted a number of doctors to its ranks. Several months later the Muslim Brothers opened their first health clinic in the town of Minuf which treated 816 patients in its first year.[100] Similar clinics were later founded in other branches. However, it was perhaps in al-Mansura that the Muslim Brothers-sponsored health service was most impressive. Here, the hospital reportedly treated some 50–100 people a day by 1938 and also provided free medicine.[101]

A similar development can be seen in the Brothers' provision of educational services, which expanded steadily throughout the 1930s. For example, in addition to the spread of Qur'an schools, a programme for "fighting illiteracy" (*muharabat al-ummiyya*) was launched at the end of the decade. Young educated Muslim Brothers were sent to teach in coffee-shops, clubs and the like, and money was raised to purchase the necessary teaching equipment and to cover travel expenses.[102] A rather surprising part of the Society's educational services was the establishment of the School for the Defence against Gas and Air Attacks, established at the MIA and in some of the largest branches at the end of the 1930s when war in Europe seemed imminent. It trained aid patrols (*firqat al-inqadh*) to assist the general public during air attacks and to instruct people on how to protect themselves in the event of gas attacks.[103]

The Muslim Brothers also extended their social work in the late 1930s and during the 1940s to include most provincial towns and villages. This gave credibility to their express commitment to social reform and became visible proof of the emergence of a new and truly popular (*sha'bi*) political force which took a genuine interest in the destiny of the lower classes in the provinces and in the poor quarters of the city. As a result, a formidable network of grass-root contacts developed which enabled the Muslim Brothers, during the 1940s, to become the largest political mass movement in Egypt. A British observer who compared the Young Egypt Party with the Muslim Brothers noted: "The more turbulent Young Egypt Movement . . . appeals rather to young men of wealthier families who are more interested perhaps in their own political advancement than in social reform after the Ikhwan [Muslim Brothers] pattern."[104] The strong commitment to social works and reform explains, at least to some extent, the Muslim Brothers' steady growth despite the fact that their newspapers and written forms of propaganda were often inferior to those of their major political rivals, like the Young Egypt Party.

The Struggle against the Missionaries

There was a close relationship between the social work undertaken by the Muslim Brothers and the activities of foreign missionaries in Egypt in the early 1930s. The schools, factories and workshops established by the Society or with their support aimed at providing education and shelter for the poor and destitute who might otherwise have been easily attracted to the schools and institutions of the Christian missions.[105] Although very few Muslims actually converted, rumours of Muslim girls being kidnapped and forcibly converted to Christianity by foreigners aroused strong feelings among many Muslims in Egypt.[106] The campaign against the missionaries had been an important factor behind the rise of Islamic associations in the 1920s and 1930s. It also had certain political implications since the government's ability to defend Muslims was put in doubt. The precursor of the Muslim Brothers, the Hassafiyya Welfare Society in al-Mahmudiyya, had regarded resistance to the missionaries as one of their main tasks.[107] This cause also became the objective of the Society's first organized campaign in the early 1930s. The campaign had three objectives. Firstly, in order to deter parents from sending their children to Christian missionary schools, the Society publicized incidents of Muslim girls being admitted to Christian schools and "forcibly converted to Christianity".[108] Secondly, the Society sought to influence the government's policies by sending petitions to King Fu'ad.

One of these petitions was submitted by the First Conference of the Society in 1933, and included a five-point plan aimed at checking the activities of the missionaries.[109] Thirdly, practical measures were undertaken by appointing branch committees in the districts which were assigned the task of warning people of the inherent dangers of using the services of the missions. Several branches in the Canal Zone and in the adjacent al-Bahr al-Saghir area formed groups to patrol villages and warn people.[110] The Society acted resolutely by "rescuing" girls who had been caught "in the claws of the missionaries" by persuading their parents to send their children to Muslim schools instead.[111] The lack of Muslim schools and charitable institutions prompted the Society to establish a few schools and workshops. It now seems clear that the Society's anti-missionary campaign of the early 1930s drew favourable attention to the fledgling Society and attracted a number of new adherents.[112] As has been noted by al-Bishri, these endeavours seem to have earned the Muslim Brothers a "special status" among the Egyptian people in the first half of the decade.[113] Most of the Society's earliest branches were founded in areas where the activities of the missionaries affected the local population. In particular, it appears that the Society's rapid expansion in the Canal Zone and in al-Bahr al-Saghir area at this time was connected to its campaign against the missionaries.[114]

Despite the campaign's limited size, it became in many ways the standard formula for the rest of the Society's campaigns in the 1930s: an intensive and sometimes inflammatory press campaign, numerous petitions to the government in which specific demands were put forward and finally a host of practical measures requiring the members' active participation. It is also illustrative of the Muslim Brothers' endeavours to concentrate on causes which united Muslims across their theological differences. These elements were all present in the Society's campaigns for religious education, the revival of *zakah*, social reform, the abolition of prostitution, anti-imperialism and the defence of Palestine. Furthermore, these issues, especially the conversion of Muslims by foreign missionaries, aroused strong feelings against the assumed indifference and inertia of the government. This merely served to highlight a crucial feature of the Muslim Brothers' ideology, namely the inseparability of politics and religion.

Sufism and Charismatic Leadership

It has often been written that Hasan al-Banna was a charismatic leader, perhaps to a greater extent than any other person in recent Egyptian history, and it has been suggested that the concept of charismatic authority could be the key to understanding the Society and the social conditions that gave rise to it.[115] However, a brief examination of the concept of charismatic authority, as defined by Max Weber, shows that it only applies to certain aspects of Hasan al-Banna's leadership. As will be discussed, it fails to provide a comprehensive model for explaining the Society's strength.[116] There were undoubtedly elements of charismatic authority in al-Banna's leadership. For instance, the Society was "based on an emotional form of communal relationship" and its administrative staff were chosen to some degree "in terms of their charismatic qualities". The Society's rules for "appointment or dismissal, career and promotion" were somewhat obscure or possibly non-existent in the beginning. Hasan al-Banna demanded "obedience and a following by virtue of his mission" and he did not "derive his 'right' from their [the followers'] will, in the manner of election". Nevertheless, contrary to Weber's definition, al-Banna's authority should be classified as stable. His position was not dependent upon "his divine mission" in the sense that "those who faithfully surrender to him must fare well". More importantly, the Muslim Brothers did develop the "bureaucratic organization of office" and at least the framework for "regulated 'career', 'advancement', 'salary' or regulated and expert training of the holder of charisma or of his aides". According to Weber, charismatic authority does not recognize these elements. The Society also had "agency of control and appeal" – checks and control mechanisms in the bureaucracy that allowed individuals to advance their claims against the bureaucracy – and it did "embrace permanent institutions", which charismatic authority does not permit. Weber's definition of charismatic authority seems to be more valid for messianic movements without any form of bureaucratic structure. Weber observed that the growing power of bureaucratic organization gave less room for charismatic authority:

> It is the fate of charisma, whenever it comes into the permanent institutions of a community, to give way to powers of tradition or rational socialization. This waning of charisma generally indicates

the diminishing powers that lessen the importance of individual action.[117]

Hence, from this brief discussion, it must be concluded that Hasan al-Banna's leadership was not based merely on charismatic authority as defined by Weber. Al-Banna's charismatic authority was confined within the framework of a bureaucratic and hierarchical organization. As has been shown, the organizational efficiency of the movement as well as its popular bases and ideological appeal accounted for its rapid growth. This suggests that the common assumption that al-Banna's charismatic leadership was fundamental to the Society's development should be qualified.[118] As will be discussed in subsequent chapters, the development of institutions and a class of cadres was an essential feature of the Muslim Brothers towards the end of the 1930s. Strong and active opposition to al-Banna's political accommodationism emerged inside the Society in the late 1930s and between 1941 and 1943. This demonstrates a strong ideological commitment among the members and contradicts the widely accepted notion of personal veneration and unquestioning obedience to al-Banna. This is not to say that his leadership was insignificant in terms of the Society's expansion. One needs, however, to determine more exactly which aspects of his leadership contributed to the Society's success and which did not.

It seems clear that there was a strong element of Sufism in Hasan al-Banna's leadership. Contrary to the Islamic Salafiyya societies, al-Banna considered true Sufism "the essence of Islamic teachings" as it provided the best way of disciplining and purifying souls.[119] In the mid-1930s al-Banna wrote a tract called *risalat al-ma'thurat*, containing formulas for the correct invocation of God (*ad'iya ma'thura*) and rules for the performance of *dhikr*.[120] There were several examples of the practising of *dhikr* among the Muslim Brothers in the 1930s. The training programme for the Battalions contained a night vigil and the practising of *dhikr*.[121] The Battalions were an organizational innovation inaugurated by al-Banna between 1937 and 1938, aiming at creating stronger organizational cohesion and enhancing the dedication of the members. In addition, weekly lectures on Sufism (*akhlaq wa tasawwuf*) were held at the headquarters in Cairo,[122] and branches were instructed to organize an "Eternity Day" (*yawm al-akhira*) once a month:

On this day the Brothers shall refine their hearts and souls, leave this world of noisiness and clamour and go to the world of tranquillity and peace. They shall visit the city of the hereafter and go to the graves for meditation and reflection.[123]

At this time there was a number of active Sufis among the Muslim Brothers and many Brothers had been members of Sufi orders before they joined the Society.[124] Although the Society was an outspoken critic of the un-Islamic and corrupt practices of some of the Sufi orders, it nevertheless expressed its sincere congratulations to the Sufi leader al-Sayyid al-Tiftazani when he was appointed to the presidency of the Society of Nobility of Islamic Morals (Jam'iyyat Makarim al-Akhlaq) in 1935. The Brothers viewed this as a promising step towards a *rapprochement* between Sufism and the Salafiyya.[125] However, this leniency towards Sufism drew the wrath of the Salafiyya societies which began labelling the Muslim Brothers "dervishes" (*darawish*).[126] There can be little doubt that by accepting a correct and reformed Sufism the Society managed to bridge the gap between traditional and modern religious practices. It therefore filled an important function for many young Muslims who were steeped in Sufi traditions or had an attachment to Sufi rituals, but who were disenchanted by the excesses and backwardness of some of the Sufi orders.

By drawing upon the traditions of Sufism, Hasan al-Banna appears to have solved the problem of obedience and authority in the Society. Al-Banna saw the relationship between himself and his followers in spiritual terms, and he used these spiritual bonds to command obedience. To reinforce this important source of informal authority, his choice of the Sufi title *murshid* (which denotes a spiritual guide and is a traditional term for a Sufi teacher or shaykh), enabled him to demand an oath of obedience (*bay'a*), as did the shaykh of a Sufi order.[127] In addition, by assuming the title *murshid* instead of more pretentious and worldly titles he eschewed the role of a leader seeking power. Thus, he consciously distanced himself from other political leaders who adopted titles like *ra'is al-jil al-jadid* (the leader of the new generation), as did Ahmad Husayn, the head of the Young Egypt Party, and *za'im* or "leader", as did Mustafa al-Nahhas Pasha, the head of the Wafd Party. This point was accentuated by the adoption of the motto "The Prophet is our leader" (*al-Rasul za'imuna*) as well as the consequent use of the metaphor "school" to describe the movement, which underlined its commitment to the education of its members, not the pursuance of the leader's personal interests.[128]

Elements from Sufism also appear to have inspired the hierarchical structure of the Society's organization; the ranks represented not only a meritocratic promotion system but were also based on the members' progress in spiritual purity and therefore involved higher degrees of initiation. The second of the three stages of initiation (the Battalions) was defined as "purely Sufi" in spiritual terms and "purely military" in practical terms.[129] Furthermore, emotional aspects of Sufism were said to be extremely important for the young Muslim Brothers.[130] The close social community, the emotional invocations of God and the "Sufi athletic" physical training were said to have helped alleviate the frustrations of puberty and sexual maturity among the youths who joined the Society.[131]

Although the Muslim Brothers adopted aspects of Sufism, they still held a strong aversion to the personal glorification and veneration of the leader which could be found in many of the Sufi orders. Some of Hasan al-Banna's most ardent followers no doubt believed that God had bestowed a divine mission on him. As one Muslim Brother asked: "Is he not the man God has chosen to bring the renewal of religion to the people? Is he not the man to steady this stumbling people and restore its greatness and glory?"[132] However, when such affection was interpreted as the veneration of Hasan al-Banna as the Prophet Muhammad, the Brothers objected.[133] When Ahmad Anis al-Hajjaji, a personal friend of the Al Banna family, announced his intention to write a biography of Hasan al-Banna in the mid-1940s, a Muslim Brother warned him against retelling miracles as was the fashion in the biographies of Sufi shaykhs:

> I believe that you might have expected to come across many miracles and supernatural episodes in his life. But I can assure you, there is nothing in the life of the General Guide that indicates such miracles.[134]

There can be little doubt that al-Banna's style of leadership encouraged a certain veneration of his virtues and deeds. His melodramatic act of undertaking single-handedly to repay the entire debt of the Society in

1932 demonstrates this point. His authority did not derive from social standing, formal learning, rank or age, but was rather a product of his sacrifices and his unrelenting struggle for the Islamic call. This was exemplified by his endless touring of Egyptian villages as well as his pledge to donate a third of his salary to the Society's fund for propagandists.[135] A letter to his father during his "internal exile" in Qena in 1941 (see Chapter 8) illustrates how Hasan al-Banna took pride in surpassing his followers in perseverance and endurance.[136] His speech to the Third Conference in March 1935 is a good example of how he saw his own role as leader:

> Dear Brethren! This hour requires efforts and action from you. If God the Exalted wishes, I will surely work and I have strengthened my determination to strive and sacrifice in His way. Those of you who wish to be by my side and carry the burden that will come on this path – they may step forward. And those of you who know in your souls that weakness will prevent you from offering these sacrifices . . . he may come later so that we will know how many we are.[137]

It seems likely that Hasan al-Banna's charisma and remarkable qualities as an agitator were developed during the course of his preaching in the early 1930s. In fact, al-Banna, according to his brother, devoted much time and effort into becoming a first-class propagandist.[138] Little was said about his oratorical skills and charisma until 1935 when articles extolling his remarkable qualities as a leader began to appear in the Society's newspaper. But these qualities had been noticed before. In January 1934, Hasan al-Banna visited the village of Bani Quraysh in the Delta province of al-Sharqiyya for two days and, as usual, he delivered speeches in the local mosque. On the second day of his visit the mosque was so overcrowded that some people had to perform their prayers on the roof. The secretary of the Muslim Brothers did not fail to notice the effect al-Banna's speeches had on the audience.[139]

From 1935 onwards, al-Banna's qualities as a leader and believer were held up as an example to be emulated by others. He was "the wise and great leader".[140] "He embodies the highest example [of a virtuous life] that I have prescribed for myself", a young admirer confessed.[141] He was widely hailed for his ability to inspire people to work for the cause of Islam, and his simplicity and selflessness aroused genuine warmth among his followers. One young Muslim Brother noticed that he did not try "to exaggerate his eloquence to impress his audience", nor did he make artificial pauses in his speeches in order to gain respect and veneration for himself. "There is nothing awe-inspiring in his clothes or his appearance which reveals that he belongs to the men of religion . . . If he had been my age, I would have forced him to become my friend", the young man concluded.[142] An observer noted in 1938 that al-Banna travelled third class on the train. Considering the non-élite background of their leader, he was immensely impressed by the Muslim Brothers' social welfare achievements. He commented: "How is all this possible? Hasan al-Banna is not a political leader, nor a prince or a minister. He does not own anything. He does not descend from the Mamluks, nor from a Sufi shaykh family!"[143] A journalist who was sympathetic to the Society's cause wrote about Hasan al-Banna in the mid 1940s that

> What distinguishes this man [Hasan al-Banna] most of all is the fact that he has kept a particular bearing throughout his life. This quality surpasses his dignity, greatness, manliness, honour, spiritual purity and noble character. This particular bearing is his simple austere lifestyle, devoid of all kinds of luxury, snobbery, haughtiness, wealth and personal glory.[144]

As the Society grew stronger (and richer) the image of the selfless leader was given added impetus by al-Banna's austere and simple lifestyle. For many of his followers this was the most convincing manifestation of the non-élite character of the movement.

In the mid-1930s al-Banna's leadership appears to have met with some opposition from local conservative notables (a'yan). Local dignitaries were often unwilling to regard the Society as anything more than a traditional bureaucratic Islamic welfare society devoid of emotional Sufi exercises and political tendencies. In 1935, controversies about the oath of allegiance surfaced in the area of al-Bahr al-Saghir in the north-eastern Delta. These branches were led by local dignitaries who resented having to take an oath of allegiance (bay'a) to a social inferior like a primary school teacher. In his speech to these dignitaries, Hasan al-Banna attempted to use an element of charismatic authority, namely the demand of "obedience and a following by virtue of his mission".[145]

You must understand us and our mission as it truly is, otherwise the
mission will leave us. God the Exalted says: If ye turn back (from
the path), He will substitute in your stead another people; then
they would not be like you [Qur'an 37:38]. We continue to depend
on you while you remain aloof and that cannot be!! If you protest
against the *bay'a* that you have given me . . . very well . . . here you
are! Take your *bay'a* and take it from my shoulders so that you can
be free from it and so let us only be friends and exchange visits.[146]

According to a local Muslim Brother deputy, his emotional speech "had
the desired effect in the souls of the people of al-Manzala [a town in
al-Bahr al-Saghir]". However, this was perhaps only wishful thinking
as al-Banna did not obtain the usual oath of obedience. Instead a
compromise was reached when some of the local members agreed to
swear the oath of allegiance *together* with Hasan al-Banna and pledged to
work for the sake of the Islamic mission. The opposition to the *bay'a*
must have taught al-Banna that the notables had to be treated differently
from the rest of the members. The establishment of honorific bodies and
various degrees of affiliation were obvious attempts to gain their loyalty
and dedication. The failure to obtain an unqualified oath of obedience
in al-Bahr al-Saghir as well as the opposition from radical cadres in the
late 1930s clearly illustrate the limits of al-Banna's charismatic leadership.
The Muslim Brothers did not obey their leader blindly. Thus, the
assumption that Hasan al-Banna's charisma was fundamental to the
Society's rapid expansion should be qualified. The reason for the Society's
remarkable expansion during the 1930s should not be reduced to Hasan
al-Banna's charismatic abilities. As has been shown throughout this and
the previous chapter, the Society's organization, ideology and modes of
action developed along different lines to traditional welfare societies,
which were dominated by notables and which were established to
serve limited non-political purposes within the realm of general Islamic
welfare. The Society's unconventional approach to politics and its
reinterpretation of traditional Islam allowed it to mobilize educated
youth from the middle classes, whose higher education had politicized
them, but who, at the same time, were strongly affected by the cultural
clashes between the traditional and Westernization. In the first half of
the 1930s the Society of the Muslim Brothers had made its first steps
towards building a mass movement. This included among other things
an ideological foundation, recruiting and training programmes, a vast

network of local branches, a financially self-reliant organization, and a meritocratic structure permitting non-élite members to assert themselves.

NOTES

1 Article 3 of the General Law of the Society of Muslim Brothers, 1934.
2 When attempting to describe the expansion of the Society, historians have usually used the number of branches as a measure. However, these branches were of varying quality, ranging from merely a group of people who had established contact with the headquarters and who met regularly, to a fully equipped branch with institutions, a range of sub-committees, a secretariat, a treasury and premises. The majority of the branches in the 1930s belonged to the former category, and an important aspect of the expansion of the Society was the strengthening and upgrading of embryonic branches. The extent of this process is hard to measure by the available sources for the early 1930s, but two surveys from 1937 and 1940 enable us to study the process of internal consolidation in the branches in the latter half of the 1930s.
3 For the the increase in number of branches and Society's organization, see Appendices I and V.
4 The Third Conference was convened during the Muslim feast *'id al-adha*, 16–19 March 1935.
5 The branches in the Canal Zone were Ismailia, Port Said, Suez, Abu Suwayr and al-Balah. The branches in al-Buhayra province were in Shubrakhit and al-Mahmudiyya. The branches in al-Daqahliyya province were in al-Manzala, al-Jamaliyya and Meet Mirajja. Finally, there were branches in Shablanja (in al-Qalyubiyya province), Tanta (in al-Gharbiyya) and Dumiyat and Abu Hamad (in al-Sharqiyya). The branches in al-Mahmudiyya, al-Manzala, al-Jamaliyya, Meet Mirajja and Suez also had sub-branches in their neighbouring villages, while the branches in Tanta, Dumiyat and Abu Hamad were still in the process of being established. See *JIM*, no. 1, 1352/1933 and *Mudh.*, pp. 166–7. These two sources differ slightly but the general picture is essentially the same.
6 Nearly all of these branches belonged to the district of al-Manzala (Judaydat al-Manzala, al-'Ajira (the name changed to al-'Aziza in 1938), Meet Khudayr, al-Bursat and al-Kafr al-Jadid). The Birmibal al-Jadida branch belonged to the nearby district of Dikirnis. The last branch was in the village of al-Basamiyyah. See *JIM*, no. 14, 1352/1933.
7 *JIM*, no. 31, 1354/1935, p. 30; *JIM*, no. 35, 1354/1935, p. 23; and *JIM*, no. 2, 1355/1936, p. 19.
8 The opening of a new branch was not always announced. Those reported in this period were: Port Fuad (in the Canal Zone), Assiyut (in Upper Egypt), Tall Bani

Tamim (in al-Qalyubiyya), Shibin al-Qanatir (in al-Qalyubiyya), Bani Quraysh (in al-Sharqiyya), Rode al-Faraj (in Cairo) and al-Qababat (in al-Giza). It appears that branches were also established or at least preliminary steps had been taken in Minyat al-Shibin (in al-Qalyubiyya), Zaqaziq, Abu al-Akhdar, al-'Uluwwiyya (all three in al-Sharqiyya), Meet al-Nahal (in al-Daqahliyya), Mahallat Diyay (in al-Gharbiyya) and in Damanhur and Kafr al-Dawar (both in al-Buhayra).

9 *JIM*, no. 19, 1352/1933.

10 The five branches in Cairo were in Shubra, Bab al-Sha'riyya, Rode al-Faraj, Ghamra and the headquarters at Harat al-Nafi'. Some of these were not formally established like the branch of Bab al-Sha'riyya. From around March 1934 the headquarters were in Harat al-Mi'mar 6, 'Abd Allah Bey Alley in Suq al-Silah Street.

11 *JIM*, no. 28, 1352/1934. A round trip made at this time by Muhammad Effendi 'Abd al-Latif, one of Hasan al-Banna's confidants, included visits to 30 branches. *JIM*, no. 29, 1352/1934.

12 *JIM*, no. 28, 1352/1934, editorial.

13 Hasan al-Banna, *Hal nahnu qawm 'amaliyun?* [are we a practical people?] (al-Mansura, Dar al-Wafa' lil-Taba'a wa al-Nashr, n.d.), p. 14.

14 'Maktab al-Irshad fi'l-'am', *JIM*, no. 43, 1354/1935, p. 8. This was a report presented to the Third Conference of the Society in Cairo in March–April 1935.

15 This can be seen by comparing the MIA's annual report of April 1935 (see *JIM*, no. 43, 1354/1935, p. 8) and reports about the opening of new branches during 1934–5. Despite the fact that the secretary had registered twenty new branches, the opening of only four branches was reported, as far as can be seen, in the Society's newspaper.

16 *JIM*, no. 14, 1355/1936, p. 9.

17 These branches were in the towns of Benha and Tukh and in the village of al-Qanatir al-Khayriyya.

18 *JIM*, no. 7, 1354/1935, p. 32.

19 Branches were reported in al-Wasita, Assiyut, al-Qusiyya, Luxor and Aswan.

20 'Pan-Islamic Arab movement', Lampson to FO, no. E3153, 28 May 1936, FO 371/19980.

21 'Pan-Islamic Arab movement', Lampson to FO, no. E2120, 8 April 1936, FO 371/19980.

22 *JIM*, 1354/1935, p. 34. See also Gershoni, 'The Muslim Brothers and the Arab Revolt in Palestine', p. 369.

23 *JIM*, no. 29, 1354/1935, p. 25.

24 For an account of Hasan al-Banna's visit to al-Mansura and Tukh, see *JIM*, no. 45, 1354/1936, pp. 22–3.

25 Mustafa Ahmad al-Rifa'i al-Liban, 'al-Jam'iyyat al-islamiyya', *Majallat al-Fath*, no. 566, 1356/1937, pp. 12–13.

26 The first annual conference was held in Ismailia in May–June 1933, the second in Port Said in January 1934, the third in Cairo in March–April 1935, the fourth in Cairo in 1937, the fifth in Cairo in January 1939 and the sixth in Cairo in January 1941.

27 For a summary of the Second General Conference of the Muslim Brothers in Port Said in January 1934 during *'id al-fitr*, see *Mudh.*, p. 185.

28 The branches were required to assist the MIA financially as much as possible. The representatives and chairmen of branches were to pay their membership fees to the MIA. The MIA was also given the right to dispatch coupons to the branches for limited amounts of money.

29 Muhibb al-Din al-Khatib's publishing house, al-Matba'a al-Salafiyya, printed the newspaper until the Muslim Brothers acquired their own printing press in 1935. Shaykh Jawhari Tantawi was a landowner in the Kafr al-Shurafa' area. He edited a 26-volume *tafsir* (commentaries on the Qur'an) entitled *al-Jawahir* (the jewels). He appears to have been considered an authority on Islamic sciences. Shaykh Tantawi had also been one of the guests of King 'Abd al-'Aziz Al Saud of Saudi Arabia at his annual banquets in Mecca during the *hajj*. He played an important role in the Society of Islamic Fraternity (Jam'iyyat al-Ukhuwwa al-Islamiyya), founded in 1938. He became the first editor-in-chief of the newspaper of the Muslim Brothers. For more information on Shaykh Tantawi, see Jamal al-Banna, *Khitabat Hasan al-Banna al-shabb ila abihi*, p. 55; 'Abd al-Halim, *al-Ikhwan al-Muslimun: ahdath sana'at tarikh*, pp. 183–5; *JIM*, no. 34, 1352/1934; and Heyworth-Dunne, *Religious and Political Trends in Modern Egypt*, p. 106.

30 *JIM*, no. 28, 1352/1934; *JIM*, no. 42, 1353/1935; and *Mudh.*, p. 218.

31 In the mid-1930s the newspaper was criticized for being too limited in its scope and focus. See 'Abd al-Halim, *al-Ikhwan al-Muslimun: ahdath sana'at tarikh*, p. 114.

32 The newspaper published ideological tracts, religious articles, announcements and summaries of the Brothers' meetings and activities. Most editions had a section called 'Fi muhit al-Ikhwan al-Muslimin' or 'Jam'iyyat al-Ikhwan al-Muslimin' reporting the activities of the local branches. The earliest comprehensive ideological tracts by Hasan al-Banna appeared for the first time in the Society's newspaper.

33 For more details, see Chapters 7 and 8 and Mitchell, *The Society of the Muslim Brothers*, p. 23. For a comprehensive account of the Society's press, see Shu'ayr, *Wasa'il al-i'lam al-matbu'a fi da'wat al-Ikhwan al-Muslimin*.

34 *JIM*, no. 43, 1354/1935, p. 8.

35 *JIM*, no. 28, 1352/1934 and *Mudh.*, p. 185.

36 For two examples, see Hasan al-Banna, *Hal nahnu qawm 'amaliyun?*, pp. 18–19 and *JIM*, no. 4, 1356/1937, p. 16.

37 Article 10 of the General Law of the Society of the Muslim Brothers (1934).

38 The representatives of the branches/districts (*nuwwab al-dawa'ir*) had the right to attend the General Conferences, but to counterbalance this the MIA had the right to summon all those who were considered to be "experienced people" (*min ahl al-khibra*) and the district deputies (whom the MIA usually appointed) to attend the conference and vote. See Article 11 of the General Law of the Society of the Muslim Brothers (1934).

39 *Mudh.*, pp. 220–1. Only the "worker" and "activist" members were entitled to be given honorific titles by the MIA.

40 *Mudh.*, pp. 224–5.

41 One of the main points of contention in the 1931–2 conflict was the allocation of the funds of the Ismailia branch. Throughout the 1930s Hasan al-Banna had to repeatedly remind the branches about their duties to forward surplus funds to the MIA. See, for example, *Mudh.*, p. 224, and *Majallat al-Ta'aruf*, no. 13, 1359/1940, p. 11.

42 *JIM*, no. 35, 1355/1936, p. 11; *JIM*, no. 41, 1355/1937, p. 15; *JIM*, no. 43, 1355/1937, p. 3; and *JIM*, no. 44, 1937.

43 *JIM*, no. 4, 1356/1937, p. 16.

44 Mitchell, *The Society of the Muslim Brothers*, p. 181.

45 For more details on the organization of the Muslim Brothers at this time, see Appendix V. The information about the districts is based essentially on *Mudh.*, p. 223; *JIM*, no. 4, 1356/1937, pp. 12–16; and *Majallat al-Ta'aruf*, no. 13, 1359/1940, p. 11.

46 This conclusion was also made by Marius Deeb. The regulations drafted by Hasan al-Banna in 1934 dealt with the administrative responsibilities and duties of the districts, not the branches, which are hardly mentioned. See Deeb, *Party Politics in Egypt*, pp. 381–2.

47 *Mudh.*, pp. 166–7.

48 Article 12 of the General Law of the Society of the Muslim Brothers (1934).

49 Article 10 in *ibid.*

50 A report about the area conferences was presented at the Third Conference in 1935. See *JIM*, no. 43, 1354/1935, p. 10. For a complete summary of one of these conferences, see *Mudh.*, pp. 187–92.

51 For the conference in Shibin al-Qanatir, see *JIM*, no. 5, 1354/1935, p. 15. Another point to be made here is that the local conferences organized in al-Bahr al-Saghir and Shibin al-Qanatir were not, strictly speaking, "area" conferences. They were in reality only large local conferences on the "district" level.

52 *Mudh.*, pp. 119–20.

53 Muhammad Shawqi Zaki, *al-Ikhwan al-Muslimun wa'l-mujtama' al-misri* (Cairo, Maktabat al-Wahba, 1954), p. 151. Zaki's book is offered as an "impartial study of the movement". His adviser, Kamal Khalifa, was a prominent member of the Society and much of the work can be said to be an "inside view". (See Mitchell, *The Society of the Muslim Brothers*, p. 33). Zaki's work has, however, a number of flaws and inaccuracies. For example, numbers and dates should not be taken at face value.

54 I have chosen to use the term "Rover Scouts" or "Rovers" rather than "Scouts" since the age of the members in the *Firaq al-Rahhalat* and *Jawwala* was reportedly between 15 and 30 years. For a fuller treatment of the Rovers, see Chapter 6.

55 Hasan al-Banna claimed in his memoirs that almost every branch established Excursion Groups shortly after their foundation. Yet, there are no references to Rover units in branches other than Ismailia, Port Said, Suez, Abu Suwayr and Cairo prior to mid-1936. Furthermore, Rover Scout groups in important

branches such as Port Said and Suez were formed only after the Third Conference. Only the Ismailia branch sent Rover Scout representatives to the Third Conference.

56 *JIM*, no. 29, 1354/1935, p. 25.

57 See, for example, *JIM*, no. 7, 1354/1935, p. 28; 'Firaq al-rahhalat', *JIM*, no. 8, 1354/1935; and 'Firaq al-rahhalat', *JIM*, no. 10, 1354/1935.

58 'La'ihat firaq al-rahhalat' in *Qanun Jam'iyyat al-Ikhwan al-Muslimin al-'amm*, p. 26. See also *JIM*, no. 43, 1354/1935, p. 18.

59 See, for example, 'al-Ikhwan al-Muslimun fi Tanta', *JIM*, no. 15, 1352/1933; *JIM*, no. 35, 1353/1935, p. 32; *JIM*, no. 20, 1354/1935, p. 7; and *JIM*, no. 21, 1354/1935.

60 *Mudh.*, pp. 276–9.

61 Article 1 of the General Law of the Society of the Muslim Brothers (1934).

62 *Mudh.*, p. 220.

63 The text of the opening address by Hasan al-Banna is reproduced in *Mudh.*, pp. 206–8.

64 Article 8 of the General Law of the Society of the Muslim Brothers (1934). A detailed description of the duties of each category is given in *Mudh.*, pp. 220–1.

65 Muhammad al-Shafi'i, 'Mazahir al-da'wah', *JIM*, no. 43, 1354/1935, p. 18.

66 *Mudh.*, pp. 225–8.

67 *JIM*, no. 4, 1356/1937, pp. 12–16 and Hasan al-Banna, *Hal nahnu qawm 'amaliyun?*, pp. 18–19.

68 al-Jindi, *Qa'id al-da'wa*, pp. 76–7.

69 al-Tilmisani, *Dhikriyat la mudhakkirat*, pp. 45–46 and al-Sa'id, *Hasan al-Banna: mata, kayfa wa li-madha?*, pp. 51–2.

70 Article 6 of the General Law of the Society of the Muslim Brothers (1934).

71 *Mudh.*, p. 221.

72 *JIM*, no. 42, 1353/1935, p. 14. See also *Mudh.*, p. 225.

73 *Mudh.*, p. 219–22.

74 An example is the policy differences between Salih Ashmawi, the editor of *al-Nadhir*, and Hasan al-Banna in mid-1938. See *al-Nadhir*, no. 12, 1357/1938, p. 4.

75 'Abd al-Halim, *al-Ikhwan al-Muslimun: Ahdath sana'at tarikh*, p. 46.

76 'Pan-Islamic Arab Movement', Lampson to FO, no. E2120, 8 April 1936, FO 371/19980.

77 Summary of the Third Conference in March 1935 in *Mudh.*, p. 219.

78 al-Tilmisani, *Dhikriyat la mudhakkirat*, pp. 39–40; al-Sisi, *Fi qafilat al-Ikhwan al-Muslimin*, pp. 18–19; and 'Abd al-Halim, *al-Ikhwan al-Muslimun: Ahdath sana'at tarikh*, pp. 37–8.

79 *Mudh.*, p. 218.

80 See, for example, decisions by Majlis al-Shura al-Markazi in Birimbal to spread the "Islamic mission" through posters in the mosques in *JIM*, no. 8, 1353/1934. For an "Islamic mission" committee established in the al-Mansura branch, see *JIM*, no. 27, 1354/1935, p. 24.

81 *Mudh.*, p. 189–91.
82 al-Tilmisani, *Dhikriyat la mudhakkirat*, p. 40.
83 *JIM*, no. 19, 1353/1934; *JIM*, no. 41, 1354/1936; and *JIM*, no. 15, 1352/1933.
84 *Majallat al-Ta'aruf*, no. 13, 1359/1940, p. 2.
85 *Mudh.*, pp. 110–13.
86 *JIM*, no. 4, 1356/1937, p. 12.
87 *Ibid.*, p. 16.
88 *Mudh.*, p. 113.
89 *Mudh.*, p. 108.
90 Hasan al-Banna, 'Sawt al-rif', *JIM*, no. 21, 1354/1935, editorial.
91 Hasan al-Banna, 'Sawt al-rif', *JIM*, no. 19, 1354/1935, editorial.
92 Hasan al-Banna, *Hal nahnu qawm 'amaliyun?*, p. 14.
93 As far as we can determine from the sources at least the branches in the Canal
    Zone, al-Bahr al-Saghir, al-Mahmudiyya, Shubrakhit and Assiyut along with a
    few other branches ran Qur'an schools prior to 1936.
94 For two incomplete surveys on the Society's institutions, see Hasan al-Banna,
    Hal nahnu qawm 'amaliyun?, pp. 14–16 and *JIM*, no. 4, 1356/1937, pp. 12–16.
95 *Zakah* is an annual alms tax of 2.5 per cent levied on wealth. For more details on
    zakah, see the Glossary.
96 *JIM*, no. 43, 1354/1935, p. 10.
97 *Mudh.*, pp. 226–9.
98 *JIM*, no. 21, 1352/1933.
99 *JIM*, no. 19, 1354/1935, p. 30.
100 *al-Nadhir*, no. 9, 1357/1938, p. 26.
101 *al-Nadhir*, no. 11, 1357/1938, p. 13; *al-Nadhir*, no. 12, 1357/1938, p. 24; and
    al-Nadhir, no. 17, 1358/1939, p. 26.
102 'al-Ikhwan al-Muslimun fi'l-Manzala', *JIM*, no. 47, 1356/1937; *al-Nadhir* no. 5,
    1357/1938, p. 21; and *al-Nadhir*, no. 9, 1357/1938, p. 26.
103 *al-Nadhir*, no. 3, 1358/1939, p. 10; *al-Nadhir*, no. 27, 1357/1938, p. 25; and
    al-Nadhir, no. 31, 1358/1939, p. 19.
104 'The Ikhwan al Muslimin Reconsidered', 10 December 1942, FO 141/838, p. 1.
105 For example, see 'Jam'iyyat al-Akhawat al-Muslimat', *JIM*, no. 24, 1353/1934;
    JIM, no. 5, 1352/1933; and *JIM*, no. 6, 1352/1933.
106 For details of some of these cases, see Barbara Carter, 'On spreading the Gospel
    to Egyptians sitting in darkness: the political problem of missionaries in Egypt in
    the 1930s', *Middle Eastern Studies*, vol. 20 (1984), pp. 18–36; Na'im, *Tarikh
    Jam'iyyat Muqawamat al-Tansir al-Misriyya*, pp. 5–11; and *Mudh.*, pp. 171–6
    (reprint of reports of an attempt to convert a Muslim girl by the Christian
    al-Salam school, forwarded to MIA).
107 *Mudh.*, p. 25.
108 For a brief summary of the Society's anti-missionary campaign, see Na'im,
    Tarikh Jam'iyyat Muqawamat al-Tansir al-Misriyya, pp. 16–18. See also *JIM*,
    no. 4, 1356/1937, p.15.
109 *JIM*, no. 6, 1352/1933 and *Mudh.*, pp. 176–8.

110 *JIM*, no. 6, 1352/1933. For the establishment of branch committees, see *Mudh.*, p. 176.
111 *Mudh.*, pp. 171–6 and *Majallat al-Fath*, no. 258, 1350/1931, pp. 8–9.
112 Shaykh 'Abd al-Latif al-Shi'sha'i, a Muslim Brother propagandist, recalled that a group of notables and merchants contacted him during his anti-missionary campaign in Tanta, expressing their desire to join the Society and found a local branch. See 'Jawlat Ustadh Shaykh 'Abd al-Latif al-Shi'sha'i fi'l-Wajh al-Bahari', *JIM*, no. 7, 1352/1933.
113 al-Bishri, *al-Muslimun wa'l-aqbat fi itar al-jama'a al-wataniyya*, p. 473.
114 Missionary activities were stated to be more intensive in these areas than elsewhere in the early 1930s. See Na'im, *Tarikh Jam'iyyat Muqawamat al-Tansir al-Misriyya*, p. 9. See also al-Bishri, *al-Muslimun wa'l-aqbat fi itar al-jama'a al-wataniyya*, p. 472.
115 The concept of charismatic authority has been suggested by Ellis Goldberg, but he does not discuss it in terms of the structure of power or leadership in the organization of the Muslim Brothers. See Goldberg, 'Bases of traditional reaction: a look at the Muslim Brothers', *Mediterranean Peoples*, vol. 14 (1981), p. 81.
116 See Max Weber, 'Legitimacy, politics and the State' in William Connolly (ed.), *Legitimacy and the State* (Oxford, Basil Blackwell, 1984), pp. 50–6. See also Weber, *The Theory of Social and Economic Organization* (New York, The Free Press, 1966), p. 360.
117 Weber, 'Legitimacy, politics and the State', p. 56.
118 Mitchell, *The Society of the Muslim Brothers*, pp. 295–300.
119 *Mudh.*, p. 26.
120 Hasan al-Banna, *Risalat al-ma'thurat* and *Mudh.*, pp. 261–4.
121 See, for example, *JIM*, no. 1, 1356/1937, editorial; *Mudh.*, pp. 261–4; *al-Minhaj*, p. 29. For the training programmes in the Battalions, see Chapter 6.
122 *JIM*, no. 1, 1355/1936, p. 19.
123 *al-Nadhir*, no. 2, 1358/1939, p. 22 and *Mudh.*, pp. 277–8.
124 *JIM*, no. 43, 1355/1937, p. 11; *JIM*, no. 37, 1354/1935, p. 23; *JIM*, no. 36, 1354/1935, p. 24; al-Sisi, *Fi qafilat al-Ikhwan al-Muslimin*, p. 42; and 'Abd al-Halim, *al-Ikhwan al-Muslimun: ahdath sana'at tarikh*, p. 457.
125 'Ladha'at hurrah', *JIM*, no. 9, 1354/1935.
126 *al-Nadhir*, no. 26, 1357/1938, editorial. For the disputes between the Muslim Brothers and some of the Salafiyya societies, see Khalil Haydar, *Adwa' 'ala mudhakkirat Hasan al-Banna* (Kuwait City, Sharika Kazima lil-Nashr wa al-Tarjama wa al-Tawzi', 1989), pp. 239–40. By labelling the Muslim Brothers "dervishes" the Salafiyya societies actually accused them of supporting excessive forms of Sufi practices which in fact the Brothers wished to distance themselves from.
127 Gilsenan, *Recognizing Islam*, p. 244. As far as is known, this title was not officially used by al-Banna until September 1932, after the first internal crisis in the Society had been brought to an end.
128 Article 9 of the General Law of the Society of the Muslim Brothers (1934).

129 Hasan al-Banna, 'Risalat al-ta'alim', *Majmu'at al-rasa'il lil-Imam al-Shahid Hasan al-Banna*, p. 274. For more information on the Battalions, see Chapter 6.
130 Interview with Jamal al-Banna, spring 1995.
131 Hasan al-Banna saw the Rover Scouts as a fruitful combination of physical training and spiritual Sufi exercises (see *Mudh.*, p. 270). However, the emotional dimension might have become too intense for some of the members. Some time in 1938–9 a few Muslim Brother youths in the Battalions reportedly became mentally deranged after having participated in Hasan al-Banna's intense and strongly emotional classes on Sufism. See al-Sisi, *Fi qafilat al-Ikhwan al-Muslimin*, p. 62.
132 *JIM*, no. 22, 1354/1935, p. 22.
133 Ahmad Husayn was one of these critics. See *Jaridat Misr al-Fatath*, no. 77, 1357/1938, pp. 3–5.
134 al-Hajjaji, *Ruh wa rayhan*, pp. 100–1.
135 During "the first pioneers in the Islamic call" (*al-ra'id al-awwal fi al-da'wa*) campaign, which began in October 1938, Hasan al-Banna surpassed his followers by donating one-third of his salary. The largest previous contribution had been one-fifth, but averaged only one-tenth. Around £E400 was raised in this campaign. See 'al-Siyasa al-maliyya lil-Ikhwan', *al-Nadhir*, no. 11, 1357/1938, p. 8.
136 Jamal al-Banna, *Khitabat Hasan al-Banna al-shabb ila abihi*, pp. 135–6.
137 Hasan al-Banna, 'Kalimat al-iftitah fi Majlis al-Shura lil-Ikhwan al-Muslimin fi in'iqadihi al-thalith' (the opening speech at the General Consultative Assembly of the Muslim Brothers), reproduced in *JIM*, no. 41, 1353/1935.
138 Jamal al-Banna, *Khitabat Hasan al-Banna al-shabb ila abihi*, pp. 106–8.
139 *JIM*, no. 26, 1352/1934.
140 *JIM*, no. 23, 1354/1935.
141 *JIM*, no. 29, 1354/1935, p. 25.
142 *Ibid.*
143 Dr Mahmud Salih, 'Fi rihal ra'is Jam'iyyat al-Ikhwan al-Muslimin', *al-Nadhir*, no. 11, 1357/1938, p. 13.
144 al-Jindi, *Qa'id al-da'wa: hayat rajul wa tarikh madrasa*, p. 131.
145 Weber, 'Legitimacy, politics and the State', pp. 50–6.
146 'Jawla fi iqlim al-Wajh al-Bahari ma' Fadilat al-Murshid (3)', *JIM*, no. 27, 1354/1935.

4

Round Trips, Networks and Patronage

It was one of Hassan al-Banna's habits to pay a visit to the
village chief or elder upon his arrival at every village . . . [Even
after a severe clash between the local Muslim Brothers and the Pasha
in Kafr al-Musaylha Hasan al-Banna insisted that] "I have
always entered this village through the 'door' . . . the
only 'door' to this village is the house of
'Abd al-'Aziz Pasha Fahmi".

'Abbas al-Sisi[1]

Hasan al-Banna's Round Trips and the Use of Traditional Religious Networks

As discussed in the previous chapter, the attention given to organizational efficiency and internal unity accounted for a great deal of the Society's progress. An essential way in which this was achieved was Hasan al-Banna's frequent round trips to the Society's branches and contacts throughout Egypt. These trips served to strengthen the bonds between the General Guidance Council (MIA) and the branches. Furthermore, during his travels al-Banna was able to ensure that the Society's policies were implemented in the branches. Although the exact date of al-Banna's first trip is not known, it is likely that this took place as soon as the Ismailia branch became firmly established in 1931. However, the first known reference to these round trips, an announcement in the Society's newspaper of the schedule for a trip to the Delta region, does not appear until 1933.[2] During the course of the next two years it is evident that al-Banna's summer trips became annual events of great significance to the Society. In the summer of 1935 al-Banna toured a large number of branches, giving speeches in local mosques and meeting members and sympathizers. Summaries from the meetings were subsequently printed in the Society's newspaper.[3]

Hasan al-Banna's round trips to the provinces have become particularly legendary in the history of the Muslim Brothers, and, as shall be seen, certain myths have been created about them. These myths are largely the result of al-Banna's own account in his memoirs of his earliest recruiting trips in the town of Abu Suwayr:

> I started to study the faces of the people in coffee-houses, shops and in the streets. Finally I reached the shop of Shaykh Muhammad al-Ajrudi. He was a man of great dignity and honour, with piety in his face and eloquence and language in his bearing . . . Seeing promising signs in him, I sat down next to him and those he was talking to in the store, and introduced myself and explained the purpose which had brought me to Abu Suwayr. I said that he had promise and could carry the burden of the Islamic call.

The coffee-shop owner thought Hasan al-Banna represented a charitable society and he invited him to deliver a sermon in the mosque or at a nearby place of prayer (*musalla*). But al-Banna chose to deliver the sermon in the coffee-shop:

> What they saw and heard was very surprising to them: this young respectable teacher is delivering religious lectures to the people in the coffee-shops! And not with the Imam in the mosque or the Shaykh of the Sufi order![4]

This story from al-Banna's memoirs has often been referred to as an example typifying his recruiting trips in the early years of the Society.[5] It undoubtedly reflects his distinct awareness of the key persons in the local community – the shopkeepers, the teachers, the religious shaykhs and the like – whose traditional links with their social inferiors – the peasants, the workers, the small tradesmen – could facilitate the mobilization of a broader mass following. The story also typifies the numerous anecdotes about Hasan al-Banna which were put forward as examples to be emulated by young Muslim Brother cadres. However, as a typical example of al-Banna's round trips of the 1930s this story is misleading. First of all, the expansion of the Society to new areas was a task usually assigned primarily to the local branches, and not to the central leadership. Branches were also founded as a result of the transfer of state functionaries, teachers and Azharite preachers (*wa'iz*) who were members of the Muslim Brothers. Secondly, as far as we know al-Banna never went on recruiting trips alone; he was usually accompanied by a large group of prominent Muslim Brothers, preferably members of local origin who knew the idiosyncrasies and traditions of the villages.[6] Thirdly, al-Banna's trips were usually well-organized and carefully planned visits to the local branches or to places where at least some preliminary local contacts had been made and a programme had been set up.[7] In many cases his visits were basically aimed at strengthening a nascent nucleus of Muslim Brother sympathizers and their links to the General Guidance Council in Cairo. Finally, as discussed in Chapter 1, there is little evidence to support the claim that preaching in coffee-shops was an important way of recruiting people. Praying and preaching in local mosques were pivotal parts of al-Banna's visits and his speeches usually served as appetizers to more detailed lectures at the houses of the Society, or in the homes of some of his adherents or sympathetic local notables.[8]

By the mid-1930s a few branches had organized Rover Scout units (*Firaq al-Rahhalat* or *al-Jawwala*) and if al-Banna visited an important town or village the Rover Scouts frequently went there to greet him, lining up at the railway station to await his arrival.[9] These Rover units, resplendent in their uniforms, parading through the streets of the town or village chanting the Muslim Brothers' official hymn, "O God's Prophet" (*Ya Rasul Allah*), must have attracted the attention of the local community and made al-Banna's arrival an event of some note.[10] The next stop was usually the mosque. Al-Banna and his associates usually seized the opportunity after prayer to deliver a short speech or lecture, calling on people to join the Society or at least to attend one of its meetings. The round trips were usually scheduled so that al-Banna arrived at an important town or village on a Friday. The Friday sermon usually drew the élite of the village and when the Society gained some momentum al-Banna was often given the honour of delivering it. After leaving the mosque al-Banna rested, then met with local Muslim Brothers, local dignitaries and possibly with the village chief (*'umda*).[11] He was always careful to pay due respect to the local élite. Al-Banna reportedly saw the village chief as "the door to the village" and tried to restrain his followers when conflicts occurred between the local Muslim

Brothers and the village chief.[12] This approach was apparently successful in winning the sympathy of the local élite whose support the Society could not afford to ignore at this early stage.

Hasan al-Banna's round trips reveal an important vehicle of the successful expansion of the Muslim Brothers: the use of traditional and religious networks in Egyptian society. The extensive religious networks of mosques and prayer-houses, the large number of people attached to the mosques, the celebration of numerous Muslim feasts and religious organizations such as Sufi orders and existing Islamic welfare societies constituted important potential platforms for recruiting new adherents. These networks could be readily used by the Muslim Brothers to recruit members, but not to the same extent by their political rivals. This was because overt political activity by these political rivals, such as the Young Egypt and the Wadfist youth, was not readily accepted by the local authorities, especially if the local notables did not support them. By using religious discourse and utilizing already existing religious networks, the Muslim Brothers evaded traditional obstacles inhibiting political activity. Their rivals would immediately incur the suspicion of the local authorities if they started preaching in mosques, as they were intrinsically political parties. The existence of mosques and places of prayer in every village provided the Muslim Brothers with a respectable pulpit and an attentive audience. The cluster of people attached to the mosque like the local prayer leader (*imam*), the mosque preacher (*khatib*), the "caller for prayer" (*muezzin*), the religious admonisher or preacher (*wa'iz*), the Qur'an reciters (*muqri*), the local Islamic scholars (*'ulama*) as well as a large number of teachers, all of whose livelihoods were directly linked to the status of Islam in Egyptian society, provided the Muslim Brothers with numerous potential sympathizers and supporters. In traditional villages and provincial towns, those relatively untouched by the process of modernization and industrialization, the religious élite still held an enormous influence over the local populace. Winning the support of the local religious élite was therefore of fundamental importance. A general call for reinstating Islamic values and traditions would naturally touch a chord with a local religious élite who had seen their social standing steadily undermined for decades by the secularizing policies of the state. When the Muslim Brothers demonstrated a willingness to do so not only through words but also by practical action, they must have found a receptive audience.

When praying in the local mosques on his frequent trips to the Egyptian countryside, al-Banna was careful to pay due respect to the local *imam*. Following the precepts of "Islamic etiquette" he always treated the *imam* as the host when he visited the mosque.[13] Although the Muslim Brothers attracted the majority of their members from non-religious occupational groups, some religious scholars were given leading positions in the Society, especially in the first half of the 1930s.[14] One such example was Shaykh Muhammad Ali Ahmad, the *imam* of the famous al-Rifa'i Mosque in the Citadel in Cairo, who was a close associate of al-Banna in 1935–6.[15] His sermons were reportedly eloquent while at the same time carrying a practical and down-to-earth message. His mosque was one of the most magnificent in Cairo and was frequently visited by educated youth. After his sermons, he used to give a short lecture while he distributed the magazine of the Muslim Brothers. The Society undoubtedly benefited greatly from the support of key figures like Shaykh Muhammad Ali Ahmad in the local communities. The importance the Society attached to local *imam*s is also reflected by the fact that they were frequently chosen to be the local representatives (*nuwwab*) of the Muslim Brothers. In fact, a survey from 1937 shows that members of the local religious élite were the second largest social/ occupational group among the Society's local representatives after civil servants and professionals.[16] Despite this, the local religious élite could not always be relied upon. For example, there were instances when they refused to allow the Muslim Brothers to deliver speeches after the Friday prayer. When the Society embarked upon the Palestine campaign in the late 1930s and attempted to use mosques as platforms for delivering vitriolic anti-imperialistic speeches, the religious élite tore down pro-Palestine posters which the Society had attached to the walls, fearing problems with local authorities.[17] As the Society grew stronger and more politicized, the utility of the local religious élite declined and the 'lay' character of the Society became more pronounced.

The spread of Islamic welfare societies in the 1920s and 1930s meant that in most large villages and provincial towns there were one or several Islamic societies with their own club, mosque and some kind of welfare work. It seems clear that al-Banna endeavoured to be on good terms with all Islamic welfare societies, partly to avoid alienating potential supporters among them. When touring the countryside he frequently delivered lectures or preached in the premises of other Islamic welfare societies, especially at the local headquarters of the YMMA with whom the Muslim Brothers had a close relationship. This was an important platform for attracting new members, particularly in towns or villages where the Society had not yet acquired a house of their own. Although no statistics are available, it seems clear that the Muslim Brothers were successful in attracting a number of zealous supporters from the YMMA.[18] Memoirs by Muslim Brother veterans show that some of them had been active members (and local leaders) of the YMMA before they joined the Muslim Brothers.[19] When the Society had become sufficiently strong by the late 1930s, it made repeated attempts to absorb or join forces with other Islamic associations in order to create an "Islamic Front".[20] From 1938 the Muslim Brothers hosted a number of meetings or conferences, which were attended by representatives of various Islamic associations, and these efforts met with some success in the sense that a number of small Islamic associations agreed to join the Muslim Brothers in the latter half of the 1930s.[21]

The Muslim Brothers gave a high priority to the celebration of Islamic feasts, which they considered a religious duty. The celebrations were preferably organized at the premises of the local branch, but as most local branches lacked a house of their own in the early 1930s, the Muslim Brothers frequently celebrated the feast in the closest main branch or at the premises of another Islamic society. These feasts were an important opportunity to propagate the ideas of the Muslim Brothers to the general public. The Society went to great lengths to organize the orderly celebration of feasts, during which modern forms of propaganda, such as the use of loudspeakers and pamphleting, were employed. For example, in 1934, on the occasion of the Prophet's Birthday, the Cairo branches organized a reportedly well-attended procession from the al-Sayyida Zaynab Mosque to the Society's headquarters.[22] A year later, in an attempt "to make the people of Cairo feel the presence of the Muslim Brothers", daily evening processions were organized in the month of the Prophet's Birthday (*Rabi' al-Awwal*, third month in the Islamic calendar). During these processions "thousands of pamphlets" announcing the Society's lectures were distributed. Although the processions were keenly watched and cheered by the local population, the Society's lectures were sparsely attended.[23] This indicates that the Muslim Brothers were not particularly successful at this early stage in attracting supporters from the general public through pamphlets and general invitations. The Society's growth in the first half of the 1930s was still based on "individual persuasion".[24] However, this all changed in 1937 when new headquarters were acquired in the Midan al-'Ataba al-Khadra', a large square in Cairo at "the heart of its Islamic life".[25] The new premises helped raise the profile of the Society and a significant increase in members was reported after the move.

The celebration of Muslim feasts offered opportunities to build networks of traditional patronage. This was done by inviting members of the local élite, who were potential sympathizers of the Muslim Brothers' ideas, to be guests of honour at the celebrations.[26] Being fully aware of the power structure of Egyptian villages and towns, Hasan al-Banna could not afford to overlook local notables (a'yan). The establishment of honorific committees in the districts consisting of "distinguished members with social standing" was clearly aimed at gaining the support of notables. Al-Banna especially encouraged sons of prominent families to join the Society, knowing that the family or the clan would then be linked to the Muslim Brothers.[27] In his memoirs al-Banna recalled how one of the celebrations at the Port Said branch had been attended by Mahmud Effendi Abd al-Latif and Umar Effendi Ghanim, both of them sons of prominent families in al-Bahr al-Saghir (in al-Daqahliyya province). After having met with al-Banna, they returned to their villages where branches were founded shortly afterwards.[28] As we have seen, this area became a Muslim Brother stronghold in the early 1930s.

In the 1930s, representatives of the local authorities and the police were invited and frequently attended the Society's celebration of Muslim feasts.[29] This might now seem surprising considering the more or less continuously outlawed and underground status of the movement since the late 1940s. However, in the 1930s it seems clear that the attendance at the Society's meetings of the *ma'mur al-markaz*, the highest governmental representative in the administrative area, who commanded the local police force, was considered an event of some significance to the Muslim Brothers, and their newspaper praised the piety of the *ma'mur al-markaz* and the local police if they attended the Society's celebrations.[30] The local branch in Port Said was for some time successful in enlisting the support of the Governor of the Suez Canal Zone who repeatedly attended the Society's celebrations.[31] The Governor also acted as the Brothers' intermediary when they petitioned the King, the Suez Canal Company and the Ministry of Endowments for the establishment of mosques in Port Said and Port Fuad, but it is not known whether these efforts produced any concrete results.[32]

Whatever support the Muslim Brothers might have had from local authorities and the local aristocracy in certain areas, there was a latent conflict between their fundamental aim and the interests of these local élites. This was already evident by the mid-1930s. For example, in a summary from the foundation meeting of the Muslim Brother branch in 1936, it was declared that they intended to fight prostitution, alcohol and other "abominations" in the town. The members then proceeded to form a committee which would contact the police and the village chief with a view to working towards the abolition of "these abominations with the power of the government". If this failed to make any satisfactory progress, the Muslim Brothers were prepared to resort to "other legal methods".[33] This amounted to nothing less than questioning the legitimacy of the local authorities and élites, politically as well as religiously. In the following years, the Brothers began to present demands which had political implications, and they began to define politics as an integral part of Islam, thereby challenging the traditional notion that politics was the preserve of the élite. This was naturally intolerable for the local aristocracy and led to an uneasy relationship in the latter half of the 1930s.[34]

The Search for Patronage

Informal networks of patronage permeated the social, political and economic life of Egyptian society of the 1930s.[35] If the Muslim Brothers were to expand their influence, it was inevitable that they should seek to gain support from members of the ruling élites. On the other hand, the Society's members, who were drawn mostly from the lower middle classes, frowned upon the luxurious lifestyle of the Egyptian upper class. Furthermore, the Society's strong commitment to an ideological programme and not to personal interests represented a major obstacle to patron–client relationships. Although such relations were sometimes portrayed as a necessary sacrifice for the Society's cause,[36] they nevertheless presented immediate ideological problems.

One way of getting influential dignitaries interested in the Society was simply to arrange meetings where leading Muslim Brothers introduced the Society and the ideas behind it. Sometimes they would offer some kind of honorary position to a sympathetic dignitary with a view to gaining funds for their welfare projects, or they would only try to secure the dignitary's goodwill and patronage. It appears that from the early 1930s the Society was on good terms with Prince Umar Tusun, a member of the royal family and one of the YMMA's main patrons.[37] There is also evidence of contacts between the Muslim Brothers and Muhammad al-Maghaji Pasha, a high-ranking dignitary from al-Buhayra who supported Islamic welfare societies.[38] The nature of both of these relationships is unknown, but they were sufficiently strong to facilitate the participation of the Muslim Brothers' leadership at one of the Prime Minister's receptions in September 1935. This important achievement is explained in more detail later.

Another way of attracting the attention of the élite was to publish open letters to politicians who could be credited for having performed virtuous deeds for Islam, or who had shown a general commitment to social and economic reform. For example, in early 1934 Hasan al-Banna wrote an open letter to the Ministers of Religious Endowments, Financial Affairs and the Interior, in which he expressed his deep satisfaction with the measures they had taken to protect the status of Islam in Egyptian society. He also praised the Ministers' deeds in order to encourage other politicians to follow their example.[39] In November 1935, al-Banna's brother wrote an article crediting another politician, Hamid al-Basil Pasha, for his devotion to Islam.[40] More overtures followed in 1936 during the caretaker ministry of Ali Mahir Pasha.[41] According to Ali Mahir, Hasan al-Banna came to see him some time in 1935. It is unknown what they discussed apart from "general affairs",[42] but al-Banna appears to have been left with a favourable impression of Ali Mahir. In April 1936, he applauded Mahir's endeavours to activate negotiations about diplomatic recognition between Egypt and Saudi Arabia.[43] Ali Mahir's programme for social reform was also praised, and his personal conduct commented upon with satisfaction. Al-Banna stated:

The Muslim Brothers are prepared to put their moderate forces in the hands of any group or institution which works for the general welfare in our country. In this they intend nothing else than to do their duty for the sake of general reform.[44]

These overtures to Ali Mahir, which in reality were attempts to offer the Society's support in return for his patronage, were made even more explicit by a second article on the same page, reminding the Muslim Brothers of "the duty to vote [in the forthcoming elections] for those who work for an Islamic and national platform . . . to colour the nation (*umma*) with Islamic teaching and legislation".[45] Thus, it seems likely that at this point al-Banna had already received positive signals from Ali Mahir and some kind of mutual understanding had been reached. As will be discussed in Chapter 7, this relationship came to play an important part in the Society's history.

In 1935, a controversy over education provided the Muslim Brothers with another opportunity to attract the attention of the élite. A new educational reform proposal which increased the number of hours allotted to foreign languages at the expense of Arabic and religion provoked a strong reaction from Azharists and Dar al-'Ulum-educated teachers.[46] The Society responded by forming "committees calling for the reform of religious education",[47] and submitted open letters and petitions to the Minister of Education and the members of the government-appointed Committee for Educational Reform. In addition, the Society's newspaper widely covered the reform proposals and devoted a series of editorials to the subject of educational reform.[48] The Muslim Brothers also gathered a large number of signatures which were included in a nation-wide petition. In September 1935, a delegation headed by Muhammad al-Maghaji Pasha and composed of various dignitaries, travelled to Alexandria and handed the petition to the Minister of Education and the Prime Minister, Tawfiq Nasim Pasha. This meeting was also attended by Prince Umar Tusun and Mustafa al-Nahhas Pasha. Among this noble and distinguished assembly Hasan al-Banna and two of his associates, Shaykh Hamid 'Askariyya and Ahmad Effendi al-Sukkari, were admitted as members of the delegation delivering the petition. This was apparently the first meeting between the Muslim Brothers and the head of the government, and as such it should be considered an important achievement of the Society's strategy to attract the attention of higher political circles.[49]

The campaign against the new educational reform proposals also brought Hasan al-Banna to the attention of Shaykh Mustafa al-Maraghi, the newly appointed Rector of al-Azhar, who was the highest religious authority in Egypt. In his memoirs al-Banna recollects his meeting with al-Maraghi in 1935. Their conversation had been marked by considerable empathy and warmth, and was the beginning of a lasting friendship between the two.[50] This meeting was not only the result of the educational campaign but had also come about through the efforts of Shaykh Ahmad Hasan al-Baquri, one of al-Banna's earliest converts. Some time after al-Baquri joined the Brothers in 1933 he became the leader of the student union at al-Azhar (Ittihad al-Jami'a al-Azhariyya), and played an important role in the campaigns and student strikes during 1934 and 1935 which aimed to force the reinstatement of the then resigned Shaykh Mustafa al-Maraghi and some 70 al-Azhar teachers who had been dismissed because of their outspoken views on the role of al-Azhar in politics.[51]

Hasan al-Banna's meetings with Ali Mahir Pasha and Shaykh Mustafa al-Maraghi and his participation at the Prime Minister's reception in 1935 illustrate that the Muslim Brothers already knew influential people at this stage who could introduce them to some of Egypt's most powerful men. These contacts might well have been too weak to bring the Society immediate benefits, but they did prepare the ground for closer and more fruitful relationships in the late 1930s.

These first encounters with members of the ruling élite appear to have paved the way for a clarification of the Society's general policies towards other political and religious bodies. In 1935, the Third Conference concluded: "every group or association which implements one of the Muslim Brothers' objectives will be supported by them in this." However, a restriction was also imposed: "If the Society supports one particular group or association, it has to make sure that it [this group] does not at any time diverge from the Society's aim."[52] Hasan al-Banna's first editorial in AH 1355 (April 1936) announced that the second aim of the Society (after the spiritual education of its members) was to spread the Islamic mission to people, particularly to the "official and unofficial men of reform".[53] Two years later, a publication distributed primarily among the most dedicated members instructed them to make contacts with and try to win the support of members of the élite "whose patronage would bring benefits" to the movement.[54] However, the

Muslim Brothers were anxious to avoid the traditional role of client. This was done by defining in detail the Society's official position *vis-à-vis* all other political and religious bodies in Egypt. These definitions were repeatedly reproduced in internal publications, thereby tying the Society's policies to an explicit ideological programme and not to the personal interests of their patrons. In the late 1930s the ideological programme was supplemented with a formula for relations with patrons. At the Fifth Conference in 1939 the Society stipulated that "the avoidance of the hegemony of notables and elders" (*al-bu'd 'an haymanat al-a'yan wa'l-kubara*) should be one of the Society's five fundamental characteristics.[55]

Thus, the Society had developed a policy on the question of patronage and contacts with the élite. The Brothers had sought to define a set of rules and restrictions which regulated these contacts, allowing for an expansion of the informal patronage networks without abandoning their commitment to an ideological programme. More importantly, the Society built an independent power basis by recruiting a mass following, by increasing its organizational efficiency and by mainly relying on its own financial resources. These factors served to protect the Muslim Brothers from ending up as puppets in the hands of their patrons. Instead, as will be discussed in Chapter 7, the Muslim Brothers began to pursue their own political agenda, even when it fundamentally conflicted with that of their patrons.

Supporters and Patrons in Saudi Arabia

The search for moral and financial support was not confined to sympathetic high-ranking dignitaries and officials in Egypt. From the mid-1930s the Muslim Brothers made efforts to establish contact with influential people in Hijaz, the north-western part of Saudi Arabia where the two holy cities of Mecca and Medina are situated.[56] Being the only truly independent state in the Middle East and at the same time strongly committed to the protection of Islam and its holy places, Saudi Arabia was looked upon very favourably by the Muslim Brothers. King Abd al-Aziz Al Saud was, in Hasan al-Banna's words, "one of the hopes of the Islamic world for a restoration of its grandeur and a recreation of its unity".[57] The young Hasan al-Banna had been eager to get an appointment as a teacher in Hijaz after his graduation in 1927.[58] Given the pan-Islamic ideology of the Brothers, it was not surprising that the Society sought to have a special relationship with the protector of the holy places of Islam.

In the mid-1930s the Muslim Brothers endeavoured to establish closer contacts with influential representatives in Hijaz. The first known attempt to approach leading Saudis came in October/November 1934 when a delegation of leading members, headed by al-Banna himself, met twice with the Governor of Medina, the capital of Hijaz, during the latter's stay in Cairo. The first meeting, initiated by al-Banna, was then reciprocated by a short visit by the Governor to the Muslim Brothers' headquarters. General Islamic affairs were discussed and, as a sign of goodwill, the Governor promised during the meeting to make special privileges for those Muslim Brothers who wished to perform the *hajj* (the pilgrimage to Mecca).[59] Following this meeting the Society's newspaper issued a special edition on Medina.[60] Shortly afterwards a campaign was launched in order to collect money for the poor and destitute in Medina, and a large sum was reportedly collected in mosques and government agencies by the Society's members in Cairo and some of the districts.[61] At the Third Conference a few months later, the Society decided to initiate a campaign to promote the *hajj* and mobilized its membership to perform this Islamic duty, which it should be noted was a cornerstone of the Hijazi economy. All branches were instructed to form committees to conduct propaganda for the *hajj*. Saving money for the *hajj* became a duty for members of higher ranks. The "worker" members would be demoted if they failed to do so. Pamphlets dealing with the rituals of the *hajj* were printed and Islamic scholars specialized in the laws of the *hajj* were sent to teach in the branches. Hasan al-Banna declared that he would do the *hajj* during the next pilgrimage season, and he ordered that a message of greetings be sent from the Third Conference to the Saudi King.[62] A few months after the Third Conference another meeting between the Muslim Brothers and the Hijazis took place, this time with the Hijazi Minister of Finance who was in Egypt at that time.[63] The sources tell us nothing about what they discussed, but it is likely that these contacts further strengthened the Society's relationship with the Hijazis. In early 1936, al-Banna left Egypt to perform the pilgrimage accompanied by a large group of members.[64] The pilgrimage at that time was the occasion for annual Islamic conferences, presided over by the

Saudi King, and with distinguished participants from Egypt as well as other Islamic states. Although not being among the official guests at the annual conference, al-Banna seized this opportunity to deliver a speech after the official speeches, making himself noticed in these prominent Islamic circles.

The Society's endeavours to establish friendly contacts with influential individuals in Hijaz coincided with the founding of the Society's publishing house, and the completion of the first volumes of the *musnad al-fath al-rabbani*, a new classification of the traditions of Imam Ahmad ibn Hanbal al-Shaybani, authorized by Shaykh Ahmad al-Banna, Hasan al-Banna's father. The first volumes were to be printed at the Society's publishing house,[65] and Shaykh Ahmad al-Banna had already completed the first volume some time in 1934 and the search for potential subscribers had begun.[66] Since the Hanbali school (*madhhab*) was the official legal school in Saudi Arabia, it was natural to look for potential subscribers there. Other Islamic associations, such as the Society of Supporters of Muhammad's Tradition (Jam'iyyat Ansar al-Sunna al-Muhammadiyya), had close contacts in Hijaz and financed part of their activities by selling books on Islamic jurisprudence to the Saudi King and leading Hijazi dignitaries.[67] It was therefore reasonable to search for reliable long-term contracts among the Hijazis, which would facilitate the continuation of Shaykh Ahmad al-Banna's laborious task, in addition to being a secure and stable income for the Society's new publishing house.

Although no direct link can be proved, it seems clear that part of the reason for the *hajj* campaign, the fund raising for the poor and destitute in Medina and the meetings with Hijazi officials in 1934–5 was to win the goodwill of Hijazi dignitaries in order to facilitate the *musnad al-fath al-rabbani* project and other Muslim Brother publications. Shortly after publishing the first volume of the *musnad al-fath al-rabbani*, Shaykh Ahmad al-Banna received letters from two prominent Hijazi notables, Shaykh Muhammad Nasif, a leading dignitary in Jeddah and an eager collector of books, and Shaykh 'Abd al-Zahir Abu al-Samh, a Salafi scholar of Egyptian origin who was the *imam* of the Royal Mosque in Mecca and the founder of Dar al-Hadith, a bookshop and publishing house there. Both were confidants of the Saudi King. Hasan al-Banna paid Shaykh 'Abd al-Zahir Abu al-Samh a visit when he was in Mecca during the *hajj* in 1936.[68] The two Hijazi dignitaries proved to be of indispensable help to Shaykh Ahmad al-Banna in the following years, when another twelve volumes of the *musnad al-fath al-rabbani* were to be printed and sold and he needed to find potential customers to finance the expensive printing operation. Although optimistic expectations of a huge order of a thousand sets of the series from the Saudi King came to nothing, they lobbied so successfully that the King agreed to subscribe to a hundred sets of Shaykh Ahmad al-Banna's voluminous work. In addition, a large number of subscriptions were gained from other Hijazi dignitaries. In the latter half of the 1930s, thirteen volumes were printed by the Society and dispatched to these subscribers.[69] The total number of copies printed must have been several thousand. Taken together with additional subscriptions for other Muslim Brother publications and their weekly newspaper, the Hijazi contacts must have been of some importance to the Society.

The Society continued to foster close relations with Hijaz in the latter half of the 1930s. A Saudi deputy for propaganda for the *hajj* in Egypt, Sayyid Ahmad Hasan Husayn, visited the headquarters of the Muslim Brothers repeatedly in 1938 and gave lectures. King Abd al-Aziz Al Saud's endeavours for the Palestinian cause, following the outbreak of the Palestine Revolt in 1936, were also highly praised in the Society's newspaper.[70] During the Palestine Round Table Conference in London in 1939, members of the Muslim Brothers reportedly served as interpreters and secretaries for the Saudi (and the Yemeni) representatives.[71]

However, in May 1939, overt criticism of the Saudi ruling élite appeared in articles in the Society's newspaper, jeopardizing Shaykh Ahmad al-Banna's and ultimately the Society's relationship with the Hijazis.[72] One of Shaykh 'Abd al-Zahir Abu al-Samh's sons had written an article, entitled 'From vagabond to king', in which he criticized and even ridiculed the "un-Islamic" lifestyle of members of the Saudi royal family, as manifested by their frequent visits to cabarets and luxury hotels in Egypt and Europe. When this came to the attention of Shaykh Abu Samh, he wrote an angry letter to Shaykh Ahmad al-Banna, castigating both him and Hasan al-Banna for "having given printing space to such nonsense". The Islamic duty of enjoining good and prohibiting evil "should not be done in this way", the Shaykh wrote, and he demanded that Hasan al-Banna "write a letter to apologize for what has been presented [in the newspaper]".[73] No apology ever appeared in the newspaper, either from Hasan al-Banna or from Shaykh Abu Samh's rebellious son. The whole affair is not only illustrative of an important aspect of the Society's ideology, namely the right and duty to correct and reproach erring rulers, but it also shows that the growing strength of the Society during the late 1930s profoundly lessened the importance of Hijazi goodwill and the *musnad al-fath al-rabbani* to the Society. Accusations that the Society worked for the interests of the Saudi King might also have put a damper on its enthusiasm for a close relationship, let alone campaigns of the kind launched in 1935.[74] On the other hand, King Abd al-Aziz Al Saud was also reported to have been very reluctant to permit the Muslim Brothers to establish branches in Saudi Arabia.[75] This probably contributed to the significant reversal from the Society's position in the mid-1930s when the patronage of King Abd al-Aziz Al Saud and Hijazi dignitaries was considered essential.

NOTES

1 'Abbas al-Sisi was a member of the Muslim Brothers from the mid-1930s. 'Abbas al-Sisi, *Hasan al-Banna: Mawaqif fi al-da'wa wa al-tarbiya* (Alexandria, Dar al-Da'wa, 1982), pp. 175–6.

2 *JIM*, no. 8, 1352/1933. A copy of Hasan al-Banna's schedule can also be found in *Mudh.*, pp. 178–9.

3 *JIM*, no. 13, 1354/1935, p. 26.

4 *Mudh.*, p. 110.

5 Goldberg, 'Bases of traditional reaction', pp. 84–5. See also al-Bishri, *al-Haraka al-siyasiyya fi Misr*, p. 44.

6 For example, during al-Banna's visit to Abu Hamad in al-Sharqiyya in the spring of 1934 he was accompanied by the heads of the al-Mahmudiyya, Ismailia, Abu Suwayr and Shubra branches. Al-Banna always asked Muhammad Hamid Abu al-Nasr, a local dignitary from Manfalut in Upper Egypt, to accompany him on his recruiting trips in Upper Egypt. See Abu al-Nasr, *Haqiqat al-khilaf bayn al-Ikhwan al-Muslimin wa 'Abd al-Nasir*, pp. 17–21.

7 *JIM*, no. 8, 1352/1933; *JIM*, no. 13, 1354/1935, p. 26; and *Mudh.*, pp. 178–9.

8 See, for example, Hasan al-Banna's visit to al-Wasita in Upper Egypt during Ramadan AH 1354 in *Mudh.*, pp. 236–7.

9 *JIM*, no. 14, 1354/1935, p. 2 and *JIM*, no. 19, 1355/1936, p. 18.

10 For the Muslim Brothers' official hymn, composed by Ahmad Hasan al-Baquri in the early 1930s, see 'Abd al-Halim, *al-Ikhwan al-Muslimun: ahdath sana'at tarikh*, pp. 165–6.

11 See, for example, Hasan al-Banna's visit to Benha where he met with two local notables and members of the Village Council (al-Majlis al-Qarawi). *JIM*, no. 43, 1354/1936, p. 22.

12 'Abbas al-Sisi, *Hasan al-Banna: mawaqif fi al-da'wa wa al-tarbiya* (Alexandria, Dar al-Da'wa, 1982), pp. 175–6. An example of how crucial the support of the local village chief was can be taken from the village of al-Marj. Here the *'umda* had reportedly taken the initiative to form a branch and "gathered a considerable number of the notables and the families of al-Marj". As a result, more than 50 of "the best people of al-Marj" joined the Muslim Brothers. Thereupon, funds for charity were made available and a clubhouse was provided for. *JIM*, no. 31, 1353/1934, p. 31.

13 Interview with Jamal al-Banna, spring 1995.

14 The four most prominent members of the MIA in 1933 were religious scholars: Shaykh Mustafa al-Tir, Shaykh 'Abd al-Hafiz Farghali, Shaykh 'Afifi 'Ituwah and Shaykh Hamid 'Askariyya. *Mudh.*, pp. 182–3.

15 Shaykh Muhammad Ali Ahmad, the *imam* and *khatib* in the al-Rifa'i Mosque, was Hasan al-Banna's only co-speaker on several important occasions. He was also a prolific writer in the Society's newspaper.

16 *JIM*, no. 4, 1356/1937, pp. 12–16.

17 'Abd al-Halim, *al-Ikhwan al-Muslimun: ahdath sana'at al-tarikh*, pp. 91–2 and *al-Nadhir*, no. 4, 1357/1938, p. 23.

18 This conclusion was also made by a contemporary observer. See Heyworth-Dunne, *Religious and Political Trends in Modern Egypt*, p. 29.

19 'Abd al-Halim, *al-Ikhwan al-Muslimun: ahdath sana'at al-tarikh*, pp. 35–7. See also Abu al-Nasr, *Haqiqat al-khilaf bayn al-Ikhwan al-Muslimin wa 'Abd al-Nasir*, p. 15.

20 *al-Nadhir*, no. 26, 1357/1938, editorial and *al-Nadhir*, no. 5, 1358/1939, p. 11.

21 These were the al-Jam'iyya al-Khayriyyah branch in Rode al-Faraj in Cairo, al-Jam'iyya al-Islamiyya lil-Barr bil-Fuqara' in Minya Qamh and Jam'iyyat al-Salafiyya bil-Hawadimiyya. See *JIM*, no. 22, 1355/1936, p. 21; *al-Nadhir*, no. 23, 1357/1938; and *al-Nadhir*, no. 31, 1357/1939, p. 20.

22 For the celebration of the Prophet's Birthday in the branches in 1934 and 1935, see *JIM*, no. 9, 1353/1934; *JIM*, no. 11, 1353/1934; and *JIM*, no. 10, 1354/1935.

23 This failure has been ascribed to the Society's somewhat dilapidated and unmarked headquarters in al-Nasiriyya Street. See 'Abd al-Halim, *al-Ikhwan al-Muslimun: ahdath sana'at tarikh*, pp. 109–110.

24 *Ibid.*, p. 149.

25 Heyworth-Dunne, *Religious and Political Trends in Modern Egypt*, p. 16.

26 See, for example, the celebration of the Prophet's Birthday at the al-'Uluwwiyya branch (in al-Sharqiyya province), to which all the village notables were invited. Another example is the celebration of the Prophet's Birthday in Port Fuad to which dignitaries, merchants and civil servants were invited. *JIM*, no. 9, 1353/1934, p. 28 and *JIM*, no. 10, 1354/1935.

27 al-Bass, *al-Ikhwan al-Muslimun fi rif Misr*, pp. 14–15. See also al-Sisi, *Fi qafilat al-Ikhwan al-Muslimin*, p. 100.

28 *Mudh.*, pp. 114–15.

29 *JIM*, no. 7, 1354/1935, p. 32; *JIM*, no. 10, 1354/1935; *JIM*, no. 29, 1354/1935; *JIM*, no. 39, 1354/1936, p. 17–18; and *JIM*, no. 45, 1354/1936, p. 23.

30 See, for example, *JIM*, no. 7, 1354/1935, p. 32.

31 *JIM*, no. 10, 1354/1935; *JIM*, no. 29, 1354/1935; and *JIM*, no. 39, 1354/1936, pp. 17–18.

32 The Society also petitioned for various social welfare projects in Port Fuad such as the construction of schools and health clinics. However, in a report from 1937, there was no mention of subsidies or donations to the branch in Port Fuad although public grants to other branches were mentioned. See *JIM*, no. 4, 1356/1937, p. 16.

33 *JIM*, no. 41, 1354/1936, p. 23.

34 On the tension between the Society and the local élite, see Chapters 6, 7 and 8.

35 See, for example, Robert Springborg, *Family, Power and Politics in Egypt* (Philadelphia, University of Pennsylvania Press, 1982) and Guilain Denoeux, *Urban Unrest in the Middle East: A Comparative Study of Informal Networks in Egypt, Iran and Lebanon* (Albany, State University of New York Press, 1993).

36 al-Tilmisani, *Dhikriyat la mudhakkirat*, pp. 52–3.

37 See the article by Ahmad al-Sukkari in *JIM*, no. 12, 1352/1933. See also al-Sisi, *Fi qafilat al-Ikhwan al-Muslimin*, pp. 20–1.

38 *JIM*, no. 11, 1352/1933.

39 *JIM*, no. 25, 1352/1934. In this edition a short article can be found in which various traditions (*hadith*) and Qur'anic verses are quoted, dealing with the virtues of collecting money. This might well have been a hint to support the Society financially.

40 'Abd al-Rahman al-Sa'ati, 'Hadiyat al-Basil Basha', *JIM*, no. 33, 1354/1935, p. 12.

41 For more information on 'Ali Mahir's ministry, see Jacques Berque, *Egypt: Imperialism and Revolution*, tr. Jean Stewart (London, Praeger, 1972), pp. 460–5.

42 *Majallat al-Da'wa*, no. 104, 1372/1953, p. 3.

43 *JIM*, no. 1, 1354/1936, p. 19.

44 Hasan al-Banna, 'Khatawat muwaffaqa' [successful steps], *JIM*, no. 3, 1355/1936, p. 16.

45 Hasan al-Banna, 'Ila al-Ikhwan al-Muslimin fi mukhtalif dawa'irihim bi-munasabat al-intikhabat' [to the Muslim Brothers in their various districts on the occasion of the elections], *JIM*, no. 3, 1355/1936, p. 16.

46 According to Hasan al-Banna the new plan for secondary schools proposed nine hours' teaching time per week for English, four for French and six for Arabic. A survey on the 1945-6 academic year shows that six hours were allotted to Arabic and between nine and fourteen hours to foreign languages in secondary schools. See Abdalla, *The Student Movement and National Politics in Egypt*, p. 27.

47 *JIM*, no. 7, 1354/1935, p. 12.

48 See, for example, *JIM*, no. 12, 1354/1935, pp. 14–15; *JIM* no. 13, 1354/1935; *JIM*, no. 14, 1354/1935; and *JIM*, no. 22, 1354/1935, p. 15.

49 Hasan al-Banna's memoirs mention that prior to 1932 the Muslim Brothers in Cairo were offered financial subsidies by the Sidqi government in return for supporting the status quo in Egypt, an offer they contemptuously rejected. There is ample reason to believe that this story is fictitious and relates to the accusation

of collusion with the Sidqi regime in the postwar years. See Lia, 'Imposing on the past the order of the present'. See also *Mudh.*, pp. 118–19.

50 *Mudh.*, pp. 284–5.
51 al-Baquri, *Baqaya dhikriyat*, pp. 25–34.
52 *Mudh.*, p. 219 (summary of the Third Conference, March 1935).
53 *JIM*, no. 1, 1355/1936, editorial.
54 *al-Minhaj* (unpublished), p. 5.
55 *al-Nadhir*, no. 35, 1357/1939, p. 12.
56 Hijaz was not a unified part of Saudi Arabia until 1932. Diplomatic relations between Egypt and Saudi Arabia were established during 'Ali Mahir's term of office in 1936.
57 Wendell (tr.), *Five Tracts of Hasan al-Banna*, pp. 96–7. The original title of the tract was 'Ila ayi shay' nad'u al-nas' published for the first time in *JIM* in 1934. For a similar statement, see *Mudh.*, p. 89.
58 *Mudh.*, p. 89.
59 *JIM*, no. 26, 1353/1934, p. 34; *JIM*, no. 28, 1353/1934, p. 33; and *JIM*, no. 43, 1354/1935, pp. 8–9.
60 *JIM*, no. 38, 1353/1935.
61 *JIM*, no. 43, 1354/1935, pp. 8–10.
62 *Mudh.*, pp. 225–6 (summary of the Third Conference, March 1935).
63 *JIM*, no. 23, 1354/1935.
64 *Mudh.*, p. 239. A member who joined the Society in the mid-1930s estimated the number of Muslim Brother pilgrims in 1935 to be in excess of a hundred. See 'Abd al-Halim, *al-Ikhwan al-Muslimun: ahdath sana'at tarikh*, p. 101.
65 It is not clear whether all volumes were printed by the Society's publishing house or whether the first volume was printed there and the rest by Shaykh Ahmad al-Banna himself. However, given Shaykh Ahmad al-Banna's central position in the Muslim Brother organization, not only by being Hasan al-Banna's father but also as a prominent columnist in the Society's newspaper and for some time as director of the Society's newspaper and publishing house, this hardly made any difference. See Jamal al-Banna, *Khitabat Hasan al-Banna al-shabb ila abihi*, pp. 51–53. See also Heyworth-Dunne, *Religious and Political Trends in Modern Egypt*, p. 16.
66 Jamal al-Banna, *Khitabat Hasan al-Banna al-shabb ila abihi*, pp. 52–3.
67 The head and founder of the Jam'iyyat Ansar al-Sunna al-Muhammadiyya, Shaykh Muhammad Hamid al-Fiqi, lived for a long time in Shubrakhit and al-Mahmudiyya, not far from the home town of the Al Banna family. According to the British he ran "a propaganda press" and was reported to be a "propagandist in Egypt on behalf of King Ibn Saud. He has many followers and goes on the Pilgrimage every year, where he gets in touch with Ibn Saud." See Appendix to Security Summary (Middle East), no. 412, 15 January 1941, WO 208/1560, p. 1. For more details on this society, see Dawud, *al-Jam'iyyat al-islamiyya fi Misr wa dawruha fi nashr al-da'wa al-islamiyya*, pp. 177–98.
68 Jamal al-Banna, *Khitabat Hasan al-Banna al-shabb ila abihi*, p. 62.

69 *Ibid.*, pp. 50–69.

70 *al-Nadhir*, no. 19, 1357/1938, p.11; *al-Nadhir*, no. 20, 1357/1938, p. 21; and *al-Nadhir*, no. 22, 1357/1938, pp. 11–13.

71 One of them was Mahmud Abu al-Su'ud, a civil servant at the Commercial Chamber in Alexandria and head of the Society's Rover units there. See 'Abd al-Halim, *al-Ikhwan al-Muslimun: ahdath sana'at tarikh*, pp. 181–2; al-Sisi, *Fi qafilat al-Ikhwan al-Muslimin*, p. 39; and *al-Nadhir*, no. 10, 1358/1939.

72 Jamal al-Banna, *Khitabat Hasan al-Banna al-shabb ila abihi*, p. 65. See also 'Abd al-Latif Abu Samh, 'Min sa'luk ila malik', *al-Nadhir*, no. 11, 1358/1939. For other criticism of the Hijazis, see *al-Nadhir*, no. 15, 1358/1939, p. 5.

73 Jamal al-Banna, *Khitabat Hasan al-Banna al-shabb ila abihi*, p. 65.

74 *Taqrir ijmali khass*, p. 20.

75 Interview with Jamal al-Banna, spring 1995. See also Harris, *Nationalism and Revolution in Egypt*, p. 160.

PART III

THE RISE OF A MASS MOVEMENT
1936–1942

5

Expansion

Brethren, you are not a benevolent organization, nor a political party, nor a local organization with strictly limited aims. Rather you are a new spirit making its way into the heart of this nation.

Hasan al-Banna[1]
1939

Growth and Expansion after 1936

The most remarkable feature of the Muslim Brothers in the 1930s was their ability to expand their organization to all parts of Egypt and recruit a mass following as a basis for political power. This and subsequent chapters will deal with the expansion of the Society after 1936 by viewing it from various angles and by revealing the main reasons behind it.[2] It is now possible to describe this expansion more exactly here than in previous studies due to the availability of new and more precise sources on the Society's growth in the late 1930s. In particular, two detailed surveys, dated June 1937 and May 1940, show that the branch organizations received the close attention of the leadership, which treated their development and growth as a top priority.[3] These surveys ranked the branches in Egypt in three categories (first, second and third degree) according to their level of development.[4] Judging by these surveys the Society's growth appears to have continued at approximately the same rate after 1936 as prior to it. In July 1936 the number of branches was reported to have exceeded 150.[5] Although this might have been a somewhat exaggerated estimate made in a moment of enthusiasm, other reports indicate that the number of branches must have passed at least 100 in the first half of 1936. By June 1937 the total number of branch organizations was 216 according to the official Muslim Brother survey, although the majority of these were still third-degree branches.[6] A year later Hasan al-Banna stated that the Society had more than 300 branches.[7] The survey published in May 1940, a few months after the defection of a dissident group, showed 265 Muslim Brother branches in Egypt. However, the setback in 1939–40 was not as dramatic as these numbers indicate. From 1937 to 1940 there had been a significant qualitative growth, doubling the number of first- and second-degree branches. This represented an important strengthening of the Society's branch organizations and it reinforces the general impression of a more or less continuous expansion, despite the crisis and the subsequent defections in late 1939. During 1940 the growth continued unabated, bringing the number of branches to 500 by January 1941.[8] Three years later the number was variously estimated at between 1000 and 1500.[9] For example, in an internal publication distributed to the heads of the administrative areas of the Society in April 1944, al-Banna wrote proudly: "God the Exalted has supported this Islamic mission greatly and opened up for it the hearts of people. Through His support, the number of branches has exceeded 1000."[10]

By the end of the 1930s the Society had spread to villages and provincial towns in every part of Egypt. The Canal Zone, the adjacent al-Bahr al-Saghir area and the province of al-Buhayra which had been Muslim Brother strongholds in the early 1930s had now definitely ceased to be the only centres of importance. While all the Delta provinces had witnessed a remarkable growth, the progress was most marked in Upper Egypt. Prior to 1936 there were few branches of importance in this region. However, by 1940 the province of Assiut in Upper Egypt had more first-degree branches than any other province. In addition, the 1940 survey also found that the Upper Egypt provinces of Qena, Bani Suwayf and Minya had witnessed the largest growth of first- and second-degree branches of all the Muslim Brother area organizations. The Society obviously found more fertile ground for its Islamic mission (*da'wa*) in Upper Egypt than in the rest of Egypt.[11] This was reflected in al-Banna's priorities. During his recruiting trips in the summer of 1936 he set aside only two weeks for visiting the Delta branches and a whole month for Upper Egypt. In 1938 he made an extra trip to Upper Egypt because "many people have responded to the *da'wa* there",[12] and in 1939 he devoted the whole summer expedition to the provinces of Upper Egypt. Touring as usual on a very tight schedule, he visited 31 villages and provincial towns in 33 days. At the end of the trip he decided to spend another 5 days among the Upper Egyptians.[13] When he returned to Cairo, he wrote with excitement:

> The people of al-Sa'id (Upper Egypt) are Arabs . . . God has removed them from the places of moral depravity, dissolution and licentiousness. He has created in their hearts a natural disposition to the Islamic mission . . . My dear brethren! I have great hopes in the people of Upper Egypt . . . from what I have seen of faith and preparedness.[14]

Such a "natural disposition to the Islamic mission" was apparently not found among the Cairenes or Alexandrians. In 1940 there were only six second-degree branches and no first-degree branches in Cairo. Alexandria had only one branch.[15] It was not until the Society became an important political force that it gained a solid foothold in most quarters of the two largest cities.[16] The initial slow growth in Alexandria might have stemmed partly from the defection of the dissident group Muhammad's Youth – which had a strong following in the city – in 1939–40. Another explanation is the relatively higher competition between Islamic associations in Cairo and Alexandria. The YMMA was especially strong in both cities and the Brothers perhaps felt that there was no need to challenge their mother organization. Moreover, the provinces and especially Upper Egypt were largely neglected by the Muslim Brothers' rivals. The Young Egypt Party, for example, usually shunned the backwardness of the countryside and had little interest in the social and educational work that the Brothers advocated.[17]

The Society's growth with regard to the number of members and sympathizers is harder to measure. The Society's own estimates were obviously somewhat exaggerated. For example, in 1936 Hasan al-Banna wrote a deeply emotional editorial to "the 20,000 Muslim Brothers in Egypt".[18] Three years later, in February 1939, he addressed the King, stating that "100,000 pious youths from the Muslim Brothers from all parts of Egypt" now waited for the prayer to begin.[19] These statements were obviously rhetorical rather factual, and the following observations might be more indicative of the actual numerical strength of the Society. A Political Police agent noted that a local conference organized by the Muslim Brothers in Zaqaziq in October 1938 gathered nearly 600 "students and fellahin [peasants]".[20] Another local conference in July 1939 in Abu Hamad was attended by around 3,000.[21] The Sixth

Conference of the Society held in Cairo in January 1941 gathered 5,000 delegates and guests of honour. When Hasan al-Banna came to the provincial town of Damanhur in October 1941, the Political Police's informers reported that more than 2,000 people came to listen to him.[22] Estimates of the total membership in July 1944 ranged from 100,000 to 500,000.[23]

The Society's numerical growth was accompanied by its increasing local and national influence. Its growing political leverage is illustrated by the strong concerns and anxiety that were expressed in higher political circles in Egypt following al-Banna's internment in October 1941. Immediately after his arrest, the Royal Councillor and the Prime Minister were inundated with petitions from all over Egypt containing more than 11,000 signatures, some of them written in an unambiguously threatening tone.[24] After releasing al-Banna in November 1941 in defiance of the orders of the British military authorities, the Prime Minister told the British Ambassador that he feared there would have been a "religious revolution" if he had been kept in prison.[25]

The Muslim Brothers in the Islamic World

The Muslim Brothers gave a high priority to keeping in touch with Islamic movements and personalities in the Islamic world. This was a natural consequence of their ideology which called for the Islamic mission (da'wa) not to be confined to Egypt but to be spread throughout the Islamic world and, ultimately, the entire world. The attention given to the Islamic world was essential because it gave the Society an "international image", and placed it firmly in opposition to any kind of traditional parochialism and racial nationalism. At the same time, the orientation towards the Islamic world represented an alternative to European influences which had been dominant among the Egyptian élite throughout the 1920s.

Upon the founding of the Society in Ismailia, Hasan al-Banna sent telegrams to a number of Islamic leaders, among them the Grand Mufti of Jerusalem, Hajj Amin al-Husayni, informing them of his new movement.[26] However, it was not until 1935 that the Society began to establish connections abroad. A visit by a delegation of Muslim Brothers to Palestine and Syria in 1935 laid the foundation for the establishment of branches abroad.[27] At the same time, Shaykh Muhammad al-Hadi Atiyya, a prominent Muslim Brother, was appointed to the Religious Institute of the Benevolent Society (Jam'iyyat al-Maqasid al-Khayriyya) in Beirut. He appears to have initiated contacts between the Muslim Brothers in Egypt and the Benevolent Society in Syria.[28] A delegation from this association visited the Muslim Brothers in Cairo in March 1936, a visit which apparently brought the Brothers to the attention of the Political Police for the first time. During the meeting inflammatory and strongly anti-imperialist speeches were made by the hosts and visitors alike, and at the end of the meeting the Syrian visitors declared that they considered themselves as "members of the Moslem Brethren Society".[29] These contacts probably paved the way for the first Syrian Muslim Brother branch which was founded in 1937 in Hama (a city which more than 40 years later was to become the scene of the most atrocious large-scale slaughter of Islamist opposition in modern Middle Eastern history). When a rebellion against French colonialism erupted during the last years of the Second World War, the Islamic movement in Syria was thoroughly reorganized under the leadership of Mustafa al-Siba'i. During this period, relations with the Egyptian Muslim Brothers were greatly strengthened by mutual visits as well as by the Egyptian Brothers' medical assistance to the Syrians during the revolt. As a sign of loyalty to the Egyptian mother organization, al-Siba'i made an oath of allegiance to Hasan al-Banna at the end of the war.[30]

According to a Muslim Brother survey from 1937, the Society had by then established several branches in Sudan, Saudi Arabia, Palestine, Syria, Lebanon and Morocco, and one in each of Bahrain, Hadramawt, Hyderabad, Djibouti and Paris.[31] Another survey from 1940 revealed an even more extensive network of connections throughout the Muslim world.[32] These appear to have been established mainly through foreign students who had been influenced by the Muslim Brothers' teachings in Cairo. A number of contacts were also facilitated through Egyptian Muslim Brothers or sympathizers who worked or studied abroad. Moreover, the Society sought to extend their networks of contacts during the Palestinian Revolt by various means. For example, in 1937 an Islamic Conference on Palestine was organized, and in October 1938 a reception was held at its premises in Cairo to honour the deputies of the Arab countries during the Inter-Parliamentary Conference on Palestine. The Society's fervent pro-Palestine campaign also gained them the support of a number of Palestinian al-Azhar students.[33] All of these efforts served to disseminate the ideas of the Society in Palestine, and paved the way for the establishment of Muslim Brother branches there.

Another aspect of the Society's targeting of its propaganda towards the Islamic world was to send representatives to attend receptions of famous Islamic personalities when they happened to visit Egypt,[34] and to make contacts with Islamic anti-colonial movements, particularly in North Africa.[35] In the late 1930s a predominant part of the Society's efforts was devoted to the struggle against imperialism in the Islamic world. Palestine was naturally the focal point of these endeavours, but countries like Libya, Syria and Morocco also received some attention.[36] The Muslim Brothers sent telegrams of protest to Egyptian newspapers during the visit of an Italian general to Cairo, denouncing "the atrocities perpetrated by Italy in Libya",[37] and their newspaper printed eyewitness accounts of Italian barbarism in Libya in an attempt to thwart Mussolini's efforts to pose as Islam's protector.[38] The Society also made contacts with Moroccan exiles in Egypt and devoted a special edition of their weekly newspaper to the fate of Moroccan Muslims under French colonial rule.[39]

By mid-1939 it is clear that the Muslim Brothers had made some progress in disseminating their ideas throughout the Islamic world. A large number of contacts had been made and a number of foreign newspapers and journals had published articles about the Society in countries like Yemen, Syria and Iran. There is, however, little evidence of the existence of active branches throughout the Islamic world before the end of the Second World War. The "branches" that were founded abroad in the latter half of the 1930s appear to have been merely based around friends and personal contacts of the Egyptian Muslim Brothers, as opposed to being active organizational units.[40] It seems clear that the formal founding of active sister organizations outside Egypt took place for the most part in the postwar years.[41] Yet the foundations for the expansion throughout the Islamic world were laid in the late 1930s when the Society's ideas were disseminated and networks of contacts and friendships were established. The spread of the Muslim Brothers to countries like Sudan, Jordan, Syria, Palestine and North Africa was an important step in the development of modern Islamism as a global phenomenon in the latter part of the twentieth century.

NOTES

1 Wendell (tr.), *Five Tracts of Hasan al-Banna*, p. 36.

2 For a graphic description of the Society's growth in the 1930s, see Appendix I.

3 'Khatawat muwaffaqa: bayan mujaz lil-Ikhwan al-Muslimin' [successful steps: a brief survey of the Muslim Brothers], *JIM*, no. 4, 1356/1937 and 'Adad khass 'an al-Ikhwan al-Muslimin' [a special edition about the Muslim Brothers], *Majallat al-Ta'aruf*, no. 13, 1359/1940.

4 The description of the classification of branches was given in the 1940 survey: "first-degree" (*al-daraja al-ula*) implied that the branch had reached the stage of "complete formation" having acquired its own premises and formed all its sub-groups, including an administration which supervised the affairs of the branch; "second-degree" (*al-daraja al-thaniya*) meant that the branch had been established, but still lacked some of the features characterizing the "first-degree" branches (such as not having its own premises); "third-degree" (*al-daraja al-thalitha*) was still "in the process of being formed", and most probably consisted of nothing more than a group of men who pledged to establish a branch and had made contacts with the MIA. See 'Adad khass 'an al-Ikhwan al-Muslimin', *Majallat al-Ta'aruf*, no. 13, 1359/1940.

5 *JIM*, no. 14, 1355/1936, p. 9.

6 *JIM*, no. 4, 1356/1937.

7 *al-Nadhir*, no. 1, 1357/1938, editorial.

8 *al-Ikhwan al-muslimun: al-mu'tamar al-dawri al-sadis*, p. 9. This estimate is also confirmed by an unpublished survey, dated 1940, which fixes the number of branches at 500. See Franz Rosenthal, 'The Muslim Brethren in Egypt', *The Muslim World*, vol. 37 (1947), p. 278. Rosenthal referred to a survey called *Ta'rif mujaz bi-maqasid al-Ikhwan al-Muslimin* (Cairo, Matba'at al-Ikhwan al-Muslimin, 1359/1940). I have been unable to study this survey. For a similar estimate, see al-Sisi, *Hasan al-Banna: mawaqif fi' al-da'wa wa al-tarbiya*, p. 156.

9 An estimate of more than 1,000 branches can be found in a British report from July 1944. The well-known Egyptian journalist Ihsan 'Abd al-Qaddus wrote in September 1945 that the Society had more than 1,500 branches. See 'Ikhwan el Muslimeen' (Secret), P.I.C. Paper no. 49 (revised), 24 July 1944, FO 371/41334, p. 5. See also al-Sisi, *Fi qafilat al-Ikhwan al-Muslimin*, p. 190.

10 *Qism al-Manatiq: nashra 'amma* (unpublished), pp. 2–3.

11 Interview with Jamal al-Banna, spring 1995.

12 *al-Nadhir*, no. 6, 1357/1938, p. 7.

13 *al-Nadhir*, no. 30, 1358/1939, p. 10.

14 *al-Nadhir*, no. 31, 1358/1939, editorial.

15 *Majallat al-Ta'aruf*, no. 13, 1359/1940.

16 For the increase of branches in Alexandria during the war, see Muhammad Labib al-Buhi, *Ma' al-Murshid al-'Amm lil-Ikhwan al-Muslimin* (Cairo, Dar al-Taba'a wa al-Nashr al-Islamiyya, 1946), pp. 58–61.

17 'The Ikhwan al Muslimin Reconsidered', 14 December 1942, FO 141/838. See also Jankowski, *Egypt's Young Rebels*, p. 23.

18 *JIM*, no. 15, 1355/1936, p. 1.

19 *al-Nadhir*, no. 2, 1358/1939, editorial.

20 British Embassy to Halifax, no. E5898, 10 October 1938, FO 371/21881.

21 *al-Nadhir*, no. 24, 1358/1939, p. 2.

22 Dar al-Watha'iq/Taqarir al-Amn/Taqarir Hikmadariyyat Bulis al-Iskandariyya (sirri siyasi), no. 382, 1941.

23 'Ikhwan el Muslimeen' (Secret), P.I.C. Paper no. 49 (revised), 24 July 1944, FO 371/41334, p. 2.

24 For instance, one entry, which the Royal Councillor marked with a red pen before submitting it to the King, contained the words "this [al-Banna's] arrest might lead to the most dangerous consequences".

25 Cairo to FO, no. 3570, 14 November 1941, FO 371/27434.

26 Hajj Amin al-Husayni, 'Qudwa hasana', *Majallat al-Da'wa*, 1374/1955, p. 3.

27 *Mudh.*, pp. 230–4. For the existence of a branch of the Muslim Brothers in Palestine prior to the Arab Revolt, see 'Pan-Islamic Arab Movement', Lampson to FO, no. E3153, 28 May 1936, FO 371/19980.

28 See 'Ustadh al-Hadi fi tariqihi ila Bayrut', *JIM*, no. 29, 1354/1935.

29 See 'Pan-Islamic Arab Movement', Lampson to FO, no. E2120, 8 April 1936, FO 371/19980.

30 al-Sisi, *Hasan al-Banna: mawaqif fi al-da'wa wa al-tarbiyyah*, pp. 231–5; Hawwa, *Hadhihi tajrubati wa hadhihi shahadati*, pp. 41–2; and R. Bayly Winder, 'Islam as the state religion: a Muslim Brotherhood view on Syria', *The Muslim World*, vol. 44, (1954), pp. 215–6.

31 *JIM*, no. 4, 1356/1937, p. 4.

32 Rosenthal, 'The Muslim Brethren in Egypt', p. 278.

33 'Muzahara fi'l-Qahira li-ta'yeed 'Arab Filastin', *Majallat al-Fath*, no. 607, 1357/1938, p. 15.

34 *JIM*, no. 4, 1356/1937, p. 15.

35 'Abd al-Halim, *al-Ikhwan al-Muslimun: ahdath sana'at tarikh*, p. 144.

36 For propaganda against French policies in Syria, see 'al-Ihtijaj 'ala nizam al-tawa'if bi-Suriya', *al-Nadhir*, no. 4, 1358/1939, p. 26. During the war, the Muslim Brothers wrote to the Syrian ambassador offering him volunteers to support the Syrian army's struggle against French colonialism. See al-Sisi, *Hasan al-Banna: mawaqif fi al-da'wa wa al-tarbiya*, pp. 231–5. For propaganda efforts for Libyan Muslims, see al-Nadhir, no. 23, 1357/1938; *al-Nadhir*, no. 1, 1358/1939, p. 25; and *Mudh.*, pp. 273–5.

37 *al-Nadhir*, no. 13, 1358/1939, p. 10.

38 *al-Nadhir*, no. 16, 1358/1939, p. 16.

39 *al-Nadhir*, no. 20, 1357/1938, p. 19 and *al-Nadhir*, no. 21, 1357/1938.

40 This is evident from the 'Abidin files. The Egyptian National Archives in Cairo contain a large number of petitions and letters of protest to the Egyptian government following the suppression of the Muslim Brothers in 1941. None

of these petitions were submitted by branches outside Egypt. For the period 1946–9, however, a number of telegrams from Syria, Palestine, Jordan can be found, protesting against the Egyptian government's policies towards the Society. See Dar al-Watha'iq, Iltimasat al-Ikhwan al-Muslimin (Box 557), 'Ta'yid al-Ikhwan min al-duwal al-'arabiyya wa'l-islamiyya 1946/12/18–1948/12/12' and 'Mawqif al-ra'i al-'amm min i'tiqal qiyadat al-Ikhwan al-Muslimin' containing a number of telegrams from Homs and Halab in Syria and from Amman in Jordan. A petition was submitted by a conference organized by the Muslim Brother Society in Haifa in October 1946. The petition was signed by deputies from east Jordan, Lebanon and Palestine.

41 See, for example, the following accounts on the founding of the Muslim Brothers in Jordan and Sudan: 'Awni Jaddu' al-'Ubaydi, *Safahat min hayat al-Hajj 'Abd al-Latif Abu Qurah, mu'assis al-Ikhwan al-Muslimin fi'l-Urdun* (Amman, Markaz Dirasat wa'l-Abhath wa'l-'Amal al-Siyasi, 1992), pp. 10–12.

6

The Making of a Class
of Cadres

To say the truth, the ideas of Hasan al-Banna probably may
not amount to much: an Islam that is simple and clear . . . He was
very open to Arabism, to nationalism . . . His ideas were very
clear, very pure and there was no ideological complexity, but . . .
as an organizing power . . . he was
something else.

Dr Hasan Hanafi[1]

As has been shown in Chapter 3, the Society had established a hierarchical
organizational structure, including a network of local branches, district
representatives and a central body (the MIA), by the mid-1930s. It had
also established a number of sub-committees for various purposes. Rover
Scout units had been developed as well as a student section and welfare
institutions. Various programmes for ideological indoctrination were also
in progress. The Society's financial independence was secured through
fund-raising among its members, and a principle of "promotion based
on merit", not on social position, had been introduced. At the same time,
the support of local notables was facilitated through special honorific
bodies.

These organizational principles were further developed in the period
up to 1941. The practical training of members was significantly expanded
in the latter half of the 1930s as special courses for propagandists (*du'ah*)
were introduced, which prepared groups of young Muslim Brothers for
recruiting tours in the Egyptian countryside. A new kind of institution
for initiated members, called Battalions (*kata'ib*), was founded in 1937,
which aimed to engender a more complete dedication to the principles
of the movement. The Rover Scout units were dramatically expanded
in this period, as witnessed by the increasing number of summer
camps by the end of the decade. These two institutions together fulfilled

a fundamental function in the organization: they were powerful vehicles of indoctrination and helped the members to internalize the Society's ideas and principles. The frequent Rover Scout parades also attracted followers to the movement, and the Rovers became an efficient instrument in paving the way for new branches and mobilizing young men for social welfare work. In addition, two new organizational bodies of great importance were established in this period. A rudimentary student movement emerged and a military wing, the "Special Section" (al-Nizam al-Khass), was founded. Apart from the expansion and diversification of the class of cadres, two essential changes in the organizational structure took place. Firstly, the fundamental principle that the individual member's position and status in the Society was determined essentially by merit became more firmly integrated in the Society's organization. Secondly, organizational changes provided for a larger degree of local initiative and lessened the Society's vulnerability to government repression; local branches were less heavily affected by the closure of other branches and/or the headquarters in Cairo.

The expansion of the Society's organization in this period was impressive. A wide range of new committees and training institutes had been founded, including a transaction company, a fund and an insurance scheme for propagandists, a school to instruct the general public on how to protect themselves in the event of gas attacks, a committee for eradicating illiteracy, scientific, medical and cultural committees as well as a committee for workers' affairs. An internal publication, dated April 1944, listed more than 25 "active departments at the general headquarters", each including from 20 to 60 "sincere" Muslim Brother youths.[2] This diversification of activities implied that the Society could attract adherents with divergent interests and occupations. The philosophy underlying this diversification can be illustrated by a saying which is attributed to Hasan al-Banna by one of his close contemporaries:

> We, the Brotherhood, are like an immense hall that can be entered by any Muslim from any door to partake of whatsoever he wishes. Should he seek Sufism, he shall find it. Should he seek comprehension of Islamic jurisprudence, he shall find it. Should he seek sports and scouting, it is there. Should he seek battle and armed struggle, he shall find it. You have come to us with the issue of "the nation". So, I welcome you.[3]

A decisive factor behind the Society's impressive expansion in the late 1930s and in the early 1940s appears to be its ability to integrate new members and encourage them to accept the Society's ideas and principles. The Muslim Brothers had an efficient organizational apparatus to absorb new adherents and turn occasional visitors at their meetings into dedicated zealots for the Muslim Brothers' cause. It thus explains, at least to some extent, why the Muslim Brothers were much more successful in recruiting new adherents than rival political and religious groups, like the Young Egypt Party and YMMA, which had a more sophisticated press and a wider network of contacts in influential political circles than the Muslim Brothers.

In this chapter we will study the dual process of recruitment and internalization by examining the most important cadre-producing bodies in the Muslim Brothers' organization. Finally, some attention will be given to the organizational changes which took place at the end of the decade.

Hijra fi Allah: The Muslim Brothers' Propagandists

The summer of 1936 witnessed the first tangible results of the Muslim Brothers' effort to educate their own propagandists. Twenty students, half of them from al-Azhar and the other half from the university at Cairo, were organized in ten "summer delegations". The "duty of preaching and guidance" would now be taken up by the individual members. Hasan al-Banna's ceaseless touring of the Egyptian countryside as well as the Prophet's *hijra* or emigration to Medina in 622 where the first Muslim community was formed, served as sources of inspiration. Each delegation was assigned a certain area, usually a few provincial centres (*marakiz*). All branches were instructed to assist and support the young missionaries or propagandists (*du'ah*) in fulfilling their duties, and donations were collected among the members to cover their expenses. Hasan al-Banna prepared a twenty-page tract in which methods of preaching to the various classes of society were explained in great detail, including a collection of useful Prophetic traditions and Qur'anic verses.[4] Before their departure, in a solemn ceremony at the Society's annual student party, the preachers received a certificate, called *risalat khitab al-da'wa*, conferring upon them the right to undertake preaching and guidance on behalf of the Society. After a one-week intensive training course, which was undertaken at the Muslim Brothers' headquarters in Cairo, the delegations left for a month of travelling and preaching in the countryside.[5]

Two developments appear to have facilitated this project. Firstly, by 1936 the Society's student section had expanded to include perhaps 100–200 students,[6] which provided the Society with a potential reservoir of zealous youth. Secondly, in cooperation with the YMMA, the Muslim Brothers had launched a fund-raising campaign for the Palestinian Arabs in May 1936. Accordingly, the summer delegations were instructed to form Palestine committees and rally support for the Palestinian victims. However, the idea of *hijra fi Allah* (emigration for the sake of God) had been conceived before the Palestine campaign started and the primary objective remained preaching the message of the Society and calling for the establishment of branches.[7] The effects of the summer delegations on the further spread of the Society appear to have been very positive. A number of new branches and Palestine committees were founded or initiated, a network of personal contacts were created, and information and brochures about the Muslim Brothers and their principles were distributed in mosques and among the general public. The delegations were also introduced to people of local influence and standing, who promised to support their efforts. Even a Sufi shaykh from the Shadhiliyya order pledged to contact the MIA and lend his support.[8] In the provincial towns of Girga and Samalut in Upper Egypt and in Meet Ghamr in the Delta, the Muslim Brothers' delegations were introduced to a number of high-ranking dignitaries.[9]

The available sources on the activities of these delegations in 1937–8 are scarce. We do know that the summer delegations had by then become a permanent part of the Society's summer programme, and that the basis for recruitment to the delegations was extended to include civil servants and *'ulama'*.[10] In 1939, the education of preachers and propagandists had been significantly expanded compared with 1936. A special department, the Summer Team for Preaching and Guidance (Firqat al-Wa'z wa'l-Irshad al-Sayfiyya), headed by Hasan al-Banna himself, undertook the practical and theoretical training of the candidates. The requirements for admittance were preferably a lower Azhar degree, but secondary school graduates were sometimes accepted as the Society initially had problems with recruiting enough members for these summer trips.

In the course of four months from June to October, eight classes of preachers were trained for two weeks each at the Society's headquarters and branches in Cairo. In addition, two deputies were dispatched to encourage similar projects in the provinces. However, this project seems to have been rather ambitious judging by the initial problems of recruiting enough candidates.[11]

In order to further stimulate the education of propagandists a system of promotion and ranks was devised in mid-1939. The first rank or degree required the candidate to fulfil various moral and social duties. These included the memorization of two-thirds of the Qur'an, the study of the Prophet's biography, Islamic history and jurisprudence and, finally, the participation in the preaching and guidance summer course. A special study requirement was *risalat al-jihad* (duty to struggle), which provided a theological basis for the duty of struggle (*jihad*) and combat (*qital*) in Islam.[12] Twice a year an examination was to be organized, followed by an "appointment celebration" to be attended by a large number of deputies from the neighbouring areas. The title "Muslim Brother" (*Akh Muslim*) would then be formally conferred upon the candidate. He was now eligible for the highest degree which involved a number of practical steps to "Islamize" his home and daily life. The religious duties at this stage were stricter and he was expected to accept heavy financial sacrifices. In addition, the candidate should produce a scientific tract about the Islamic mission, which was to "fill gaps in the Islamic library". If the tract was approved by the scientific committee of the Society, the candidate had the right to call himself a "Muslim Brother Propagandist"(*da'iya min du'at al-Ikhwan al-Muslimin*). He would then be entitled to carry a special badge and would become eligible for membership in the highest executive organ of the Society, the MIA, or for other positions like the deputy of a province. Little is known about the actual implementation of this system, but it certainly provides us with yet another example of how the Brothers strove to integrate the principle of "status based on merit" in the organizational structure.

The policy of educating preachers seems to have been continued in the 1940s.[13] There can be little doubt that the attention given to the training of a class of propagandists recruited among the educated youth was an essential factor in the successful expansion of the Society. Mahmud Abd al-Halim, a prominent Muslim Brother, explained this success by the fact that volunteering young preachers were a novelty at that time. They represented a rejuvenation in a field dominated by old-fashioned government-appointed preachers:

> For the first time people saw missionaries [*du'ah ila al-din*] who were young and who were not linked to religion in any formal way. At that time people questioned the faith of University students and looked upon them with mistrust, because students frequently changed their habits and traditions and became like strangers in their home villages. Hence, it was a surprise to people when they saw these young men who came to the mosques and addressed people with the sweetest and most beautiful words, reciting glorious verses from the Koran.[14]

Another important factor appears to have been the oratorical style employed by these propagandists. It was stated to differ from the sedate and dispassionate style of the government-appointed preachers:

> A wa'iz [a government-appointed preacher] talks with the tongue of knowledge and Islamic jurisprudence [*fiqh*]. A da'iya [a Muslim Brother propagandist] overflows with the spirit of the Islamic mission and faith. A wa'iz presents to his audience nice words that reach their ears and brains. A da'iya inspires his listeners with a spiritual message that shakes their feelings and moves their hearts.[15]

The mere existence of youth preachers who employed a new and more vigorous style of preaching constituted in itself a challenge for the traditional religious élite and established Islamic officialdom in Egypt. It conveyed an image of a new rejuvenating force challenging the reactionism and social irrelevance that had in many people's eyes tainted the Islamic camp.

The Rover Scout Units

The initial problems of recruiting enough candidates to the Summer Section for Preaching and Guidance in 1939 might indicate that the summer delegations demanded too great a personal sacrifice. The prospect of spending the hottest months of the year touring and preaching in the primitive Egyptian countryside might have scared off even the most dedicated member. The Rover Scout units (*jawwala*) represented a far more attractive alternative. The Rover Scouts embodied the ethos of *futuwwa* (noble manliness, chivalry, bravery, courage and perseverance), and the uniforms, flags, banners and hymns aroused fascination among the youth as did the paramilitary parades and marches. The appeal of these values and paraphernalia were greatly enhanced by the ascendancy of new militaristic powers in Europe who were successfully challenging the old colonial powers of Great Britain and France. In addition, the new military spirit was also seen as a modern rejuvenating force which stood in stark contrast to the inertia of the old generation. A contemporary student of the Society probably grasped the underlying motives of many young men for joining the Rover Scouts:

> Imperialism and its obvious effects are the main reasons that urge youth to join the Muslim Brothers' Rover Scout units . . . [The Rovers] are a living idea which brings forth masculinity and strength in the souls of the youth at a time when effeminacy and softness have enfeebled the youth as a whole.[16]

Hasan al-Banna was greatly influenced by the new militaristic trends from Europe and attempted to define an Islamized version of the new militarism which would encompass its virtues but avoid its aggressiveness. Consequently, between December 1936 and January 1937 al-Banna produced an ideological tract in which he elaborated the concept of "the militarism in Islam" (*al-jundiyya fi'l Islam*):

> Similarly, the renascent nations need strength, and need to implant the military spirit in their sons . . . Islam did not overlook this factor, but as a matter of fact made it a stringent duty, and did not differentiate in any way between it and prayer and fasting. In the entire world, there is no regime which has concerned itself with this factor . . . to the extent that Islam has in the Koran . . . The modern nations have paid close attention to this [militarism]. They have been founded on these principles: we see that Mussolini's Fascism, Hitler's Nazism and Stalin's Communism are based on pure militarism. But there is a vast difference between all of these and the militarism of Islam, for Islam has sanctified force, but it has preferred peace.[17]

As discussed in Chapter 3, Rover Scout units had already been founded by the mid-1930s in some of the oldest branches and an organizational framework had been developed. In 1935, the total number of Rover Scouts appears to have been just a few hundred, and a major recruiting drive was undertaken to expand the Rover units. Although the ambitious aim of forming units in every branch was not reached, impressive progress was made towards the end of the 1930s. The earliest Rover units (*firqat al-rahhalat*) consisted theoretically of four clans (*'asha'ir*) which in turn were subdivided into five sections (*aqsam*), consisting of ten Scouts each.[18] A complete unit thus contained 200 Scouts. However, this system was subsequently modified and a more practical one devised by dropping the last subdivision and making the clan the basic unit, consisting of seven to ten Rover Scouts and headed by a companion (*rafiq*). In 1938 the minimum entry age was seventeen; a year later it was lowered to fifteen.

In 1938-9 the Society's Rover Scout units were formally registered in the Egyptian National Scout Movement,[19] which included not only Muslims but also Scout groups from the Christian, Jewish and the national minorities in Egypt. Formal registration brought material benefits, such as reduced prices on uniforms, subsidies and the use of national facilities. There was also another, and perhaps unanticipated, advantage of registering the Society's Rover Scouts. On 10 February 1938, in the aftermath of general disorder and clashes between Young Egypt's Green Shirts and the Wafd's Blue Shirts, the government issued a decree ordering the dissolution of all paramilitary groups in Egypt. This decision was a victory for the Palace-backed government since the Wafdist Blue Shirts far outnumbered the pro-Palace Green Shirts. According to Muslim Brother veterans, formal registration in the National Scout Movement served to protect the Brothers' Rover Scouts from being dissolved together with the other paramilitary groups.[20] Yet in any event it is doubtful whether the Society's Rover units were associated with paramilitary units at this stage. There is no evidence to support the claim made in some studies that the Rover Scouts had played a prominent role in the clashes between the Green and Blue Shirts during the political crisis of late 1937.[21]

The Rover Scouts were reorganized in line with the requirements of formal membership of the National Scout Movement,[22] and a Higher Council of the Rover Scouts (al-Majlis al-A'la lil-Jawwala) was established. Mahmud Labib, a retired army lieutenant, became the general inspector of the Society's Rover Scouts. He had fought in the war against the Italians in Libya with other notables such as General Aziz al-Misri Pasha, Abd al-Rahman Azzam Bey and Salih Harb Pasha. Like most veterans from the Libyan War as well as a number of Watani politicians, Mahmud Labib had spent several years in exile in Turkey and Germany. He later came to play an important part in recruiting army officers to the Muslim Brothers during the war and became a central figure in the Society's military wing.[23] The aura of national glory that surrounded him made him an important asset for the Muslim Brothers.

In the latter part of the 1930s the Rover Scouts began to organize general summer camps for Scouts from all over Egypt, and these became a main focus of the Society's summer programme. In 1938 a two-month summer camp was set up in the village of al-Dikhayla outside Alexandria. Hasan al-Banna stayed at the camp for most of the summer and turned it into temporary headquarters for the Society. "Military" and physical training,[24] religious education and social activities were undertaken, and the al-Dikhayla camp appears to have been the starting-point for efforts to educate Rover instructors.[25] In the following year another larger training camp was planned, which was to offer a series of 10-day training courses between early June and late September. However, this plan was slightly modified as half a dozen temporary regional camps were instead set up for 10 days over the summer. In addition, a 50-day camp was established in Helwan outside Cairo, which Hasan al-Banna described as "a splendid success".[26] At the same time renewed efforts were made to encourage the branches to form Rover Scout units of all "worker" members (*'amilun*).[27] By May 1940 one or several Rover units had been formed in more than 42 towns or districts and a number of new units were in the process of being set up. The total number of Rovers in early 1941 was estimated at 2,000. Most units had been formed in provincial centres and towns, but only rarely in villages.[28]

The Rover Scout units became a vital part of the Society's organization, not only because of their sheer size but also because of the essential functions they fulfilled. The Rover Scouts were responsible for maintaining order and security at larger meetings and conferences. However, their primary importance lay in their ability to attract new members. It appears that Hasan al-Banna saw the Rover units as an efficient instrument to familiarize young people with religion in a gradual

and appealing way. A weekly programme for newly established Rover
units, devised in 1938, designated the first three days to various social
activities to introduce the members of the group to each other. The
remaining four days were set aside for Scout activities, camping, tours
and charitable work. Religious lectures were only an optional choice.
Only after a certain period of time did religious education and training
become more pronounced, and even then the study of Islamic subjects
was made more attractive through organized examinations with prizes
given to successful candidates.[29]

The Rover Scouts focused heavily on physical training and athletics.
At the Fifth Conference, al-Banna described the Rover units as "the
Athletic Training Institute" of the Society. The Rover Scouts appear to
have played an important role in forming football teams in the latter
half of the 1930s.[30] This marked the beginning of a remarkable growth in
athletics and sports, organized under the auspices of the Muslim Brothers.
Prior to the dissolution of the Society in late 1948, it had 99 football
teams, 32 basketball teams, 27 table tennis teams, 19 weightlifting teams,
16 wrestling teams and a number of other forms of organized athletics.[31]
Members who distinguished themselves in athletics were given honours
by the Society. During the King's wedding celebrations in 1938 the
world weightlifting champion, Sayyid Nasir, was given the honour of
carrying the banner of the Muslim Brothers and led the parade of Rover
Scouts.[32] There can be little doubt that the Muslim Brothers' emphasis
on sports was fundamental to their ability to recruit and integrate young
men in the organization.

In the late 1930s, the Rover Scouts became an important instrument
in establishing new branches. Judging by reports in the Muslim Brothers'
newspaper, a number of branches were directly established as a result of
the efforts of the Rovers. In 1939 these endeavours were intensified
and Rover Scouts were instructed to join the Section for Summer Tours
(Qism al-Rahalat al-Sayfiyya) in order to visit the suburbs of Cairo every
Friday and spread the Islamic mission.[33] Surveying the bulk of reports
about new branches, the impression is however that the final initiative
was seldom taken by the Rovers, but instead by prominent Muslim
Brothers from neighbouring branches who commanded sufficient
respect and status in the local community. Yet the ground was certainly
prepared by the Rover Scouts who organized frequent marches to
neighbouring villages, carrying their banner and singing their hymns. A

description of the visit to a village of Bani Ayub near al-Qitawwiyya in 1939 is illustrative of their style:

> The 20 Rover Scouts from al-Qitawwiyya marched in their uniforms to the village of Bani Ayub some five miles away. They carried the banner of Muslim Brothers and the Glorious Koran. A crowd of people on bicycles followed them . . . The Islamic slogans of the Brothers resounded all over the village and their hymns were heard everywhere. Then they were received by Hajj Abd al-Aziz Nasr Allah and . . . they went to the mosque. The Rover Scouts explained their mission and called for the creation of a Rover Scout group in the village.[34]

Rover Scout parades in Cairo often used loudspeakers mounted on cars, and if the parades were conducted in the evening the Rovers also carried torches. Royal celebrations often served as pretexts for these parades, but as a previous member noted, "the essential point was to show the strength of the Society, and its military appearance."[35] This strategy appears to have been quite successful. British intelligence agents observed that people were greatly impressed by the Rover Scout parades:

> In the poorer districts of Cairo daily parades of the Gawalah [Rover Scouts] dressed in uniforms showing their appropriate ranks have taken place. Onlookers have been powerfully impressed by these displays and many have hastened to enlist.[36]

The Rover Scouts have usually been seen as the first manifestation of the increasingly militant mood that came to characterize the Society in the late 1930s. During the war some observers drew parallels to the fascist youth formations in Europe. For example, British intelligence paid some attention to rumours that Hasan al-Banna intended "to use the Gawala [the Rover Scouts] just as Mussolini used the Balilla".[37] It appears, however, that the Rovers as a whole seldom participated in violent demonstrations although individual members certainly did.[38] However, this changed in the postwar years when disturbances erupted throughout Egypt. A certain military mood was undoubtedly an inherent part of the Rover Scout units. Their military drills and exercises coincided with a stronger emphasis on struggle and resistance against imperialism and Zionism. An early member recalled how the Rover Scouts were trained in the use of guns made of wood during military exercises.[39] Yet it should be noted that the Rover units were not designed for military purposes. As will be discussed later, the rudiments of a military wing came into being around 1940. This was kept strictly separate to ensure complete secrecy. The Rover Scout units on the other hand were an officially recognized organization and the names of all local and central leaders were published in the Society's newspaper. Scout activities, sports and social welfare work, not military training, constituted the predominant part of the Rover Scouts' activities. The Rover Scouts served as a reservoir of trained youth who could be easily rallied to social welfare services and public health projects which became a preoccupation of the Society during the war; the Muslim Brothers organized mobile units which helped improve public health in villages and towns by cleaning streets and alleys, instructing people of the importance of cleanliness, performing minor first aid, and encouraging the use of hospitals and modern scientific medical procedures.[40] In many provinces these activities probably created more goodwill for the Society among the local population than the paramilitary parades did.

The Battalions

Ideological education or indoctrination was a fundamental instrument in preparing cadres for the efficient propagation of the Muslim Brothers' mission. Up to 1937 the means of education had been confined to lectures, meetings, prayers, Qur'anic study groups, the Society's weekly journal and the Rover Scout units. This was apparently not sufficient to produce the "mighty spiritual strength" which Hasan al-Banna desired to bring forth.[41] Consequently, in the autumn of 1937, a new organizational unit was inaugurated, variously called the Battalion of the Supporters of God (Katibat Ansar Allah), the Battalion of Glory (Katibat al-Majd) or usually just the Battalion (Katiba). The beginning of the Battalion institution coincided roughly with the launching of a new strategy for the Society's future development, which outlined the various stages of the Islamic mission. According to al-Banna:

> The path of the Muslim Brothers is drawn and well-defined: its stages and future steps are not left to be determined by circumstances or

pure coincidences. The stages of this path are three: acquaintance – formation – execution [*ta'rif – takwin – tanfidh*].[42]

Up until 1938 the Society had essentially been in the first stage. The Society's mission had been disseminated among people, branches had been formed, various welfare services had been undertaken and reform programmes had been submitted to the authorities. This stage had now been "completed", al-Banna told his followers in 1938, and it was time to initiate the next stage, "formation" or the "special call" (*da'wa khassa*). However, the divide between the stages was not to be watertight. Al-Banna explained in early 1939, "for the most part these three stages go side by side, in accordance with the unity of our Islamic mission."[43] It seems clear that the inauguration of a new stage did not represent a dramatic change of policy for the Society as a whole. It basically meant that a group of dedicated cadres would be selected. Only those who understood the Society's mission well, had implemented its principles in their own lives and were prepared to "carry the burden of struggle" were eligible.[44] While all the branches, their organization and operation remained in the first stage, the selected group of initiated and virtuous members represented the Society's second stage, the "stage of formation".[45] This group was to be supported by "some influential dignitaries from among the leading personalities" in Egypt which obviously meant that some sort of patronage and protection could be counted on.[46]

The Battalions were essentially a vehicle for the completion of the "stage of formation". A Battalion was composed of between 10 and 40 members between the ages of 18 and 40. Only people with some background in the Society were eligible to become members, and the integrity and sincerity of candidates had to be attested to by the other members of the Battalion. Each Battalion was headed by a chief (*naqib*), who was elected by a secret ballot in the presence of an MIA deputy. It was usually subdivided into "companionships" (*'ishrah*), each headed by a deputy (*mandub*) and consisting of 10 members. All members were to be registered in meticulous detail in personal files in the "archives" of the Battalion. Loyalty to the organization and to the brethren in the Battalion was expressed through a special oath of allegiance called "the oath of association" ("I swear by God to [commit myself to] obedience, action and secrecy"), and disciplinary steps were to be taken against disobedient or negligent members.[47]

The training programme began after an initial period of four weeks during which new members were recruited. When this period expired, the Battalion became a closed unit aiming at "creating the highest example of the Muslim youth, described by Muslim forefathers as the 'monks at night and the knights by day'".[48] The means of achieving this was described broadly as "spiritual and physical training based on obedience, order, sincerity, sanctification of duty and complete preparedness".[49] The members usually met once a week for training, involving a rigorous night vigil with only a few hours' sleep. Physical training, prayers, invocation of God, *dhikr* (the practice of the collective invocation of God) and Qur'anic recitation were scheduled to occupy a large part of the night. However, *dhikr* and the recitation of special prayers, *ma'thurat*, were perhaps too closely associated with traditional Sufism and aroused some controversy in the Society. These rituals were criticized by other members, especially the Salafi adherents, who considered them a violation of the Prophet's tradition (*Sunna*).[50] In the earliest Battalions, Hasan al-Banna had led these night sessions himself, the high point of which was his spiritual guidance on a variety of subjects ranging "from Sufism to sex".[51] For the young bachelors in the Society, it was an important symbol of al-Banna's devotion to the cause that he "left his house, his wife and his children", preferring to spend the night in vigil with the Brothers.[52] Time was also set aside for studies of "matters concerning the Battalions". The core curriculum consisted of two tracts called *risalat al-ta'alim* (message of the teachings) and *al-minhaj* (the programme). The former outlined in detail the "spirit of the Brothers" and represented a kind of covenant between the leadership and the individual member, specifying 38 duties which the Battalion members were obliged to fulfil.[53] It did not address the membership in general but only "the 'Brother Activists' [*al-Ikhwan al-Mujahidun*] who believe in the loftiness of their mission and the sanctity of their ideology and who are firmly determined to live and die for the sake of it".[54] Al-Banna had written *al-minhaj* in the spring of 1938 and it was to be distributed among the members of the Battalions only. It outlined the policies of the Brothers in considerably greater detail than his general tracts which were published in the Society's weekly newspaper. The programme announced among other things the Brothers' intention to enter the Egyptian Parliament, a decision which was not made official until the Sixth Conference in January 1941. Muslim Brother veterans who participated in the Battalions recalled that al-Banna used to tell them confidential details about his policies, his contacts in political circles and other information which was withheld from the general membership.[55] In sum, there can be little doubt that the Battalions were meant to represent an advanced stage of initiation or an inner circle, consisting of the most dedicated cadres.

In the Battalion system, the principle of "status based on merit" was clearly recognized. For example, a member was awarded an honorific prize by the MIA when he had attended more than 40 weekly meetings, memorized the elementary curriculum, acquainted himself with the Society's laws and fulfilled his duties. By then, he was qualified to become a chief (*naqib*) of new Battalions and the MIA would confer on him the title of "an official Muslim Brother propagandist" (*da'iya min du'at al-Ikhwan al-rasmiyyin*). The Battalion formations were closely connected to the Rover Scout units. One previous member described the two systems as "almost inseparable".[56] For example, the Battalion members were instructed to register officially as Rover Scouts and acquire their own Rover Scout uniforms to be used at all gatherings. The Battalions also had daytime meetings and practised various forms of sports and "military training", not unlike the Rover Scouts. It appears that there were links between the Battalion-units and the organizational formation which came to be known as the "Special Section" (the military wing). With their heavy emphasis on secrecy, initiation and obedience, combined with a rigorous spiritual and physical training programme, the Battalions obviously served as a precursor to the military wing.

The heavy emphasis on militancy and struggle in the ideological preparation of the Battalions led the British to believe that they were training to be "suicide squads", and that they were partly modelled on the German Schutzstaffel (SS):

> It is known that in the past the Ikhwan [the Muslim Brothers] made a careful study of the Nazi and Fascist organizations and modelled a part of their organization upon them. The Gawala or Rovers . . . may be compared with Sturmabteilungen [SA], and the "kata'ib" [Battalions], special trusted men, with Schutzstaffel [SS]. They are also stated to be "suicide squads", though these have not yet had an opportunity to put their training into practice . . . There seems no doubt that the Ikhwan have sought to buy arms, and that they could bring out shock-troops in a time of disturbance. In

September 1941 Hasan al-Banna is reported to have said that he had 2,000 hand-picked armed men ready to obey his orders; the reference is probably to the "kata'ib".[57]

During the war the British Intelligence Service described most anti-imperialistic groups in Egypt as "pro-Axis", "fifth-column" and "fascist". However, when the British position in Egypt had been secured after the critical battle of El-Alamein in 1942 they reported, "there is however very little evidence of their contact with Axis agents since the outbreak of the war . . . Though the Ikhwan have perhaps imitated the Nazi–Fascist organization, they have no particular sympathy for their ideology as far as is known."[58]

The Battalions never came to play the dominant role that Hasan al-Banna envisaged for them in 1938 when he began advocating their formation in every village in Egypt. Inspired by the Prophetic tradition "Never shall 12,000 men be defeated because they are too few", he envisaged a four-year growth period aimed at creating 300 Battalions and 12,000 "fully equipped Brothers, both materially and spiritually".[59] However, by 1939 it was obvious that this schedule had not been fulfilled, although a number of new Battalions were reported. Al-Banna put this delay down to the fact that branches had not been able to implement the system of the Battalions properly.[60] In 1940, the project of mobilizing dedicated members in Battalions was given high priority and the Committee for the Organization of Battalions (Lajnat Tanzim al-Kata'ib) became a focal point in the Society's organizational apparatus. These efforts resulted in a significant increase in the number of Battalions during the early years of the Second World War.

The Battalions performed an essential function by paving the way for a more efficient mobilization of the active members. Although the Battalions were replaced by a new scheme, the Family System (*nizam al-usar*) or Families, in 1943,[61] their ideas and principles were reflected in this new system. The hierarchical structure of the Family System was composed of tightly-knit chains of command and basic units consisting of only five persons. In fact, the Families represented a more comprehensive formula for the creation of a close-knit socio-religious community, including social insurance, social welfare and mutual responsibility. The weekly meetings of the Families were conducted outside the branch headquarters, usually at the homes of the members in rotation. This enabled the Society to function efficiently even if branches were closed and the leadership arrested. The Family System has been described correctly as "the real basis of the power in the Society".[62] However, the foundations for this organizational strength were laid during the early experiences of building close-knit organizational units of dedicated cadres in the Battalions.

The Founding of a Military Wing:
The Special Apparatus

Since the British colonial power crushed the Urabi revolt in 1881, a number of "terrorist groups" had emerged in Egypt.[63] In the 1920s the Wafd Party and the Nationalist Party (al-Hizb al-Watani) had their own secret military wings which aimed to weaken British imperialism through "terrorist" attacks and assassinations. The murder of Sir Lee Stack, the British High Commander of Sudan, in 1924 by the Wafdist military wing was the most notable of these attacks.[64] In the 1930s, however, these parties became increasingly associated with the older generation's tacit acceptance of British colonial domination. Radical youth then began to look for other alternatives and flocked to the Muslim Brothers and the Young Egypt Party, as they were perceived as being more rigorously opposed to imperialism.

The background for the Muslim Brothers' military wing is some-what complex and our knowledge about it is still quite rudimentary. The formation of a military wing might be considered a natural consequence of the Society's ideology of the mid-1930s, which stressed that it was the religious duty of Muslims to repel aggression against the Islamic nation. The heavy emphasis on actions and deeds in the Brothers' propaganda, as opposed to the inertia of the established political parties, gave an added impetus for military action to be taken against the imperialists. The military wing (or the Special Apparatus) is said to have grown out of the Rover Scout units. Egyptian historians have tended to portray the Society's Rover units as a devious way of recruiting young men to the military wing. A comprehensive study of the Special Apparatus by Abd al-Azim Ramadan asserts that Hasan al-Banna began "building a large army under the innocent name of 'excursion groups'". Slowly and consciously these Scout formations "were transformed into a secret military organization".[65] There is, however, little evidence to support the claim that Hasan al-Banna and the Society's leadership devoted a lot of their time and energies into enticing young men to join the military wing. To the contrary, youths were more than willing to join secret societies which offered an opportunity to engage in adventurous subversive activities against the occupying power. There can be little doubt that strong internal pressure from radical members, as opposed to some preconceived plan hatched by Hasan al-Banna, was the major factor behind the formation of the military wing. As will be shown in Chapter 8, there had been growing pressure from young and militant cadres since 1937 for the Society to adopt a more radical and militant course, and individual members deliberately disobeyed the leadership's instruction to avoid clashes with the government. It appears that some members were involved in activities that could have brought repressive measures on the movement, and in mid-1938 the Wafdist press urged the Ministry of the Interior to take action against the Brothers, claiming that the Society trained young people in the use of firearms.[66] At the same time, according to British intelligence sources, some of the Society's members were sending funds and arms to the Palestinian Arab rebels and attempted to organize the manufacture of explosives for them.[67]

Prior to the Fifth Conference in 1939 some of the more impatient Brothers had been demanding the implementation of the third stage, "execution", which involved "uncompromising struggle".[68] At the Conference Hasan al-Banna argued that at that time only a very few members were able to "carry the burdens of fierce struggle and violent action" (*al-jihad al-shaq wa'l-'amal al-'anif*). "These activists", he said prophetically, "might take the wrong course and miss the target." Only after having recruited and thoroughly prepared the 300 Battalions, numbering 12,000 partisans, as envisaged in the programme of 1938, would he launch the third stage.[69] By late 1939 this policy of restraint had led to a serious crisis which resulted in the secession of some of the Society's most zealous cadres, and a rival society, Muhammad's Youth, had been formed. Against this background the founding of a military wing appears to have presented a solution. It offered opportunities for those who wished to prepare for armed struggle, thereby reducing the internal pressure for militant action. At the same time it strengthened the image of the Muslim Brothers as a movement which was preparing its members for armed struggle against the British. The rumours surrounding the military wing also gave the Society a touch of mystique and secrecy which usually tends to attract the young. People who worked for the British Intelligence Service, like Heyworth-Dunne, acknowledged the difficulty of obtaining reliable information about the Muslim Brothers:

> Whenever agents were sent to watch and report on the activities of the Ikhwan, they always succumbed to the leader . . . As a rule the information that was acquired was always second-hand, and even the sympathies of officials in the Governorate were towards the Ikhwan.[70]

Thus, it is very likely that rumours about subversive activities which reached the British also reached some segments of the population. The early activities of the military wing thus served to bring additional attention to the Muslim Brothers.

Two important factors enabled the formation of the Special Apparatus. In the late 1930s the Society had begun to enjoy the patronage of the Royal Councillor, Ali Mahir Pasha. His protégés in the Egyptian police were thus reluctant to act on British calls for the suppression of the kind of anti-British activities in which the Muslim Brothers were indulging.[71] In addition, the basic 'military' training being given to the Rover Scout units and some of the student groups at that time was fully in accordance with the policies of Ali Mahir Pasha, who as Prime Minister had issued orders in 1939 that all schools teach students military drill and manoeuvres.[72]

Another important factor was the Society's contacts with Hajj Amin al-Husayni, the Grand Mufti of Jerusalem, and members of the German Legation in Cairo. Documents seized in the flat of Wilhelm Stellbogen, the Director of the German New Agency (Deutsches Nachrichtenbüro) affiliated to the German Legation in Cairo, show that prior to October 1939 the Muslim Brothers received subsidies from his organization. Stellbogen was instrumental in transferring these funds to the Brothers, which were considerably larger than the subsidies offered to other anti-British activists. These transfers appear to have been coordinated by Hajj Amin al-Husayni and some of his Palestinian contacts in Cairo, including Awni Abd al-Hadi, Muhammad Ali Tahir and Shaykh Sabri 'Abedin.[73]

Muslim Brother veterans confirmed that the pro-Palestine propaganda efforts and the Secret Apparatus were partly financed by funds from Hajj Amin al-Husayni, transferred to them through his agents in Cairo.[74] The receipt of German funds in 1938–9 helps explain the mysterious statements made by some of the Brothers in the military trials of 1954–5, that Mahmud Labib, the leader of the Society's Rover Scouts and one of the leading figures in the military wing, had "called upon the services of German officers in shaping the Special Apparatus".[75] As the total income of the MIA from November 1938 to June 1939 was only £E807, the receipt of the German–Palestinian funds must have been of some importance even though these funds were most probably cut off after the outbreak of the Second World War in late 1939 when Stellbogen was interned and deported by the British military authorities. In addition to financing the pro-Palestine propaganda, these funds provided the Muslim Brothers with money for arms.

There are many uncertainties surrounding the founding of the Special Apparatus, but it seems clear that it was formed some time in 1940 and included a number of leading figures in the Muslim Brothers.[76] In a later reprint of his famous *risalat al-ta'alim* (message of the teachings), Hasan al-Banna recalled that the first group to swear allegiance to the principles of the "third stage", or "execution", took their oath on 5 Rabi' al-Awwal AH 1359 (April 1940). Several of the leading members of the Supreme Council of the Rover Scouts, like Husayn Kamal al-Din, Mahmud Labib and Abd al-Aziz Ahmad were reportedly among the founding members of the Special Apparatus.[77] This enabled the leaders to pick out those cadres from the Rover Scouts who met their requirements. The first part of the training programme in the military wing consisted of intensive 'ideological education'. A tract called *risalat al-jihad* (duty to struggle), which dealt with the inescapable duty of fighting the enemies of Islam, served as a core curriculum. The practical training programme included praying, fasting and intense physical exercise as well as various assignments, such as distributing pamphlets in secrecy and practising escape procedures like jumping from the third floor.[78] The determination of the individual member was tested by ordering him to purchase a revolver with his own money.[79] The building up of arms caches then began and the members of the military wing received basic training in the use of firearms.[80] Weapons were bought from arms dealers in the deserts.[81] (The abandoned dumps of arms in the Western Desert were a major source of concern to the British in the latter half of the war.)[82]

The military wing also developed an 'intelligence service' network. It was reported that the Muslim Brothers were making contacts with employees on the railways and in British military workshops and depots. Information was gathered about British troop movements, and plans were made for the sabotage of British military installations and lines of communication. Reports about the activities of the Special Apparatus were met with concern at the British military headquarters. These taken together with the repeated reports of anti-British propaganda and the less well-confirmed reports of sabotage plans led the British authorities to request the Prime Minister to intern Hasan al-Banna and his second-in-command, Ahmad al-Sukkari, in October 1941. The combined factors of a mass following, sabotage plans and Palace support resulted in the British Intelligence Service identifying the Muslim Brothers as "the most serious danger to public security".[83]

With a few exceptions,[84] the Special Apparatus remained quiet during the war years, even during the critical battle of El-Alamein in 1942. An uprising similar to the al-Kaylani rebellion in Iraq in 1941 did not occur. Hasan al-Banna did not want to jeopardize the Society's future by rash and foolhardy action, especially since the growing influence of the Society increased the prospects of attaining power by Fabian methods. However, the problems of meeting the demands of an increasingly impatient membership remained unresolved. Although the founding of a military wing might have served to temporarily offset the pressure for revolutionary action, the increasing power of the military wing eventually proved fatal to the Society in the latter half of the 1940s.

"Islam of the Effendia": The Beginning of an Islamic Student Movement

Students were an important part of Egyptian political life ever since the Egyptian revolution in 1919, although they had mainly been acting under the auspices of the Wafd Party until the student uprising of 1935–6. The independent role played by the student body during the disturbances in 1935–6 marked the beginning of what has been correctly dubbed " the years of the youth" or "the years of youthful disenchantment with the professional politicians".[85] A number of various groups and rival camps began to appear within the student body. The Wafd's hegemony over the student movement was increasingly challenged by non-Wafdist student groups. Until 1938 the Young Egypt Party was the main rival to Wafdist domination. The Muslim Brothers' student following was one of these new camps or factions which emerged within the student movement in the latter half of the 1930s, and by the mid-1940s it had grown to become one of the most dominant groups within the student body. Despite the essential role it came to play in the 1940s, the origins. of the Society's student body has been largely ignored by historians.

It is clear that the students came to occupy a special position in the Muslim Brother organization. Hasan al-Banna's deep concern for the educated youths' departure from Islam made him devote special attention to the students. In 1933, for the first time, students from the university at Cairo joined the Muslim Brothers. Hearing about this "great conquest", al-Banna reportedly broke off one of his journeys in the Delta to return to Cairo to meet the six students as soon as possible. "It was a blessed moment", he enthused in his memoirs, "when they joined the Islamic call [da'wa] and pledged to work for it."[86] There is no doubt that al-Banna attached a fundamental importance to student cadres. A saying frequently attributed to him is that "a student from one of the University faculties will be more useful to the Islamic mission than a whole village."[87] In one of his tracts, called *To the Youth and Especially the Students,* al-Banna stated:

> The four indispensable elements for the success of the Islamic mission are firm belief, sincerity, zealotry and action. These elements can only be found among the youth . . . [The youth are] the firm pillar of any developing and renascent nation.[88]

Consequently, students were given a very prominent place in the Society's organization. In 1936, two students, Hamdi Effendi al-Jarisi and Muhammad Tahir al-Arabi, were reportedly the most active cadres at the headquarters in Cairo. The former was a driving force in the Society's pro-Palestine campaign, and the latter served as al-Banna's personal secretary. Muhammad Tahir al-Arabi also assumed the important position of secretary of the Muslim Brothers' Palestine Committee and served as the liaison officer between the Society and the YMMA during the Palestine campaign in mid-1936. Apart from recruiting some of his best cadres among the students, al-Banna began to use meetings arranged by the Society's Student Section (established in 1933) to present the Muslim Brothers' policies on various matters.[89] For example, the Society's official entry into politics was announced at the Student Conference in February 1938, not in the first issue of *al-Nadhir* (May 1938) as is usually assumed.[90]

The special position of students in the Society was also evident in al-Banna's personal attitude towards student members. There are many testimonies of his efforts to build a close relationship of paternal love and affection between himself and the young students.[91] He took particular interest in their personal lives and studies, and visited them at home if any of them were ill. Special arrangements were also made for student members. For example, if a student member failed his exams, he was exempted from his duties at the headquarters, allowing him to devote all his time to his studies.

Personal contacts and initiatives remained the most important way of recruiting new student members. The Society began organizing special "mutual acquaintance" parties or end-of-term celebrations to which student members were urged to bring friends and colleagues. The Student Section appointed deputies for each university faculty, who were assigned the task of getting to know all the Muslim Brothers at the university at Cairo and acquainting them with each other. Islamic celebrations offered an opportunity to invite colleagues and teachers to the Society's special student gatherings. Tours, hiking, camping and military training were also organized by some of the student groups, not unlike the Rover Scouts. An important way of recruiting students was the campaign of support for the Palestinians during the Arab Revolt of 1936–9. A special Palestine committee for students was organized in May 1936 to complement the Society's general Palestine Aid Committee. The student element was an essential part of the pro-Palestine sub-committees organized by the Society during the revolt.[92] There is little doubt that the Society's unrelenting pro-Palestine campaigns contributed to the influx of students in the latter half of the 1930s.[93]

The Muslim Brothers' student body appears to have grown steadily since the first six students joined the Society in 1933. The same year a few student groups were formed by the Muslim Brothers at university faculties and other educational institutes. It was at this stage that the

Student Section was set up at the headquarters and a special column in the Society's newspaper was devoted to articles written by students. The Student Section reportedly consisted of 100 students in 1936 and more than 300 were said to have attended the Society's annual student party in Cairo in 1937.[94] The increasing number of students enabled the Muslim Brothers to organize a general student conference in mid-February 1938. Regional student conferences were convened some months later in several provincial towns (for example, hundreds of students reportedly attended conferences in al-Mansura, Zaqaziq and Assiut). In 1939 the Student Section announced the opening of several new student branches at secondary schools and regional religious institutes. The student following in Cairo had by then increased significantly and it had become a dominant element in the organization. Al-Banna felt that his weekly "Tuesday talks" (*hadith al-thulatha*), which were the weekly highlight for members in Cairo and its suburbs, were not sufficient to address the problems of the Society's growing student body. Accordingly, a series of special student lectures scheduled for Thursdays was initiated by Hasan al-Banna at the Society's headquarters in the autumn of 1939.[95] By 1940 the Committee for Student Affairs (the successor of the Student Section) had become the single largest committee in the Muslim Brothers' organization. From then on, the Society's student body was considered "the central nerve in the strength of the general movement", and it undoubtedly commanded the Society's most powerful segment of articulate and active opinion.[96]

The Society's efforts to recruit students were best rewarded in secondary schools. In contrast to the al-Azhar and the university at Cairo, these educational institutes were considered peripheral by most political groupings, and were thus left more accessible to political newcomers like the Brothers. Hence, part of the Society's strategy for winning over the student body was to focus particularly on the recruitment of secondary school students as a way of strengthening the future following at the university.[97] Its efforts at some of the regional religious institutes also bore fruit. The Religious Institute of Zaqaziq had become a staunch Muslim Brother stronghold by the turn of the decade and a significant following was reported at the religious institutes in the Shubra and al-Sayyida Zaynab quarters in Cairo as well as in Assiut.[98] As will be discussed in the following chapter, this success was not accompanied by similar progress at al-Azhar.

By 1939 the Society had made some headway in recruiting students at the university in Cairo, although not as much as al-Banna had hoped for. There were clear signs of a nascent student movement at the university at this point. The rivalry between the Young Egypt Party and the Muslim Brothers in 1938–9 stemmed mainly from the fact that the Brothers had begun to penetrate a student body which the Young Egypt Party regarded as its natural supporters. Furthermore, a number of Young Egypt's student activists switched to the Muslim Brothers.[99] The Society's deputies at the university became more involved in student affairs at the faculties. For example, they began raising the issue of prayer facilities, directing complaints to the administration about small, inadequate or non-existent prayer-rooms in the faculties. However, as there was a tendency at the university to associate religious devotion with reactionism and backwardness, these demands for prayer-rooms were sometimes ridiculed by professors.[100] The Society's deputies also ran a number of fund-raising campaigns for the Palestinian Arabs at the faculties and organized private lectures under the auspices of the Society's student body. In addition, the student deputies were particularly active in distributing the Society's newspaper in the faculties.

In February 1939 a group of Muslim Brothers founded the Union for Economic, Political and Islamic Studies (Rabitat al-Buhuth al-Iqtisadiyya wa al-Siyasiyya wa'l-Islamiyya) at the Faculty of Commerce. Its aim was to "study the true Islamic economic and political system anew and translate these excellent studies into French and English and exchange these with foreign universities". Its programme included such topics as the "Economic System of Islam" and "Commerce in Islam", and political issues such as "Politics in Islam", "Umar Ibn al-Khattab: the Father of the First Real Democracy" and "Islam between Democracy and Dictatorship or Islam the Dictatorial 'Consultation' [shuriyya]". The Union's laws demanded strict discipline at the meetings. Discussions were to be "scientific and devoid of emotional excitement", and failure to attend weekly meetings would result in fines. Money was also set aside for the publication of scientific tracts. The Union also established an honorific committee, Hay'at Sharaf al-Rabita, consisting of some of the professors. Little is known about the Union's further activities. It is worth noting, however, the strong commitment to a "scientific" method in the search for an economic and political system based on Islam as well as their desire to exchange their works with foreign universities. It reflects a different world view than that usually attributed to the Muslim Brothers. It represents in many ways the beginning of what was seen as a wholly new phenomenon in this period: the "Islam of the effendia".[101] This entailed the creation of a new image which repudiated the ingrained images of reactionism and religious inertia which had been the hallmark of established Islam. The importance of this new image can hardly be overstated and it was a major factor contributing to the steady influx of students into the Muslim Brothers in the 1940s.

Purges and Reorganization

An important part of Hasan al-Banna's rhetorics was to warn his followers that sooner or later tribulation and persecution would come, and he incessantly urged those who were not prepared to assume the burden of the Islamic mission to leave the Society or join it later when they felt they were prepared.[102] This essentially reflected his vision of a movement whose core consisted of a class of zealous cadres who would devote themselves completely to the cause. In al-Banna's eyes, only the most zealous and dedicated members would be reliable soldiers during the struggle that lay ahead. These considerations reportedly led him to convene a closed meeting, the "Committee of 24 Men", in the summer of 1938, attended by members who due to family relations and bonds of friendship had been given prominent positions in the organization, but who lacked the "will to sacrifice". They had thus become "a burden for the Islamic mission". When they were asked to join a new committee which would be assigned burdensome tasks, involving the possibility of heavy personal sacrifices, a number of them resigned. This move served to purge the organization of a number of uncommitted members in leading positions. This strategy was pursued further in a comprehensive reorganization initiated by al-Banna in November 1938. The essential aim of the new structure was "to put an end to empty titles" among the Brothers and "purge the ranks of every idle member whose contributions to the Brothers' cause are nothing but useless discussions".[103] The MIA was the testing-ground for the new organizational structure for seven months, and in the autumn of 1939 al-Banna proceeded to implement it in the branches. In the following section I will briefly sketch this new structure and try to assess its effects on the recruitment of new cadres to the Society.

The regulations that Hasan al-Banna drafted in 1934 gave the branches a virtually free rein in organizing their administrative and executive bodies. The organizational structure, adopted at the Third Conference in 1935, sought to strengthen the MIA *vis-à-vis* the branches by specifying certain prerogatives for its deputies and the right to veto local decisions. Nonetheless, the local branches were left to elect their own leaders. Given the power structure in Egyptian society at that time, one can safely assume that leading positions were allotted to local dignitaries. Surveying the reports of new branches in 1938–9 a pattern is clearly discernible: the local *'umdah, shaykh al-balad* or *'alim* were usually appointed as presidents or presidents of honour, while an *effendi* was appointed as secretary. However, the dominance of local conservative dignitaries had by 1939 led to tensions within the Society in a number of branches, precipitating the emergence of "two different camps: an administrative slow-paced and stumbling group and another camp of serious, active and fast-working members". According to al-Banna, these tensions had been created by the fact that the "positions of prestige and honour" in the Society were allotted to "administrative people who represent the Society" but who did not understand its ideas. Nor were they "committed to work for the sake of the Society". The system at that time, al-Banna argued, created "titles and names" which had no practical meaning, but which were used "for false display and personal purposes". The rights of the active members who did not have a high social standing were thus neglected and suppressed. It led to the loss of "the true basis for esteeming and appreciating the productive workers in the Society".

Consequently, al-Banna introduced organizational changes which became the basis for a new executive structure in the Society, swaying the balance of the power decisively in favour of the MIA and its loyal cadres in the provinces. This was done by detaching the honorific committees from the executive boards of branch organizations. Instead, the honorific bodies were assigned various consultative and representative tasks, such as giving recommendations in matters of great importance, representing the Society at formal receptions and participating in welfare projects. The real power of the branch was now vested in the executive body, called the General Supervisory Committee (Lajna Muraqiba 'Amma). This committee consisted of only three members appointed by the MIA after thorough consultation with local Muslim Brothers. This implied that locally elected leaders were replaced by centrally appointed deputies. Day-to-day administration and contacts with the MIA and other branches were the exclusive responsibility of the General Supervisory Committee, and its members represented the branch at all the Society's internal meetings. It was empowered to appoint local cadres to positions like secretary and treasurer amongst others, and was responsible for the supervision of various aspects of the activities at the branch.

The new executive structure placed a great importance on the office of local spiritual guide. The spiritual guide was to be appointed "from among those who have knowledge of jurisprudence, are pious and righteous, have a firm understanding of the Islamic mission and adhere to the principles of the Society". His duties were to divide the members into groups according to "their spiritual preparedness" and to hold weekly lectures for each group. Furthermore, he was to supervise their conduct, "guide them to good deeds" and "straighten the path of the corrupt". In executing his mission, he was not to be subjected to any formal or administrative restrictions. The spiritual guide represented Hasan al-Banna directly and wielded his authority in spiritual matters. Apart from his spiritual function, the spiritual guide may also be considered as one of the checks on the abuse of power or negligence of duties which the new organizational structure envisaged. Another check was provided by an annual consultation between the MIA and the members of the branches in which the incumbent General Supervisory Committee would be evaluated and, if necessary, replaced.

The new structure which substituted local elections with appointments represented a continuation of the process of strengthening the powers of the MIA, a process which can be traced back to the Second and Third Conferences in 1934 and 1935.[104] This new structure both aimed to make the Society more independent of local conservative dignitaries and to implement the principle of "position based on merit" more fully throughout the organization. It even perhaps reflected a new assertiveness in the Society, owing to its increasing influence as the largest Islamic society in Egypt. More importantly, the new executive structure grew out of Hasan al-Banna's experience of the first confrontation with the government during the Society's pro-Palestine campaign in 1938–9 when he realized the dubious loyalty of local conservative dignitaries. When demonstrations and clashes with the police occurred, a number of elder Muslim Brothers with high social standing withdrew their support from the Society.[105] The fact that leading positions in the Society were open to anyone who proved himself dedicated, zealous and qualified, regardless of class and social background, was fundamental to the successful recruitment of an efficient class of cadres. Thus, the Muslim Brothers came to represent an attractive option for ambitious young men from the lower echelons of the educated middle class, who sought political influence and upward social mobility.[106] Contrarily, the dominant popular party in the 1920s and 30s, the Wafd Party, never attempted to bring more people into the political process by expanding its membership, thus denying non-élites any access to the policy-making process. Its leadership preferred to recruit and then satisfy more upper-class constituents.[107]

The Society's new structure also addressed the problem of vulnerability to repressive measures. The new organizational changes were described as "implementing the principles of 'decentralization'",[108] or in Hasan al-Banna's words: "we are combining the advantages of complete 'centralization' (close supervision and the power invested in one body, the MIA) with the advantages of 'decentralization' (every deputy is given full freedom to act independently in fulfilling his mission)." Although the new structure amounted to a strengthening of the central authority, rather than a decentralization, measures were taken to ensure that the branches were able to function without central directives. For example, the new structure specified in more detail the distribution of responsibilities and duties of each organizational body, thereby increasing the ability of each body to act independently. This principle was labelled the Committee System (*nizam al-lijan*).[109]

In 1940 a more complete reorganization furthered this trend. The organizational hierarchy was now amended. While the previous system had mostly failed to produce efficient organizational levels between the local branches and the MIA, the new system created medium levels by vesting real power in the hands of the largest local branches, situated in provincial capitals or district towns. The formal structure established in the mid-1930s, consisting of areas (*manatiq*), districts (*dawa'ir*) and branches (*shu'ab*), was replaced by a system of four levels: areas (*manatiq ra'isiyya*), main branches (*shu'ab ra'isiyya*), district branches (*shu'ab markaziyya*) and sub-branches (*shu'ab far'iyya*).[110] The main branches were instructed to supervise the neighbouring district branches which in turn supervised the sub-branches nearest to them. Only "in cases of dire necessity" was the MIA to be consulted in affairs concerning district branches and sub-branches.

The reorganizing efforts of the Society also included the establishment in 1941 of a new central consultative body, the Constituent Assembly (al-Hay'a al-Ta'sisiyya), which consisted of 100 hand-picked representatives. It was to meet once a year, but could be convened more frequently if required. The selection of members to the Constituent Assembly was largely in the hands of the MIA and Hasan al-Banna, although the selection of candidates was guided by the principles that all districts should be represented and that seniority in the Society's mission was to be preferred. At its first meeting in 1941 the Constituent Assembly elected a 7-member committee, the Membership Committee (Lajnat al-'Udwiyya), to be responsible for nominating new candidates for the Constituent Assembly when seats became vacant, but these appointments were not to exceed 10 a year. The Membership Committee was also to supervise the moral conduct of the members of the Assembly, in addition to investigating complaints and meting out appropriate penalties accordingly. The new assembly effectively replaced the previous General Assembly with a centrally appointed body, although the Constituent Assembly became self-recruiting through the Membership Committee. The Constituent Assembly was partly a result of the increasing number of members and branches, which made it difficult to convene the General Assembly as it consisted of representatives of all branch organizations. The fact that the Constituent Assembly was appointed by the MIA in Cairo reflected the general trend towards centrally appointed deputies (replacing locally elected leaders), a process which had begun in the mid-1930s and which had a very important impact on the whole organization during the late 1930s.

During the war the experience of arrests and internment led to more far-reaching experiments in achieving a decentralized structure which would be resistant to government repression. This included the appointment of prefects or local substitute leaders, social insurance for members falling victim to political persecution and the establishment of the Family System. A British intelligence report from 1944 noted that as a result of the Society's decentralized structure:

> the activities of the organization should no longer be handicapped
> or disrupted by the closing of meeting places or by the arrest of

leading members, and many of the smallest sections are now able to operate without the direction of a senior body.[111]

The importance of the attention given to organizational efficiency can hardly be overstated. Not only did it enable the Muslim Brothers to sustain repression but it also demonstrated their ability to build a power base independent of the élite. This power base gave credibility to the Society's claim of representing the middle and lower classes in Egypt. It also contributed to the Brothers' identity as a new political force based on ideology not on patronage networks. This will be studied in the next chapter.

NOTES

1 Dr Hasan Hanafi quoted in François Burgat and William Dowell, *The Islamic Movement in North Africa* (Texas, University of Austin), p. 35 (italics added for emphasis). Dr Hanafi is currently Professor of Philosophy at Cairo University in Egypt and an important representative of the 'Islamic left'.

2 *Qism al-manatiq: nashra 'amma*, p. 3.

3 Khaled Mohi El Din, *Memoirs of a Revolution: Egypt 1952* (Cairo, AUC Press, 1995), p. 22.

4 'Abd al-Halim, *al-Ikhwan al-Muslimun: ahdath sana'at tarikh*, p. 79.

5 *JIM*, no. 10, 1355/1936, p. 18 and *Mudh.*, pp. 235–40.

6 Mahmud 'Abd al-Halim roughly estimated that 100 students were involved in the Society of the Muslim Brothers in 1935. A British intelligence report dated April 1936 stated that a Muslim Brother meeting in Cairo on the occasion of a visit of a Syrian delegation was attended by around 200 people, most of them al-Azhar and university students. See 'Abd al-Halim, *al-Ikhwan al-Muslimun: ahdath sana'at tarikh*, p. 79 and 'Pan-Islamic Arab Movement', Lampson to FO, no. E2120, 8 April 1936, FO 371/19980.

7 This is evident from the first announcement of *Hijra fi Allah* which makes no mention of the Palestine issue. See *JIM*, no. 10, 1355/1936, p. 18.

8 *JIM*, no. 17, 1355/1936, p. 19.

9 *JIM*, no. 13, 1355/1936, p. 20; *JIM*, no. 15, 1355/1936, p. 19; and *JIM*, no. 16, 1355/1936, p. 21.

10 *JIM*, no. 4, 1356/1937, p. 5; *Mudh.*, pp. 268–70; and *al-Nadhir*, no. 2, 1357/1938, p. 13.

11 *al-Nadhir*, no. 16, 1358/1939, p. 15.

12 Wendell (tr.), *Five Tracts of Hasan al-Banna*, pp. 133–61.

13 See, for example, *Majallat al-Ta'aruf*, no. 6, 1940, pp. 9–11.

14 'Abd al-Halim, *al-Ikhwan al-Muslimun: ahdath sana'at tarikh*, pp. 79–80. A Muslim Brother veteran from Alexandria recalled that people were usually surprised when they saw young men attending the sermons in the mosques. See al-Sisi, *Hasan al-Banna: mawaqif fi al-da'wa wa al-tarbiya*, p. 57.

15 al-'Ubaydi, *Safahat min hayat al-Hajj 'Abd al-Latif Abu Qurah, mu'assis al-Ikhwan al-Muslimin fi'l-Urdun*, pp. 9–10.

16 Zaki, *al-Ikhwan al-Muslimun wa'l-mujtama' al-misri*, p. 159.

17 See Hasan al-Banna's editorials in *JIM*, nos. 38–40, 42, 43, 45 and 46 (1936/1937). These editorials correspond roughly to *nahwa al-nur*, printed and translated in *Five Tracts of Hasan al-Banna*, pp. 103–31.

18 'La'ihat firaq al-rahhalat', *Qanun Jam'iyyat al-Ikhwan al-Muslimin al-'amm al-mu'addal 1354h: mulhaqat* (Cairo, Matba'at al-Ikhwan al-Muslimin, AH 1354/1934), pp. 26–7.

19 Mitchell erroneously dated the official registration of the Rover Scouts to the end of the war. Zaki's study, on which Mitchell has relied, has recorded a much earlier date (around 1940). The handbook of the Battalions (*kata'ib*), written by Hasan al-Banna in the spring of 1938, instructed all Battalion members to register with the National Scout Movement in order to obtain permission to use scout uniforms. Another internal publication from mid-1939 reported that a number of Rover Scout units had already been registered with the National Scout Movement and the remaining units were in the process of being registered. See Mitchell, *The Society of the Muslim Brothers*, p. 202; Zaki, *al-Ikhwan al-Muslimun wa'l-mujtama' al-misri*, p. 155; *al-Minhaj*, p. 30; and *Taqrir ijmali khass*, p. 7.

20 'Abd al-Halim, *al-Ikhwan al-Muslimun: ahdath sana'at al-tarikh*, pp. 129–31. For more details on the Green and Blue Shirts, see Jankowski, *Egypt's Young Rebels* and 'The Egyptian Blue Shirts and the Egyptian Wafd, 1935–1938', *Middle Eastern Studies*, vol. 6 (1970), pp. 77–95.

21 al-Sa'id, *Hasan al-Banna: mata, kayfa wa li-madha?*, pp. 106–7. For more details on the Wafd–Palace struggle, see Chapter 7.

22 Zaki, *al-Ikhwan al-Muslimun wa'l-Mujtama' al-Misri*, pp. 155–7.

23 Mahmud Labib wrote memoirs of his military adventures in the Libyan War. See Mahmud Labib, *Humat al-Sallum* (Cairo, Dar al-'Arabi, 1950). For more details about Mahmud Labib, see al-Sisi, *Fi qafilat al-Ikhwan al-Muslimin*, pp. 29–30; Bayumi, *al-Ikhwan al-Muslimun wa'l-jama'at al-islamiyyah fi'l-hayah al-siyasiyya al-misriyyah*, p. 130; and Husayn Muhammad Ahmad Hammuda, *Asrar harakat al-Dubbat al-Ahrar wa'l-Ikhwan al-Muslimun* (Cairo, al-Zahra' lil-I'lam al-'Arabi, 1985), pp. 28–9.

24 "Military" in the sense that marches and parades were organized. I have found nothing about training in the use of firearms at these camps. For more information on the summer camps, see 'Abd al-Halim, *al-Ikhwan al-Muslimun: ahdath sana'at al-tarikh*, p. 167; Abu al-Nasr, *Haqiqat al-khilaf bayn al-Ikhwan al-Muslimin wa 'Abd al-Nasir*, pp. 25–8; al-Sisi, *Fi qafilat al-Ikhwan al-Muslimin*, pp. 29–30; and *al-Nadhir*, no. 6, 1357/1938, p. 22.

25 Zaki, *al-Ikhwan al-Muslimun wa'l-mujtama' al-misri*, pp. 155–6 and *Taqrir ijmali khass*, p. 6.

26 Rover Scout camps were initially planned in Suez, Port Said, Zaqaziq, Ismailia, al-Matariyya, Assiut, al-Minya, Bani Suwayf, Ra's al-Barr, al-Mansura and Alexandria. These plans were not fulfilled, but regional camps were organized in Port Said, al-Manzala, Ismailia, Suez and Assiut. See *al-Nadhir*, no. 18, 1358/1939, p. 26; *al-Nadhir*, no. 27, 1358/1939, p. 22; and *Mudh.*, pp. 289–90. For the quotation, see *Taqrir ijmali khass*, p. 6.

27 See Hasan al-Banna's report to the branches after his trip to Upper Egypt in 1939 in *al-Nadhir*, no. 34, 1358/1939, editorial.

28 See the survey of Rover Scout units in *Majallat al-Ta'aruf*, no. 13, 1359/1940, p. 12. Zaki fixed the number of Rover Scouts in early 1941 at 2,000 and at 15,000 by the end of 1942. At the end of the war the Muslim Brothers had between 20,000 and 45,000 Rover Scouts, according to two different estimates (Salah 'Isa and 'Abd al-'Azim Ramadan). At its height in 1947–8, the Society reportedly had nearly 75,000 Rover Scouts. See Zaki, *al-Ikhwan al-Muslimun wa'l-mujtama' al-misri*, pp. 157–9. For Ramadan's and Salah 'Isa's estimates, see Ahmad Abdalla, *The Student Movement and National Politics in Egypt*, p. 48 and p. 241.

29 See, for example, *al-Nadhir*, no. 7, 1358/1939, p. 23.

30 *al-Nadhir*, no. 9, 1357/1938, p. 26; *al-Nadhir*, no. 6, 1358/1939, p. 13; and *al-Nadhir*, no. 9, 1358/1939, p. 13.

31 Zaki, *al-Ikhwan al-Muslimun wa'l-mujtama' al-misri*, p. 152.

32 al-Sisi, *Fi qafilat al-Ikhwan al-Muslimin*, pp. 53–4.

33 *al-Nadhir*, no. 12, 1358/1939, p. 7.

34 *al-Nadhir*, no. 11, 1358/1939, p. 25.

35 Kamal, *al-Nuqat fawq al-huruf*, p. 62–4.

36 Extract from 'Defence Security Summary of Egyptian Affairs', 27 July – 2 August 1944, WO 208/1580.

37 Security Summary (Middle East), no. 81, 19 September 1942, WO 208/1561/ SSME.

38 See, for example, the large demonstrations organized by the Muslim Brothers in early August 1938. The Rover Scouts participated in a few peaceful marches in Meet Ghamr and al-Manzala, not in the violent demonstrations in Ismailia, Rashid and Alexandria. See *al-Nadhir*, no. 11, 1357/1938, p. 18.

39 'Abd al-Halim, *al-Ikhwan al-Muslimun: ahdath sana'at al-tarikh*, p. 161.

40 Nancy Elizabeth Gallagher, *Egypt's Other Wars: Epidemics and the Politics of Public Health* (Cairo, AUC Press, 1993), p. 110.

41 Wendell (tr.), *Five Tracts of Hasan al-Banna*, p. 86.

42 *al-Minhaj*, p. 1. See also Hasan al-Banna's editorial in the first edition of *al-Nadhir* in May 1938.

43 *al-Nadhir*, no. 35, 1357/1939, p. 13.

44 *al-Minhaj*, p. 3.

45 *Majmu'at al-rasa'il lil-imam al-shahid Hasan al-Banna* (Beirut, al-Mu'assasa al-Islamiyya lil-Taba'a wa'l-Sahafa wa'l-Nashr, n.d.), p. 274.

46 *al-Minhaj*, p. 3.
47 *Ibid.*, pp. 27–32.
48 *al-Nadhir*, no. 30, 1357/1938, p. 22.
49 *al-Minhaj*, p. 27.
50 'Adil, *al-Nuqat fawqa al-huruf*, p. 68.
51 Mitchell, *The Society of the Muslim Brothers*, p. 196.
52 'Abd al-Halim, *al-Ikhwan al-Muslimun: ahdath sana'at al-tarikh*, pp. 152–3.
53 The first *risalat al-ta'alim* was written for the Society's summer camp in al-Dikhaylah outside Alexandria in 1938. By mid-1939 it was reportedly used as the basic curriculum for the Battalions. Later, it became the primary indoctrination text for the rank-and-file membership. See *al-Minhaj*, p. 5; *Taqrir ijmali khass*, p. 14 and p. 38; and *Majmu'at al-rasa'il lil-Imam al-Shahid Hasan al-Banna*, pp. 266–82.
54 *Majmu'at al-rasa'il lil-Imam al-Shahid Hasan al-Banna*, p. 267.
55 'Adil, *al-Nuqat fawqa al-huruf*, p. 69.
56 'Abd al-Halim, *al-Ikhwan al-Muslimun: ahdath sana'at al-tarikh*, p. 163.
57 'The Ikhwan al Muslimin Reconsidered', 14 December 1942, FO 141/838. See also Security Summary (Middle East), no. 81, 19 September 1942, WO 208/1561/SSME.
58 'The Ikhwan al Muslimin Reconsidered', 14 December 1942, FO 141/838.
59 *al-Minhaj*, pp. 5–6.
60 *Taqrir ijmali khass*, p. 7.
61 For more detail on the Family System, see Mitchell, *The Society of the Muslim Brothers*, pp. 197–200; 'Abd al-Halim, *al-Ikhwan al-Muslimun: ahdath sana'at al-tarikh*, pp. 256–7; and 'Ikhwan el Muslimeen' (Secret), P.I.C. Paper no. 49 (revised), 25 July 1944, FO 371/41334, p. 2.
62 Mitchell, *The Society of the Muslim Brothers*, p. 198.
63 V. S. Koshelev, 'Iz istorii tainykh antibritanskikh organizatisii v Egipte', *Narody Azii i Afriki* (1980), pp. 111–19.
64 For more details, see Deeb, *Party Politics in Egypt*, pp. 83–4; Goldschmidt, 'The National Party from spotlight to shadow', *Journal of Asian and African Studies*, vol. 16 (1982), p. 26; and Koshelev, 'Iz istorii tainykh antibritanskikh organizatisii v Egipte', pp. 118–19.
65 Ramadan, *al-Ikhwan al-Muslimun wa al-tanzim al-sirri*, p. 37 and p. 40. See for a similar view, al-Sa'id, *Hasan al-Banna: mata, kayfa wa li-madha?*, pp. 122–35.
66 al-Sisi, *Fi qafilat al-Ikhwan al-Muslimin*, p. 62; *al-Nadhir*, no. 10, 1357/1938, p. 20; *al-Nadhir*, no. 11, 1357/1938, pp. 4–6; and *Majallat al-Ta'aruf*, no. 16, 1359/1940, editorial.
67 'The Ikhwan al Muslimin Reconsidered', 14 December 1942, FO 141/838.
68 'Risalat al-ta'alim', *Majmu'at al-rasa'il lil-Imam al-Shahid Hasan al-Banna*, p. 274.
69 *al-Nadhir*, no. 35, 1357, p. 15.
70 Heyworth-Dunne, *Religious and Political Trends in Modern Egypt*, p. 91.
71 British Embassy, Alexandria, to Halifax, no. 1077, E5896/10/31, 26 September 1938, FO 371/21881.

72 al-Nadhir, no. 28, 1358/1939, p. 17.
73 'Notes on Wilhelm Stellbogen', 23 October 1939, WO 208/502 and 'The Ikhwan al Muslimin Reconsidered', 14 December 1942, FO 141/838. The transfer of German funds to the Muslim Brothers was also noted by Seth Arsenian who served in the Bureau of Overseas Intelligence at the Office of War Intelligence during the Second World War. See Arsenian, 'Wartime propaganda in the Middle East', *The Middle East Journal*, vol. 2 (1948), p. 425.

Shaykh Sabri 'Abedin had been one of the Muslim Brothers' contacts in Jerusalem since 1936. During the war he was also reported to be an active agent in Egypt for the exiled Palestinian leader Hajj Amin al-Husayni, "distributing funds to Palestine refugees and propagandists". See Appendix to Security Summary (Middle East), no. 642, 25 October 1941, WO 208/1560; Appendix to Security Summary (Middle East), no. 513, 14 May 1941; and *JIM*, no. 4, 1356/1937, p. 4.
74 'Abd al-Halim, *al-Ikhwan al-Muslimun: ahdath sana'at al-tarikh*, p. 260.
75 al-Husayni, *The Moslem Brethren*, p. 139.
76 Mahmud al-Sabbagh, *Haqiqat al-tanzim al-khass wa dawruhu fi da'wat al-Ikhwan al-Muslimin*, pp. 126–7; 'Abd al-Halim, *al-Ikhwan al-Muslimun: ahdath sana'at al-tarikh*, pp. 258–9; and Anwar Sadat, *Revolt on the Nile* (London, Allan Wingate, 1957), pp. 28–30. The head of the Special Section in the 1950s stated in 1955 that it was founded around 1942 or possibly even a little earlier. See Muhammad Khamis Humayda's testimony in *Mahkamat al-Sha'b: al-madbata al-rasmiyya li-mahadir jalasat Mahkamat al-Sha'b*, p. 1026.
77 'Abd al-Halim, *al-Ikhwan al-Muslimun: ahdath sana'at al-tarikh*, p. 258 and Zaki, *al-Ikhwan al-Muslimun wa'l-Mujtama' al-Misri*, p. 156.
78 'Abd al-Halim, *al-Ikhwan al-Muslimun: ahdath sana'at al-tarikh*, pp. 258–9.
79 al-Sabbagh, *Haqiqat al-tanzim al-khass wa dawruhu fi da'wat al-Ikhwan al-Muslimin*, p. 127–8.
80 'Ikhwan el Muslimeen' (Secret), P.I.C. Paper no. 49 (revised), 25 July 1944, FO 371/41334, pp. 5–6.
81 'Abd al-Halim, *al-Ikhwan al-Muslimun: ahdath sana'at al-tarikh*, pp. 258–9.
82 'Ikhwan el Muslimeen' (Secret), P.I.C. Paper no. 49 (revised), 25 July 1944, FO 371/41334, pp. 5–6.
83 Security Summary (Middle East), no. 66, 30 July 1942, WO 208/1561/SSME.
84 A previous member recalled that a bomb was thrown into the British Club in Cairo on Christmas Eve to frighten the soldiers. See 'Abd al-Halim, *al-Ikhwan al-Muslimun: ahdath sana'at al-tarikh*, p. 263.
85 Abdalla, *The Student Movement and National Politics in Egypt*, p. 42.
86 *Mudh.*, pp. 183–184; *JIM*, no. 4, 1356/1937, pp. 1–2.
87 'Abd al-Halim, *al-Ikhwan al-Muslimun: ahdath sana'at al-tarikh*, p. 73.
88 Hasan al-Banna, *Ila al-shabab wa ila al-talaba khassatan* (Alexandria, Dar al-Da'wa lil-Taba'a wa al-Nashr wa al-Tawzi', n.d.), p. 4.
89 See, for example, two important speeches by Hasan al-Banna in the spring of 1937 at the annual end-of-term celebrations in *JIM*, no. 1, 1356/1937, editorial (or *Mudh.*, pp. 261–4) and *JIM*, no. 4, 1356/1937, pp. 1–2.

90 For the speeches delivered at the Student Conference, see *Kalimat mu'tamar talabat al-Ikhwan al-Muslimin* (unpublished).
91 'Abd al-Halim, *al-Ikhwan al-Muslimun: ahdath sana'at al-tarikh*, p. 73.
92 Lampson to FO, no. E3153, 28 May 1936, FO 371/19980 and *JIM*, no. 7, 1355/1936, p. 15.
93 The students' interest in the Palestine question was considerable. In November 1938 the General Student Conference for the Support of the Palestinian Arabs was attended by more than 5,000 students. See *Majallat al-Fath*, no. 627, 1357/1938, pp. 16–17.
94 *JIM*, no. 4, 1356/1937, pp. 1–2. For an estimate of the Muslim Brothers' student following in 1936, see 'Abd al-Halim, *al-Ikhwan al-Muslimun: ahdath sana'at al-tarikh*, p. 79.
95 For a survey of the student lectures held by Hasan al-Banna in the period December 1939 to April 1940, see al-Sisi, *Fi qafilat al-Ikhwan al-Muslimin*, p. 80.
96 In the 1940s the head of the Muslim Brothers' student movement was one of the most powerful positions in the Society. See Mitchell, *The Society of the Muslim Brothers*, p. 180. For the quotation, see interview with the previous Muslim Brother activist Muhammad Farid 'Abd al-Khaliq in 'Abd al-Sattar al-Maliji, *Tarikh al-haraka al-islamiyya fi sahat al-ta'lim 1933–1993* (Cairo, Maktabat al-Wahba, 1994), p. 19.
97 Interview with Jamal al-Banna, spring 1995.
98 In 1941, more than 300 students from the Religious Faculty of Zaqaziq signed letters of protest against the detention of the Muslim Brothers' leadership. Students from the religious institutes in Shubra and in al-Sayyida Zaynab were also represented among the petitioners. See Dar al-Watha'iq, Qasr 'Abedin/ 'Iltimasat al-Ikhwan al-Muslimin' (Box 557). For other sources on the Society's following at the religious institutes, see British Embassy, Alexandria, to Halifax, no. E5898, 26 October 1938, FO 371/21881; *al-Nadhir*, no. 16, 1357/1938, p. 7; *al-Nadhir*, no. 28, 1357/1938, p. 23; and *al-Nadhir*, no. 30, 1357/1938, p. 26.
99 Jankowski, *Egypt's Young Rebels*, p. 40 and 'Abd al-Halim, *al-Ikhwan al-Muslimun: ahdath sana'at al-tarikh*, pp. 124–8.
100 *al-Nadhir*, no. 30, 1357/1938, p. 26.
101 al-Jindi, *Qa'id al-da'wa: hayat rajul wa tarikh al-madrasa*, p. 84, and Bayumi, *al-Ikhwan al-Muslimun wa'l-jama'at al-islamiyya fi'l-hayah al-siyasiyya al-misriyya*, p. 309.
102 For two examples, see *JIM*, no. 41, 1353/1935, editorial and *al-Nadhir*, no. 10, 1358/1939, editorial.
103 The following section is based on *Taqrir ijmali khass*, pp. 26–34.
104 This was modified in the laws adopted by the General Assembly in September 1945. Only the head of the local branch was to be appointed by Hasan al-Banna, with the other twelve members of the administrative board to be elected by the general assembly of the branch. See Articles 37–43 of the Basic Law of the Organization of the Muslim Brothers (1945).

105 This point has also been made by Mahmud 'Abd al-Halim. During pro-Palestinian demonstrations in Rashid, his home town, in 1938 a dozen Muslim Brother activists were arrested. At the same time a number of local dignitaries (a'yan) resigned from the Society. See 'Abd al-Halim, *al-Ikhwan al-Muslimun: ahdath sana'at al-tarikh*, pp. 178–9.

106 After the 1936 treaty the Egyptian army became another channel of upward social mobility for lower-middle-class youth (though the higher ranks continued to be the preserve of the upper class). For more details about the social classes from which Islamic radical movements in Egypt recruited their members, see Davis, 'Ideology, social classes and Islamic radicalism in modern Egypt'.

107 Selma Botman, *Egypt from Independence to Revolution 1919–1952* (New York, Syracuse University Press, 1991), p. 32.

108 *Majallat al-Ta'aruf*, no. 13, 1359/1940, p. 2.

109 For more details, see al-Sisi, *Hasan al-Banna: Mawaqif fi al-da'wa wa al-tarbiya*, pp. 154–61.

110 See Appendix III.

111 'Ikhwan el Muslimeen' (Secret), P.I.C. Paper no. 49 (revised), 25 July 1944, FO 371/41334, p. 3.

7

An Ideological–Political Party

If someone should say to you "this is politics!", say: "This is Islam, and we do not recognize such divisions." If someone should say to you "you are agents of revolution!", say: "We are agents of the truth and of peace in which we believe and which we exalt. If you rise up against us and offer hindrance to our message, God has given us permission to defend ourselves."

Hasan al-Banna[1]
1939

The Politicization of Islam:
Revolt against the Politics of Notables

The so-called Islamic revival in general and the rise of political Islam in particular have frequently urged scholars to examine the "political" nature of Islam. It has been argued that Islam does not recognize the Christian distinction between Church and State, and its allegedly holistic nature makes it more politicized than other religions. This ideational thesis is further backed up with socio-economic and cultural explanations. The exacerbating economic crisis in Egypt coupled with a rapid process of Westernization are said to have created propitious conditions for a Muslim reactionary backlash, resulting in a reassertion of religious traditions and a retreat from modernity.[2] However, as has been pointed out by Eric Davis, these models fail to explain why some Muslims are attracted to Islamic political movements while other Muslims are not.[3] He has suggested that the ideology of the Islamist radicals is, to a great extent, a reflection of class interests. More specifically, it reflects the class interests of the professional urban middle class. By drawing upon existing surveys of the social background of Islamist activists, Davis has shown that since the 1930s the radical Islamic groups have recruited an overwhelming proportion of their members from this class, particularly among those who were recent immigrants to urban areas. Davis argued that the Muslim Brothers did not attract their main following from the traditional classes of urban lumpenproletariat, but from professionals, civil servants and students whose high level of education should, at least in Western eyes, indicate a secular and "modern" world-view.[4] Davis's results should be slightly qualified however. His sources were mainly drawn from the upper echelons of the Society's leadership and do not reflect the rank-and-file membership of the Muslim Brothers which included wide sections of the lower classes, especially in the 1940s. A survey of the 11,000 signatures gathered by the Muslim Brothers in 1941 shows a high percentage of peasants, small landowners, petty traders and artisans.[5] Yet Davis's conclusion is correct when analysing the articulate and policy-making sections of the Muslim Brothers.

Davis's perspective appears to be a better starting-point for the study of the background of the Society's official entry into the political arena in 1938, rather than some vague notion about the political nature of Islam as opposed to the other-worldliness of Christianity. This chapter will argue that the political outlook of the Muslim Brothers in many ways represented a revolt against the "politics of notables and patronage networks" which dominated the Egyptian political scene.[6] This was a closed world for the expanding and restless urbanized middle class. Ralph Coury, the biographer of the Egyptian politician Abd al-Rahman Azzam (who was to become the first Secretary-General of the Arab League), described this upper-class world as:

> a "social round", a continuous movement of political and societal personalities between various "poles" of the city, the hotels, the Palace, the embassies, the newspaper offices and various clubs and private homes . . . The activity of all of these clubs was listening to jokes and pleasantries and news of intrigues, disasters and scandals.[7]

Other contemporaries related "the pleasurableness of this Cairene cafe society between the two world wars" to the fact that the peasants and workers were still "in a state of political weakness".[8] Politics was essentially the domain of this closed world of notables, dignitaries and upper-class families in the 1930s, and laws strictly forbade civil servants as well as voluntary organizations to engage in politics.[9] Channels of political expression open to the middle and lower classes were confined to the student activism of the Young Egypt Party and the Wafd, the workers' syndicates and the emerging voluntary organizations, especially the Islamic associations. None of these were entirely independent. They usually relied heavily on the patronage of members of the ruling establishment who sought to exploit the mass following of the popular movements for their own interests. The Wafd Party usually controlled the students at the university in Cairo and a substantial part of the syndicates,[10] the Palace controlled the majority of the al-Azhar students and enlisted the support of the Islamic societies, and the local and national dignitaries controlled most of the voluntary organizations through subsidies and patronage. The ability to control and mobilize these popular elements against political rivals was an essential part of the political strategy of the élite. Members of the non-élite classes were, however, seldom co-opted into the ruling élite. Selma Botman has noted that the only political party with a broad popular following at the elections, the Wafd Party

> . . . could have acted as a mobilizer of the masses and aggressively brought more people into the political process by expanding its own membership, allowing non-élites to influence policy in the party, and embracing issues of social and economic reform. Wafdist leaders, however, chose not to activate peasants, workers, and members of the lower middle class, preferring instead to recruit and then satisfy the more upper class constituents . . . For most of the liberal period [the Wafd] simply chose not to fight for social change, fearful of creating a movement it would not be able to control . . . As a result of Wafdist restraints on the political process, the masses' connection to mainstream political life in Egypt remained weak.[11]

Despite the restrictions placed upon the political involvement of Islamic associations, these organizations nevertheless offered an opportunity for political expression in various forms. Islamic causes, like the persecution of Muslims in Libya, the desecration of the al-Aqsa Mosque and the Palestine Revolt, provided platforms for expressing political views on the foreign policies of the Egyptian government and its relationship with Britain. Other issues, like the declining status of religion in Egyptian schools, served as a starting-point for the Islamic associations' involvement in the domestic policies of the government. The call for Islamic law was another powerful instrument of political expression, given Egypt's extremely fragmented and foreign-dominated judicial system. These causes formed the platform for the Muslim Brothers' entry into the political arena.

The ideological foundation for a politicized Islam was laid by Hasan al-Banna in 1938, although as has been shown in Chapter Two religious issues with political implications had been raised by the Muslim Brothers since 1932. The intention to enter the political arena and deal openly with politics was announced at the Society's Student Conference in February 1938, and al-Banna's speech to the conference represents the earliest and most illustrative source on the politicization of the Society. In his speech, al-Banna sought to define an ideological basis for a politicized Islam. He stressed that Islam was a total concept, embracing all aspects of life – politics included. According to al-Banna, the traditional and narrow interpretation reduced Islam to "an imperialist, submissive and despicable Islam", and therefore Muslims needed to free themselves from the shackles imposed by their enemies, by expanding the interpretation of Islam to include politics:

> O ye Brethren! Tell me, if Islam is something else than politics, society, economy, law and culture, what is it then? Is it only empty acts of prostration, devoid of a pulsating heart? . . . O ye Brethren! Did the Koran reveal a complete, perfect and elaborate system to mankind just for this? . . . This narrow interpretation of Islam and these closed boundaries to which Islam has been confined is exactly what the adversaries of Islam want in order to keep the Muslims in place and make fun of them.[12]

In Hasan al-Banna's eyes, the acceptance of the totality of Islam represented a "liberation", confirming that a Muslim, "by virtue of his adherence to Islam, has the right to have a voice in all aspects concerning the nation". Al-Banna defined the execution of this right as a duty: "A Muslim will never become a real Muslim if he is not political and has a view for the affairs of his people." Thus, if Islam was correctly understood it meant a kind of empowerment of Muslims. The role of politics in society, as defined by Hasan al-Banna, was to organize the affairs of government, clarify its prerogatives and duties, control and supervise the rulers, obey them if they behaved well and criticize them if they erred. Islam had specified the general rules and objectives for a just Islamic society. It had also imposed on mankind the duty to realize these objectives. Islam had left all details and minor issues to be solved by people, according to the general circumstances. Al-Banna particularly stressed the principle of the sovereignty of the people and the importance of holding the ruler accountable:

> Islam has enjoined, confirmed and recommended the principle that power belongs to the nation. The Muslims should be supervising the acts of their governments, giving advice and support and holding them accountable.[13]

Islam also imposed on the ruler the duty to work for the general welfare of his people. Al-Banna continued: "If the ruler goes astray, the people are obliged to force him to abide by the law and return him to the origin of justice." By this interpretation of Islam, the Muslim Brothers could forcefully assert their right to political participation and demand a voice in the political affairs of the country.

Having produced an ideological platform for his entry into the political arena, Hasan al-Banna went a step further by launching an attack on the existing political parties.[14] He made an important distinction between politics (*siyasa*) and party politics or partyism (*hizbiyya*), identifying the latter as useless and damaging in the Egyptian context:

> Even though it is viable in some circumstances in some countries, party politics is not feasible in Egypt at all. Especially at this time when a new era has begun, we have to cooperate, join forces, make use of all talents to build a strong nation. We need firm stability and complete devotion to all aspects of reforms.[15]

The existing political parties in Egypt were, according to al-Banna, "more artificial than real". Their *raison d'être* was more "personal than national", and the rivalries between the political parties were, in al-Banna's eyes, rooted in personal disputes not real political differences. The wrangles over posts and positions had only served as a pretext for foreign intervention in Egyptian politics. He also criticized the existing political parties for lacking a social and economic reform programme and for being uninterested in the welfare of the people. He even went as far as to characterize the political parties as "the parasites of this people" which represented "the greatest obstacle to our development".[16]

The Muslim Brothers' vitriolic attacks on the party system soon drew harsh criticism from the Wafd Party, the largest popular party in

Egypt, which described the call for a non-party system (*al-la hizbiyya*) as "nothing but a deceitful call to treason". According to a Wafdist newspaper, the party system was the firmest pillar for democracy since without it the parliamentary delegates "would become pawns in the hands of an autocrat [i.e. the King]". Against this the Muslim Brothers pointed out that the political parties had lost credibility, because they submitted to the British in order to achieve power, and they served as the imperialists' most reliable lackeys. There can be little doubt that this argument had strong appeal. It has been noted in a recent study on the nationalist movement that

> the Wafd's position in relation to power was the crucial factor affecting its stance on the nationalist question . . . But once in a position of political responsibility it abandoned its demands, needing British support to remain in power . . . the repetition of this pattern was a major cause of faltering belief especially among many of the youth in the steadfastness of the political parties and their ability to lead the National movement against the British since these parties were always prepared to co-operate with the forces of occupation in order to gain and to hold on to power.[17]

Some Brothers also called for the replacement of the parliamentary system with "a just tyrant"(*mustabidd 'adil*) who should appoint councillors from among "the morally and intellectually most suitable Egyptians".[18] This had also been the position of the greatly respected Islamic reformer Shaykh Muhammad 'Abduh, but it never became the official policy of the Society, which remained committed to a kind of representative political system. Islamic politics, al-Banna maintained, did not contradict "constitutional consultative rule" (*hukm dusturi shuri*). In his speech to the Fifth Conference of the Society in 1939, he stated:

> When one considers the principles that guide the constitutional system of government, one finds that such principles aim to preserve in all its forms the freedom of the individual citizen, to make the rulers accountable for their actions to the people and finally, to delimit the prerogatives of every single authoritative body. It will be clear to everyone that such basic principles correspond perfectly to the teaching of Islam concerning the system of government. For this reason, the Muslim Brothers consider that of all the existing systems of government, the constitutional system is the form that best suits Islam and Muslims.[19]

However, al-Banna made an explicit reservation by insisting that the constitutional regime should function within a non-party system, and he advocated a "national body" (*hay'a wataniyya*) composed of representatives of all political parties and bodies, including experts, technocrats and specialists in various fields. Only a coalition of this kind could accomplish the desired reforms and lead Egypt to independence, the two fundamental objectives that the political parties had failed to fulfil.

The Brothers' vehement criticism of the political parties cannot be understood without taking into consideration the fact that politics in the Egypt of the 1930s was still an exclusive domain for the élite and its patronage networks. Influence-peddling and political clientism dominated the political scene. However, the 1930s represented a watershed in modern Egyptian history, marking the beginning of a difficult transition from a notable-based political system to a system dominated by ideological parties and mass politicization, and the rise of the Muslim Brothers was an essential element of this process. Thus, in this light the Muslim Brothers' condemnation of party politics can be understood as a rejection of a malfunctioning political system, not necessarily as a rejection of democratic principles *per se*. The essence of the Muslim Brothers' message was an overall rejection of the fundamental principles on which the class-divided and patron–client-dominated Egyptian society rested, and the Society explicitly defined itself in opposition to the notables. For example, Hasan al-Banna defined "the avoidance of the hegemony of notables and elders" as one of the Society's five fundamental characteristics, giving instead primacy to the ideological consciousness of the membership:

> The essential thing among the Muslim Brothers is to what degree the member has absorbed the principles [of the Society] and to what degree he has struggled to implement these principles even if he has no high social standing among people, no titles or no appearance of dignity whatsoever.[20]

This position was further underlined by explicitly condemning the class system. When a member of the royal family drew upon Islam to defend the class system in Egypt in 1939, al-Banna castigated him and insisted on a diametrically opposite interpretation of Islam:

No! This has not been enjoined by Islam. Islam is equal for all people and prefers nobody to others on the grounds of differences in blood or race, forefathers or descent, poverty or wealth. According to Islam everyone is equal . . . However, in deeds and natural gifts, then the answer is yes. The learned is above the ignorant . . . Thus, we see that Islam does not approve of the class system.[21]

This lack of deference for traditional authority and paternalism permeated he Society's political propaganda, especially in the latter half of the 1930s. The Muslim Brothers in particular stressed their commitment to an "objective" ideological programme, transcending the differences of the traditional political parties and the interests of a small élite.[22] This was one of the most recurrent themes in the Society's propaganda. As Ahmad al-Sukkari argued: "We [the Muslim Brothers] do not work for a particular group, a particular party or for some particular person. We work for the sake of a principle and a goal: that is Islam and nothing but Islam."[23]

In 1938 the Muslim Brothers began to raise their own political agenda with increasing militancy, openly defying the élite's monopoly on politics. In the first editorial of *al-Nadhir*, al-Banna announced that the Muslim Brothers were now entering a new phase:

We are moving from propaganda alone to propaganda accompanied by struggle and action. We will direct our Islamic mission to the leadership of the country: the notables, the government, rulers, elders, legislators and political parties . . . We will place our programme in their hands and demand that they lead this country . . . on the path of Islam with courage without hesitation. If they respond to our call and adopt the path to our aim, we will support them. But if they resort to double-crossing and evasion and hide behind false excuses and pretexts, then we are at war with every leader, every president of a party and every organization that does not work for the victory of Islam and does not move in the direction of re-establishing the rule of Islam [*hukm al-Islam*].[24]

This rejection of the existing power structures in Egyptian society paved the way for the emergence of a movement based on ideological appeal and the class interests of the middle and lower segments of the population. The ideological–political appeal of the Muslim Brothers was of crucial importance. It enabled them to pose as spokesmen for the lower classes in Egypt, in particular the educated lower middle class. This will be studied in the following section.

Spokesman for the Educated
Lower Middle Class

It has often been claimed that the Muslim Brothers presented an incomplete and highly ambiguous programme of reform which was either intentionally or unconsciously made obscure to avoid "doctrinal disputes" and to conceal its inconsistencies.[25] Although this contention has been refuted in a recent Egyptian study,[26] little has been done to show why the Muslim Brothers' ideological programme had such a strong appeal. Whilst a complete theoretical basis for an Islamic social system and Islamic economy was not elaborated until the postwar period,[27] a deep commitment to social, economic and political reform, based on an Islamic world-view, can be found in the Brothers' political and economic programmes of the 1930s.[28] This section will examine some of the most salient features of the Society's reform programmes and relate these to the classes to which the Society appealed. Three factors appear to have contributed to the wide appeal of the Society's reform programmes, despite inherent inconsistencies and weaknesses. First, the programmes were formulated and advocated by non-élites. The Muslim Brothers' reform plans sounded much more credible than those presented by the wealthy Pashas who controlled the political parties, simply because the Society's leaders belonged to the middle class themselves. The identity of the Muslim Brothers became closely linked to that of the lower classes of society, a crucial point which was never missed in the Society's propaganda:

> The members of the Muslim Brothers are from the very core of this society. They belong to various parts of the lower classes. Even our leadership is not among those who live in mansions or have their own cars.[29]

Secondly, the Society's programme in the 1930s was not, as has sometimes been assumed, confined to calls for moral regeneration or religious revival. The Muslim Brothers displayed a profound and persistent commitment to reform, including social, economic, political, religious, educational, health and family reforms. Their reform proposals aimed at being all-inclusive, and were characterized by a heavy emphasis on social equality and economic development, with particular attention given to practical implementation. The credibility of the Society's programmes was further strengthened by "their solid achievements in social and educational works", as one observer noted.[30] Thirdly, as we have already seen, the Brothers attempted to base their programmes on an ideology, independent of names, families and parties. The commitment to an "objective" ideological programme, transcending the differences of the traditional political parties, became a pivotal and successful aspect of the Society's propaganda.

The Society's reform programme appealed particularly to the educated lower middle class, not only because of its fervent anti-imperialistic stance towards the colonial powers but also because of the attention given to the worsening economic position of the effendia, in particular junior civil servants and professionals. One British report noted that amongst the effendia "the highest percentage of dislike and mistrust of Great Britain is to be found".[31] There can be little doubt that the Society's anti-imperialism, such as its demand in 1938-9 for the amendment of the 1936 Anglo-Egyptian Treaty (the legal foundation of the British military presence in Egypt), was well-received by this class. The launch of its military wing and the rumours about its activities further strengthened the Society's image as an uncompromising anti-colonial force. In addition, the general socio-economic interests of the educated lower middle class, especially junior civil servants, were clearly reflected in the Society's programme. However, the Muslim Brothers also addressed the economic grievances of wider sections of the lower middle classes, including petty traders, small landowners and artisans, and to a lesser extent peasants and workers. Pre-revolutionary Egypt was subjected to a series of laissez-faire economic policies which favoured the upper class and foreign interests at the expense of the population as a whole. Thus, the Society's call for nationalization and a larger degree of interventionism and state corporatism, in order to provide a basis for social welfare programmes, found a receptive audience. The absence of a strong Marxist or socialist party in the political arena left it open to the Muslim Brothers,[32] and the Society's social profile in ideas as well as in deeds made contemporary observers think of it as an emerging Labour party alternative to the increasingly bourgeois Wafd Party. A British observer noted in 1942 that

> . . . there was no mistaking about the genuineness of the movement's social programme. An Ikhwan [Muslim Brother] speaker declared that the present poverty of the masses was due to the tyranny of the rich . . . In their general outlook the Ikhwan are social democrats, and might conceivably some day take the place in Egypt of a labour party in opposition to the petit-fonctionnaire Wafd and the minute plutocratic parties of the present opposition . . . Politically, time is probably on the side of the Ikhwan. They stand for a wider education, social and moral reform, whereas the Wafd is slowly but surely losing ground and its leader's reputation has suffered from the presence of corrupt influences around him. The day may arrive when the Ikhwan will seriously compete with the Wafd for office and power in its own name and on its own programme.[33]

The administrative, economic and social reform programmes presented by the Society attempted to address the problem of upper-class dominance in the state bureaucracy and the plight of underpaid junior civil servants. For example, the Society demanded that the government administration should be thoroughly reorganized and purged of inefficiency, incompetence, nepotism and bribery. The budgets of the ministries should be thoroughly reviewed with a view to ending the lavish spending on privileges for senior civil servants and on their salaries, and in 1940 a reform programme called for a radical reduction of all salaries exceeding £E20, fixing the maximum salary at £E100 (at the time a minister's salary was £E2,500). This onslaught against élite dominance was further emphasized by a proposal to "allot a proportion of the capital and the property of the wealthy classes to national defence".[34] At the same time, the Brothers proposed that the salaries of junior civil servants should be raised. Such a policy was in accordance with the Society's general principle of "bringing the classes closer together".[35]

Bureaucratic efficiency combined with social welfare policies was another characteristic of the Society's reform programmes. For example, the Muslim Brothers called for a "revolt against the ingrained routine" of the government's socio-economic policies.[36] They strongly advocated that a ministry for social affairs should be established, and heaped much praise upon Ali Mahir Pasha when he did so in 1939. The Muslim Brothers also proposed that each ministry should include a Supreme

Council of Specialists to develop and implement public projects. In addition, they called for the tax system to be amended according to Islamic laws prescribing *zakah*, a tax levied on properties equivalent to £E12.5 in gold or above (non-Muslims were to pay an equivalent tax rate). In the 1940s the Brothers raised demands for various "social taxes", which were to follow a progressive scale. The Society further advocated the expansion of public enterprises and the introduction of various benevolent projects in order to put an end to Egypt's chronic unemployment. Industrial exploitation of various natural resources, like mining and the development of water sources and wasteland, should also be sponsored. The need for rapid industrialization was increasingly stressed throughout the 1940s with the encouragement of small-scale domestic industries as a preliminary step. To achieve this "a modern Islamic banking system" should be established to provide interest-free loans for industrial, agricultural and commercial purposes, with a view to promoting private enterprises and local initiative.[37] Given the foreign control of the Egyptian economy, the Society argued forcefully for all foreign firms and enterprises to be Egyptianized and for all foreign capital to be replaced by Egyptian capital. At the Sixth Conference in 1941, Hasan al-Banna devoted a significant part of his speech to foreign economic dominance.[38] National companies and factories must be founded he argued, and custom barriers should be enacted to protect native industries. The debt crisis among Egyptian property owners had to be settled, and a diversification of agriculture should be encouraged to end the dependence on fluctuating cotton prices. Special attention was to be given to the strengthening of economic links and the reduction of commercial barriers between Arab, Islamic and Eastern countries. In addition to the attention given to state interventionism, the Muslim Brothers emphasized the need to "accustom people to economy and thrift". Self-reliance and self-sufficiency were two other keywords.

Social welfare was another crucial aspect of the Muslim Brothers' programme. They advocated allowances for the unemployed and public housing for the growing number of beggars, orphans and elderly people. The coffee-shops should be utilized to teach illiterates reading and writing. The masses should be protected against "the oppression of the monopolistic companies", which should be heavily regulated by the state.[39] Labour legislation was also to be introduced to protect the workers against the exploitation of capitalists. In the countryside, cooperative societies were to be sponsored and advice on modern farming methods should be provided in order to raise the productivity of the peasants. The villages should also be reformed, including health and literacy programmes for peasants and the purification of their water supply. To ease the pressure on government budgets the Society recommended that social reform projects could be undertaken by mobilizing voluntary youth groups and the armed forces. The Muslim Brothers set a good example by using their own followers for various "wiping out illiteracy" projects,[40] and from 1939 instructions went out that all branches should strive to establish evening schools, clinics and special committees for social welfare work among the poor.

The question of the distribution of private land does not seem to have occupied the Muslim Brothers significantly until the late 1940s. The defence of private property was firmly embedded in their reform proposals.[41] This attitude was typical of the whole political spectrum, with the exception of the communist movement. It perhaps indicated that the active core of the Muslim Brothers' membership, the young urbanized professional middle class, had strong family ties with the small and conservative landowners of the villages. It has been argued that these ties made the urban middle class less susceptible to radical changes in the rural socio-economic structure.[42] It was not until 1948 that the Brothers made demands for a review of the system of land property in Egypt and for the immediate distribution of government properties among the smallest property owners. However, as early as the late 1930s the Muslim Brothers were unequivocal in their condemnation of the ruling class of large landowners in Egypt:

> This class among whom you will find the rulers who have made the rule of this country a private matter for themselves, this class will be our arch-enemies, because our Islamic mission restricts their avidity, puts an end to their greed and opens the eyes of people to their evil deeds and disgraceful acts.[43]

This challenge to the socio-economic interests of the ruling élites was also noticed by contemporary observers. In 1944 the British noted: "the landowners are not generally enthusiastic over the Society since they fear that they might lose authority over the fellahin [the peasants] if the principles of the Ikhwan were too closely adhered to."[44] Mitchell observed that three of the thirteen counts made against the Muslim

Brothers in the court case of 1949 following the suppression of the Society in late 1948, "conjured up the image of economic and social revolt". He suggested that this, and not just the anger at the assassination of Prime Minister al-Nuqrashi by a Muslim Brother, accounted for "the fierceness by which the Society was suppressed".[45]

The Muslim Brothers' strong commitment to educational and social reforms earned them the allegiance of a large section of the primary and secondary school teachers in Egypt. Hardly any other occupational group became so involved in the Society. British observers who had noticed this phenomenon noted that the Society's "genuine, if fanatical and impractical, ideals as well as their more solid achievements in social and educational work make an appeal".[46] Hasan al-Banna had a sharp eye for the benefits accruing from the support of local teachers. In his memoirs he recalls the advantages of appointing the local principal as the head of the Society's branch in Abu Suwayr:

> Shaykh Abdallah Badawi is the principal of the primary school. He is also a virtuous Islamic scholar and eager to educate people . . . He has position among people. They respect him and keep closely in touch with him. Furthermore, he has time. He is free after the classes are finished and has more time than the merchants and artisans.[47]

By the mid-1930s it was already evident that several of the Society's branches were closely linked to local schools. Sometimes schools served as the local headquarters of the Muslim Brothers until a proper location could be found. From the end of the 1930s, and perhaps even earlier, close relations were established between the Teachers' Syndicate and the Brothers.[48] The Syndicate, which was one of Egypt's largest occupational unions, began to hold their conferences at the house of the Society in Cairo in the early 1940s. Many of the teachers were reportedly "converted" and brought the Society's ideas to their villages.[49] A previous member characterized the cooperation with the Teachers' Syndicate as "one of the most blessed steps for the Islamic mission".[50] The example of the teachers was not unique. In the late 1930s a section of doctors was established at the Society's headquarters. By the 1940s a wide range of professional groups were attached in various ways to the Muslim Brothers.[51]

A question which has frequently been raised is how the Society's heavy emphasis on issues like public morality, Islamic laws and the position of women found such support among the classes from which the Society recruited its members. One reason appears to be that a significant proportion of the Society's members were still bachelors and usually recent immigrants to cities. It has been argued that the unfamiliar moral permissiveness and the mixing of sexes which confronted them in their new urban environments caused sexual frustrations as it intensified a deep concern with "finding a 'pure' woman who would be suitable for marriage".[52] Yet more fundamental to the Society's appeal was its ability to link issues which were usually associated with reactionism and backwardness, such as Islamic laws and strict public morality, to the national issues of independence and development. A good example of this is the Society's demand for Islamic laws. In 1937 Prime Minister Mustafa al-Nahhas condemned this call as a "plot" to frustrate the negotiations on the abolition of the Capitulations in Montreux. In response, Hasan al-Banna argued that the demand for Islamic laws was essentially a demand for independent national legislation, and reminded the Prime Minister that every sovereign state must have the right to pass its own legislation free from the influence of foreigners.[53] The Muslim Brothers also skilfully connected moral issues to the question of the horrendous social inequality in Egypt. Thus, the campaigns for public morality and Islamic values frequently assumed the character of attacks on the upper classes. The Brothers seized every opportunity to condemn the extravagant lifestyles of the ruling élite, where the "money of the poor is wasted".[54] Ultimately, the political élite were criticized for being brought up in a Western and "unIslamic" environment, with the inevitable result that they acted either consciously or unconsciously in collusion with the colonial power.[55]

The Muslim Brothers also sought to demonstrate that their programme was essentially compatible with the most modern developments in the West.[56] For example, the handbook of the Battalion members from 1938 instructed the Brothers to "explain Islamic laws to foreigners and ignorants and teach them that Islamic legislation is compatible with the most modern systems of legislation". Western authorities were sometimes quoted to underpin these arguments. One Muslim Brother compared *zakah* and Adam Smith's theories of taxation in order to prove the modern features of *zakah*.[57] The German threat against the less populous France of the late 1930s was frequently referred to when justifying the necessity of encouraging early marriage and family life.[58]

As has been shown in Chapter 2, the Society was remarkably open to Western innovations and ideas as long as these strengthened the movement and underpinned its ideas, and it has been noted that Hasan al-Banna managed to "colour the Western principles with a religious hue".[59] There can be little doubt that the Society's success was due to its ability to propagate an Islamic programme that the educated middle class no longer associated with religious reactionism and backwardness.

The continuous appeal of the Muslim Brothers among large sections of the educated middle class has also been explained in terms of the "ideological and civilizational independence" that the Society sought to build.[60] One should not underestimate the appeal of a "native and authentic" ideology in countries where Western values were associated with imperialist domination and the extravagant lifestyles of the upper class. More important, such an ideology represented an attempt at "intellectual" liberation from European domination. However, the theoretical framework for an Islamic social, economic, judicial and cultural system was still rudimentary in this period, and it thus seems premature to stress the intellectual aspects of the Muslim Brothers' alternative world-view. In sum, a fundamental cause of the success of the Society was that it championed the causes of large segments of the middle and lower middle classes which had been antagonized by the "politics of notables" and which were largely excluded from the political process.

The Palace and the Limits of Political Alignment

Most studies on the Muslim Brothers in the late 1930s have emphasized the Society's relations with the Palace and Palace politicians, in particular the Royal Councillor from 1937, Ali Mahir Pasha, and his protégés, Abd al-Rahman Azzam Bey, General Aziz al-Misri and Salih Harb Pasha. Shaykh al-Azhar Mustafa al-Maraghi is also included in this 'Palace clique'. However, apart from sketchy details, little information is available about the nature of the relationship between the Palace and the Society. It is known that Azzam Bey's contact with the Society probably began in the early 1930s when he was approached by some of the disenchanted YMMA members who intended to join the Muslim Brothers. By 1939 the relationship was sufficiently warm for Hasan al-Banna to describe him as "one of the Muslim Brothers' friends". General Aziz al-Misri met al-Banna for the first time in 1937, and by 1940 their friendship had developed to such an extent that al-Banna felt able to offer himself as intermediary between al-Misri and the young army officer Anwar Sadat, who sought to organize nationalist elements in the Egyptian army. Salih Harb Pasha was close to the Brothers from the latter half of the 1930s, especially after he became head of the YMMA in 1940. He attended several conferences and meetings organized by the Muslim Brothers. Apart from the existence of personal bonds of friendship between the Society's leadership and a number of pro-Palace politicians, little is known about the nature of the Society's overall relationship with the Palace. The accepted wisdom is that the Muslim Brothers firmly supported the Palace against the Wafd Party and acted as one of Ali Mahir Pasha's clients.[61] However, as will be discussed, the Brothers' relationship with the Palace and the Royal Councillor was considerably more uneasy than earlier studies have acknowledged. Far from being an obedient tool of the Royal Councillor, the Brothers rejected central elements of his political strategy, namely the Islamic image of the "Righteous King" and the Caliphate aspirations, thereby undermining Ali Mahir Pasha's primary objective in this period of achieving the ascendancy of a royal autocracy under his leadership, supported by a popular following.

We have already seen that the Muslim Brothers profoundly mistrusted the upper classes, partly because of their monopolization of political power and partly because of their luxurious and "unIslamic" lifestyles. Taken together with the strong ideological component in the movement, this should have discouraged any relations with Palace circles. Yet the Society found some common ground with Ali Mahir Pasha. His efforts to establish a Ministry of Social Affairs in 1936 as well as his attention to Arab–Islamic causes were wholeheartedly supported by the Brothers. The initial alignment with Ali Mahir Pasha must be seen in the context of the political role of Islamic associations in Egyptian politics in the 1930s. Islamic societies were considered the domain of the Palace. For example, the Brothers' mother organization, the YMMA, was closely associated with the Palace, and other Islamic associations, especially the Benevolent Islamic Society (al-Jam'iyya al-Khayriyya al-Islamiyya), served as salons and clubs for the royal family and the aristocracy supporting the Palace.

The Society's contacts with Shaykh al-Maraghi and Ali Mahir Pasha were established in 1935. In May 1937 it appears that rumours of Hasan al-Banna's friendly relations with the Royal Councillor, the enemy of the Wafdist government, had become so rife that al-Banna found it necessary to issue a denial to his followers that the Brothers were "serving the interests of a particular political group".[62] However, events in 1937 had serious implications for al-Banna's relations with Ali Mahir. In December 1937, an intensifying struggle between the Wafdist government and the Palace culminated in widespread demonstrations in which pro-Palace and pro-government groups clashed. In this struggle the Palace-backed opposition used Islam as a weapon against the Wafdists, denouncing them as a "Coptic clique". An important element in the Palace-orchestrated campaign was to imbue the young King with an "Islamic image", portraying him as the "Righteous King" (al-Malik al-Salih). His attendance at Friday prayers received wide attention in the pro-Palace press, and he was proclaimed more or less officially as Caliph or "Commander of the Faithful" (Amir al-Mu'minin).[63] This propaganda campaign obviously infuriated Muhammad al-Shafi'i, who had recently become the editor and owner of the Society's newspaper. He found it difficult to take the Palace's professed piety at face value, and in January 1938 he wrote several editorials criticizing the anti-Coptic propaganda and Caliphate campaign orchestrated by Shaykh al-Maraghi during the King's wedding celebrations.[64] Al-Shafi'i wrote: "The prostitutes and alcoholics are cheering for the 'Commander of the Faithful'. Is that the way the Caliphate should be? . . . The celebration of the King's marriage is nothing but political propaganda which violates the principles [of Islam]."[65]

As a result of this criticism Hasan al-Banna disassociated himself from Muhammad al-Shafi'i and ordered the Muslim Brothers to sever all links with the Society's newspaper. However, this decision did not stem from enthusiasm for the Palace-sponsored "Islamic campaign". The Society remained largely aloof from the political confrontation between the Wafd Party and the Palace. There was no anti-Wafdist propaganda in the newspaper in late 1937, nor is there any evidence to claim that the Brothers took to the streets in support of the King as has been assumed in several studies. After the fall of the Wafdist government and the accession of a Palace-backed ministry, Hasan al-Banna openly questioned whether the new government would be any better than the previous one.[66] All the same, al-Banna's efforts to obtain the patronage of Ali Mahir Pasha and al-Maraghi had already met with some success, and accordingly he could not afford to allow his newspaper to become a mouthpiece of Wafdist anti-Palace propaganda. If a choice had to be made the Society naturally inclined towards the Palace, and on 3 March 1938 the Society hosted a conference of Islamic associations in al-Mansura, passing a resolution strongly condemning the Wafdist campaign against Shaykh al-Maraghi and petitioning the King to put an end to "these lies". Two months later a delegation of Muslim Brothers met Ali Mahir Pasha at the Royal Council (al-Diwan al-Maliki) and handed him a petition asking for the replacement of all political parties with a national unified body, a move which was seen as an attack on the Wafd Party.[67] In the summer of 1938 al-Banna's relationship with Ali Mahir Pasha was sufficiently strong to facilitate his first audience with the King. During the Muslim Brothers' summer camp in al-Dikhayla a delegation of Rover Scouts, headed by al-Banna himself, marched into nearby Alexandria and was introduced to King Farouq by Ali Mahir Pasha outside the Sayyidi Jabir Mosque. Further signs of royal favour came in the autumn of 1938, when the benefits of Ali Mahir's patronage became more evident. According to the British, the Royal Councillor's associates in the Egyptian police were too lenient on the Society's anti-British activities.[68] Funds were also finding their way to the Muslim Brothers at the behest of the Royal Councillor.[69] Apart from direct subsidies to the Society, it appears that Ali Mahir's patronage may have been instrumental in obtaining financial support for the Society's social work in some provinces.[70]

However, elements of conflict between the Palace and the Muslim Brothers were in the making. When Hasan al-Banna in the spring of 1938 formulated the Society's ideological position towards the Palace, he took the liberty to stress their right to criticize the Palace if they deemed it necessary:

> The King is the legitimate ruler of this country . . . The position of the Muslim Brothers towards the Palace is that of allegiance and love. The General Guidance Council [MIA] strives to strengthen the bonds [of allegiance and love] and make the Palace understand this fact. However, this does not prevent us from giving fair advice and uttering a word of truth if the MIA notices anything which makes this necessary.[71]

In late 1938 and 1939 the political activism of the Society aroused the government's suspicion and funds from municipal authorities were cut off temporarily. The Muslim Brothers were also subjected to government harassment and restrictions because of their anti-British propaganda. The Royal Councillor's failure to protect the Muslim Brothers indicates that his patronage was limited and not as extensive as previous studies have assumed. In any case Hasan al-Banna did not want the Society to become a pawn in the hands of Ali Mahir Pasha. He zealously guarded the interests of his movement. When the Young Egypt Party, apparently with the firm support of General Aziz al-Misri, an associate of the Royal Councillor, began to press for a merger between the two groups to create a pro-Palace Islamic party, al-Banna rejected this outright. The issue was again raised in January and July 1939, throughout the summer of 1940 and in April 1942, and the pressure on al-Banna to agree to such an alliance must have been considerable. Undoubtedly, this must have put a damper on his enthusiasm for closer relations. He was careful to avoid overt pro-Palace propaganda in his newspaper, and he severely censured his editor when the latter went too far in criticizing the Wafd Party. There could be no compromise on the principle of non-partyism, which meant that politicians and parties should be judged solely by their deeds and work for the Islamic cause. Nor could they evade the ideological imperative of correcting and reproving erring rulers. When the Society acquired a new newspaper, *al-Nadhir*, in May 1938 the Palace was repeatedly criticized, despite al-Banna's friendship with Ali Mahir Pasha. In this respect the Muslim Brothers differed fundamentally from the Young Egypt Party and other pro-Palace groups who openly called for a ministry headed by the Royal Councillor. By contrast, the Muslim Brothers' newspaper contained numerous veiled attacks on the Palace. Criticism of the Palace usually assumed the form of denunciations of royal night parties. The belly-dancers, the consumption of alcohol and the mixing of sexes at these parties were nothing less than abominations in the eyes of the Brothers. In 1939 the editor of *al-Nadhir* did little to conceal his grave doubts about the King's widely advertised piety:

> Who has dared to place a naked or half-naked ballerina who performed dances with provocative and suggestive movements . . . in front of our King, the Pious, may God protect him? They have committed a serious crime against Islam. They have hurt our King

Farouq whose piety we have heard of and who cannot possibly have accepted this.[72]

In mid-1939, perhaps even earlier, a series of malicious rumours surfaced about the nocturnal escapades of the young and newly married King Farouq.[73] This was only the beginning of a flow of rumours of moral corruption throughout the 1940s, which more than anything else scandalized the Egyptian monarchy. The Muslim Brothers had by 1939 sharpened their criticism of the upper classes,[74] with even the so-called "Righteous King" failing to escape their condemnation. Overt criticism of the Palace began to appear in the Society's press. For example, the Palace was criticized for its friendly relations with the wealthy Jewish family of al-Qitawi who, it was stated, supported the Zionists in Palestine.[75] The political parties created by the Palace (*Hizb al-Sha'b* and *Hizb al-Ittihad*) were at one point labelled "the Parties of Satan" (*ahzab al-shaytan*).[76] More importantly, the Palace's Caliphate ambitions, a pivotal point in Ali Mahir Pasha's strategy, were criticized by the Brothers who stated that Egypt's claim to the leadership of the Islamic world was "nonsense" as long as it remained so demonstratively uncommitted to Islamic reform.[77] In an editorial called "Where is the 'Commander of the Faithful'?", Hasan al-Banna made reference to the Saudi King who was one of King Farouq's principal contenders for title of Caliph:

> In the Arabian peninsula there is a respectable community of leaders of opinion and spiritual guides for the lands of Islam. They should proclaim their judgment and state their opinion on the Palestinian issue in the name of Islam. We expect a clear and unwavering position. We further expect that their decision will be supported by all Muslims.[78]

This call for Saudi leadership of Muslim opinion was made a few days before the Inter-Parliamentary Conference on Palestine in Cairo in October 1938 during which various pro-Palace groups hailed King Farouq as Caliph and "Commander of the Faithful". In addition to Hasan al-Banna's overt support for the Saudis, the Society's reserved press coverage of King Farouq's presence at the Conference left little doubt that the Muslim Brothers were less than enthusiastic about his Caliphate ambitions.[79] With this kind of sensitive propaganda appearing in al-Banna's editorials, one can only assume that more outspoken criticism was propagated at the Society's meetings. The Society's stance resulted in harassment from the Palace and in May 1939 al-Banna wrote:

> Egypt has become a breeding ground for missionary activities. Despite this, where do the informers of the Royal Secret Police gather? On the premises of the Islamic associations, in their lectures and in their clubs! My dear people, what is this?[80]

True, the Society did pay the necessary lip-service to the King on important occasions. The Rover Scouts vigorously took part in the celebration of King Farouq's accession to the throne in July 1937. In February 1939, when the King escaped a dangerous accident in one of the provinces, the Muslim Brothers rallied their Rover Scouts to greet him upon his return to Cairo. Rover Scout parades were an efficient way of attracting new members to the Society and royal celebrations were consciously used by the Brothers to display their Rover Scouts.[81] Yet the basic position of the Society towards the Palace remained highly ambiguous and frequently hostile. A Muslim Brothers' meeting in Alexandria in March 1940 is a good illustration of this. According to informers of the Egyptian Political Police, the branch had received a telegram from the Palace in response to their telegram of congratulation on the occasion of the King's birthday. After having read the telegram, two of the leading Muslim Brothers gave long speeches denouncing the moral corruption of the "aristocratic classes".[82]

The "unIslamic" lifestyles of the King and his court and the hollowness of the Caliphate propaganda proved to be firm obstacles to an alignment between the Brothers and the Palace, even if Hasan al-Banna might have wished for closer cooperation. When Ali Mahir Pasha formed his own ministry (1939–40), which included a number of "friends of the Muslim Brothers" as al-Banna put it, the limits of cooperation became more evident. Al-Banna had expected a privileged role for the Muslim Brothers, especially in the newly formed Territorial Army, but he was rebuffed.[83] The Society's initial praise of Ali Mahir Pasha's "spirit of reform" gave way to satirical articles attacking the government for its failure to deliver on the expected military projects and social reform programmes.[84] Following this criticism, the Ministry of the Interior revoked the licence of the prestigious Islamic magazine *al-Manar*, which al-Banna had managed to acquire. In addition, *al-Nadhir*, the Society's newspaper, ceased production, ostensibly because of internal dissent. However, the abrupt end of both publications in October 1939 and the fact that the editor and owner of *al-Nadhir*, Abu Zayd Uthman, left the Brothers in 1940, and not at the time of the secession of Muhammad's Youth in 1939, strongly suggests that government orders had been issued against *al-Nadhir* as well. Seven months later the licence to publish *al-Manar* was regained but government restrictions continued to delay its production. This was the first time in the Society's history that any of its publications had been subjected to government bans, and it must have taught al-Banna an important lesson about the vagaries and limitations of patronage networks. When Ali Mahir was forced to resign in the summer of 1940, al-Banna once again avoided making any commitment to join a unified pro-Palace Islamic party.[85] Al-Banna's sense of caution was heightened when, following an offensive launched by the British-backed government against all of Ali Mahir's "creatures", he was transferred to the town of Qena in Upper Egypt in the spring of 1941.[86]

Al-Banna was aware of the dangers of becoming dependent on Ali Mahir's untrustworthy patronage as early as 1938 and as a result he began searching for support from other groups. A friend of the Muslim Brothers in the Ministry of Agriculture introduced al-Banna to the Prime Minister and head of the Liberal Constitutionalist Party, Muhammad Mahmud Pasha. Cordial relations reportedly developed between the Muslim Brothers and some of the Liberal Constitutionalists.[87] In the summer of 1939 a number of "pro-Islamic" delegates from various political parties were invited to a reception hosted by the Muslim Brothers on 5 July at the fashionable Palace of Al Lutf in Zamalek in Cairo. The objective was "to honour the respectable senators and deputies of the Parliament" who had supported the Islamic cause.[88] Ibrahim Disuqi Abaza, who later became the leader of the Liberal Constitutionalists, expressed "his pleasure and happiness with the activities of the Islamic societies and their *jihad* for the sake of Islam". The reception was a tangible sign of the increasing favour that the Society enjoyed in political circles. Even representatives of the Wafd Party attended.[89] Despite the Muslim Brothers' frequent attacks on al-Nahhas and Wafdist secular Egyptian nationalism, they still cultivated relations with the Wafd Party. There were apparent cordial relations between Wafdists and the Muslim Brothers in several provinces.[90] A number of leading Muslim Brothers, such as Abu al-Nasr, Umar al-Tilmisani and Mahmud Abd al-Halim, had been active Wafd members before they joined the Society. Thus, it is not surprising that the Society had reliable contacts among the Wafdists.[91] Even in late 1938, when Hasan al-Banna's relations with Ali Mahir Pasha were close, reports were received by British intelligence that the Muslim Brothers were funded by the Wafd for their anti-British propaganda.[92] Although there are no independent sources to verify the extent or indeed even the existence of Wafdist subsidies to the Society, this is not unlikely. The growing strength of the movement attracted numerous potential patrons. For example, during al-Banna's annual tour of Upper Egypt in 1939 he was sought out by several Members of Parliament,[93] and during the early years of the war, the Muslim Brothers were courted by the Sa'dist Party and the Liberal Constitutionalists in addition to the Wafdists.[94] The Society exploited these opportunities and expanded its networks of contacts, even in prominent pro-British circles, as with Prince Muhammad Ali, a close friend of the British ambassador and one of Ali Mahir Pasha's enemies.

Ali Mahir Pasha is stated to have been the chief patron of the Muslim Brothers throughout 1940–1, although British intelligence observed that their relations had "never been very close".[95] His anti-British policies obviously made him more palatable ideologically to the Society than the Wafd. In the summer of 1941, after al-Banna's return from Qena, the Palace ordered provincial officials to allow the Muslim Brothers free rein to conduct their activities. Ali Mahir increased his financial aid to the Society and through his control of the Special Branch of the Egyptian police – which he managed to retain despite his fall from office in 1940 – he sought to conceal the extent of the Muslim Brothers' subversive activities and sabotage plans against British military installations. However, British intelligence, acting on rumours about these activities, forced the Prime Minister to arrest al-Banna and his chief lieutenant, Ahmad al-Sukkari, in October 1941. Immediately following the arrests, considerable pressure was brought to bear upon the Prime Minister to release them, especially from Ali Mahir's associates. The 11,000 signatures that the Society gathered for the release of its leaders must have convinced Ali Mahir Pasha of the potential power of this organization. In November 1941, the Prime Minister ordered the release of both al-Banna and al-Sukkari in defiance of British orders.[96]

These efforts still failed to convince al-Banna of the need to fit in with Ali Mahir's schemes. He had learnt the rules of the political game in Egypt and was not prepared to jeopardize the Society's future by serving the interests of others. In the months before the British military intervention of 4 February 1942, when the King was forced to appoint a Wafdist government which would be more compliant with the British war effort, al-Banna ordered his followers to keep a low profile and not to play a conspicuous part in the disturbances which Ali Mahir encouraged in order to force the British to accept him as the strongman of Egyptian politics.[97] This strategy was rewarded when Ali Mahir Pasha and most of his associates, with the exception of the Muslim Brothers, were interned until 1944. The new Prime Minister, Mustafa al-Nahhas, defied British demands to reintern the Society's leadership as this would make them look like martyrs and increase their popularity at the expense of the Wafd. Instead, he tried to make a deal with the Brothers to persuade them to confine their activities to the religious sphere and leave politics to the Wafd Party.[98]

The essential difference between the Muslim Brothers and other pro-Palace groups has been overlooked by historians. Western as well as Egyptian studies have failed to take note of the Society's verbal attacks on the Palace in the late 1930s, which were reciprocated with restrictions and surveillance.[99] This section has attempted to provide an explanation of the puzzling contradiction in the historiography on the Muslim Brothers in the 1930s: how could the Society recruit a large following from the educated lower middle class if it at the same time acted as an obedient pawn in the political game of the Palace? The simple fact is that the Muslim Brothers did not fit in with the Palace politics of Ali Mahir Pasha. There was an uneasy relationship resulting from fundamental conflicts over moral issues as well as class interests. The attempts by politicians to exploit the mass following of the Muslim Brothers became less successful with the steady increase of the Society's power base. In 1942 it was acknowledged that the Society was the only serious rival to the Wafd Party.[100] This power base enabled the Muslim Brothers to benefit from an increasing number of generous patrons without having to abandon their ideological programme. This represented the rise of an new political force, unwilling to accept the role of client. Instead, the Society sought to build a power base strong enough to challenge the traditional political forces and pursue its own political agenda.

The Muslim Brothers and al-Azhar

The conventional wisdom concerning the Muslim Brothers' relationship with al-Azhar has been that their basic approach to al-Azhar was hostile, even if leading Brothers took pains to publicly dispel the belief in Egypt that there were tensions between the two groups. More vociferous members repudiated al-Azhar as the voice of Islam in Egypt, claiming that it had failed in its assigned role of spokesman for a living and dynamic Islam. Al-Azhar had persisted in a "time-worn, anachronistic approach to Islam and its teachings – dead dry, ritualistic and irrelevant to the needs of living Muslims". Moreover, it had failed to resist occupiers, imperialists and corrupt governments. Al-Azhar's Islam was a resigned and submissive Islam, "the Islam supported by the imperialists".[101] These factors had created the "gap" in religious life in Egypt that the Islamic associations, first and foremost the Muslim Brothers, were to fill. Despite these ideological incompatibilities between the two groups, authoritative studies like Mitchell's and Bayumi's have asserted that al-Azhar students came to form an important and active core of the membership of the Society. It is further claimed that the Society managed to attract a significant number of al-Azhar students in the late 1930s, and that the Muslim Brothers were "controlling a large part of al-Azhar student body" by the early 1940s.[102] The Muslim Brothers' student following at al-Azhar at this time appears to have been misjudged in the above studies.[103] As will be seen below, the Society's attempts to gain a foothold at al-Azhar in these years failed and the active support for the Brothers among al-Azhar students remained limited.

Available sources show that the Azharite component of the Society's following in the 1930s was not significant. For example, a survey of the delegates at the Second and Third Conferences (in 1934 and 1935) reveals a majority of *effendi* titles – not the *shaykh* title of the Azharists – among the leading members in the Society.[104] This signified a predominance of people with a non-religious education in leading positions in the Society's branch organization. The "lay" character of the core of the Society's membership became more evident by the close of the decade. A ranking list of the Society's cadres in Cairo in 1939 shows that only 7 out of 87 bore the title *shaykh*.[105] A similar result can be found in a survey listing the heads of the administrative districts of the Muslim Brothers in 1944, which shows that only 10 out of 91 bore the *shaykh* title.[106] Given the high proportion of students among the cadres, one can assume that this also reflects the Azharite component of the Society's student body. This assumption is supported by the fact that there is, as far as we can see, no trace of an active student section under the Society's auspices at al-Azhar in this period, although the Society had active student organizations at other educational institutes.

As discussed in Chapter 4, Hasan al-Banna had established friendly relations with Shaykh Mustafa al-Maraghi, the Rector of al-Azhar, by the mid-1930s. This relationship tended to soften the Society's criticism of al-Azhar in the 1930s. Al-Banna considered his relationship with al-Maraghi a valuable asset and did his best to obtain the approval of al-Azhar. In his writings he stressed the importance of al-Azhar as an indispensable Islamic centre of learning,[107] and in his proposals for educational reform he envisaged a dominant role for it.[108] He stressed that the Muslim Brothers should make "incessant efforts to strengthen and elevate al-Azhar's position", and instructed his followers to endeavour to convince

> the Islamic scholars of al-Azhar that the success of the Muslim Brothers is also the success of al-Azhar and that a union between them is natural . . . It is necessary to win over as many Islamic scholars and students from al-Azhar as possible and at any price. The Brothers must also win the support of the Office of Preaching and Guidance (Hay'at al-Wa'z wa'l-Irshad) and of the imams of the mosques and cooperate with them.[109]

Since the creation of the Office of Preaching and Guidance at al-Azhar in the 1920s, Azharite preachers had been appointed to all provinces in Egypt and they represented an important religious network which al-Banna was keen to use. In 1939 he approached Shaykh Mustafa al-Maraghi to ask him to extend the services of these preachers to the Muslim Brothers all over the country. This request was granted informally and all Azharite preachers were instructed to cooperate with the Society's branches.

Despite this favour, it seems clear that a conflict was already in the making. Al-Banna told his followers in 1938: "There are men at al-Azhar who have not yet understood the Brothers and look upon us as rivals."[110] A year later, he remarked that there were men at al-Azhar who "think badly of the Muslim Brothers and envy our success and attempt to distance us from al-Azhar students".[111] Heyworth-Dunne noted that "the ulama began to think that he [Hasan al-Banna] was interfering with their work and undermining their position".[112] Al-Banna denounced all attempts by his political opponents to "stir up the animosity . . . of al-Azhar against us".[113] However, despite al-Banna's conciliatory attitude towards al-Azhar, criticism of al-Azhar's submissive role in Egyptian politics began to surface in the Society's newspaper.[114]

It appears that as long as Shaykh al-Maraghi controlled al-Azhar, the Muslim Brothers remained less vociferous in their criticism of al-Azhar's stagnation and inertia. This was reciprocated with a certain benevolence from al-Azhar. The Sixth Conference of the Muslim Brothers in January 1941 was attended by the Vice-Inspector of the Office of Preaching and Guidance, who gave a speech praising the efforts of the Society.[115] This was more a gesture from Shaykh al-Maraghi than an indication of a power base among the Azharists. Nevertheless, relations between the Society and al-Azhar began to take a downturn when, in early 1940, a large group of Azharists lobbied to prevent new legislation that would undermine al-Azhar's monopoly to certain government positions. Instead of strongly supporting the Azharists' cause, al-Banna reproached them for their yearning for jobs and positions. He then challenged the Azharists to accept voluntary employment in the Society's district organization. A year later, al-Banna became even more direct in his criticism of the Azharists, bluntly attacking them for "committing sins by being lazy and evading their duties".[116] As a prominent Muslim Brother recalled, there was "no affection and friendship" between al-Azhar and the Society and only a "handful" of Azharists joined the Muslim Brothers.[117] When Shaykh al-Maraghi lost influence at al-Azhar after the British installed a Wafdist government in 1942, a new dominant figure at al-Azhar, Shaykh Muhammad al-Banna (no relation), took the initiative to recommend the closure of the Muslim Brothers' provincial branches. A year later, it was evident that the Azharists no longer ranked high in the priorities of the Society. Nor did the Society have a sufficient following among the Azharists to influence events when disturbances broke out at al-Azhar in the spring of 1943. The main grievance prompting the riots was the rejection of the Azharists' plea that al-Azhar diplomas should be admissible in competition for junior civil service posts on a par with degrees from Cairo University. As Hasan al-Banna was eager to lift the government's ban on the activities of the Society, he condemned the al-Azhar demon-strations and urged his followers to take no part in the demonstrations. His position incurred the wrath of the Azharists. Even Shaykh Abd al-Latif Diraz to whom Hasan al-Banna had strong personal ties, urged all Azharists to boycott the Muslim Brothers.[118] These findings should urge us to qualify the general assumption that there was no active opposition to the Society from al-Azhar as a body. More importantly, they show that the Society already had a marked "lay" and *effendi* character in the 1930s. The Muslim Brothers' failure to win a significant student following at al-Azhar, as well as the ideological conflict between the two, illustrate a facet of the general theme of this chapter, namely the rise of an ideological–political party which began to challenge the pillars of the traditionalist regime in Egypt: al-Azhar, the Palace and the élite's monopoly of power and patronage. By the end of the decade, the Society of the Muslim Brothers had emerged as an important voice in Egypt for a disenchanted class made up of educated lower middle class youth. The Society's mass following and its solid organizational structure allowed it to go beyond the role of client in Egyptian politics. As a consequence, the relationship with the Palace grew uneasy. This is an important development which has been ignored in previous scholarship, and which foreshadowed the fatal clash between the Society and the Monarchy in 1948–9. The politicization of Islam was the kernel of the Society's revolt. This interpretation of an Islam with political dimensions became a powerful tool in the hands of the Muslim Brothers, and allowed them to undermine the traditional legitimacy of the bastions of power in Egyptian society, represented by the Palace, al-Azhar and the established political parties, controlled by notables.

NOTES

1 Wendell (tr.), *Five Tracts of Hasan al-Banna*, p. 36.
2 For a typical proponent of this view, see Safran, *Egypt in Search of a Political Community*. A similar view can be found in Goldberg, 'Bases of traditional reaction', pp. 79–96.
3 Davis, 'Ideology, social classes and Islamic radicalism in modern Egypt', pp. 135–6.

4 While most Islamic radicals in urban areas tended to be professionals or part of a white-collar salariat, those in the countryside tended to contain a heavy proportion of secondary school teachers. For statistical material on the class composition of the Muslim Brothers in the 1930s and 1950s, see Davis, 'Ideology, social class and Islamic radicalism in modern Egypt', pp. 142–3.

5 Dar al-Watha'iq, Qasr 'Abedin/'Iltimasat al-Ikhwan al-Muslimin' (Box 557). The assumption that the Muslim Brothers lacked support among peasants has been made by Uri Kupferschmidt. However, his study lacks statistical data to support his argument. See Kupferschmidt, 'The Muslim Brothers and the Egyptian village', pp. 157–70.

6 I have borrowed this notion from Sami Zubaida. See his book *Islam, the People and the State: Essays on Political Ideas and Movements in the Middle East* (London, I. B. Tauris, 1993), p. 50.

7 Ralph Moses Coury, 'Abd al-Rahman Azzam and the development of Egyptian Arab nationalism' (Ph.D. thesis, Princeton University, 1983), p. 385.

8 See Fathi Radwan, 'al-'Asr wa al-rijal' quoted in *ibid.*, pp. 385–6.

9 When Hasan al-Banna was transferred to Qena on government (and British) orders, the official reason given was that as a civil servant he had violated the law of non-involvement in politics. See Muhammad Hasanayn Haykal, *Mudhakkirat fi al-siyasa al-misriyya* (Cairo, Dar al-Ma'arif, 1978), pp. 177–8.

10 For more information on the syndicates, see Marius Deeb, 'Labour and politics in Egypt 1919–1939', *IJMES*, vol. 10 (1979), pp. 187–203.

11 Botman, *Egypt from Independence to Revolution*, pp. 32–3.

12 'Kalimat Fadilat al-Murshid al-'Amm' in *Kalimat mu'tamar talabat al-Ikhwan al-Muslimin*, p. 21. Parts of this document have been reprinted in Hasan al-Banna, *Ila al-tullab* (Cairo, Dar al-Nashr wa al-Tawzi' al-Islamiyya, n.d.).

13 *Ibid.*, p. 23–4.

14 The aversion to political parties was one of the most characteristic features of the political outlook of the Muslim Brothers. See, for example, *al-Nadhir*, no. 13, 1357/1938, p. 17; *al-Nadhir*, no. 15, 1357/1938, p. 15; *al-Nadhir*, no. 16, 1357/1938, p. 14; and *al-Nadhir*, no. 28, 1357/1938, p. 11.

15 *Kalimat mu'tamar talabat al-Ikhwan al-Muslimin*, p. 32. For a discussion of Hasan al-Banna's rejection of party pluralism, see Ghanim, *al-Fikr al-siyasi lil-Imam Hasan al-Banna*, pp. 350–1.

16 *al-Nadhir*, no. 27, 1357/1938, editorial.

17 Hoda Gamal Abdel Nasser, *Britain and the Egyptian Nationalist Movement, 1936–1952* (Reading, Ithaca Press, 1994), p. 57.

18 *al-Nadhir*, no. 13, 1357/1938, p. 17.

19 'al-Ikhwan al-Muslimun fi 'ashar sanawat' in *al-Nadhir*, no. 35, 1357/1939, p. 22.

20 *Taqrir ijmali khass*, pp. 26–7.

21 *al-Nadhir*, no. 17, 1358/1939, editorial.

22 "Objective" in the sense that it should be independent of the subjective interests of persons and parties.

23 Speech by Ahmad al-Sukkari in Dar al-Watha'iq, Taqarir al-Amn/Taqarir Hikimadariyyat Bulis Misr (sirri siyasi), no. 2461, 20 November 1941.
24 Hasan al-Banna, 'Khatwatuna al-thaniya' [our next step], *al-Nadhir*, no. 1, 1357/1938, editorial.
25 For a summary of the positions of Egyptian leftist historians on this issue, see Meijer, 'Contemporary Egyptian historiography of the period 1936–1952', pp. 135–45. See also Bayumi, *al-Ikhwan al-Muslimun wa'l-jama'at al-islamiyya fi'l-hayah al-siyasiyya al-misriyya*, pp. 319–22.
26 Ghanim, *al-Fikr al-siyasi lil-Imam Hasan al-Banna*; see especially introduction.
27 *Ibid.*, p. 367. See also Mitchell, *The Society of the Muslim Brothers*, pp. 272–3.
28 This can be seen from documents like *al-Minhaj* (the programme), the handbook for the members of the Battalions (published in 1938), and *Risalat nahwa al-nur* (mission towards the light), published in 1937.
29 *Majallat al-Ta'aruf*, no. 12, 1359/1940, p. 3.
30 'The Ikhwan al Muslimin Reconsidered', 10 December 1942, FO 141/838.
31 'The Effendi Class', 5 March 1947, FO 141/1223.
32 Prince 'Abbas Halim founded a Labour party in 1931 which lasted for only two months. He made another attempt in 1937, probably encouraged by King Farouq who hoped it would be "a troublesome thorn in the side of the Wafd". See Deeb, 'Labour and Politics in Egypt', pp. 187–203.
33 'The Ikhwan al Muslimin Reconsidered', 14 December 1942, FO 141/838.
34 *Majallat al-Ta'aruf*, no. 16, 1359/1940, p. 4.
35 *al-Minhaj*, pp. 17–27.
36 *al-Ikhwan al-Muslimun: al-mu'tamar al-dawri al-sadis*, p. 23.
37 *al-Minhaj*, p. 25.
38 *al-Ikhwan al-Muslimun: al-mu'tamar al-dawri al-sadis*.
39 Wendell (tr.), *Five Tracts of Hasan al-Banna*, pp. 126–31.
40 *Majallat al-Ta'aruf*, no. 13, 1359/1940, p. 11.
41 Gabriel Baer, 'Egyptian attitudes towards land reform, 1922–1952' in Walter Z. Laqueur (ed.), *The Middle East in Transition* (New York, Praeger, 1958), pp. 80–1.
42 For more details, see Deeb, *Party Politics in Egypt*, p. 323.
43 *al-Nadhir*, no. 10, 1358/1939, editorial.
44 'Ikhwan el Muslimeen' (Secret), P.I.C. Paper no. 49 (revised), 25 July 1944, FO 371/41334, p. 2.
45 Mitchell, *The Society of the Muslim Brothers*, p. 182.
46 'The Ikhwan al Muslimin', 10 December 1942, FO 141/838.
47 *Mudh.*, pp. 111.
48 The Syndicate of Secondary School Teachers included nearly 25,000 teachers and 6,000 schools. When 'Abd al-Rahman 'Azzam attempted to revive the project of an "Islamic party" in the service of the King in 1942, he approached both the Muslim Brothers and the Syndicate of the Secondary School Teachers with which the Brothers had maintained close relations. See Appendix to Security Summary (Middle East), no. 36, 13 April 1942, WO 208/1561/SSME.
49 'Abd al-Halim, *al-Ikhwan al-Muslimun: ahdath sana'at tarikh*, pp. 115–6.

50 *Ibid.*, p. 116.
51 *al-Nadhir*, no. 19, 1358/1939, p. 24. See also Gilsenan, *Recognizing Islam*, p. 220.
52 Davis, 'Ideology, social class and Islamic radicalism in modern Egypt', pp. 144–5.
53 *al-Nadhir*, no. 6, 1357/1938, editorial.
54 *al-Nadhir*, no. 3, 1357/1938, editorial.
55 Ghanim, *al-Fikr al-siyasi lil-Imam Hasan al-Banna*, p. 351.
56 For a reference to the conservative family policies of Germany in the 1930s, see *JIM*, no. 9, 1352/1933. For religious education in the West, see *JIM*, no. 6, 1354/1935, p. 31 and *JIM*, no. 12, 1354/1935, editorial. For military training of youth in Europe, see *al-Nadhir*, no. 5, 1357/1938, pp. 12–13.
57 Salih 'Ashmawi, 'al-Dara'ib al-jadida', *al-Nadhir*, no. 13, 1357/1938.
58 *JIM*, no. 45, 1354/1936, p. 19 and *al-Nadhir*, no. 24, 1358/1939, p. 17.
59 Husayni, *The Moslem Brethren*, p. 93.
60 See "New Introduction" in al-Bishri, *al-Haraka al-siyasiyya fi Misr*.
61 See, for example, al-Bishri, *al-Muslimun wa'l-aqbat fi itar al-jama'a al-wataniyya*, pp. 543–5 and Tripp, 'Ali Maher and the Palace politics', pp. 198–203, 208–9 and 232–6.
62 *JIM*, no. 1, 1356/1937, editorial (in *Mudh.*, pp. 261–4).
63 For more details, see Tripp, 'Ali Maher and the Palace politics', pp. 121–62. See also 'Abd al-Rahman al-Rafi'i, *Fi a'qab al-thawra al-misriyya* (Cairo, Dar al-Ma'arif, 1951), pp. 58–62.
64 *JIM*, no. 30–1, 1356/1938, editorial and p. 14.
65 *JIM*, no. 32, 1356/1938, editorial
66 The claim that the Muslim Brothers participated vigorously in the demonstrations that brought down the Wafdist government in December 1937 stems from Rif'at al-Sa'id's biography on Hasan al-Banna. However, the newspapers he quoted to underpin his arguments (*al-Ahram* and *al-Balagh*) do not say a word about the Muslim Brothers, nor about their alleged pro-Palace demonstrations. See al-Sa'id, *Hasan al-Banna: mata, kayfa wa li-madha?*, pp. 106–7.
     For Hasan al-Banna's views on the old and new government, see his editorial 'Adbarat wizara wa aqbalat ukhra: fa-hal hiya lam tataghayyar?' in *JIM*, no. 28–9, 1356/1938, and his article 'Tatawwur jadid fi al-siyasa' in the same edition (p. 19).
67 For the petitions submitted by the Brothers to the King, to Prince 'Umar Tusun, Prince Muhammad 'Ali and to the heads of the political parties in May 1938, see Hasan al-Banna, 'Mudhakkirat 'an al-da'wa wa al-da'iya', *JIMY*, 14 December 1947 and *al-Nadhir*, no. 1, 1357/1938, p. 25. For Wafdist criticism of the Muslim Brothers' call for the dissolution of political parties, see *al-Nadhir*, no. 15, 1357/1938, p. 7.
68 British Embassy, Alexandria, to Halifax, no. 1077, E5896/10/31, 26 September 1938, FO 371/21881.
69 Yusuf Nasir, a Palace agent, reported that the Muslim Brothers received annual subsidies from Ali Mahir Pasha. See Mitchell, *The Society of the Muslim Brothers*, p. 17. See also FO 141/838 15322 (12 March 1942) and 'Security Summary Middle East', WO 208/1561, (17 January 1942).

70 As early as the mid-1930s the Muslim Brothers began receiving financial support from municipal councils in several parts of Egypt. It appears that the first government support came in the form of a grant from the municipal council in al-Buhayra province for a charitable institution for children run by the Muslim Brothers in al-Mahmudiyya and Shubrakhit (see *JIM*, no. 13, 1352/1933 and *JIM*, no. 4, 1356/1937, p. 16). These funds seem to have been facilitated by 'Abd al-Salam al-Shadhli Pasha, the governor of al-Buhayra and a friend of Ali Mahir Pasha. In 1937 it was reported that the al-Mahmudiyya and Shubrakhit branches received £E149 in annual subsidies from the municipal authorities (*JIM*, no. 4, 1356/1937, p. 16). In 1938 the Ministry of the Interior allotted an annual grant of £E150 to the Brothers in Abu Tij in Upper Egypt, and the provincial council in Assiut gave another £E50 to the Society's local branch (*al-Nadhir*, no. 6, 1357/1938, pp. 10–11).

71 *al-Minhaj*, p. 10.

72 *al-Nadhir*, no. 4, 1358/1939, pp. 5–6.

73 Lampson to FO, no. 402, J2616/1/16, 3 July 1939, FO 371/23306.

74 See, for example, *al-Nadhir*, no. 10, 1358/1939, editorial and p. 14; *al-Nadhir*, no. 17, 1358/1939, editorial and pp. 13–14; and *al-Nadhir*, no. 21, 1358/1939, p. 14.

75 *al-Nadhir*, no. 15, 1357/1938, p. 17.

76 *al-Nadhir*, no. 26, 1357/1938, editorial.

77 *al-Nadhir*, no. 17, 1357/1938, editorial.

78 Hasan al-Banna, 'al-Nafir: ayn Amir al-Mu'minin?', *al-Nadhir* , no. 19, 1357/1938, editorial.

79 *al-Nadhir*, no. 19, 1357/1938, editorial and *al-Nadhir*, no. 20, 1357/1938, p. 6.

80 *al-Nadhir*, no. 17, 1358/1939, editorial.

81 'Adil, *al-Nuqat fawq al-huruf*, pp. 62–4.

82 Dar al-Watha'iq, Taqarir al-Amn/Taqarir Hikimadariyyat Bulis al-Iskandariyya (sirri siyasi), no. 46, 23 February 1940.

83 *Mudh.*, pp. 298–301.

84 For criticism of Ali Mahir Pasha's ministry, see *al-Nadhir*, no. 34, 1358/1939, p. 5; *Majallat al-Ta'aruf*, no. 3, 1359/1940, editorial; *Majallat al-Ta'aruf*, no. 9, 1359/1940, p. 12; and *Majallat al-Ta'aruf*, no. 12, 1359/1940, p. 3.

85 Tripp, 'Ali Maher and the Palace politics', p. 233.

86 Lampson to FO, no. 787, 29 March 1941, FO 3/1/2/429.

87 See 'Abd al-Halim, *al-Ikhwan al-Muslimun: ahdath sana'at tarikh*, p. 145. See also Bayumi, *al-Ikhwan al-Muslimun wa'l-jama'at al-islamiyya fi'l-haya al-siyasiyya al-misriyya*, p. 89.

88 For the quotation, see *al-Ahram*, no. 19689, 1358/1939, p. 10. See also *al-Nadhir*, no. 19, 1358/1939, p. 10; *al-Nadhir*, no. 20, 1358/1939; and *al-Nadhir*, no. 21, 1358/1939.

89 *al-Ahram*, no. 19689, 1358/1939, p. 10.

90 *JIM*, no. 21, 1355/1936, p. 22 and *al-Nadhir*, no. 22, 1357/1938, p. 21.

91 Abu al-Nasr, *Haqiqat al-khilaf bayn al-Ikhwan al-Muslimin wa 'Abd al-Nasir*, p. 9; Abd al-Halim, *al-Ikhwan al-Muslimun: ahdath sana'at tarikh*, pp. 36–7; and

Ibrahim Qa'ud, *'Umar al-Tilmisani shahidan 'ala al-'asr: al-Ikhwan al-Muslimun fi da'irat al-haqiqa al-gha'iba* (Cairo, al-Matba'a al-Tijariyya al-Haditha, 1988), p. 43.

92 See FO 371/21881, no. 1077, 26 September 1938.

93 *al-Nadhir*, no. 31, 1358/1939, editorial.

94 Lampson to FO, no. 3597, 16 November 1941, FO 371/27434.

95 'The Ikhwan al Muslimin Reconsidered', 10 December 1942, FO 141/838. See also Tripp, 'Ali Maher and the Palace politics', pp. 208–9 and 232–6.

96 See Lampson to FO, no. 3597, 16 November 1941, FO 371/27434; Lampson to FO, no. 3628, 18 November 1941, FO 371/27434; and Appendix to Security Summary (Middle East), no. 665, 21 November 1941, WO 208/1560/SSME.

97 Tripp, 'Ali Maher and the Palace politics', pp. 236–7 and 'The Ikhwan al Muslimin Reconsidered', 10 December 1942, FO 141/838, p. 3.

98 Lampson to FO, no. 711, 5 March 1942, FO 371/31569.

99 Tripp, 'Ali Maher and the Palace politics' and al-Bishri, *al-Muslimun wa'l-aqbat fi itar al-jama'a al-wataniyya*, pp. 543–5.

100 Security Summary (Middle East), no. 22, 20 February 1942, WO 208/1561/SSME.

101 Mitchell, *The Society of the Muslim Brothers*, p. 212.

102 *Ibid.* and Bayumi, *al-Ikhwan al-Muslimin wa'l-jama'at al-islamiyya fi'l-hayah al-siyasiyya al-misriyya*, p. 267.

103 Bayumi believed that the Society unequivocally supported the al-Azhar students in a conflict with the Dar al-'Ulum students in 1939. He argued that this move strengthened the Society's position among the Azharists. He also observed that the Azharists played a prominent role in disturbances which the Muslim Brothers were stated to have organized in 1941-2. See Bayumi, *al-Ikhwan al-Muslimin wa'l-jama'at al-islamiyya fi'l-hayah al-siyasiyya al-misriyya*, pp. 261–71. Al-Azhar students were, however, very much controlled by the Palace and Shaykh al-Azhar Mustafa al-Maraghi, and it seems clear that the role of the Muslim Brothers in these demonstrations were less than he has assumed

104 *JIM*, no. 28, 1352/1934 and *Mudh.*, pp. 208–29. See also 'Pan-Islamic Arab Movement', Lampson to FO, no. E2120, 8 April 1936, FO 371/19980.

105 *Taqrir ijmali khass*, pp. 34–5.

106 *Qism al-Manatiq: nashra 'amma*, pp. 21–6.

107 *al-Minhaj*, pp. 10–11 and Heyworth-Dunne, *Religious and Political Trends in Modern Egypt*, pp. 31–4.

108 See a series of editorials by Hasan al-Banna in *JIM* in mid-1935 about religious education.

109 *al-Minhaj*, pp. 10–11.

110 *Ibid.*

111 *Taqrir ijmali khass*, pp. 17–18.

112 Heyworth-Dunne, *Religious and Political Trends in Modern Egypt*, p. 33.

113 *Majallat al-Ta'aruf*, no. 16, 1359/1940, editorial.

114 *al-Nadhir*, no. 23, 1357/1938, pp. 18–21 and *al-Nadhir*, no. 26, 1357/1938, editorial.

115 *al-Ikhwan al-Muslimun: al-mu'tamar al-dawri al-sadis*, pp. 3–4. See also interview with Mustafa al-Maraghi's son in Zuhair Mardini, *al-Ladudan: al-Wafd wa'l-Ikhwan al-Muslimun* (Beirut, Dar al-Iqra', 1984), p. 191.

116 Dar al-Watha'iq, Taqarir al-Amn/Taqarir Hikimadariyyat Bulis Misr (sirri siyasi), no. 2461, 1941.

117 Interview with Jamal al-Banna, spring 1995.

118 Security Summary (Middle East), nos. 119 (19 February 1943), 120 (24 February 1943), 121 (3 March 1943), 126 (5 April 1943) and 137 (19 June 1943), WO 208/1562/SSME.

8

Political Activism
and Radicalism

The Muslim Brothers anticipate serious action, like clashes
with the government. They always express their desire to
enter the battlefield! No, my dear Brethren! Clash
with yourselves first.

Hasan al-Banna[1]
1939

The Campaign for the Palestinian
Arabs 1936–1939

The Palestinian Revolt against British mandatory rule in Palestine in
1936–9 had a profound impact in Egypt and significantly altered the
environment in which the Muslim Brothers operated.[2] The continued
immigration of Jews, their large-scale purchases of land and the strengthening of the Zionist *Yishuv* community represented a serious threat to
the Arab Islamic identity of Palestine. The Partition Plan, recommended
by a royal commission headed by Lord Peel in July 1937, raised the
disconcerting prospect of a Jewish state in Palestine. The symbolic and
religious significance to Muslims of Palestine and its capital, Jerusalem,
can hardly be overstated.[3] Moreover, many Egyptians expressed their
apprehension that the future security of Egypt and its favourable position
as a cultural and economic focal point in the Middle East would be
endangered if a Zionist state were to be established on its borders. These
and other considerations produced a definite change in Egyptian public
opinion – from indifference in the late 1920s to a deep sympathy for the
Palestinian Arabs in the late 1930s. This strongly reinforced the shift of
public opinion from secular Egyptian nationalism and Westernization
towards an Arab Islamic orientation, thus closer to the position of
the Muslim Brothers. Furthermore, the Palestinian Revolt and the

relative inaction of the Egyptian government served to undermine both the legitimacy of the regime and the 1936 treaty between Egypt and Great Britain. The architect of this treaty, the Wafdist leader Mustafa al-Nahhas Pasha, had described it as the attainment of complete independence for Egypt. However, the inability of the Egyptian government to provide efficient support to the Palestinian Arabs strengthened the belief that Egypt was only outwardly "ruled by nationalist rulers, but in reality they were rulers who relied on the imperialists for support".[4] Thus, the Palestinian Revolt and its repercussions served to undermine the legitimacy of traditional political forces in Egypt. At the same time it drew more supporters to the anti-imperialist position of the Muslim Brothers and their call for the amendment of the 1936 treaty.[5]

Prior to the Palestinian Revolt Egyptian involvement in the Palestine issue was mainly concentrated around various Islamic organizations, especially the mother organization of the Muslim Brothers, the prestigious YMMA, which had been involved in the Palestine issue since the violent Wailing Wall riots in 1929.[6] At the outbreak of the Palestinian Revolt in May 1936 the YMMA convened a conference, including leaders of Islamic organizations in Egypt, representatives of Syro-Palestinian bodies operating in Egypt and a number of leading politicians. As a result of a resolution passed at the conference, an umbrella organization, the Supreme Committee for Relieving Palestinian Victims, was established. Hasan al-Banna and one of his associates represented the Muslim Brothers in the committee. From May 1936 onwards associations and groups from all sections of society became involved in the Palestinian campaign, including, rather surprisingly, groups like the Merchants of Bab al-Luq and the Association for the Revival of Tribes, as well as the Egyptian Feminist Movement, headed by the famous Madame Huda Sha'rawi, who became particularly active in the campaign in the late 1930s, much to the dismay of the British.[7] The most prominent place in the campaign was taken by the YMMA.

The campaign for the support of the Palestinian Arabs continued throughout the summer and autumn of 1936 until the end of the general strike in Palestine in September 1936. A temporary lull followed until the spring of 1938, but this was eventually interrupted by agitation and demonstrations following the publication of the Partition Plan for Palestine in July 1937 and the deportation of the Palestinian leadership of the Higher Arab Committee in the autumn of 1937.[8] In 1938, when the Palestinian Revolt escalated to guerrilla warfare, the pro-Palestinian campaign in Egypt became particularly intense and most political groups became involved, including the Young Egypt Party which joined the campaign with the excessive zeal of a latecomer. The Wafd Party also began fund-raising and campaigning from 1938. By this stage the Palestine question had become a central political issue in Egyptian politics, leading to the convention of the World Inter-Parliamentary Congress in Cairo in October 1938 and the St James's Conference on Palestine in London in 1939.

The beginning of the Muslim Brothers' campaign for the Palestinian Arabs can be dated back to May 1936. Until then their involvement had been confined to articles in the press and a visit to the President of the Supreme Muslim Council in Jerusalem, the Grand Mufti Hajj Amin al-Husayni, by two prominent members of the Society.[9] The two young Muslim Brother envoys were accompanied to Jerusalem by the exiled Tunisian leader Abd al-Aziz al-Tha'alibi, a prominent figure in Islamic circles in Cairo. In Jerusalem, Amin al-Husayni took the two deputies under his personal patronage and facilitated their trip to Syria by supplying them with letters of introduction to the Islamic organization Jama'at al-Hidaya al-Islamiyya in Damascus.[10] This was the start of a lasting friendship between the Muslim Brothers and the Grand Mufti of Palestine.

On 7 May 1936 the Grand Mufti, now also the head of the Higher Arab Committee in Palestine, and thereby the leader of the Palestinian national movement, made an impassioned speech, addressing a call to Arabs and Muslims throughout the world to extend assistance to Palestine.[11] Shortly afterwards, on 16 May, Hasan al-Banna convened a meeting of the Muslim Brothers in Cairo to discuss the situation in Palestine.[12] A few days later, a comprehensive plan to assist the Palestinian Arabs was launched. A supreme body, the Central Committee for Aid to Palestine (al-Lajna al-Markaziyya al-'Amma li-Musa'adat Filastin), was established. The importance which the Muslim Brothers attached to this issue can be seen from the fact that this committee included virtually the entire leadership of the Society. A series of decisions was made: a fund-raising campaign should be launched and the contributions should be transferred to the Higher Arab Committee in Palestine; instructions went out to set up sub-committees for fund-raising in the branches;

committees were established for propaganda in mosques and schools; the publication of articles in the local press attacking British policy in Palestine was to be expanded; telegrams of protest to the British authorities and the Secretariat of the League of Nations were formulated; a call was issued for the boycott of Jewish merchants in Egypt; high-ranking dignitaries who were known for their sympathies for Islamic and Arab causes, like Prince Umar Tusun, Muhammad Alluba Pasha (a Senator and former Minister of Education) and Dr Abd al-Hamid Saʿid (a Member of Parliament and head of the YMMA), were to be requested to organize groups to assist the Palestinians; and, unofficially, the Brothers also decided to send delegates to Palestine to monitor the situation. Similar resolutions were passed at a larger YMMA-sponsored meeting in mid-June, which proposed to send a delegation of dignitaries to Palestine in order to "express the Egyptians' sympathy with the [Palestinian] Arabs" and to "publish a report on the situation". However, British intelligence became aware of these plans and ordered that the necessary visas be refused.[13]

The pro-Palestine campaign of the Muslim Brothers reveals some of those elements from which the Society drew its strength. Its organizational efficiency can be seen in the prompt establishment of its Palestinian campaign in May 1936. During the subsequent pro-Palestine unrest, the Society staged solidarity rallies and organized special 'Palestine days'. Pro-Palestine propaganda was disseminated in mosques and petitions of protest were dispatched. The branches were also permitted to send their own letters of protest which served to enhance the active participation of the members. In the countryside some of the Society's branches were instructed to allot a part of the "wheat alms" (*zakat al-qamh*) to the Palestinian victims. In accordance with their commitment to spiritual education, the Muslim Brothers also prescribed a special prayer, *qunut*, for the Palestinians.[14]

The subsequent fund-raising and propaganda activities show the importance of dedicated cadres. In May–June 1936 the Brothers mobilized a number of members for fund-raising campaigns in Upper Egypt. The YMMA had long complained about the inefficiency of its fund-raising campaign and at a meeting in June 1936 the YMMA ascribed the lack of progress "to the obstacles made by the British". The Muslim Brothers' representative, by contrast, reported their fund-raising mission to be "a complete success" and resolved to dispatch another 8 propagandists for the Palestine cause to Upper Egypt.[15] In 15 successive collection drives undertaken in 1936 the Muslim Brothers raised some £E430 in schools, university faculties, mosques, market-places, coffee-shops, railways, government departments and so on. The total amount raised by the YMMA's umbrella organization, the Supreme Committee for Relieving Palestinian Victims, during the entire period of the revolt amounted to nearly £E6,800, but this came from wealthy donors, Palace circles, official parties, commercial companies and large financial bodies.[16] In contrast, the Brothers' fund-raising campaign clearly reflected the lower-middle-class character of the movement. In the Society's newspaper the small donor was hailed as a hero, while senior civil servants and members of the upper classes who declined to contribute were censured.[17] The lists of donors published by the Muslim Brothers included only a handful of dignitaries; the overwhelming majority came from among the rural and urban middle classes. As has been noted in a study by Israel Gershoni, the Muslim Brothers were the only organization in Egypt who worked intensively and continuously in small towns and provincial villages for the cause of the Palestinian Arabs.[18] Thus, the ability of the Muslim Brothers to raise £E430 in a few months in 1936 among these segments of the Egyptian society testifies to the dedication of their cadres and the efficiency of their organization.

A detailed treatment of all aspects of the Society's involvement in the Palestine issue is naturally outside the scope of this study. What concerns us here is the relationship between the Palestine Revolt and its repercussions in Egypt on the one hand and the development of the Muslim Brothers on the other. In Egyptian historiography the debate about the Muslim Brothers' Palestine involvement clearly reflects the division between Islamists and leftists. Egyptian Islamist historians stress the immense efforts the Brothers exerted in supporting the Palestinians by petitions, fund-raising campaigns, demonstrations, mass meetings and other means of propaganda. These efforts helped sway Egyptian public opinion from indifference to commitment to the cause of the Palestinian Arabs.[19] By contrast, Egyptian leftist historians have considered the Muslim Brothers' involvement in the Palestine issue as "insincere". The Brothers are stated to have "exploited the Palestine issue for the selfish purpose of promoting themselves throughout the Arab world".

The Society's involvement in the issue is also described as a part of its support for the Palace's "Islamic campaign" against the Wafd Party in the late 1930s.[20]

The view of these leftist historians is also echoed in Western studies in slightly more sophisticated forms. An early British study asserted that "through the relationship and the work done by the Ikhwan for the Palestinian Arabs . . . Hasan al-Banna came to the fore and was able to expand very rapidly in Egypt". The Muslim Brothers' participation in the propaganda campaigns against British mandate policies in Palestine "enabled him [Hasan al-Banna] to get his share of the 'news-value' of the Palestinian–Arab rebellion". Another advantage accruing from their involvement in Palestine was that it brought the Society into close contact with influential politicians like Ali Mahir Pasha and Abd al-Rahman Azzam Bey who gave the Society essential protection and support.[21] A recent study by Gershoni attempted to develop a thesis of the Society's "exploitation" of the Palestine issue. He identified a "general tendency to exploit the pro-Palestinian campaign as a material and ideological springboard for domestic expansion". Gershoni asserted that "the Palestine issue [was] the principal springboard to prominence" for the Muslim Brothers, providing them with "a network of contacts with various political forces". The Society managed, through its "special 'Palestinian' bodies", to exploit the expression of sympathy for the Palestinians "in a clearly instrumental way, to strengthen its own ranks and expand its activities". In other words, the Palestinian campaign became "the principal catalyst for the remarkable augmentation in members and branches", quadrupling the number of active branches in the five years from 1935. The campaign for the Palestinian Arabs is also said to have been "the main proving ground for the Society's special militant bodies". The campaign generated "the most noticeable change in the essential character of the Society during the 1930s – the transition from religious preaching and education to . . . dynamic political activism". In sum, the benefits that the Society reaped from its Palestine involvement "were essential to the transition to the 'golden age' in the latter half of the 1940s".[22]

This thesis of "exploitation" is of course fascinating because it provides ready answers to the remarkable transformation of the Society in the 1930s, including its increasing size, politicization and influence in political circles as well as its growing militancy. For those who wish to condemn the Muslim Brothers the obvious moral implications of Gershoni's thesis must be equally attractive, especially because it severely undermines the historical legitimacy which the Muslim Brothers derive from their prominent role in the Palestinian campaign. However, a fundamental weakness of the exploitation theory is that it rests heavily on the assumption that the Muslim Brothers misappropriated the funds which they raised for the Palestinian Arabs. Gershoni states: "from the very beginning, the Muslim Brothers had not intended to transfer any but the smallest part of the donations [from the fund-raising campaigns] to Palestine, and had earmarked most of them for domestic use."[23] This claim is at best an exaggeration, at worst completely unfounded. A dissident group which seceded from the Muslim Brothers in 1939 accused Hasan al-Banna in February 1940 of "financial manipulation", including the misuse of Palestinian funds. Of the £E570 collected for the Palestinians in 1938–9, only £E465 had been forwarded to Palestine, the secessionists claimed. However, they conceded: "when Hasan al-Banna had ascertained of the right position of Islam on this topic, he renounced his former position and promised to recollect the missing amount and send it to the Palestinians."[24] There is some uncertainty concerning the funds, collected in 1936–7. A former member of the Society wrote in his memoirs that the donations collected for the Palestinians were used for propaganda purposes in Egypt, in accordance with orders received from the Higher Arab Committee in Palestine.[25] However, there is evidence of at least three transfers from the Society to the Palestinians in June–July 1936, amounting to £E152.[26] What happened to the rest of the £E436 collected by October 1936 is uncertain, but it has been reported that money was sent secretly by "special messengers" to avoid British interference.[27] The continued close relationship and cooperation between the Muslim Brothers, the YMMA and the Palestinian leadership make the misappropriation of funds less likely. Indeed, as was discussed in Chapter 6, money from German and exiled Palestinian sources was transferred to the Muslim Brothers in 1939 in order to finance their pro-Palestine and anti-British activities.

If the moral question of exploitation or not is left aside, the crucial questions appear to be what were the effects of the Society's involvement in the Palestine issue on its growth and expansion, and how did it influence the Society's character? There are several reasons to believe that the Palestine issue was less fundamental to the Society's growth than has been assumed by earlier studies, and Gershoni's study in particular. As was seen in Chapter 5, the Society had already established branches and contacts in more than 100 villages and towns prior to the outbreak of the Palestine Revolt in 1936. This has also been acknowledged by Gershoni. He noted: "During this year [1935] . . . there was a remarkable increase in new membership – 'several thousands' according to the reports of the official press."[28] This observation is not included in his final analysis. The Society's continued rapid expansion following the Palestinian campaign shows that it was not dependent on the campaign for recruiting followers. However, it appears to have been the case, as Gershoni has correctly observed, that the fervent participation of the Muslim Brothers in pro-Palestine activities attracted new adherents. Memoirs by Muslim Brothers who joined the Society in the mid-1930s confirm that the intense pro-Palestine agitation had a strong appeal among the youth.[29] The advantages of the Palestinian campaign were, however, partly outweighed by a number of negative effects. As will be seen, policy differences on the Palestine question caused tensions within the Society in 1938–9, precipitating a serious internal crisis in 1939 which was said to have brought the Society's headquarters in Cairo to a standstill for several months.[30] This internal crisis slowed down the spectacular growth which characterized the movement in the 1930s. Similarly, the Society's intensive campaigning for the Palestinians attracted the attention of the Political Police and the British Intelligence Service, resulting in restrictions being imposed on the movement in late 1938 and 1939. These negative effects of the Muslim Brothers' Palestinian campaign have passed unnoticed in Gershoni's study.

The claim that the Palestine issue was essential for the Muslim Brothers, in the sense that it provided them with "a network of contacts with various political forces", appears to be exaggerated. True, the Palestine issue brought the Society into closer contact with important politicians like Abd al-Rahman Azzam Bey, Muhammad Alluba Pasha, Ali Mahir Pasha and others. However, as discussed in Chapter 4, some of these contacts had already been made in 1935. The Society's most important patrons, Ali Mahir Pasha and Shaykh al-Maraghi, had been approached successfully during that year. The most obvious manifestation of the Society's connections in political circles, the reception in Zamalek in 1939 to honour the "pro-Islamic forces" in the Parliament, was not related to the Palestine issue, but to the issue of religious education.[31] Thus, the Palestine campaign cannot have been indispensable in providing the Society with contacts in the highest political circles.

Finally, the assertion that the Palestine issue produced "the transition from religious preaching and education to . . . dynamic political activism" must be qualified. As seen in Chapter 3, the first British intelligence report on the Muslim Brothers clearly shows that they were fervently anti-imperialistic *before* the outbreak of the Palestinian Revolt. We have also observed that the Society dropped the provision of non-involvement in politics in its General Law in 1934. At the same time the Society faced accusations of being "a political group" (see Chapter 2). Nor does it seem likely that the politicization of the Muslim Brothers was merely a side-effect of the Palestinian campaign as Gershoni's study suggests.[32] The Palestine issue received no attention in Hasan al-Banna's first ideological treatise on Islam and politics in 1938.[33] Yet Gershoni has correctly observed that the Society's pro-Palestine agitation became a platform for political propaganda against the British and the Egyptian regime. The Palestinian campaign thus served to reinforce and accelerate a development towards political involvement which began during the first half of the 1930s. However, the most far-reaching consequence of the Muslim Brothers' pro-Palestinian campaign was the radicalization of segments within the Society, leading the Society on a course towards a confrontation with the authorities. In the following sections the process of radicalization and its effects on the Society will be discussed.

Already by the autumn of 1936 the political implications of the Palestinian campaign had become obvious, not only through the sharp condemnation of the British policies in Palestine but also because the Egyptian government was increasingly being criticized for its weak position on the issue. More specifically, the use of Egyptian labour in the service of the British army in Palestine was repeatedly condemned by the Brothers as "an unlawful and abominable act".[34] When the campaign resumed in late 1937 and during 1938, the Palestine question became a fundamental issue in the political struggle of the Muslim Brothers and served as one of the criteria by which the Brothers measured politicians and governments. The direction of their Palestinian involvement was changed to a more overtly political campaign against the inaction of the Egyptian government and its dependence on the British.

In late 1937 and during 1938 the Brothers' campaign for the Palestinian Arabs expanded to include a number of new means of propaganda; the Society's newspaper published several special editions on Palestine, the fund-raising campaigns were continued and propaganda efforts in mosques were intensified. Pamphlets were printed and distributed on the university campus, in shops and coffee-houses, among civil servants and in the provinces. Posters describing atrocities perpetrated by the British in Palestine were fixed to the walls of buildings and mosques. The call for a boycott of Jewish merchants was now backed up by the distribution of lists of names and addresses of Jewish stores and merchants in Cairo. Vitriolic attacks on Zionists and on Jews *qua* Jews (Jews as Jews as opposed to Jews as Zionists) were published in the Society's newspaper, describing them as a "societal cancer".[35] The Muslim Brothers frequently referred to the Qur'anic verse, "Strongest among men in enmity to the Believers wilt thou find the Jews and Pagans", as a theological basis for the campaign against the Jews.[36] However, the official policy of the Muslim Brothers never came close to that of the Nazis in Europe. Apart from calling for the boycott of Jewish merchants, attacks remained verbal. The Brothers' anti-Jewish propaganda was inextricably connected to the Palestinian Revolt. Anti-Jewish sentiments were kindled by the unwillingness of Egyptian Jews to support the Palestinian Arabs and the involvement of Egyptian Jewish associations in the financing of Zionist organizations in Palestine.[37] In this respect it is worth noting that throughout 1933–6 there were no anti-Jewish articles in the Society's press, and even during the Revolt many Muslim Brother writers attempted to uphold the essential distinction between Jews and Zionists. Whatever hatred the Muslim Brothers might have felt against the Jews, it was not sufficiently strong to prevent one of their football teams from playing matches against the team of the Jewish Makabi Society in 1939, although this event aroused some controversy afterwards.[38]

In the late 1930s the Brothers acquired a reputation for intensive pamphleteering. The head of the Society's printing press recalled that their printing capacity was dramatically expanded to include two dozen employees and a large printing press which ran only at night to avoid police surveillance. Pamphlets were also printed and smuggled into Palestine.[39] The Muslim Brothers' capacity for pamphleteering far exceeded that of other organizations working for the Palestine cause and, according to a British intelligence report, "most of the pamphlets in Egypt dealing with the Palestine Rebellion were published by them".[40] The ability to disseminate anti-British propaganda on a large scale was clearly connected to the Society's efficient class of cadres. Another important factor was the funds which were forthcoming from German and exiled Palestinian contacts in Cairo in 1938–9. The Society's most famous publication was *al-Nar wa al-Dimar fi Filastin* (fire and destruction in Palestine), a booklet containing detailed descriptions and pictures of British and Jewish atrocities against Palestinian Arabs.[41] The dissemination of such scurrilous anti-British propaganda led to police action against the Society. In July 1938 the Society's premises in Cairo were searched by the police and anti-British publications were confiscated. The Brothers responded by ridiculing the Islamic image of the Palace-backed government, the so-called "Righteous Rule" (*al-hukm al-salih*). They accused the authorities of giving in to British pressure by sending police forces to "search for the book that had infuriated our dear allies!"[42] The Brothers demanded that the legal authorities commence proceedings against them, insisting on their right to continue the struggle "in the courtroom" and to "lodge our protests against what goes on in Palestine in the court protocols."[43] As a lawsuit against pro-Palestine activists was apparently considered too delicate an affair given the strong pro-Palestinian sentiments of public opinion, no further legal action was taken despite the fact that police surveillance was intensified.

The uneasy relationship with the authorities was exacerbated by two new elements in the Society's campaign: mass meetings and demonstrations. In October 1937 the Muslim Brothers reportedly sponsored a demonstration of several thousand people that marched to the 'Abidin Palace to protest against British activities in Palestine. The police were called in to disperse the crowd with the result that clashes occurred. From May to September 1938 a series of pro-Palestinian demonstrations were launched by the Society. The most conspicuous event must have been the nationwide demonstrations organized on 7 August when marches were organized simultaneously in dozens of Egyptian towns and major villages. The evidence suggests that violence was limited, with clashes with the police occurring only in Cairo, Ismailia, Alexandria and Rashid.[44] Sympathy with the Palestinians was running high and in the provinces the police were apparently keen to avoid confrontation. Those demonstrators who were arrested were usually quickly released.[45] However, police action against the Muslim Brothers was stepped up and a well-publicized "Week for the Victory of Palestine" in Port Said in August was reportedly subjected to police harassment. Shortly afterwards the Brothers published an unambiguous warning to the government:

> We wonder whether he who ordered this vicious attack was the Minister of the Interior in the era of the so-called "Righteous Rule" [al-hukm al-salih]? Was he inspired only by himself or was he inspired by the British? . . . O ye Rulers! Know that we are a Muslim people who do not tolerate injustice! . . . When you continue to oppress the Islamic nation, you will only destroy yourselves! You are already walking with long steps towards annihilation and perdition.[46]

The Society reported that spies from the Political Police conducted surveillance on its premises. The houses of Muslim Brothers in Cairo, Ismailia, Port Said and Rashid were repeatedly searched, pro-Palestine demonstrations suppressed and demonstrators arrested.[47] Hasan al-Banna was himself arrested for the first time during a demonstration in Ismailia and was detained for four days.[48] With branches submitting petitions in protest against police actions, militancy was clearly gaining momentum. A large youth conference convened in Zaqaziq on 5 September 1938, attended by some 600 delegates, put forward the hitherto most radical resolutions: British and Jewish goods were to be boycotted, youths were strongly encouraged to volunteer for "the defence" of al-Aqsa Mosque in Jerusalem and demands would be sent to the Egyptian government to permit volunteers to travel to Palestine. A fortnight later the Brothers proceeded to publish the banned booklet *Fire and Destruction in Palestine* in their newspaper.[49] By this stage the British authorities were becoming increasingly concerned about the Brothers' "undesirable activities". The Egyptian Director-General of Public Security was instructed to take action "with the object of putting a stop to any further anti-British manifestations on the part of religious organizations".[50] This resulted in a police clamp-down on the Society and scores of activists were arrested in Cairo while collecting contributions for the Palestinians.

The Palestinian campaign now threatened to get out of hand. Hasan al-Banna did not want his radical followers to put the political future of the Society in jeopardy. As he was anxious to play a role in the forthcoming Inter-Parliamentary Congress on Palestine to be held in Cairo in October 1938, he adopted a more accommodating stance. The Society's pro-Palestine campaign was restricted to verbal attacks on the government's Palestine policies, especially its intention to participate at the Palestine Round Table Conference (the St James's Conference) in London scheduled for January 1939. The reversal of the Society's policy of confrontation became more conspicuous when al-Banna changed his position on the Round Table Conference after it became clear that Ali Mahir Pasha and his protégé Abd al-Rahman Azzam Bey, and not the ageing Prime Minister Muhammad Mahmud Pasha, would head the Egyptian delegation to London. When the delegates returned from London, they were welcomed by a "crowd of Muslim Brothers filling the whole area of the airport, chanting 'God is Great! Praised be the Lord!' and greeting Ali Mahir Pasha as 'the Friend of the Arabs'".[51] This euphoric celebration for a Palace politician infuriated a number of Brothers since it was interpreted as a gross violation of the fundamental principle of "non-partyism". One disgruntled Brother noted: "The Muslim Brothers never extol persons. They praise nobody but God and acclaim only productive work and struggle!"[52] The reversal from a radical anti-government policy was again witnessed by the Society's reception in July 1939 in Zamalek. Strong tensions between radicals and moderates were building up within the Society. In late 1939 the conflict culminated in a serious crisis and the secession of a group of leading members. This will be the subject of the following section.

The Secession of Muhammad's Youth

There are a number of interpretations of the internal crisis in the Muslim Brother organization which resulted in the secession of a group called the Society of Our Master Muhammad's Youth (Jam'iyyat Shabab Sayyidina Muhammad), or simply Muhammad's Youth (Shabab Muhammad), in 1939–40. Two early Western studies maintained that the *rapprochement* between the Muslim Brothers and Ali Mahir Pasha constituted the main background for the split. Within the Society "there was a marked aversion . . . to any kind of political liaison, especially as they had joined the Movement for religious reasons".[53] The secessionists held that the Society "should concentrate exclusively upon social and religious objectives", and not the kind of political involvement which Hasan al-Banna had initiated.[54] Egyptian leftist historians have given it another twist, by claiming that the secessionists opposed al-Banna's pro-Palace policies. The dissidents had "refused to hail the King, knowing how corrupt he was". They are said to have had Wafdist sympathies and began to oppose al-Banna "when he permitted the Society to become an instrument in the hands of the Palace to crush the Wafd Party".[55] Mitchell's authoritative study also stressed this factor, but identified two other issues which contributed to the crisis: the use of funds collected for the Palestinians and the issue of "imperatives, moral and theological, by which the Society should be guided". According to Mitchell, the moral issue was the most important element in the conflict, but it was only vaguely described as a demand for the fulfilment of the Muslim Brothers' mission which was defined as "the moral salvation of this country, if necessary 'with force of the hand'".[56]

The confusion about the basic issues of the dispute stems partly from the fact that there were several crises and expulsions in the late 1930s, each with different motives. The first serious crisis seems to have occurred in January 1938 when al-Banna and the Society severed all contacts with Muhammad Effendi al-Shafi'i, the editor of the Society's newspaper. As discussed in Chapter 7, this crisis was related to the Palace-sponsored campaign against the Wafd Party and al-Shafi'i's scathing criticism of the Caliphate propaganda of Shaykh al-Maraghi, which al-Banna obviously felt was damaging his relations with al-Maraghi and the Palace.

The crisis, which ended in the expulsion (or secession)[57] of Muhammad's Youth in late 1939, was not connected to questions of morality versus politics or whether politics was an integral part of Islam or not. The dissidents wholeheartedly embraced al-Banna's 'political' interpretation of Islam, perhaps even more vigorously than al-Banna himself, at least judging by their own words that "Islam is politics and politics is Islam".[58] Nor does it appear to be connected to the struggle between Ali Mahir Pasha and the Wafd Party. In their final statement about the causes of the secession in February 1940, the dissidents made no mention of Ali Mahir Pasha who was Prime Minister at the time of the defection. Indeed, Muhammad's Youth supported the candidacy of Salih Harb Pasha, one of Ali Mahir's closest protégés, for the chairmanship of the YMMA in June 1940. In 1942, following the installation of a Wafdist government by the British and al-Banna's decision, taken under threat of internment and suppression, to accommodate it, Muhammad's Youth seized the opportunity to condemn his "ignominious capitulation" and tried to win the support of Muslim Brother members who felt alienated by his policies. In a communiqué announcing the final break with the Muslim Brothers, the dissidents voiced their grievances against al-Banna's autocratic leadership and failure to expel members "whose moral conduct and manners are not above suspicion". The use or misuse of funds was also mentioned. The main cause for dissension was, however, al-Banna's willingness to enter into political compromises:

> The Islamic mission [da'wah] can only can be successfully accomplished through the "spontaneous power of the people" [quwah al-sha'b al-dhatiyyah] and sincere Islamic guidance of public opinion without being dependent on the rulers. However, Hasan al-Banna has deviated from this principle by declaring that the success of the Islamic mission is dependent on pleasing the rulers and working under their party banners.[59]

Thus, the dispute appears to have been concerned less with the choice between al-Nahhas or Ali Mahir than with the question of policy towards the government of the day. This is also evident in al-Banna's answer to the statement by the dissidents in February 1940.[60] While strongly repudiating the assertion that "the success of the Islamic mission is dependent upon pleasing the rulers and working under their party banners", he stressed the need to "bring the Islamic mission to the rulers . . . and make it known to them". This strategy, al-Banna stated, was "one of the most useful and efficient methods of achieving the aims of the Islamic mission". Al-Banna further pointed out that there was no justification for opposing the ruler in every circumstance:

> [The ruler] might stand up against the enemies of Islam and prevent them from reaching their aims. It would be foolish and contrary to Islam if the Muslims were to embarrass those who frustrated the enemies of Islam in their attempts to reach their aims . . . In any case, it is better that the ruler supports the Muslim Brothers in their efforts to educate people . . . than standing in their way and opposing their aims. The Brothers view all rulers, irrespective of party allegiance, from the position of preachers for the Islamic cause [du'ah] and not as partisans [ashiya'].[61]

Muhammad's Youth's programme was not much different from that of the Muslim Brothers. They were firmly committed to the causes which the Brothers strove to achieve, such as Islamic laws, the liberation of all Islamic countries from imperialist rule, Islamic unity, the return of the Caliphate, social justice and internal reform (although it did assume a more extreme position in certain questions concerning public morality, in particular the veiling of women). The essential differences, however, were confined to the pace of implementation and the means of enforcement. In principle Muhammad's Youth repudiated any accommodation with the government of the day. They refused to accept any kind of subsidies for welfare projects from the Ministry of Social Affairs (created by Ali Mahir's government in 1939). In practice, the financial hardship of the Muhammad's Youth evidently forced them to approach politicians with a view to acquiring funds. Due to the minor following of the group they were mostly ignored or suppressed, and this probably perpetuated their radicalism. In the postwar period for example, they began advocating preparation for a total revolution against the British and permission to carry arms for all.[62] From a longer-term perspective, the Muslim Brother–Muhammad's Youth divide has become the historical antecedent for today's schism between moderate Islamists and radical Islamic militants.

There is some uncertainty about when Muhammad's Youth came into existence. There are indications that a precursor to the group was formed as early as 1937, perhaps under the leadership of Muhammad Izzat Hasan, a member of the MIA and a deputy of al-Qalyubiyya province. In June 1937 he took the liberty of formulating the course to be adopted by the Muslim Brothers. An unrelenting struggle against the tyranny of materialism was unavoidable, he announced. The first task of the Brothers should be "to annihilate this idol perching on the chest of mankind" and to "destroy the pillars [of this economic and political system]".[63] This militant position was strongly reproached by al-Banna, who argued: "The nature of our Islamic mission is building, not destruction! [The Brothers] prefer peacefulness and love to confrontation and war."[64] However, the dissent resurfaced during the Palestinian campaign in the autumn of 1937, and Muhammad Izzat Hasan was severely censured by al-Banna for his desire to "speed up [the pace of] our programme". Such a course would only "ostracize everyone" and put the Society's "fruitful results in jeopardy". He stressed that "the

Islamic mission of the Prophet was nothing but stages and steps, the one following the other."[65]

Nevertheless, al-Banna did respond to the call for a more militant course. In May 1938 he announced what has been interpreted as the beginning of the political struggle of the Society. In a militant tone he declared that the Muslim Brothers were now "moving from propaganda alone to propaganda accompanied by struggle and action". If the authorities failed to implement the Society's programme, "then we are at war with every leader, every party and every organization that does not work for the victory of Islam!"[66] Shortly after his impassioned declaration of "war", al-Banna learnt that his followers interpreted his words literally. In June 1938, during the Palestine Revolt, a group of young Muslim Brothers defied the instructions of the MIA to refrain from demonstrations in accordance with police orders. They took to the streets of Cairo and clashed with the police, which resulted in numerous arrests. A minor crisis of authority seems to have arisen. Several proclamations of loyalty to al-Banna were printed in the Society's newspaper,[67] and Muhammad Izzat Hasan's group was dismissed from all positions in the Society, ostensibly because their tendencies conflicted "with the fundamental aims of the Muslim Brothers".[68] Yet feelings were running high and the desire for immediate action for the Palestinians could not be suppressed. The radical approach was gaining support and the Muhammad's Youth group came to the fore. At the Muslim Brothers' conference in Zaqaziq in September 1938, the group managed to push through a radical proposal calling for Egyptian volunteers to go to Palestine in order to "defend" al-Aqsa Mosque. Some months later there were rumours that two of the radicals who had been dismissed together with Muhammad Izzat Hasan himself had been arrested following an aborted attempt to travel to Palestine.[69] At the same time open criticism of al-Banna's conciliatory attitude to al-Azhar appeared in the Society's newspaper,[70] and al-Banna had to renew his efforts to bring the radicals under control. Prior to the Fifth Conference in January 1939, he issued something close to an ultimatum to those who opposed his policies "only because of irresponsible rashness and emotional zealotry".[71]

The tensions within the Society were clearly reinforced by the propaganda of the Young Egypt Party, which was one of the most radical political groupings in the late 1930s. With firm support from Palace circles the Young Egypt Party tried to challenge the Wafd Party, and employed militant methods like paramilitary youth units and revolutionary rhetoric. However, the swelling ranks of the Muslim Brothers threatened to undermine the Young Egypt Party's position as the dominant political youth formation and leading challenger to the Wafdists, and in 1937 the party's paramilitary Green Shirts began to mock the Muslim Brothers' Rover Scouts for not being real paramilitary units. The Green Shirts also criticized the Brothers for being "quietists and not revolutionaries".[72] The rapid growth of the Society meant that the Young Egypt Party was eclipsed by the Muslim Brothers by the late 1930s. This led to rivalry between the two for the allegiance of the youth, erupting in open verbal conflicts in October 1938, probably triggered off by the Inter-Parliamentary Congress for Palestine at which both groups were eager to play a prominent role. Tensions further increased when the Brothers proudly announced that "the first drops of rain sent by God" had come with the conversion of a number of Young Egypt activists to the ranks of the Society. In an effort to regain its former supremacy among the youth movements, the Young Egypt Party abandoned its Greater Egypt nationalist propaganda in favour of the pan-Islamic causes from which the Muslim Brothers seemed to derive their success. It tried to outbid the Society by propagating Islamic causes with excessive radicalism. From mid-November 1938 its previous concentration on peaceful organizational work was replaced by militant activism, and it began to use the word "revolution" (*thawra*) in its propaganda, calling for volunteers to support Palestinian Arabs. The party also carried out a series of violent attacks on bars in Cairo, Alexandria and elsewhere, and organized protest marches against prostitution. This new militant course was widely believed to be an attempt to "surpass the Muslim Brothers by deeds and actions", in order to appear more deserving of the youth's allegiance. Their new militancy would make the Muslim Brothers "look like pensioners without vigour and energy".[73]

In a daring attempt to defeat the Muslim Brothers, Ahmad Husayn, the leader of the Young Egypt Party, orchestrated a provocative campaign for Islamic laws, calling for the abolition of the constitution and parliamentary system. For this he was brought to trial, as he had intended. The Muslim Brothers were incensed by this campaign which enabled Ahmad Husayn to pose as a martyr since he was being prosecuted for having called for the implementation of the *shari'a*. They immediately demanded that they too should be summoned to court for having advocated Islamic laws and the overthrow of the constitutional system. However, the Brothers were not prepared to risk their political future by following Ahmad Husayn's revolutionary course, and shortly afterwards the Society's leaders backed down by professing their allegiance to the constitution and legal means of struggle. The direct action of the Young Egypt Party against the bars was denounced outright: "We do not agree to this defiance of the law. It is not our programme to embark on such a course."[74] Al-Banna was treading a perilous path between his radical supporters and the political realities of the day. At the widely publicized Fifth Conference of the Society in January 1939, he addressed the issue of whether the Muslim Brothers intended "to use force to achieve their objectives" and whether they "planned a general revolution against the social and economic system in Egypt". After discussing at length the need for "practical" force and productive work, he stated: "the Muslim Brothers never think of revolution, nor do they believe in its usefulness and results." He repeated his old thesis that the social and economic crisis itself might generate a revolution if social reforms were not rapidly enacted.[75]

The Young Egypt Party's revolutionary course brought numerous trials and prison sentences upon its leadership, culminating in total suppression in 1941. By contrast, al-Banna remained firmly committed to an accommodation with the government. However, the call for radical action and confrontation gained more adherents during 1939. In April, clashes occurred between police and some of the Rover Scouts in the provincial town of Shibin al-Kawm, during which a police officer was wounded. A number of Muslim Brother activists were arrested and reportedly beaten up and tortured by the police.[76] A storm of protest showered over the MIA, demanding that direct action should be taken against the authorities, but the leadership strongly impressed upon its members to remain quiet and obey the orders of MIA. This call was repeated in a special comprehensive report (*taqrir ijmali khass*), which is one of the best sources on the internal situation in the Society at this time. In this report, written and distributed among the members in mid-1939, al-Banna stressed the potentially fatal results of confrontation with the government. Police surveillance of the branches had already been tightened. Governors and district prefects had issued orders to cut off financial support to the Society's social welfare projects. Threats and persuasion were used to induce civil servants who were members of the Muslim Brothers to break with the Society. Senior civil servants in the provinces who sympathized with the Brothers' cause had almost completely ceased to visit the local clubs of the Society, fearing the consequences of overt contact with them. Al-Banna told his followers that he had had a series of meetings with the Director of Public Security to "remove the obstacles for reform . . . and pave the way so that we can work for the general welfare only". He impressed upon his followers that they "must be wise in their behaviour and avoid bringing harm upon themselves", and he instructed them to "purge their ranks and their meetings of people with 'sick hearts' and 'suspicious aims'". Above all, they should "not resort to words when a sign is enough, not to lashes when a word suffices and not to violence where the end can be achieved with gentleness".[77]

The beginning of Ali Mahir Pasha's ministry on 19 August 1939 might have justified al-Banna's call for accommodation. The government's initial and well-publicized commitment to social and military reforms made such a compromise easier. The Muslim Brothers could also wholeheartedly support Ali Mahir Pasha's rejection of British pressure to abandon neutrality and declare war on the Axis powers. However, the outbreak of war increased the demand for immediate action. When a war in Europe seemed imminent in early 1939, al-Banna had been in the forefront of those who urged the government to take advantage of British weakness to obtain independence. He wrote enthusiastically: "The unsettling, confused and disordered international situation which shakes the heart and nerves of the imperialists is our opportunity. This is our only chance!"[78] Needless to say, such a message kindled the revolutionary mood among the youth. At the outbreak of war in the autumn of 1939, al-Banna once again tried to restrain his revolutionaries. He recalled:

I still remember 3 September when I was in Esna and the Second World War was declared. In the afternoon that day I travelled to Asfun al-Mata'ina and there I was received by people firing their guns. I looked at them and said: "By your Prophets, the battlefield is not here! Nor are we entering the battlefield today!"[79]

In an attempt to channel zealotry into peaceful and harmless action, al-Banna proposed a plan for internal spiritual struggle and action:

> Now the time for action has come! The Muslim Brothers anticipate serious action, like clashes with the government. They always express this desire to enter the battlefield! No, my dear Brethren! Clash with yourselves first and struggle with the individual practices that are contrary to Islam. Soon I will call you to change your clothes in order to approach the "external appearance of Islam" [*mazhar al-Islam*]. I will call upon you to grow a beard so that you will look different from and in opposition to the foreigners. I will call upon you to change your time schedules. We shall sleep after the evening prayer ['*isha*] and get up before dawn [*fajr*]. I will call upon you to furnish your houses with Islamic furniture and to discipline [*ta'dib*] your wives, daughters and sisters according to Islam.[80]

These suggestions were greeted with scepticism, even from some of al-Banna's closest allies. An open conflict with the radicals was probably inevitable. By October 1939 Muhammad's Youth groups had spread to the provinces and acted like an independent entity within the Society's organization, and was presumably headed by Muhammad Ali al-Mughlawi, the Secretary of the General Committee of Students and Workers in the Society. He belonged to the group of "hotheads" who had defied MIA orders during the pro-Palestine demonstrations in 1938. Al-Mughlawi joined forces with Husayn Yusuf, a prominent Young Egypt Party dissident, who was reportedly disillusioned by the lack of a "religious element" within the party and of "courage" among the Muslim Brothers.[81] In February 1940 the breach between Muhammad's Youth and the Society was sealed. Muhammad Izzat Hasan and some 16 other young Muslim Brothers joined the new movement. Many of them had held important positions in the Muslim Brothers' organization, such as deputies of provinces and members of the MIA. With the defection of Mahmud Abu Zayd, the editor of the Society's weekly, the Brothers also lost their mouthpiece.

Given the background of this split there can be little doubt that formidable pressure for revolutionary action was building up inside the Society. Al-Banna could not ignore this pressure if the Society was to retain its favoured position among the youth movements in Egypt. The duty of struggle could not be confined to words and occasional demonstrations if the Muslim Brothers were to perpetuate their image as a truly anti-imperialist force. As we have seen, the founding of the Special Apparatus took place shortly after Muhammad's Youth's secession. This suggests that internal pressure and the 1939 crisis must have been important elements behind the decision.

In the aftermath of the political activism of the 1930s and the 1939 crisis the political tactics of the Muslim Brothers became more discernible. The Society was strongly committed to an anti-British policy including activist methods and occasional confrontations. Nevertheless, it was by no means prepared to sacrifice its legal existence and face an uncertain future as an underground movement. The expulsion of Muhammad's Youth and the official decision to present candidates for the parliamentary elections two years later, in 1942, show that the Society intended to reform the political system from within rather than by demolishing it through revolution.

Between Confrontation and Accommodation 1940–1942

By 1940 the Society of the Muslim Brothers had become the largest Islamic society in Egypt. Its organization had reached a stage of maturity. The growth in the number of branches had continued unabated since the early 1930s, and was only interrupted by the defection of Muhammad's Youth in 1939. In January 1941 the Society had around 500 branches. Three years later the number was variously estimated at between 1,000 and 1,500. In 1941 the Society had one or several Rover units in more than 50 towns or districts with a total number of nearly 2,000 Rovers. At the same time as the system of Battalions was being improved, a military wing was in the making. Another source of strength was the Society's student organization which commanded its most powerful segment of articulate and active opinion. Thus, by 1940, the Society's organization was stronger than ever before, and for many of the younger Muslim Brothers it was time to translate this organizational strength into political power and influence. Contacts had already been initiated between the Society and politicians from right across the political spectrum. Although seeking political influence as clients through traditional patronage networks was ideologically an anathema to the Society, it was tolerated to a certain extent for pragmatic reasons.

It is obvious that by the turn of the decade the Muslim Brothers had begun to prepare themselves for a larger role in the Egyptian political arena. This is evident from their declaration, in an internal programme from 1938 (later publicized at the Sixth Conference in 1941), of the Society's intention to present candidates for the next parliamentary elections.[82] However, the outbreak of the Second World War presented immediate obstacles for the realization of the Society's political ambitions. Despite a number of attempts to advance a political agenda during the war, the Muslim Brothers were forced to postpone their overtly political struggle until the end of the war. The Society had already been subjected to increasing restrictions, harassment and arrests in the late 1930s for its vitriolic anti-imperialistic propaganda during its Palestine campaign. When the war broke out, the Egyptian government was requested by the British to take draconian measures against anti-British activities to prevent the emergence of a "fifth column" in Egypt. This included the imposition of martial law as well as strict censorship of post, telegraphs, telephones and the press. This resulted in a partial paralysis of political life during the war due to the suppression or silencing of a number of opposition politicians.[83] During the first half of the war a number of Egypt's most prominent (or notorious) opposition figures ended up in prison or under house arrest, including the Young Egypt Party's Ahmad Husayn, the leader of the YMMA Salih Harb Pasha and the previous Royal Councillor and ex-Prime Minister Ali Mahir Pasha.

However, the extraordinary political restrictions imposed by the British during the war presented the Muslim Brothers with unexpected opportunities. Being originally a religious welfare society, the Muslim Brothers operated mainly through local grass-root networks of mosques, welfare institutions and branch organizations, not through traditional political channels where surveillance was stricter. The British military authorities admitted that they could not ban the Society's meetings as long as they were held in mosques.[84] Thus, the Muslim Brothers could evade some of the obstacles posed by the wartime policies of the British, and the dual politico-religious character of the Society undoubtedly accounted for its ability to survive when such policies forbade political and anti-imperialistic activities. At the same time, the traditional political parties experienced a steady erosion of their political support bases during the war, not only because of political restrictions but also because of being too closely associated with the British. This was particularly true of the Wafd Party when on 4 February 1942 British troops surrounded the Palace and forced King Farouq to appoint a Wafdist government. The traditional parties began to look to the Muslim Brothers for support against their rivals, offering to withstand British pressure to suppress the Society in return for its support. This enabled the Muslim Brothers to form several beneficial alliances which secured its legal existence throughout most of the war. There is little doubt that these factors contributed greatly to the continuation of the impressive growth of the Society during these years.

At the outbreak of the war the Muslim Brothers had firmly supported the stance of the Ali Mahir government of refusing to abandon neutrality by declaring war on the Axis powers. The Society did not wish the government to go beyond the limits of the 1936 Anglo-Egyptian Treaty, but they urged the government to take advantage of existing circumstances to achieve independence. However, the Muslim Brothers significantly scaled down their overtly political and anti-British propaganda. In the new wartime conditions political propaganda was proving very costly. Intemperate criticism of the government's failure to honour its declared social and Islamic policies led to the closure of the Society's newspapers in late 1939 (see Chapter 7). Surveillance of the Society's meetings became tighter and the dissemination of anti-British propaganda frequently led to arrests. The Society adapted to these conditions by stressing the need for political accommodation. The strategy of the day was to keep a low profile. One Muslim Brother veteran described the Society's strategy during the war as "avoiding a direct confrontation with the enemy", "refraining from political issues" and concentrating on "proliferation and formation of branches".[85] The Achilles' heel of the Society's wartime policy was that its young and restive membership did not automatically accept the need for political accommodationism and an indefinite postponement of the political struggle. After all, the political message of Islam as propagated by the Muslim Brothers was a major reason why many young members had joined the Society. It was the cornerstone of the Society's ideology. The Muslim Brother preachers tried to allay their disillusionment by declaring that the Society was following the Prophet's strategy between the Battle of Hudaybiyya (when he entered into a temporary compromise with his adversaries in Mecca), and the Battle of Badr where the Prophet finally defeated his opponents:

> The best description that could delineate our current policies is the position and action of the Prophet before the Battle of Badr. That is thinking logically before using weapons. Is this not sufficient for those who ask what is the current message of the Muslim Brothers? Our Prophet Muhammad worked for the dissemination of the Islamic message among different tribes and clans, recruiting adherents, inculcating the spirit of sacrifice . . . This is what we mean by forming branches in the neighbourhoods of Cairo, in the provincial cities and in rural villages. Could this bring shame on the Muslim Brothers? There are thousands of cries for reform.[86]

To ensure compliance with the Society's wartime strategy the leadership repeatedly stressed the absolute necessity of obedience:

> Hasty and short-sighted perspective is fatal to the Islamic mission. The policies of every Islamic call require high capabilities and special talents. The soldier must only obey, suggest and be informed about the orders he should assume. He should not criticize or put his leader in a situation of debate which indicates belittlement and could result in internal disputes, factionalism and the spread of whimsical ideas.[87]

The Society appears to have managed to offset some of the pressure for anti-imperialistic action by taking up other less sensitive political issues, such as the need for socio-economic reforms. A trend towards a more deeply rooted social awareness of the fundamental inequalities of Egyptian society had already begun in the early 1930s, but it was accelerated during the war. It not only included criticism of the government's social policies and the extravagant lifestyles of the Egyptian upper classes, but also extended to direct support for trade unions, as well as attempts to organize workers' unions under the aegis of the movement.[88] The Society's welfare programmes were significantly expanded during the war. The campaign against illiteracy gained pace, evening schools were formed and alms were collected. The Society made important humanitarian efforts to relieve the suffering of the victims of the Axis bombing of Egyptian cities. All branches were instructed to keep their premises open to people who had lost their homes as a result of air raids.

Nevertheless, the Society's leadership appears to have abandoned their efforts to discourage overtly political and anti-imperialistic propaganda from mid-1940. This coincided roughly with the fall of Ali Mahir Pasha's ministry in the summer of 1940. Following Italy's declaration of war on the Allies in June 1940, the British once again pressed Egypt to join the war. As Prime Minister Ali Mahir Pasha refused to comply with this demand he was soon replaced by a more pro-British politician, Hasan Sabri Pasha. The change in government affected the Muslim Brothers in so far as, despite their differences with Ali Mahir, they retained an "ideological and psychological affinity" with him.[89] As a leading opposition figure, Ali Mahir found it worthwhile to encourage the Muslim Brothers to join his cluster of protégés in an anti-British and anti-government campaign. After the fall of his ministry, he retained control of the Special Branch of the Egyptian Police, and with its support the Society's leadership felt confident in embarking on an overtly political course. The Society's press attacked "the dominance and monopoly of foreigners in all aspects of life, to the detriment of national Egyptians". Hasan al-Banna explicitly reiterated his former position that Egyptians should seize "this opportunity to get rid of the foreign rule".[90] Such temerity to criticize British dominance in Egypt proved costly, and in early autumn 1940 the government permanently revoked the Society's licence to publish the prestigious Islamic journal *al-Manar*. The Society also found it increasingly difficult to acquire journals which could serve as its mouthpiece. Another obstacle was put in place by the Husayn Sirri Pasha's ministry which assumed power after Hasan Sabri Pasha's death in November 1940. In a bid to limit the influence of the Muslim Brothers and its sister organization the YMMA, the government passed a law which explicitly banned any kind of political involvement by Islamic welfare organizations.

Despite these moves, the overall weakness of the pro-British minority governments of Hasan Sabri Pasha and Husayn Sirri Pasha permitted Ali Mahir's opposition coalition to offer substantial support to the Muslim Brothers. In January 1941 the Society was able to hold its Sixth conference in Cairo with the participation of thousands of district deputies as well as prominent political and religious figures, among them the previous Defence Minister and head of the YMMA Salih Harb Pasha. The speeches made at the conference and the resolutions passed were explicitly political and anti-British. For the first time the

Muslim Brothers openly advocated the nationalization of the Suez Canal Company, an extremely sensitive political issue. A large part of Hasan al-Banna's speech was devoted to the need to limit British and foreign dominance in Egypt. The Society's enhanced position was further underlined by the fact that several of its leaders were given the honour of delivering Friday speeches in the prestigious al-Azhar Mosque where King Farouq sometimes prayed.

The Society's Sixth Conference was undoubtedly perceived by the government and the British as provocative and ominous. During the war mass rallies of all kinds were treated with the utmost suspicion. British intelligence was greatly disturbed by reports about contacts being made between German and Italian agents and Egyptian opposition figures, including members of the YMMA and the Young Egypt Party.[91] Although no link to the Muslim Brothers was proved at this point, it seems probable that they came under heavy scrutiny given their pre-war association with members of the German Legation in Cairo (see Chapter 6). The British began pressing the government to take action against people they perceived as being Ali Mahir's "creations".[92] The final move against Hasan al-Banna was probably triggered by his own writings in which he criticized Husayn Sirri Pasha's government for its departure from Qur'anic principles.[93] In late February 1941 (and not on 19 May as cited elsewhere),[94] the Ministry of Education ordered al-Banna to transfer from Cairo to a school in Qena, a town some 300 miles away in Upper Egypt where refractory government officials were commonly sent to "expiate their offences".[95] This caused considerable perturbation among the Muslim Brothers. The MIA passed a resolution which advised al-Banna not to abide by the government's order, and a memorandum was sent to the Ministry of Education informing it of this decision. In the meantime, however, a military order had been issued to enforce the Ministry's decision. Upon this "some important personalities" reportedly intervened and offered to undertake mediation in order to resolve the crisis. As a result of this, al-Banna accepted the Ministry's order and left for Qena. Ahmad al-Sukkari, who headed the Society in Cairo in al-Banna's absence, went to great lengths to calm tensions and convince the membership that this, after all, was the best course to take, despite the apparent violation of a decision by the MIA, the Society's highest executive body. At a large meeting in Cairo, to which some 80 district deputies were summoned on short notice, al-Sukkari explained that the leadership had given al-Banna permission to leave for Qena only "for a limited period". This decision was motivated by their wish not to reject the mediation offered and also to dispel the impression of the Muslim Brothers as "mischief-makers". Al-Sukkari stressed that the Brothers should permit those who had "not yet understood us and our mission, to fully grasp our intentions . . . that we are a group who want peace more than anyone else". His admonitions were supported by Salih Harb Pasha, the head of the YMMA, who urged the Brothers to obey their leaders. Al-Sukkari impressed upon all district deputies to "explain our position to your Brothers", and to calm tensions among the rank and file.[96]

The Society did not suffer greatly from al-Banna's transfer to Qena, although to a certain extent it exacerbated existing tensions between radicals and moderates within the Society. In the late 1930s, Upper Egypt had already become a major recruiting ground for al-Banna, and his four months of "internal exile" in Qena gave him ample opportunities to concentrate on streamlining the district organizations there. In the meantime, moves were being made by a number of the Society's influential patrons to secure al-Banna's return. Tawfiq Pasha Duss, a prominent Coptic Member of Parliament, made an interpellation in Parliament following al-Banna's transfer in response to a pledge made by influential local Muslim Brothers in Duss's own constituency in Upper Egypt.[97] In addition, a number of MPs from the Liberal Constitutionalist Party intervened to put pressure on the Minister of Education as well as the Prime Minister to reverse their decision.[98] These moves were not merely the result of the Society's own network of patrons. For various reasons, the opposition in Parliament seized upon the transfer to embarrass the weak government of Husayn Sirri Pasha. The result was that after four months in internal exile, al-Banna was allowed to return to Cairo.[99] In the meantime, political opposition groups associated with Ali Mahir Pasha had become more active. The Young Egypt Party boasted that it was reasonably "immune from police interference" since the key persons in the Egyptian police were sympathetic to its cause. Ahmad Hussein, the party's leader, was obviously aware of the tensions within the Society, and resorted to tactics similar to those he had employed in the late 1930s in order to outbid the Muslim Brothers. Realizing the precarious position of al-Banna in exile in Qena, he challenged the Muslim Brothers by asking them to encourage student demonstrations. However, the Society continued to keep a low profile as long as al-Banna was in Upper Egypt. When Ali Mahir Pasha's coalition organized a large rally in April 1941, at which Abd al-Rahman Azzam Bey described the ongoing al-Kailani revolt against the British in Iraq as "a striking example of a country's resolution to free itself from foreign bondage", the Society was noticeably absent.[100]

Shortly before al-Banna was allowed to return to Cairo at the end of June 1941, another government move against the Muslim Brothers took place. Ahmad al-Sukkari, the Society's second-in-command, was arrested. Papers had been found which linked him to the prominent opposition figure General Ali Aziz al-Misri, who had been Commander-in-Chief of the Egyptian Army until the British granted him "sick leave" in February 1940 and subsequently pensioned him off. The General, a long-standing associate of Ali Mahir Pasha, was violently anti-British. During the al-Kailani revolt in April–May 1940, he had made several attempts to leave Egypt and join the insurgents. In one such attempt his plane developed engine problems and the pilot was forced to make an emergency landing in the desert shortly after take-off. General al-Misri was finally arrested on 6 June 1941, and the story of his attempted escape was widely reported in the Egyptian press. Al-Sukkari's quick release from prison in late June suggests that the Muslim Brothers played no major role in this operation, although the sources are scant on this point. One of General al-Misri's pilots later became a well-known Muslim Brother figure, but at the time of the escape attempt he was reportedly not associated with the Society. The other accomplice, Anwar Sadat, had been in touch with the Society since the beginning of the war.

Al-Sukkari's arrest exacerbated tensions between the leadership and some of the young activists in the Society, who were keen to pursue a more anti-government course and objected to the leadership's subordination to government harassment. At this point, al-Banna dispatched an explicit ultimatum, ordering all members to "keep completely quiet". He would not tolerate "even a single petition or protest to the government". Al-Banna sent his envoys to the provinces to ensure that his orders were followed. He promised that al-Sukkari's arrest would not last long, but at the same time warned all branches and members that they "would be excluded from the Society if they in any way went beyond the order of the Society".[101] Al-Banna managed to maintain order. His position proved to pay off and at the end of June he had been transferred back to Cairo and al-Sukkari had been released.

After al-Banna's return to Cairo the pro-Palace Ali Mahir Pasha group sought to make better use of the Muslim Brothers' extensive organization. According to British intelligence reports, orders issued by the Palace instructed provincial officials to allow the Brothers free rein to conduct their activities. Police reports about the Society dried up and British intelligence inferred that "the Palace had begun to find the Society useful, and had thrown its aegis over them".[102] It is obvious that by September 1941 the Society had been granted special permission by the head of the Egyptian Police to hold meetings, a concession not granted to other Islamic societies. In October 1941 the British discovered a report that the King himself had issued orders to the governors of the provinces not to interfere with the Muslim Brothers, who were "working without any personal ambition whatsoever for the welfare of the country".[103] Ali Mahir Pasha, who headed the pro-Palace coalition, reportedly increased his financial aid to the Society. Through his control of the Special Branch he sought to conceal the extent of the Muslim Brothers' anti-British activities and sabotage plans against British military installations. However, despite a number of unconfirmed reports about subversive activities, there was in fact very little evidence to the claim that the Society actually planned an uprising similar to the al-Kailani revolt in Iraq.[104] Nevertheless, British military intelligence felt increasingly threatened by the rumours about the Society's activities and the support it enjoyed in Palace circles. On 17 October 1941, at the behest of the British, Prime Minister Husayn Sirri Pasha ordered the arrest of both al-Banna and al-Sukkari. The Society's press was closed down, and meetings and any reference in newspapers to the Society were forbidden.

Prior to his arrest, al-Banna had been cautious not to provide the authorities with any direct pretext to suppress the Society. At several meetings in the provinces he had adhered to instructions to stick to purely religious issues, and to avoid disturbances at the Society's meetings. His followers were, however, less guarded in their anti-British pronouncements. In any case, the British were merely looking for an excuse to order the arrest of the Society's leadership. This was provided in early October 1941 when al-Banna made an intemperate speech in the provincial town of Damanhur in front of some 2,000 people.

Al-Banna reportedly condemned the current unIslamic legislation and called for the application of Islamic laws. Worse still, he attacked the "imperialistic policies" in the Islamic world and urged the crowd to "rise up as one man to defend their religion and their honour". He impressed upon them that the time was right "to demand our right because the Imperialist is in a hard-pressed situation". Al-Banna raised the expectations of his audience by promising that "the coming days will bring great events" and he urged them to "follow the call at the very first glimpse of hope". One can only speculate as to what prompted al-Banna to abandon his usual circumspection; perhaps his rapidly growing organization and the support of the Palace might have made him slightly overconfident.

The arrest of al-Banna and al-Sukkari in October 1941 prompted the Society's organization to its hitherto most impressive show of strength. In the course of a few weeks the Society's district and branch organizations mobilized its members and activists to gather signatures for petitions for the release of their leaders. The result was astonishing and convincing proof of the Society's mass following. Hundreds of petitions from all over Egypt including more than 11,000 signatures were showered upon the Royal Councillor and the Prime Minister. Some of them were written in an unambiguously threatening tone, including passages like "this might lead to the most dangerous consequences". Judging by archival sources, the Royal Secretary marked several of the most threatening passages with a red pencil before submitting them to the Royal Councillor. The arrest also provoked violent denunciations of the British among the Muslim Brothers in the provinces. As was the case during the Palestine campaign in the late 1930s, the Society's "hotheads" could no longer remain idle and decided to take direct action against the authorities. On 11 November the Society's Student Committee planned a protest rally in Cairo, but the Ministry of Interior had already issued specific orders to deny permission and police officers were stationed at the Society's premises to enforce these orders. According to a police report, a group of some 200 Muslim Brother students refused to obey police instructions to disperse and instead started a demonstration which led to clashes with the police and around 30 arrests.

The Society's patrons were not slow to react to al-Banna's and al-Sukkari's arrest. Considerable pressure was brought upon Prime Minister Husayn Sirri Pasha to release them. The Society had become so influential

in higher political circles that even a minister from the government
visited al-Banna in prison.[105] It was clearly in the interests of Ali Mahir's
pro-Palace coalition to secure the release of the Society's leadership. This
would embarrass the government and demonstrate to the British that
Ali Mahir was the only politician powerful enough to control the
country and its unruly elements. Thus, Ali Mahir Pasha's associates in
the Ministry of Interior and in the Security Department of the Police
recommended the release of al-Banna in mid-November, less than a
month after his arrest.[106] The Prime Minister was left caught between
the Palace and the British, but he was also worried by impending signs
of civil disorder.[107] The scale of the Society's petition campaign as well as
the clashes between the police and the Muslim Brother activists were a
bad omen for a country in the midst of a war. Fearing disturbances at
the forthcoming opening of Parliament, Husayn Sirri Pasha hoped to
calm the situation by releasing al-Banna and al-Sukkari, although this
implied open defiance of his British allies. After having released them
without consulting the British authorities, the Prime Minister told the
British Ambassador that "there would have been a 'religious revolution'
if he had kept these people interned". He further sowed doubts about
the reliability of the informers of British military intelligence who had
reported al-Banna's seditious speech in Damanhur.[108] Shortly afterwards
the Prime Minister also ordered the release of another prominent member
of the Muslim Brothers who had been on a hunger strike, again without
consulting his British allies. By this stage, British military intelligence
was extremely irritated and disturbed by these developments:

> The Prime Minister evidently finds it easier to condone the activities
> of elements hostile to us than to resist pressure from Ali Maher's
> entourage and possibly from the Palace . . . In Cairo the meetings
> of the YMMA have recently been a rendezvous for leading Islamic
> preachers, high Palace officials and various notable personalities. For
> instance, on 21 November the Rector of Al Azhar, the King's Imam,
> Abd al-Rahman Azzam and the Afghan Minister were present.
> Congratulations were exchanged on the release of Hasan al-Banna
> and the others. These gatherings at the premises of the YMMA
> seem to represent something like a unified Moslem front against
> Great Britain and for the protection of subversive elements.[109]

The British were by now convinced that the Prime Minister and the police were trying to "whitewash the Ikhwan [the Muslim Brothers] in the eyes of the British authorities".[110]

In addition to strong British pressure for the suppression of the Society, al-Banna found himself confronted with internal opposition to his rule after his release. Pamphlets had been distributed in several provinces accusing him of "running the Islamic mission as he pleases guided by his own personal interest and greed". Similar pamphlets appeared at the Religious Institute in Tanta where the Society had a certain following, and provoked a great uproar among the Society's local student committee. The pamphlets were labelled "British propaganda" by some of the Brothers. Protest letters were submitted to the Prime Minister, and all branches were warned against this sort of propaganda. Although one cannot completely dismiss the possibility that the British had sponsored the spread of such propaganda, these pamphlets fit well into the pattern of increasing tensions within the Society's ranks stemming from policy differences over how to face the current political realities.

His internment had a great impact on al-Banna and subsequently affected his relationship with his pro-Palace patrons. It was obvious to him that he could not rely on their protection. Moreover, the Muslim Brothers had reaped scant reward from Ali Mahir Pasha during his ministry in 1939–40. Consequently, al-Banna did not want to jeopardize his chances by throwing the full weight of his movement behind the Ali Mahir coalition. His imprisonment intensified his instinct for caution and he generally avoided hostile references to the British in his public speeches, although anti-British speeches were reported in the provinces.[111] In December 1941 the British observed that the Muslim Brothers were "moderately quiet". However, by the end of January 1942 food shortages in Cairo and German advances in the western desert precipitated student strikes and demonstrations. These disturbances hastened the fall of Husayn Sirri Pasha's government, and the pro-Palace coalition organized a campaign calling for a ministry headed by Ali Mahir Pasha. Through demonstrations and "spontaneous disorder" Ali Mahir hoped to force the British to accept him as the strongman of Egyptian politics.[112] British military intelligence reported:

> On 3 February, in the interval between the fall of Hussein Sirri and the Wafd government, about 5,000 students presented a petition at

the Palace, in which they demanded that Ali Mahir should form a government, to include Salih Harb and Abd al-Rahman Azzam; that Aziz al-Misri . . . and all political internees should be released; and that the British should undertake not to interfere in any Egyptian political or internal questions. If their demands were not accepted, they threatened general strike and widespread sabotage. Amid shouting for the King and Ali Maher, there were shouts of "We are all Axis soldiers, advance Rommel, down with Churchill."[113]

The speed with which the demonstrations were organized led the British to believe that they were "instigated" by the Muslim Brothers and the pro-Palace coalition. Despite this, al-Banna ordered his followers not to play too conspicuous a part in the disorder encouraged by Ali Mahir's group.

However, Ali Mahir's ambitious plan backfired when British military intervention on 4 February 1942 forced the Palace to accept a Wafdist government. During the following months Ali Mahir and most of his protégés were interned, with the notable exception of the Muslim Brothers. Although the British Ambassador repeatedly pressed for the reinternment of the Society's leadership, the new Prime Minister Mustafa al-Nahhas preferred to treat them otherwise.[114] Al-Banna's reinternment would probably have unleashed large-scale petition campaigns and organized disturbances, as had been the case during Husayn Sirri's Ministry in late 1941. Furthermore, it seems probable that al-Banna's restraint prior to British intervention might have led al-Nahhas to believe that al-Banna was amenable to some sort of accommodation with the Wafdist government. After all, in the early 1940s there was not yet any marked hostility between the Muslim Brothers and the Wafd Party.

As the new government prepared for general parliamentary elections in March 1942, the Society decided to put forward a modest number of 17 candidates. Al-Banna himself was to stand for Ismailia. The membership was excited by the decision to participate in the elections, and the opposition press gave coverage to the Society's election campaign. A newspaper went so far as to propose al-Banna as a possible leader of the opposition. During the election campaign al-Banna was careful not to make any public expression of anti-British feeling, and his election speeches chiefly concentrated on the necessity of Islamic laws.[115] However, the government thought it unwise to permit the Society to run for

Parliament. British pressure was probably an important factor behind this decision, although Prime Minister al-Nahhas himself appears to have thought that by forcing al-Banna to surrender to his demands he would weaken the Society significantly. In the middle of March 1942, al-Nahhas summoned al-Banna and ordered him to withdraw his candidature and cancel the Society's participation in the forthcoming elections. He also asked al-Banna to make a written statement in which he declared his loyalty to the government and the 1936 Anglo-Egyptian Treaty. If not, he and his leading associates would be reinterned. Faced with this ultimatum, the MIA came to the decision that al-Banna had no option but to refuse to comply with al-Nahhas's demands. However, as had happened in March 1941 when al-Banna was transferred to Upper Egypt, he overruled the MIA's decision. In an open letter to the Prime Minister, published in *al-Ahram*, al-Banna declared his support for the government's adherence to the 1936 treaty. This was naturally interpreted as an ignominious surrender and drew widespread criticism from many of his followers. However, his compliance with the government's demands allowed al-Banna to conclude an informal agreement with the Wafdist government which permitted the Society to continue its activities and intensify its recruiting efforts. There is little doubt that the Muslim Brothers benefited considerably from this organizational freedom. The Society experienced a great leap forward during the Wafdist ministry.

The Society's election campaign in 1942, its subsequent withdrawal and realignment with the Wafdist government were major events which represented a watershed in the history of the movement. For the first time the Muslim Brothers had opted for the parliamentary route, but were denied access. This was an ominous sign for the future, not only because it strengthened the radicals and revolutionaries within the Society, but also because it demonstrated the hollowness of the parliamentary system in Egypt. The repercussions of al-Banna's submission to the government were far stronger in 1942 than during his "exile" in Qena in the spring of 1941. This time a temporary split occurred within the Society.[116] It appears that al-Banna's unilateral decision provoked strong resentment, and opposition to his leadership crystallized around his second-in-command Ahmad al-Sukkari.[117] The rift was soon patched up, but it reappeared on several occasions during the war. It highlighted the recurring conflict between advocates of accommodation and confrontation, which was a major source of tension in the Society of the Muslim Brothers.

Epilogue: Sinister Forebodings

The conflict between the demands for a radical anti-government course and the political realities of the day was the central divisive issue within the Society in the late 1930s. These tensions increased during the war when Hasan al-Banna was forced to make a number of humiliating compromises with the government in order to avoid suppression. A number of British intelligence reports about the Society during the war described al-Banna's difficulties in restraining an increasingly restive and impatient membership.[118] However, the persistence with which al-Banna's policy of political accommodation was pursued, despite this increasing internal dissension, convinced the British that the Muslim Brothers were not "likely to jeopardize their future by precipitate and rash action when their prospects of attaining power by Fabian methods are considerable".[119] They also believed that al-Banna's "temperament and religious background favour a policy of peaceful development, not of violence which might involve the Movement's ruin".[120] However, a policy of "peaceful development" became increasingly difficult to maintain since the demands for radical action were nurtured by oppressive measures against the Society during the war, such as the arrest and internment of the leadership in 1941, and the pressure on al-Banna to withdraw from the parliamentary elections of 1942. The rigging of the 1945 elections, which resulted in al-Banna's defeat in the Muslim Brother stronghold of Ismailia, once again denied the Brothers access to Parliament, although they commanded a mass following comparable only to the Wafd Party. The development of a military wing, founded partly to check and control the militants, became too powerful to be contained by those who wished to pursue al-Banna's course of accommodation. These incompatibilities were the seeds of the downfall of the movement in 1948–9. Shaykh Ahmad al-Baquri, a prominent Brother, recalled that al-Banna tried to calm his furious followers after his defeat in the 1945 elections when he called upon them to "replace a revolution against the government with another way". His call was not heeded and shortly afterwards the Prime Minister, Ahmad Mahir Pasha, was assassinated. This was the first in a wave of political violence that ravaged Egypt in the latter half of the 1940s. Although the Muslim Brothers' involvement in Ahmad Mahir's murder is disputed, there seems to be little doubt that by 1945 radical Muslim Brothers were preparing for violent action of this kind.[121] The involvement of elements of the military wing of the Society in political violence between 1945 and 1949 is also well established.

Nevertheless, whatever responsibility the Society's leadership had for the political violence of the postwar years, there were no concerted attempts to topple the government by violent methods. Furthermore, the political violence of the Society's military wing took the form of revenge and blood feuds which are still widespread in the Egyptian countryside, rather than systematic attempts to destabilize the regime. This reinforces the general impression of a movement which sought accommodation and reform, not confrontation and revolution. In 1948–9 the Muslim Brothers had a larger following than any other political group in Egypt. For all that, the Society had no seats in Parliament, nor was it consulted in the policy-making of the government. The inability or unwillingness of the ruling élite to acknowledge the growing power of the Society and co-opt it into the political system produced the bitterness and revolutionary zeal which led to violence. This lesson has not been learnt by the present regime in Egypt which persistently refuses to recognize the existence of non-violent and law-abiding Islamists. By its monopolization of power, not unlike that of the ruling élites in pre-revolutionary Egypt, the present regime nurtures forces which inevitably lead to violence and murder.

The West also has a lesson to learn. A story attributed to Sayyid Qutb, the main ideologue of today's Islamic militants, says that he became a radical Islamist during his stay in the United States in 1949 when he saw the gloating American press coverage of al-Banna's assassination. This story might well be apocryphal. However, journalists who attended the military court case against the Egyptian Muslim Brothers in the autumn of 1995, observed a bitterness among the Brothers' supporters. They questioned the complete indifference of Western countries to human rights abuses perpetrated against moderate Islamists, while the fate of human rights activists in Nigeria received full media attention.[122] By supporting oppressive and illegitimate regimes in the Middle East and turning a blind eye to state violence against the moderate Islamist opposition, the West will probably strengthen the heirs of Muhammad's Youth and not al-Banna's legacy of pragmatism and moderation.

NOTES

1 *al-Nadhir*, no. 23, 1358/1939, editorial.
2 For repercussions of the Palestine issue in Egypt prior to the Second World War, see Jankowski, 'Egyptian responses to the Palestinian problem in the interwar period' and 'The government of Egypt and the Palestine question 1936–1939', *Middle Eastern Studies*, vol. 17 (1981), pp. 427–53; and Gershoni, 'The emergence of pan-nationalism in Egypt'. For studies of the Muslim Brothers' involvement in the Arab–Zionist conflict in Palestine in the 1930s, see Gershoni, 'The Muslim Brothers and the Arab revolt in Palestine'; El-Awaisi, 'The conceptual approach of the Egyptian Muslim Brothers towards the Palestine question'; Jankowski, 'Egyptian responses to the Palestinian problem in the interwar period'; and Ghanim, *al-Fikr al-siyasi lil-Imam Hasan al-Banna*.
3 Palestine is the birthplace of a number of prophets. Its capital "Jerusalem", is considered the Third Holy Place of Islam. The city is also the site of numerous holy places, especially the al-Aqsa Mosque. Various Qur'anic verses deal with the Prophet Muhammad's Midnight Journey to Jerusalem, and the celebration of the Prophet's visit to Palestine is an important Islamic feast (*'Id al-mi'raj wa'l-isra*). See El-Awaisi, 'The conceptual approach of the Egyptian Muslim Brothers towards the Palestine question', pp. 225–30.
4 al-Baquri, *Baqaya dhikriyat*, p. 45.
5 Following the announcement of the 1936 treaty, the Muslim Brothers published a series of articles which denounced the treaty and Prime Minister al-Nahhas's suggestion of a national holiday called the Feast of Independence (*'id hurriyat al-istiqlal*), to celebrate the signing of the treaty. In 1938–9 the Muslim Brothers began publicly to call for the amendment of the treaty. See *JIM*, no. 21, 1355/1936, editorial; *JIM*, no. 24, 1355/1936, pp. 3–4; *JIM*, no. 32, 1355/1936, p. 17; and *al-Nadhir*, no. 30, 1357/1938, editorial.
6 Jankowski, 'Egyptian responses to the Palestinian problem in the interwar period', p. 12.
7 Lampson to FO, no. E4415/3217/31, 3 July 1936, FO 371/20035.
8 The Grand Mufti Hajj Amin al-Husayni managed to escape arrest and deportation by fleeing to Syria and then Iraq. This served to enhance his reputation in the Arab world. See also Zvi Elpeleg, *The Grand Mufti Haj Amin al-Hussaini: The Founder of the Palestinian National Movement* (London, Frank Cass, 1993), pp. 32–44.
9 These were 'Abd al-Rahman al-Sa'ati, Hasan al-Banna's brother, and Muhammad al-As'ad Hakim.
10 *Mudh.*, pp. 230–4 and *JIM*, no. 17, 1354/1935, p. 6.
11 For the outbreak of the Palestine Revolt, see Elpeleg, *The Grand Mufti Haj Amin al-Hussaini*, pp. 32–44.
12 For the beginning of the Muslim Brothers' Palestine campaign, see *Mudh.*, pp. 240–4; *JIM*, no. 6, 1355/1936, pp. 19–20; Lampson to Sir Arthur Wauchope

(High Commissioner for Palestine), no. E3217/3217/31, 28 May 1936, FO 371/20035; and Lampson to FO, 'Pan-Islamic Arab Movement', no. E3153, 28 May 1936, FO 371/19980.

13 Kelly to FO, no. E3629/3217/31, 17 June 1936, FO 371/20035.

14 *Mudh.*, pp. 244–5.

15 Lampson to FO, no. E4415/3217/31, 3 July 1936, FO 371/20035. See also 'Min abna' al-Lajna al-Markaziyya', *JIM*, no. 8, 1355/1936.

16 Gershoni, 'The Muslim Brothers and the Arab revolt in Palestine', p. 380.

17 See, for example, *JIM*, no. 9, 1355/1936, p. 3.

18 Gershoni, 'The Muslim Brothers and the Arab revolt in Palestine', p. 375.

19 See, for example, Ghanim, *al-Fikr al-siyasi lil-Imam Hasan al-Banna*, pp. 473–506.

20 See Meijer, 'Contemporary Egyptian historiography', pp. 73–4; al-Sa'id, *Hasan al-Banna: Mata, kayfa wa li-madha?*, p. 98; and al-Bishri, *al-Haraka al-siyasiyya fi Misr*, pp. 47–8.

21 Heyworth-Dunne, *Religious and Political Trends in Modern Egypt*, pp. 22–3.

22 Gershoni, 'The Muslim Brothers and the Arab revolt in Palestine', pp. 381–2, 390.

23 *Ibid.*, p. 381.

24 'Mawqifuna al-niha'i min al-Ikhwan al-Muslimin', *al-Nadhir*, no. 1, 1358/1940, pp. 2–3.

25 'Abd al-Halim, *al-Ikhwan al-Muslimun: ahdath sana'at tarikh*, p. 174.

26 *Majallat al-Fath*, 1355/1936, p. 23; Lampson to FO, no. E4415/3217/31, 3 July 1936, FO 371/20035, pp. 194–6; and *JIM*, no. 16, 1355/1936, p. 14.

27 Lampson to FO, no. E4415/3217/31, 3 July 1936, FO 371/20035, pp. 194–6.

28 Gershoni, 'The Muslim Brothers and the Arab revolt in Palestine', p. 369.

29 'Abd al-Halim, *al-Ikhwan al-Muslimun: ahdath sana'at tarikh*, p. 173–4.

30 *Ibid.*, pp. 205–10.

31 *al-Nadhir*, no. 20, 1358/1939; *al-Ahram*, no. 19689, 1358/1939, p. 10; *al-Nadhir*, no. 21, 1358/1939; and *Mudh.*, pp. 285–7.

32 Gershoni, 'The Muslim Brothers and the Arab revolt in Palestine', p. 383.

33 *Kalimat mu'tamar talabat al-Ikhwan al-Muslimin*, pp. 18–37.

34 *JIM*, no. 25, 1355/1936, p. 13.

35 See, for example, Dr Mahmud Salih, 'Khatar al-yahud 'ala al-'alam al-islami wa'l-masihi', *al-Nadhir*, no. 9, 1357/1938, p. 17.

36 Surat al-Ma'ida [The Table], Qur'an 5:85. See *JIM*, no. 11, 1355/1936, pp. 1–3 and *JIM*, no. 22, 1356/1937, p. 4.

37 For the Muslim Brothers' official view on Egyptian Jews, see *al-Nadhir*, no. 24, 1357/1938, pp. 4–6 and *al-Nadhir*, no. 24, 1358/1939, p. 15.

38 *al-Nadhir*, no. 9, 1357/1938, p. 13.

39 Interview with Jamal al-Banna, spring 1995. He supervised the Society's printing press in the late 1930s.

40 'The Ikhwan al Muslimin reconsidered', 10 December 1942, FO 141/838, p. 1.

41 Part of the booklet was published in *al-Nadhir*, no. 18, 1357/1938.

42 *al-Nadhir*, no. 11, 1357/1938, p. 18.

43 'Awwal al-ghayth', *al-Nadhir*, no. 9, 1357/1938.

44 Peaceful demonstrations were reported in Bani Suwayf, Suez, Meet Salsil, Meet Ghamr, Zifta, Manfalut, al-Manzala, Awlad Yahya al-Hajir and al-Bilbays. See *al-Nadhir*, no. 11, 1357/1938.

45 al-Sisi, *Fi qafilat al-Ikhwan al-Muslimin*, pp. 37–8.

46 'Fi muhit al-Ikhwan', *al-Nadhir*, no. 13, 1357/1938.

47 *al-Nadhir*, no. 11, 1357/1938, p. 18; *al-Nadhir*, no. 14, 1357/1938, p. 17; and 'Abd al-Halim, *al-Ikhwan al-Muslimun: ahdath sana'at tarikh*, pp. 174–7.

48 'al-Ikhwan al-Muslimun yaghdabun li-Filastin: al-muzaharat fi jami' anha' al-qutr', *al-Nadhir*, no. 11, 1357/1938; 'Mudhakkirat 'an al-da'wa wa al-da'iya', *JIMY*, no. 507, 1367/1947; and *JIMY*, no. 508, 1367/1947.

49 'al-Nar wa al-dimar fi Filastin', *al-Nadhir*, no. 18, 1357/1938, pp. 10–48.

50 British Embassy to Halifax, no. E5898, 26 September 1938, FO 371/21881.

51 *Majallat al-Da'wa*, no. 104, 1372/1953, p. 3; *Mudh.*, pp. 303–4; and *al-Nadhir*, no. 7, 1358/1939, p. 23.

52 *Mudh.*, pp. 303–4.

53 Heyworth-Dunne, *Religious and Political Trends in Modern Egypt*, p. 27.

54 Harris, *Nationalism and Revolution in Egypt*, p. 179.

55 al-Sa'id, *Hasan al-Banna: mata, kayfa wa li-madha?*, p. 110 and *Safha min tarikh Jama'at al-Ikhwan al-Muslimin* (Cairo, Sharikat al-'Amal lil-Taba'a wa al-Nashr, 1990), pp. 101–2; and al-Bishri, *al-Haraka al-siyasiyya fi Misr*, pp. 48–9.

56 Mitchell, *The Society of the Muslim Brothers*, pp. 17–19.

57 Hasan al-Banna wrote in his letter to the group: "You have insistently requested to be expelled by your intentions and by the actions which you planned." See 'Mawqifuna al-niha'i min al-Ikhwan al-Muslimin', *al-Nadhir*, no. 1, 1358/1940, pp. 2–3 and al-Sisi, *Hasan al-Banna: mawaqif fi al-da'wa wa al-tarbiya*, p. 155.

58 See an article by a Muhammad's Youth writer in July 1940 quoted in Bayumi, *al-Ikhwan al-Muslimun wa'l-jama'at al-islamiyya fi'l-hayah al-siyasiyya al-misriyya*, p. 134.

59 'Mawqifuna al-niha'i min al-Ikhwan al-Muslimin', *al-Nadhir*, no. 1, 1358/1940, pp. 2–3. For a reprint of this article, see al-Sisi, *Hasan al-Banna: mawaqif fi a-da'wa wa al-tarbiya*, pp. 149–62.

60 A reprint of Hasan al-Banna's letter to the dissidents can be found in al-Sisi, *Hasan al-Banna: mawaqif fi a-da'wa wa al-tarbiya*, pp. 154–62.

61 *Ibid.*, pp. 158–9.

62 For a brief review of Muhammad's Youth in the 1940s, see Bayumi, *al-Ikhwan al-Muslimun wa'l-jama'at al-islamiyya fi al-hayah al-siyasiyya al-misriyya*, pp. 132–7.

63 Muhammad 'Izzat Hasan, 'Ila al-amam ila al-amam al-Ikhwan al-Muslimun fi'l-midan', *JIM*, no. 4, 1356/1937, p. 6.

64 *JIM*, no. 4, 1356/1937, pp. 1–2 and *JIM*, no. 1, 1356/1937, editorial.

65 Hasan al-Banna, 'Ila akh 'Izzat Effendi li-sahib al-fadilat al-Murshid al-'Amm', *JIM*, no. 23, 1356/1937, editorial. For an article by Muhammad 'Izzat Hasan, see 'Makan Filastin min al-Ikhwan al-Muslimin', *JIM*, no. 22, 1356/1937, p. 12.

66 Hasan al-Banna, 'Khatwatuna al-thaniya', *al-Nadhir*, no. 1, 1357/1938, editorial.

67 See, for example, *al-Nadhir*, no. 6, 1357/1938, p. 13.

68 'Mudhakkirat 'an al-da'wa wa al-da'iya', *JIMY*, no. 501, 1367/1947 and 'Bayan min al-Maktab al-Irshad al-'Amm', *al-Nadhir*, no. 4, 1357/1938.
69 These two were Ahmad Rif'at and Sadiq Amin. See 'Takdhib isha'a', *al-Nadhir*, no. 34, 1357/1939, p. 26.
70 Muhammad Ibrahim Disuqi, 'Lam yu'addi risalatahum', *al-Nadhir*, no. 25, 1357/1938.
71 Hasan al-Banna, 'Fi samim al-da'wa', *al-Nadhir*, no. 34, 1357/1938, p. 11.
72 *JIM*, no. 4, 1356/1937, pp. 1–2.
73 'Abd al-Halim, *al-Ikhwan al-Muslimun: ahdath sana'at tarikh*, p. 126.
74 *al-Nadhir*, no. 33, 1357/1939, editorial and p. 25.
75 *al-Nadhir*, no. 35, 1357/1939, pp. 19–20. The issue of a revolution in Egypt generated by the horrendous social inequality had been raised before. See, for example, Hasan al-Banna, 'Mudhakkirat al-Ikhwan al-Muslimin', *al-Nadhir*, no. 7, 1357/1938, editorial.
76 *al-Ahram*, 1939, p. 11 and *al-Nadhir*, no. 8, 1358/1939, p. 14.
77 *Taqrir ijmali khass*, pp. 19–26.
78 *al-Nadhir*, no. 9, 1358/1939, editorial; *al-Nadhir*, no. 19, 1357/1938, editorial; and *al-Nadhir*, no. 26, 1357/1938, p. 11.
79 *Mudh.*, p. 291.
80 Hasan al-Banna, 'Wajibat al-Ikhwan fi'l-'adat wa'l-libas wa'l-manzar', *al-Nadhir*, no. 23, 1358/1939, editorial.
81 'Abd al-Halim, *al-Ikhwan al-Muslimun: ahdath sana'at tarikh*, pp. 212–13.
82 *al-Minhaj*, pp. 7–8 and *al-Ikhwan al-Muslimun: al-mu'tamar al-dawri al-sadis*.
83 Abdel Nasser, *Britain and the Egyptian Nationalist Movement*, p. 42.
84 Security Summary (Middle East), no. 119, 19 February 1943, WO 208/1562/SSME.
85 'Abd al-Halim, *al-Ikhwan al-Muslimun: ahdath sana'at al-tarikh*, pp. 219–20.
86 Abu Hamid, 'Ula'ik alladhin hada Allah', *al-Ta'aruf*, no. 4, 1940, p. 9.
87 Muhammad 'Abd al-Hamid Ahmad, 'Min wahi al-Ikhwa', *al-Ta'aruf*, no. 4, 1940, p. 4.
88 Interview with Jamal al-Banna, spring 1995.
89 'Abd al-Halim, *al-Ikhwan al-Muslimun: ahdath sana'at al-tarikh*, p. 312.
90 See, for example, Hasan al-Banna, 'Hadhihi al-harb al-mubaraka. A-la nastafid min barakatiha?', *al-Ta'aruf*, no. 21, 1940.
91 See, for example, Appendix to Security Summary (Middle East), no. 447, 27 February 1941, WO 208/1560/SSME.
92 Lampson to FO, no. 787, 29 March 1941, FO 371/27429.
93 'The Ikhwan al Muslimin reconsidered', 10 December 1942, FO 141/838, p. 2.
94 Mitchell, *The Society of the Muslim Brothers*, p. 21 and p. 23. For a reliable source on the dates of Hasan al-Banna's transfer, see Jamal al-Banna, *Khitabat Hasan al-Banna al-shabb ila abihi*, pp. 133–5.
95 'The Ikhwan al Muslimin reconsidered', 10 December 1942, FO 141/838, p. 2.

96 Appendix to Security Summary (Middle East), no. 456, 10 March 1941, WO 208/1560/SSME. Dar al-Watha'iq, Taqarir al-Amn/Taqarir Hikmadariyyat Bulis Misr (sirri siyasi), no. 398 and no. 469, 23 March 1941.

97 Abu al-Nasr, *Haqiqat al-khilaf bayn al-Ikhwan al-Muslimin wa 'Abd al-Nasir*, pp. 33–6.

98 Haykal, *Mudhakkirat fi al-siyasa al-misriyya*, pp. 177–8.

99 Jamal al-Banna, *Khitabat Hasan al-Banna al-shabb ila abihi*, pp. 135–7. Charles Tripp's account is obviously erroneous when he writes that " . . . within *a few weeks* al-Banna returned to Cairo . . ." (italics added). See Tripp, 'Ali Maher and the Palace politics', p. 234.

100 Appendix to Security Summary (Middle East), no. 495, 29 April 1941, WO 208/1560/SSME.

101 Dar al-Watha'iq, Taqarir al-Amn/Taqarir Hikimadariyyat Bulis Misr (sirri siyasi), no. 1058, 10 June 1941.

102 'The Ikhwan al Muslimin reconsidered', 10 December 1942, FO 141/838, p. 2.

103 *Ibid.*

104 *Ibid.*

105 The visit of the Minister of Supply to Hasan al-Banna in the Zaytun prison is referred to in Ahmad Husayn's testimony at the Muslim Brothers' trial in 1949 as well as in several security reports. See Bayumi, *al-Ikhwan al-Muslimun wa'l-jama'at al-islamiyya fi'l-hayah al-siyasiyya al-misriyya*, p. 98.

106 Appendix to Security Summary (Middle East), no. 4, 12 December 1941, WO 208/1560/SSME.

107 Tripp, 'Ali Maher and the Palace politics', p. 236.

108 Cairo to FO, no. 3570, 14 November 1941, FO 371/27434.

109 Security Summary (Middle East), no. 5, 16 December 1941, WO 208/1560/SSME.

110 'The Ikhwan al Muslimin reconsidered', 10 December 1942, FO 141/838, p. 2.

111 Security Summary (Middle East), no. 8, 24 December 1941, WO 208/1560/SSME; Security Summary (Middle East), no. 11, 5 January 1942, WO 208/1561/SSME; Security Summary (Middle East), no. 13, 17 January 1942, WO 208/1561/SSME.

112 Tripp, 'Ali Maher and Palace politics', pp. 236–7 and 'The Ikhwan al Muslimin reconsidered', 10 December 1942, FO 141/838, p. 3.

113 Security Summary (Middle East), no. 20, 12 February 1942, WO 208/1561/SSME.

114 Security Summary (Middle East), no. 22, 20 February 1942, WO 208/1561/SSME and Lampson to FO, no. 711, 5 March 1942, FO 371/31569.

115 'The Ikhwan al Muslimin reconsidered', 10 December 1942, FO 141/838, p. 4.

116 Security Summary (Middle East), no. 34, 7 April 1942, WO 208/1561/SSME and Security Summary (Middle East), no. 40, 27 April 1942, WO 208/1561/SSME.

117 'First fortnightly meeting with Amin Osman Pacha held at the Embassy' (Secret), 18 May 1942, FO 141/838.

118 Hasan al-Banna's accommodationist policies were particularly evident during the Wafdist ministry in 1942–4. For this he had to make exceptional efforts to control his unruly followers who advocated a more aggressive policy towards the government and the British. See, for example, Security Summaries (Middle East), nos. 102 and 105, 7 and 17 December 1942, WO 208/1561/SSME and Security Summaries (Middle East), nos. 122 and 126, 8 March and 5 April 1943, WO 208/1562/SSME.

119 'The Ikhwan al Muslimin reconsidered', 14 December 1942, FO 141/838.

120 *Ibid.*

121 Recent memoirs by a previous member of the Secret Apparatus state that although they made plans for the assassination of Ahmad Mahir Pasha, the assassin, Mahmud al-'Isawi, acted first. However, other studies claim that Mahmud al-'Isawi, though officially a member of the Nationalist Party, in reality belonged to the Muslim Brothers. See al-Sabbagh, *Haqiqat al-tanzim al-khass wa dawruhu fi da'wat al-Ikhwan al-Muslimin*; Ramadan, *al-Ikhwan al-Muslimun wa al-tanzim al-sirri*, pp. 57–9; and Khayri Tal'at, *al-Ightiyalat wa'l-'unf al-siyasi fi Misr 1882–1952* (Minya, Dar Hira', 1991), pp. 234–5.

122 Steve Negus, 'Military trials degenerate further', *Middle East Times*, vol. 13, no. 47, 19–25 November 1995.

Conclusion

The Muslim Brothers have usually been viewed in varying degrees as an aggressive reassertion of religious traditionalism. Mitchell's work of 1969 viewed the Society as a "defender of tradition" and a movement of "conservative transition" which only reluctantly and perhaps even unconsciously had had to come to terms with some of the elements of the modern Western world.[1] Though he refuted the common assumption that "any references to modern Western developments" were automatically excluded, "the Society's hallmark on the Egyptian scene" was identified as "rigidity and puritanism". The "call to return to Islam was vitiated by a sterility born of obedience to inherited forms".[2] This religious conservatism, according to Mitchell, was coupled with intolerance as well as militant and violent means of enforcement. His study focused heavily on the question of violence. Although he stressed the relevance of socio-economic pressure, the presence of a colonial power and the malfunctioning of the political system, he identified "the sense of mission" as the main cause of the Society's involvement in political violence.[3] The "religious element generated . . . a self-righteous and intolerant arrogance which opened an unbridgeable gap between the Society and its fellow citizens", resulting in "a violence inspired by a social and religious exclusiveness".[4] Mitchell further reinforced the image of an authoritarian traditionalist movement by accentuating the importance of obedience, discipline and the venerated leader. These represented "the organizational dynamics" of the Society.[5] The fatal weakening of the movement in 1954 was described as "the ultimate consequence" of attempts to transform "a Society whose function was largely based on the spiritual and personal ties between the leader and the led to one in which the constitution suddenly emerged as relevant".[6] While not articulated as such, Mitchell's thesis conforms with the widely accepted view of the Muslim Brothers as a pathological and xenophobic response to the process of secularization, Westernization and modernization.

The findings of this book represent a radical breach with this traditional view. They indicate that the rise of the Muslim Brothers in the 1930s was an essential part of the rise of modern mass politics in Egypt, and not an aggressive reassertion of religious traditionalism. The Muslim Brothers represented a growing and self-conscious Muslim middle or lower middle class. By addressing the latter's demands for political participation, socio-economic reforms as well as religious renewal the Muslim Brothers became the spokesmen for disenchanted young men who had been alienated by the traditional political parties, which were controlled and manipulated by the ruling élite. Initially an Islamic welfare society, the Muslim Brothers from the early 1930s began to reinterpret Islam and traditional religious values as a basis for their demands for political participation and programmes for reform. The pillar of the Society's growth was not the appeal of religious traditionalism. This is evidenced by the predominant *effendia* character of the movement in addition to its failure to win a significant following at al-Azhar. The Brothers' appeal was instead linked to their ability to distance themselves from the image of religious reactionism (*raj'iyya*) which was the hallmark of the Islamic establishment at that time. The Society's steady expansion was based on ideological appeal, modern organization and the interests of the lower middle class. By virtue of its organizational efficiency, mass following and lower-middle-class character, the Society became the first non-élite political force to challenge the ruling classes in Egypt. These elements were the most fundamental reasons behind the rise of the Muslim Brothers.

The attention given to the development of human resources was fundamental to the rapid expansion of the Muslim Brothers. In the late 1920s the idea of educating "sincere youth propagandists" had already taken shape in Hasan al-Banna's mind. The education of cadres began in Ismailia at the School of Moral Discipline where members underwent an "Islamic study programme", including practical training in preaching. By the mid-1930s the training of cadres became more systematic and delegations of propagandists began touring the countryside and disseminated the Society's ideas in local mosques. The Society's Rover Scout formations, which were founded in Ismailia, were expanded and became important vehicles in attracting new adherents by their frequent parades and recruiting tours in the provinces and lower-class districts. The Battalions, established in 1937, served as an inner circle of initiated members and aimed to produce a more complete dedication to the principles of the Society. The class of cadres was indispensable to the Society's impressive proselytizing capacities, and the efficiency of the Society's pro-Palestine campaign testifies to the importance of this class.

The successful education of cadres was linked inextricably to a fundamental principle in the Society's organization: promotion based on merit, achievement and dedication, not on social status and prestige. Considering the hierarchical structure of Egyptian society at the time and the omnipresence of patron–client networks, one cannot understate the importance of this principle. As has been shown, this principle was firmly integrated in the organizational structure of the Society and served to attract members from the lower middle classes. It preserved the non-élite character of the movement and stimulated an enterprising spirit which permeated the Society.

A successful point in the Muslim Brothers' propaganda was their professed non-reliance on government subsidies or funds from other political groups. The Muslim Brothers raised funds by subscriptions, internal fund-raising and donations from local sympathizers. Only in the latter half of the 1930s did some of branches begin to receive subsidies from local municipals. Funds were also received from some politicians and in 1938–9 from German and exiled Palestinian sources. However, these funds never became indispensable to the Society's economy, and the Muslim Brothers' organization did not collapse when a patron deserted them, as was often the case of weak political groups. Funds were forthcoming from the Society's dedicated cadres as well as the membership at large. For example, the "First Pioneers" campaign of 1938, in which around £E400 was collected from the monthly salaries of the cadres, demonstrates the Society's financial independence.

The non-élite character of the Society was further enhanced by its policy to establish and maintain relations with the local aristocracy and members of the ruling élite which was spelled out in the latter half of the 1930s. An ideological basis for the Society's relations with all other political and religious bodies was defined, and initiated members (mainly from the Battalions) were instructed to make contacts with and try to win the support of members of the élite whose patronage would be of benefit to the Society. At the same time the principle of "the avoidance of the hegemony of notables and elders" was maintained through the establishment of separate honorific bodies in the organization for influential sympathizers. These measures as well as the Society's ideological commitment and financial self-sufficiency accounted for its relative independence from traditional patronage networks.

This study has shown that Hasan al-Banna's leadership of the Society displayed elements of charismatic authority, and that his extraordinary qualities undoubtedly inspired a certain amount of personal veneration among some of his more enthusiastic followers. However, the importance of his leadership has probably been overstated. We have seen that the expansion of branches was a locally initiated process rather than a result of al-Banna's personal proselytizing. We have also seen a number of examples of open opposition to al-Banna's policies inside the Society. Thus, the widely accepted view of blind obedience and unqualified authority cannot readily be accepted. His leadership made an appeal by embodying the virtues of the lower middle class, such as thriftiness and an austere lifestyle. Al-Banna focused almost unilaterally on dedication and productive work as criteria for the attainment of position in the Society, as opposed to traditionally accepted norms such as social standing, "names and titles". The fact that he avoided the traditional role of the political leader, and also his modest social background, introduced a new element into Egyptian political life. He represented a new kind of leader who demanded a following not by virtue of his social position, family background or political contacts, but because of his "mission" and personal dedication to fulfilling it. Thus, in secular terms, his was an authority based on personal qualifications and ideology. This represented an important breach with the established norms of traditional paternal authority.[7]

The modes of action which characterized the Muslim Brothers' political involvement in the 1930s were highly modern. Their committees, petitions, press campaigns, pamphleteering, propaganda tours, mass demonstrations, and so on, were manifestations of the rise of mass politics as opposed to a reassertion of religious traditionalism. Furthermore, their political activism represented a breach with the sedate meetings of notables which dominated Egyptian political life. More importantly, modern methods of political propaganda were applied in the traditional settings of mosques, provincial villages and "popular" city quarters where politics was regarded as the preserve of the élite. Thus, in defiance of the élite's political exclusivism, the Muslim Brothers brought politics to traditionalist and politically unconscious classes and thereby broadened the basis for political participation.

The politicization of Islam was one of the Society's most fundamental ideological characteristics. Hasan al-Banna's interest in politics was first evident in the late 1920s when he printed and distributed a petition on educational reforms. The Society's politicization was initiated in the aftermath of its first internal crisis in 1931–2. The provision of political non-involvement, which all Islamic welfare societies included in their general laws, was dropped. The Society's objective was defined in terms of "achieving the nation's goals and ambitions", and not in merely providing welfare for a local community of Muslims by building charitable institutions. As seen in Chapter 7, al-Banna called for a "liberation of Islam". Islam as understood by the Muslim Brothers conferred the right to political participation on every Muslim, and the Society's reinterpretation of Islam imposed a duty on them to confront and "correct erring rulers". Islam was also understood as a revolt against the traditional submissiveness of the politically excluded Muslim masses.

The Muslim Brothers were unequivocal in their denunciation of the political practice of the notable-dominated parties. The Society's rejection of partyism and party politics was closely linked to its claim to represent an "objective" ideological programme which transcended all personal and familial interests. The Muslim Brothers repeatedly submitted proposals for reform to the ruling élites, and pledged to be fully committed to their ideological programme regardless of changing governments and external pressure. Although this principle of non-partyism was sometimes disregarded, the strong reactions which any deviation from this principle provoked (see Chapter 8) show how highly this principle was regarded by the members.

Social justice became an integral part of the Society's ideology. Contrary to what has been previously assumed, the Society had developed a programme for political, social and economic reforms by the latter half of the 1930s. This programme was based on the interests of the lower classes, especially the educated lower middle class, and the Society's commitment to social reform was also demonstrated in its expanding social and educational work.

Despite the vicissitudes of Egyptian politics in the latter half of the 1930s and during the Second World War, the Society grew rapidly.

This suggests a much greater independence from the dominant political forces than has usually been assumed. Indeed, the section about the Society's relations with Ali Mahir Pasha, the Royal Councillor, and Shaykh al-Azhar al-Maraghi (who are universally accepted as the Society's main patrons in this period) shows that these relations did not prevent the Society from ridiculing fundamental elements in the political strategy of these two: the "Islamic image" of the King and his Caliphate ambitions. Furthermore, the Muslim Brothers repeatedly rejected proposals for a merger with the Young Egypt Party to form a unified pro-Palace party. The Society also harshly criticized Ali Mahir's ministry for its failure to enact social and military reforms. This unwillingness to serve as a loyal client was reciprocated by police surveillance and restrictions, most clearly demonstrated by the government's revocation of permission to publish *al-Manar* in 1939. In Chapter 8, it was seen that the secessionists in Muhammad's Youth were opposed to Hasan al-Banna's political accommodationism, not his alleged pro-Palace stance. These findings strongly suggest that the Society's dependence on patrons and politicians was limited. The Society refused to accept the traditional role of client in Egyptian politics. It skilfully expanded its own network of contacts while slowly but steadily building a power base of its own. This made the Muslim Brothers the first major political force in Egypt to be controlled by non-élites, a quality which was of fundamental importance to the Society's appeal.

As has been repeatedly stressed throughout this book, the success of the Muslim Brothers was in no small measure linked to the class interests of certain segments of Egyptian society. The unwillingness or inability of the traditional political parties to co-opt lower-middle-class elements to a large extent accounts for the Society's successful recruitment of this class. By heavily emphasizing the need for comprehensive reforms, social welfare and ideological commitment, the Muslim Brothers became spokesmen of an increasingly disgruntled middle class who saw its interests being steadily undermined by deteriorating economic conditions and a regime which excluded them from the political process. By bringing these groups into the political landscape and acting as a mouthpiece for their interests, the Muslim Brothers were de facto a democratizing element in Egyptian society, despite occasional anti-democratic outbursts in their propaganda. The Society's role as a spokesman for non-élite groups was strongly reinforced by its growing grass-roots activities in the educational and social field. The Muslim Brothers represented a modernizing force which did not shun the backwardness and the discomfort of provincial villages and "popular" city quarters as did many of their political opponents. The illiteracy campaigns, the founding of hospitals and evening schools, the organization of *zakah* and social cooperatives were fruits of an enterprising spirit which permeated the organization of the Muslim Brothers. These practical efforts to produce lasting changes for the lower echelons of society bear little resemblance to the spirit which Mitchell identified as "violence inspired by a social and religious exclusiveness".[8] This brings us to the question of political violence which has dominated the debate on the Muslim Brothers.

As has been shown, the Society had assumed a strongly anti-imperialistic character by the mid-1930s. In the course of the campaign for the Palestinians the Society proved itself as one of the most fervently anti-colonial forces in Egypt. However, as discussed in Chapter 8, the Muslim Brothers were not prepared to embark on a revolutionary course. It appears that the military wing was devised to contain the militants and to perpetuate the anti-imperialist image of the Society. Although strong demands for a radical and perhaps revolutionary course were coming from the ranks of the Society's cadres, the leadership tried to restrain rather than encourage these sentiments. These findings suggest a reappraisal of the Society's role in the political violence and assassinations of the postwar years and especially the widely accepted belief that the Society instigated violence and created an atmosphere in which violence was encouraged. Considering the fact that these tragic events took place more than 17 years after the foundation of the Society and involved only a small group of members from an estimated total membership of 500,000, one is inclined to think that the political violence was in the main acts of disobedience on the radical fringes rather than a sponsored policy in the Society as a whole.

The Muslim Brothers' relationship with the traditional religious forces in Egypt has also been examined in this study. As we have seen, al-Banna's choice of education, his preaching in coffee-shops and his conflicts with the religious élite in Ismailia gave an early warning of the Society's challenge to the conservative Islam of al-Azhar. The failure to achieve a student following at al-Azhar and the strong *effendia* character of the articulate segment of the movement further indicate that the Muslim Brothers were not associated with religious conservatism. The Brothers' youth preachers represented a new element in the Egyptian religious landscape, and they soon faced opposition from the traditional religious élite who felt that the Society was undermining their authority. The challenge to religious conservatism was also evident in al-Banna's earliest religious tracts in which he severely censured the Islamic establishment for its inability to communicate Islam to the Egyptian youth. The Society's profound commitment to religious renewal went beyond theological debate by addressing the practical and mundane problems of modern Muslims. A crucial point was the abandonment of theological disputes and the acceptance of minor differences in religious questions. This was coupled with a conscious pragmatism which allowed for the adoption of aspects of Sufism as well as beneficial aspects of "all other missions". The Muslim Brothers were considerably more open to Western innovations and influences than has usually been assumed and should not be lumped together with the doctrinaire Salafiyya societies, such as the Society for Religious Legality (al-Jam'iyya al-Shar'iyya) which embodied religious rigidity in the 1930s. The Muslim Brothers' pledge to develop a comprehensive ideology based on Islam meant that a lasting process of renewal was initiated in which religion was related to the modern age and all aspects of modern life. This process of "practical reinterpretation" was initiated in the early 1930s by professing that Islam was an all-inclusive societal system and culminated in the politicization of Islam in 1938 which became the core of the Society's ideology. More than any other theological reinterpretation of Islam, this has secured the relevance of Islam for modern generations, and it is probably not an overstatement to say that al-Banna's reinterpretation of Islam will remain the most far-reaching Islamic renewal this century.

This study has questioned a number of traditional views of the early history of the Muslim Brothers. In particular it has refuted the widely held belief that the Muslim Brothers were a product of deplorable societal conditions, an alien element or the manifestation of a sick society. The conception of Islamism as "societal cancer" is as widespread and deeply embedded in Western minds as is the belief in Egypt that Islamism is sponsored from the "outside" (for example, by the Palace and the British in pre-revolutionary Egypt and by Iran today). What this study has sought to demonstrate is how a strong belief in the ability of non-élite groups to force the ruling establishment to accommodate their needs was transformed into a political mass movement. Gradually the project of forming a new political–religious movement materialized, based on the reinterpretation of traditionalist values. The findings of this book point to the need for a study of the mechanisms of grass-roots mobilization. There exists no comprehensive study of the social, educational and economic welfare projects of the Muslim Brothers in the pre-revolutionary period, not even in Arabic. This task should be given higher priority than studies of the Society's ideology of which there are already many. The discussion on the differences between the Salafiyya societies and the Muslim Brothers should encourage a comparative study of the Muslim Brothers and other Islamic groups. This may shed interesting light on the social–religious setting in which the Muslim Brothers operated. More importantly, scholars should devote more attention to the process in which Islamists and Islamist movements absorb and integrate modern principles and ideas within their ideological framework, instead of analysing Islamism within a paradigm which a priori counterpoises Islamism with so-called "Western values" (whatever they may be). This process of the adoption of modern ideas cannot be studied merely by textual analysis of isolated ideological tracts. More attention should be given to the political practice, organization and activities of Islamist movements. Such an approach may yield new results about why Islamism has such a remarkable endurance despite recurring cycles of repression by the regimes in the Middle East.

NOTES

1 Mitchell, *The Society of the Muslim Brothers*, p. 331.
2 *Ibid.*, p. 325.
3 *Ibid.*, pp. 320–31.
4 *Ibid.*, p. 319.
5 *Ibid.*, pp. 295–306.
6 *Ibid.*, p. 303.
7 Yunan Labib Rizq, 'Bayn al-mawdu'iyya wa'l-tahazzub fi kitabat tarikh al-ahzab al-siyasiyya fi Misr' in Ahmad 'Abd Allah (ed.), *Tarikh Misr bayn al-manhaj al-'ilmi wa al-sira' al-hizbi*, pp. 363–4.
8 Mitchell, *The Society of the Muslim Brothers*, p. 319.

Glossary of Arabic Terms

'alim (pl. *'ulama'*): scholar of the Islamic religious traditions who has graduated from one of the great mosque academies, such as al-Azhar University in Egypt, and is therefore a qualified interpreter of the Qur'an, *Sunna* and the stipulations of Islamic laws.

al-'alimiyya: learnedness, scholarliness; a rank of scholarship, conferred by diploma, of al-Azhar University and the Great Mosque in Tunis.

wali (pl. *awliya*): "friends of God".

amir al-mu'minin: (lit. "Commander of the Faithful"). Often used as an equivalent to caliph.

a'yan: a loose term usually denoting village notables of some wealth and standing.

basha (pl. *bashawat*): pasha, title awarded by the King to members of the aristocracy. Usually associated with the pre-revolutionary élite of large landowners in Egypt.

bay'a: traditionally an oath of allegiance or fealty to a sovereign. This term was used for the oath of loyalty taken by the chiefs and lords of the tribes before the Caliph, and formally involved the mutual taking of hands as well as the swearing of an oath of obedience and submission. *Bay'a* is also the oath of allegiance sworn by a disciple (*murid*) to the head of a Sufi order (*shaykh*).

bid'a: unlawful innovations; deviation from Islamic tradition.

khalifa (caliph): to Sunni Muslims this title denotes the successor of Muhammad as leader of the Islamic community.

da'wa: (lit. "call" or "the call to Islam"). This signifies missionary and propaganda works and proselytization in order to spread and confirm the message of Islam. In Muslim Brothers vocabulary, the term usually meant the Society's principles and ideas.

dhikr: (lit. "mentioning", "citing"). In the context of Sufism, a litany consisting of the glorification of the names of God, selections from the Qur'an and special prayers. Public communal *dhikr*s are often performed by members of Sufi orders in the larger mosques and generally entail specific bodily postures and movements, as well as varied breathing techniques, while uttering the formulae and sacred names.

effendi (pl. *effendia*): gentleman (when referring to non-Westerners wearing Western clothes and the fez or *tarboush*). In pre-revolutionary Egypt the *effendia* denoted civil servants and white-collar employees from the middle classes, educated at non-religious faculties and schools.

fatwa (pl. *fatawi*): a formal religio-juridic verdict or a legal opinion issued by a recognized Islamic scholar (*mufti*).

fiqh: Islamic jurisprudence, religious laws.

fitna (pl. *fitan*): sedition/discord as caused by misleading ideas that result in social disorder and strife. It also denotes the first civil strife in the Muslim community following the Prophet Muhammad's death in AD 632. The "history book" of the Muslim Brothers, Mahmud Abd al-Halim's memoirs, uses this term with reference to the internal conflicts in the Society.

hadith: (lit. "conversation" or "narration"). A story in which some act or saying of the Prophet Muhammad is recorded. Ideally, the *hadith* should go back to an actual eyewitness who was present at the time, and whose exact words are scrupulously reported, as well as the exact words uttered by the Prophet.

hadra: (lit. "presence"). A Sufi gathering.

hajj: the pilgrimage to Mecca, one of the five pillars of Islam or duties incumbent on all adult Muslims.

hijra: emigration of Muhammad from Mecca to Medina in AD 622 (or in year 0 in the Islamic calendar), where he established the first Muslim community state.

'id al-adha: (lit. "feast of sacrifice"). The most important Muslim feast, which takes place on the last day of the *hajj*.

'id al-fitr: (lit. "festival of the breaking of the fast"). An important Muslim feast at the end of the month of Ramadan.

'id al-isra' wa'l-mi'raj (*al-isra*): the annual celebration of the Prophet Muhammad's Midnight Journey to the Seven Heavens on 27 Rajab.

Ikhwan: brethren or brotherhood. Here, it means the Muslim Brothers (*al-Ikhwan al-Muslimun*).

imam: leader, religious and sometimes political. Usually, it denotes a prayer leader in the mosque. It has, however, numerous connotations, all revolving around the idea of "leadership". As a title, it may refer to the individual who leads the communal prayer in a mosque, a renowned religious teacher or scholar, for example the founders of the four orthodox schools of Islamic law, or even the Caliph himself.

Among the Shiites, with their much greater emphasis on the theocratic aspects of the supreme Islamic office, the term *imam* is used instead of caliph.

Islam: lit. "submission to the will of God".

jihad: (lit. "earnest effort"). In Islamic law, the so-called "holy war" is the only kind of war since war between Muslims is forbidden. Because Islam in the early days aimed at universal dominion, *jihad* was a communal obligation which had to be fulfilled by subjection and conversion of the non-Muslim world. Christians and Jews, referred to as "People of the Book", were allowed to retain their religion if they submitted to the rule of Islam and agreed to pay the *jizya* (a tax for Christians and Jews). Theoretically, all other people who could be designated "idolaters" were compelled to accept Islam, slavery, or extinction. Largely conceived of as offensive, *jihad* could be defensive if the domain of Islam was threatened by an external enemy.

khatib: preacher who delivers the sermon (*khutba*) in the mosque on Fridays. (It also has other meanings such as suitor, speaker or orator.)

kibar al-a'yan: members of the national élite considered significantly above the *a'yan* or notables of some local influence. They were recruited to parliament and the higher ministerial posts.

kuttab: a Qur'an school. It was usually the lowest elementary school in Egyptian villages.

madhhab: recognized school of Islamic jurisprudence. Sunni Islam has four schools of Islamic jurisprudence: al-Maliki, al-Shafi'i, al-Hanafi and al-Hanbali.

ma'dhun: traditionally an official authorized by the Muslim judge, the *qadi*, to perform civil marriages.

mahdi: divinely guided leader who is to come in the future to establish God's rule on earth, a socially just society.

muezzin (or *mu'adhdhin*): announcer of the hour of prayer.

mufti: specialist on Islamic law competent to deliver a *fatwa* or legal interpretation.

munkarat: reprehensible and forbidden actions.

musnad: a compilation of traditions or *hadith* which can be traced in ascending order to its first authority.

qahwa (pl. *qahawi*) (colloq.): Turkish coffee or a traditional Egyptian coffee-shop.

qasida (pl. *qasa'id*): an ancient Arabic poem having as a rule a rigid tripartite structure.

qibla: the direction faced by Muslims at prayer – towards Mecca.

qunut: a special prayer which is offered when calamities have befallen Muslims.

sadaqa: voluntary charity for the poor.

salah: prayer of worship observed five times daily.

salat 'id al-fitr: the prayer during *'id al-fitr*.

Salafiyya: the upholders of the tradition represented by the "Great Ancestors", the "Fathers of the Muslim Community". A religious reform movement initiated by Muhammad Abduh in Egypt at the turn of the century. It advocated religious renewal and reinterpretation by returning to the pristine Islam of the Prophet and the first generations of Muslims. In the 1930s, the term "Salafiyya societies" (*jam'iyyat salafiyya*) usually denoted the Society of Religious Legality (al-Subkiyya or al-Jam'iyya al-Shar'iyya) and the Society of Supporters of Muhammad's Tradition (Jam'iyyat Ansar al-Sunna al-Muhammadiyya). These societies were associated with religious rigidity and hatred of Sufism and popular Islam.

Shi'a: originally "the party of Ali", who believed that leadership of the Muslim community after the Prophet Muhammad should have passed to Ali, the Prophet's cousin and son-in-law. Today, it is the largest religious minority in Islam. Most Shiites live in Iran, Lebanon, Tadzhikistan, Azerbaijan and Bahrain.

shura: usually unbinding consultation sought by the ruler from colleagues or scholars, or in the modern interpretation, from the people.

Sunna: (lit. "beaten path", "clear-cut way"). By analogy, the customary law and folkways of a people or tribe, for example the *Sunna* of the pre-Islamic Bedouins. In Islam, the *Sunna* is the beliefs and practices of the Prophet and the Companions, whose living examples thus became a commentary on the Qur'an and its ethical and legal prescriptions, and therefore the models for all Muslims after them.

'umda: the head of a village. He often acted as arbiter between the government authorities and the village community.

umma: community, either in an ethno-cultural or in a religious sense. Also used about "people" or "nation", although it traditionally refers to the community of Muslims.

zakah: an alms tax prescribed by Qur'anic decrees. An ordinary form of *zakah* is the *zakat al-fitr* which is the obligatory donation of foodstuffs at the end of Ramadan, the month of fasting. The *zakah* is a tithe which is usually 2.5 per cent of the value of the accumulated wealth and assets held for one year. It is not regarded as charity, since it is not really voluntary, but instead it is owed to the poor by those who have received their wealth as a trust from God's bounty.

Appendix I

The Growth of Branches in Egypt in 1928–1945

Surveys published in June 1937 and May 1940 classified the Society's branches in Egypt according to following standards:

(1) First degree (*al-daraja al-ula*): the branch had reached the stage of "complete formation" having acquired its own premises and all sub-groups having been formed, including an administration which supervised the affairs of the branch.

(2) Second degree (*al-daraja al-thaniya*): the branch had been established, but it still lacked some of the features characterizing first degree branches, such as not having its own premises or that some of the sub-groups were not yet formed.

(3) Third degree (*al-daraja al-thalitha*): the branch was "still in the process of being formed". The typical third degree branch was most probably only a group of persons who had pledged to establish a branch and had made contact with the MIA.

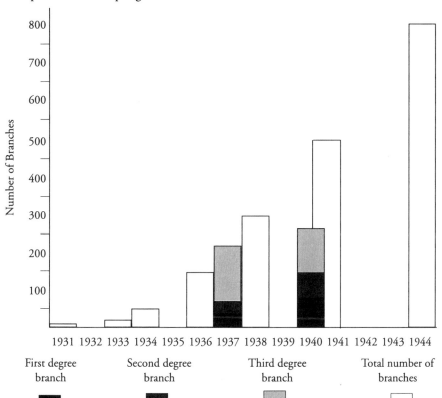

Appendix II

The Central Organization of the Muslim Brothers in 1940

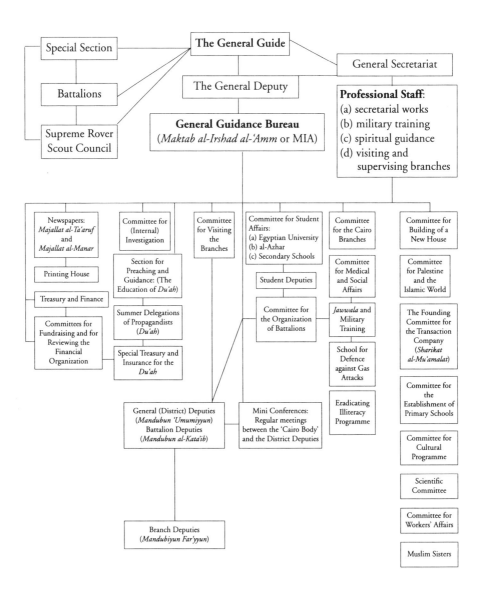

Appendix III

The Field Organization of the
Muslim Brothers in 1940

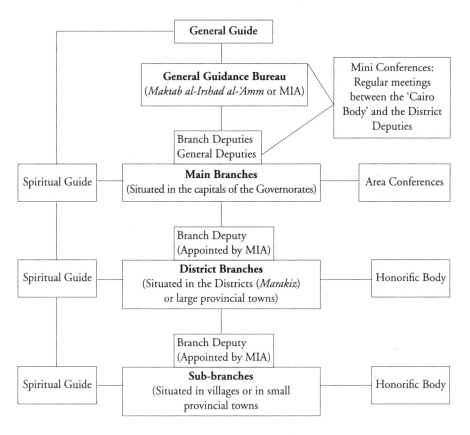

Organizational units in the branches:

| Du'ah (spreading the da'wa to neighbouring villages) | Committees: a) Treasury b) Secretariat c) supervision d) alms-giving e) fighting illiteracy f) lectures g) the house etc. | Athletic or Sports Units | Rover Scout Unit | Battalion |

Appendix IV

The Rover Scout Organization 1938–1940

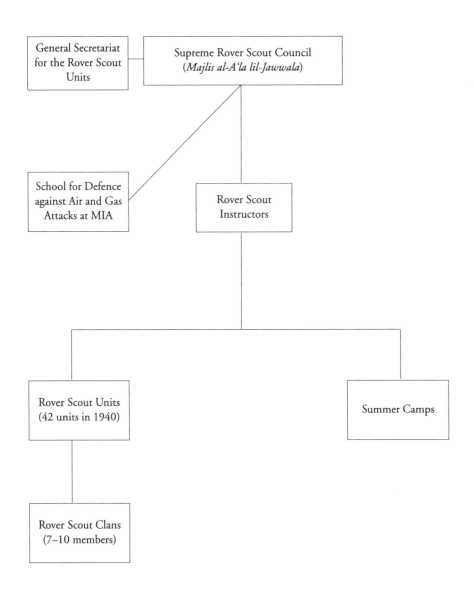

General Secretariat for the Rover Scout Units

Supreme Rover Scout Council
(*Majlis al-A'la lil-Jawwala*)

School for Defence against Air and Gas Attacks at MIA

Rover Scout Instructors

Rover Scout Units
(42 units in 1940)

Summer Camps

Rover Scout Clans
(7–10 members)

Appendix V

The Organization of the Muslim Brothers in 1935

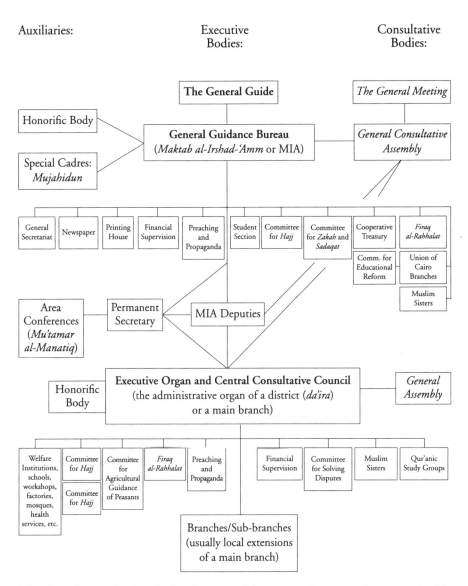

Auxiliaries:

Executive Bodies:

Consultative Bodies:

Most branch organizations had only some of these committees or sub-groups. A wide range of sub-groups and committees were founded and adapted to local idiosyncrasies. The above branch structure must be considered only as a general suggestion.

Bibliography

Unpublished Egyptian Sources and Archives

Archives

Dar al-Watha'iq, al-Hay'a al-'Amma lil-Kitab, Cairo:
(i) Qasr 'Abdin, *Iltimasat al-Ikhwan al-Muslimin* (Box 557)
    Qasr 'Abdin, *Iltimasat al-jam'iyyat al-diniyya* (Box 206)
(ii) *Taqarir al-amn al-'amm 1940–1*

Muslim Brothers Documents

Mudhakkira fi al-ta'lim al-dini [memorandum about religious education], Cairo, Matba'at al-Salafiyya, AH 1348/AD 1929.

Bayan mujaz: min Maktab al-Irshad al-'Amm bil-Qahira lil-Ikhwan al-Muslimin [a brief survey: from the General Guidance Bureau in Cairo to the Muslim Brothers], AH 1352/AD 1933.

Qanun Jam'iyyat al-Ikhwan al-Muslimin al-'amm [the general law of the Society of the Muslim Brothers], Cairo, Matba'at al-Ikhwan al-Muslimin, AH 1353/AD 1934.

Qanun Jam'iyyat al-Ikhwan al-Muslimin al-'amm al-mu'addal 1354h: mulhaqat [the general law of the Society of the Muslim Brothers as amended in AH 1354/AD 1935], Cairo, Matba'at al-Ikhwan al-Muslimin, AH 1354/AD 1935.

Kalimat mu'tamar talabat al-Ikhwan al-Muslimin [speeches at the student conference of the Muslim Brothers], AH 1356/AD 1937.

al-Minhaj: bayanat khassa [the programme: special announcements], AH 1357/ AD 1938.

Taqrir ijmali khass [a special comprehensive report], AH 1358/AD 1939.

al-Ikhwan al-Muslimun: al-mu'tamar al-dawri al-sadis [The Muslim Brothers: the sixth Periodic conference], AH 1359/AD 1940.

Qism al-Manatiq: nashra 'amma [section for the administrative areas: a general publication], AH 1363/AD 1943.

Qanun al-nizam al-asasi li-hay'at al-Ikhwan al-Muslimin [the basic law of the organization of the Muslim Brothers], AH 1364/AD 1944.

Pamphlet by the 1932 Secessionists
Taqrir marfu' lil-ra'i al-'amm al-isma'ili mubayyin fihi a'mal ra'is Jam'iyyat
  al-Ikhwan al-Muslimin [report submitted to the general public in
  Ismailia explaining the actions of the president of the Society of
  the Muslim Brothers], Zaqaziq, al-Matba'a al-Haditha, 1932.

Unpublished UK Sources

Archives
Public Record Office, London:
(i) Foreign Office:
    FO 141 (Egypt: Embassy and Consular Archives)
    FO 371 (General Correspondence)
(ii) War Office:
    WO 201 (Military Intelligence HQ, Middle East)
    WO 208 (Military Intelligence, Middle East and Egypt)

Theses
Coury, Ralph Moses. 'Abd al-Rahman Azzam and the development of
  Egyptian Arab nationalism', Ph.D. thesis, University of Princeton,
  1983.
Meijer, Roel. 'Contemporary Egyptian historiography of the period
  1936–1952: a study of its scientific character', MA dissertation,
  University of Amsterdam, 1985.
—'The quest for modernity: secular liberal and left-wing political thought
  in Egypt, 1945–1958', Ph.D. thesis, University of Amsterdam,
  1995.
Tripp, Charles. 'Ali Maher and the Palace politics 1936–1942', Ph.D.
  thesis, University of London, 1984.

Published Sources in Arabic

Newspapers and Journals
al-Ahram
al-Balagh

Jaridat al-Ikhwan al-Muslimin (JIM)
Jaridat al-Ikhwan al-Muslimin al-Yawmiyya (JIMY)
Jaridat Misr al-Fatah
al-Khulud
Majallat al-Da'wa
Majallat al-Fath
Majallat al-Ikhwan al-Muslimin
Majallat al-Manar
Majallat al-Nadhir (al-Nadhir)
Majallat al-Ta'aruf

Memoirs and Biographical Accounts
'Abd al-Halim, Mahmud. *Al-Ikhwan al-Muslimun: ahdath sana'at al-tarikh. Ru'ya min al-dakhil*, vol. 1, Alexandria, Dar al-Da'wa, 1979.

'Abd al-Khaliq, Farid. *Al-Ikhwan al-Muslimun fi mizan al-haqq*, Cairo, Dar al-Sahwa, 1987.

'Abd al-Ra'uf, 'Abd al-Mon'em. *Arghamtu Faruq 'ala al-tanazul 'an al-'arsh: Mudhakkirat 'Abd al-Mon'em 'Abd al-Ra'uf*, Cairo, al-Zahra' lil-I'lam al-'Arabi, 1988.

Abu al-Nasr, Muhammad Hamid. *Haqiqat al-khilaf bayn al-Ikhwan al-Muslimin wa 'Abd al-Nasir*, Cairo, International Press, 1987.

'Ashmawi, Hasan. *Al-Ayyam al-hasima wa hassaduha: janib min qissat al-'asr*, Cairo, Dar al-Tawzi' wa al-Nashr al-Islamiyya, 1991.

—*Hassad al-ayyam wa mudhakkirat harib: janib min qissat al-'asr*, Cairo, Dar al-Fath, 1992.

'Assaf, D. Mahmud. *Ma'a al-Imam al-Shahid Hasan al-Banna*, Cairo, Maktabat 'Ayn Shams, 1993.

al-'Assal, Fathi. *Hasan al-Banna kama 'ariftuhu*, Cairo, al-Maktaba al-Misriyya, 1952.

—*Al-Ikhwan al-Muslimun bayn 'ahdayn: qissat al-ifsad al-dini*, Cairo, Matabi' al-'Asima, 1992.

al-Baghdadi, 'Abd al-Latif. *Mudhakkirat 'Abd al-Latif al-Baghdadi*, Cairo, Maktab al-Misri al-Hadith, 1977.

Bahi, Muhammad. *Hayati fi rihab al-Azhar. Talib wa ustadh wa wazir*, Cairo, Matba'at al-Wahba, 1983.

al-Banna, 'Abd al-Basit. *Fi mawkab al-dhikra – taj al-islam wa malhamat al-Imam*, Cairo, n.d.

al-Banna, Hasan. *Mudhakkirat al-da'wa wa al-da'iya*, Cairo, Dar al-Tawzi' wa al-Nashr al-Islamiyya, 1986.

al-Baquri, Ahmad Hasan. 'Malamih al-dhikriyat', *al-Muslimun*, 6 April – 28 September 1985.

—*Baqaya dhikriyat*, Cairo, Markaz al-Ahram, lil-Tarjama wa al-Nashr, 1988.

al-Bass, Ahmad. *Al-Ikhwan al-Muslimun fi rif Misr*, Cairo, Dar al-Tawzi' wa al-Nashr al-Islamiyya, 1987.

al-Buhi, Muhammad Labib. *Ma'a al-Murshid al-'Amm lil-Ikhwan al-Muslimin*, Cairo, Dar al-Taba'a wa al-Nashr al-Islamiyya, 1946.

Dawh, Hasan. *Alam wa amal fi tariq al-Ikhwan al-Muslimin*, Cairo, Dar al-I'tisam, 1989.

al-Hajjaji, Ahmad Anis. *Ruh wa rayhan*, 2nd edn, Cairo, Maktabat Wahba, 1981.

—*al-Imam*, vol. 1, Cairo, Matba'at Wadi al-Muluk, 1950.

Hammuda, Husayn Muhammad Ahmad. *Asrar harakat al-Dubbat al-Ahrar wa'l-Ikhwan al-Muslimun*, Cairo, al-Zahra' lil-I'lam al-'Arabi, 1985.

Hawwa, Sa'id. *Hadhihi tajrubati wa hadhihi shahadati*, Beirut, Dar 'Ammar, 1988.

Haykal, Muhammad Hasanayn. *Mudhakkirat fi al-siyasa al-misriyya*, 2nd edn, vol. 2, Cairo, Dar al-Ma'arif, 1990.

al-Jarisi, Mahmud Hamdi. *Al-Islam yata'adda al-madhahib wa al-diyan*, Cairo, Dar al-Turath al-'Arabi, 1976.

al-Jindi, Ahmad Anwar. *Hasan al-Banna: hayat rajul wa tarikh madrasa*, Cairo, Dar al-Taba'a wa al-Nashr al-Islamiyya, 1365/1946.

Kamal, Ahmad 'Adil. *Al-Nuqat fawq al-huruf: al-Ikhwan al-Muslimun wa al-Nizam al-Khass*, 2nd edn, Cairo, al-Zahra' lil-I'lam al-'Arabi, 1989.

Labib, Mahmud. *Humat al-Sallum*, Cairo, Dar al-'Arabi, 1950.

al-Sabbagh, Mahmud. *Haqiqat al-tanzim al-khass wa dawruhu fi da'wat al-Ikhwan al-Muslimin*, Cairo, Dar al-I'tisam, 1989.

al-Samman, Muhammad 'Abbas. *Hasan al-Banna: al-rajul wa'l-fikra*, Cairo, Dar al-I'tisam, 1977.

Shadi, Salah. *Safahat min al-tarikh: hassad al-'umr*, Kuwait City, Sharikat al-Shi'a', 1981.

al-Sisi, 'Abbas. *Hasan al-Banna: mawaqif fi al-da'wa wa al-tarbiya*, Alexandria, Dar al-Da'wa, 1982.

—*Fi qafilat al-Ikhwan al-Muslimin*, 2nd edn, vol. 1, Alexandria, Iqra-Dar al-Taba'a wa al-Nashr wa al-Sawtiyyat, 1986.

al-Tilmisani, 'Umar. *Dhikriyat la mudhakkirat*, Cairo, Dar al-Tawzi' wa al-Nashr al-Islamiyya, 1985.

Collections of Hasan al-Banna's Letters, Speeches and Tracts
'Ashur, Ahmad 'Isa. *Hadith al-thulatha'*, Cairo, Dar al-Qu'ran, 1985.
al-Banna, Hasan. Anja' al-wasa'il fi tarbiyat al-nash' – tarbiya islamiyya khalisa' (lecture given by Hasan al-Banna in the YMMA club in Cairo, *c.* 1930) in Muhibb al-Din al-Khatib (ed.), *al-Muntaqa min muhadarat Jam'iyyat al-Shubban al-Muslimin*, vol. 2, Cairo, al-Matba'a al-Salafiyya, AH 1349/AD 1930.
—*Hal nahnu qawm 'amaliyun?*, al-Mansura, Dar al-Wafa' lil-Taba'a wa al-Nashr, n.d.
—*Ila al-shabab wa ila al-talaba khassatan*, Alexandria, Dar al-Da'wa lil-Tab'a wa al-Nashr wa al-Tawzi'*, n.d.
—*Ila al-tullab*, Cairo, Dar al-Nashr wa al-Tawzi' al-Islamiyya, n.d.
—*Majmu'at al-rasa'il lil-Imam al-Shahid Hasan al-Banna*, Beirut, al-Mu'assasa al-Islamiyya lil-Tiba'a wa'l-Sahafa wa'l-Nashr, n.d.
—*al-Ma'thurat*, Alexandria, Dar al-Da'wa, n.d.
al-Banna, Jamal. *Khitabat Hasan al-Banna al-shabb ila abihi*, Cairo, Dar al-Fikr al-Islami, 1990.
al-Mut'ani, 'Abd al-'Azim Ibrahim. *19 risala min Hasan al-Banna ila qiyadat al-da'wa al-islamiyya*, Cairo, Dar al-Ansar, 1979.

Arabic Secondary Sources
'Abbas, Ra'uf. 'Al-Ikhwan al-Muslimun wa'l-Injiliz', *Majallat Fikr lil-Dirasat wa'l-Abhath*, no. 8 (1985), pp. 144–58.
'Abd Allah, Ahmad (ed.). *Tarikh Misr bayn al-manhaj al-'ilmi and al-sira' al-hizbi* (collection of papers from a Cairo conference on Egyptian historiography in 1987), Cairo, Dar Shuhdi lil-Nashr, 1988.
Abu al-Nur, Sami. *Dawr al-qasr fi'l-hayah al-siyasiyya 1936–1952*, Cairo, Maktabat al-Madbuli, 1988.
al-'Adawi, Mustafa. *'Umar al-Tilmisani bayn hamasat al-shabab wa hikmat al-shuyukh*, Cairo, Dar al-Aqsa lil-Kitab, 1987.
Ahmad, Muhammad Hasan. *Al-Ikhwan al-Muslimun fi'l-mizan*, Cairo, Matba'at al-Akha', n.d.

'Arif, Jamil. *Safahat min al-mudhakkirat al-sirriyya li-awwal amin 'amm lil-Jami'a al-'arabiyya: 'Abd al-Rahman 'Azzam*, Cairo, al-Maktab al-Misri al-Hadith, 1977.

'Atiq, Wajih. *Al-Malik Faruq wa Almaniya al-naziyya: khamas sanawat min al-'alaqat al-sirriyya*, Cairo, Dar al-Fikr al-'Arabi, 1992.

al-Banna, Jamal. *Al-Da'wat al-islamiyya al-mu'asira ma laha wa ma 'alayha*, Cairo, Maktabat al-Islam, 1978.

—*Nahwa haraka niqabiyya muthaqqafa wa dawr al-kuttab fi dhalika*, Cairo, Dar al-Fikr al-Islami, 1990.

—*Mas'uliyyat fashl al-dawla al-islamiyya fi'l-'asr al-hadhith wa buhuth ukhra*, Cairo, Maktabat al-Islam, 1993.

Bayumi, Zakariyya Sulayman. *Al-Ikhwan al-Muslimun wa'l-jama'at al-islamiyya fi'l-hayah al-siyasiyya al-misriyya 1928–1948*, 2nd edn, Cairo, Maktabat Wahba, 1991.

al-Baz, Na'm. *Al-Baquri: tha'ir taht al-'amama*, Cairo, al-Hay'a al-'Amma al-Misriyya lil-Kitab, 1988.

al-Bishri, Tariq. *Al-Haraka al-siyasiyya fi Misr 1945–1952*, 2nd edn, Cairo, Dar al-Tawzi' wa al-Nashr al-Islamiyya, 1983.

—*Al-Muslimun wa'l-aqbat fi itar al-jama'a al-wataniyya*, 2nd edn, Cairo, Dar al-Shuruq, 1988.

—'Al-Sira' al-fikri wa atharuhu fi'l-iltizam wa'l-mawdu'iyya fi kitabat al-tarikh – dirasa fi bahth al-Ustadh Ahmad Sadiq Sa'd' in Ahmad 'Abd Allah, *Tarikh Misr bayn al-manhaj al-'ilmi wa al-sira' al-hizbi*, Cairo, Dar Shuhdi lil-Nashr, 1988.

Dawud, 'Abd al-'Aziz. *Al-Jam'iyyat al-islamiyya fi Misr wa dawruha fi nashr al-da'wa al-islamiyya*, Cairo, al-Zahra' lil-I'lam al-'Arabi, 1992.

Dissuqi, 'Asim. *Al-Fikra al-qawmiyya 'inda al-Ikhwan al-Muslimin 1928–1954*, Cairo, Matba'at Jami'at 'Ayn Shams, 1976.

Ghanim, Ibrahim al-Bayumi. *Al-Fikr al-siyasi lil-Imam Hasan al-Banna*, Cairo, Dar al-Tawzi' wa al-Nashr al-Islamiyya, 1992.

—'Al-Gharb fi ru'yat al-haraka al-islamiyya al-misriyya', *Majallat al-Qahira*, September 1993, pp. 58–69.

Haydar, Khalil 'Ali. *Adwa' 'ala mudhakkirat Hasan al-Banna*, Kuwait City, Sharika Kazima lil-Nashr wa al-Tarjama wa al-Tawzi', 1989.

Imam, 'Imad Jum'a. *Al-Baquri bayn al-Ikhwan wa al-thawra: hal khan al-Baquri al-Ikhwan al-Muslimin?*, Cairo, I. J. Imam, 1992.

'Isa, Salah. 'Al-Ikhwan al-Muslimun: ma' sat al-madi wa mushkilat al-mustaqbal' (introduction to the Arabic translation of Richard Mitchell, *The Society of the Muslim Brothers*) in *al-Ikhwan al-Muslimun*, Cairo, Maktabat al-Madbuli, 1977.

al-Jabari, 'Abd al-Mit'al. *Li-madha ughtil al-Imam al-Shahid Hasan al-Banna*, Cairo, Dar al-I'tisam, 1978.

al-Jami'i, 'Abd al-Mon'em Ibrahim. *Ittijahat al-kitaba al-tarikhiyya fi tarikh Misr al-hadith wa'l-mu'asir*, Cairo, 'Ein lil-Dirasat wa'l-Buhuth al-Insaniyya wa'l-Ijtima'iyya, 1994.

Jawhar, Sami. *Al-Samitun yatakallamun*, Cairo, al-Maktab al-Hadith, 1975.

al-Khatib, Muhammad 'Abd Allah. *Al-Ikhwan al-Muslimun tahta qabbat al-barlaman*, Cairo, Dar al-Tawzi' wa al-Nashr al-Islamiyya, 1991.

Mahdawi, Tariq. *al-Ikhwan al-Muslimun 'ala madhbah al-munawara 1928–1986*, Beirut, Dar Azal, 1986.

al-Maliji, 'Abd al-Sattar. *Tarikh al-haraka al-islamiyya fi sahat al-ta'lim 1933–1993*, Cairo, Maktabat Wahba, 1994.

Mardini, Zuhair. *Al-Ladudan: al-Wafd wa'l-Ikhwan al-Muslimun*, Beirut, Dar al-Iqra', 1984.

Muhammad, Muhsin. *Man qatala Hasan al-Banna?*, Cairo, Dar al-Shuruq, 1987.

Mustafa, Halah. *Al-Islam al-siyasi min harakat al-islah ila jama'at al-'unf*, Cairo, Markaz al-Dirasat al-Siyasiyya wa'l-Istratijiyya, 1992.

Na'im, Khalid. *Tarikh Jam'iyyat Muqawamat al-Tansir al-Misriyya 1933–1937*, Cairo, Kitab al-Mukhtar, 1987.

Qa'ud, Ibrahim. *'Umar al-Tilmisani shahidan 'ala al-'asr: al-Ikhwan al-Muslimun fi da'irat al-haqiqa al-gha'iba*, Cairo, al-Mukhtar al-Islami lil-Taba'a wa al-Nashr wa al-Tawzi', n.d.

Radi, Nawwal 'Abd al 'Aziz Mahdi. *Sidqi wa'l-Ikhwan al-Muslimun wa wafd al-Sudan 'amm 1946*, Cairo, al-Matba'a al-Tijariyya al-Haditha, 1988.

al-Rafi'i, 'Abd al-Rahman. *Fi a'qab al-thawra al-misriyya*, 2nd edn, vol. 3, Cairo, Dar al-Ma'arif, 1989.

Ramadan, 'Abd al-'Azim. *Al-Fikr al-thawri fi Misr qabla thawrat 23 yulyu*, Cairo, Maktabat Madbuli, 1981.

—*Al-Ikhwan al-Muslimun wa al-tanzim al-sirri*, Cairo, Maktabat Ruz al-Yusuf, 1982 .

—*Mudhakkirat al-siyasiyyin wa'l-zu'ama' fi Misr 1891–1981*, Cairo, Maktabat Madbuli, 1984.

—*Al-Sira' bayn al-Wafd wa'l-'Arsh 1936–1939*, Cairo, Maktabat Madbuli, 1985.

—*Tarikh Misr wa'l-muzawwarun*, Cairo, al-Zahra' lil-I'lam al-'Arabi, 1992.

Raslan, 'Uthman 'Abd al-Mu'izz. *Al-Tarbiya al-siyasiyya 'inda Jama'at al-Ikhwan al-Muslimin fi al-fatra min 1928 ila 1954 fi Misr*, Cairo, Dar al-Tawzi' wa al-Nashr al-Islamiyya, 1990.

Rizq, Jabir. *Al-Imam al-Shahid Hasan al-Banna bi-aqlam talamidhatihi wa mu'asirihi*, al-Mansura, Dar al-Wafa', 1985.

al-Sa'id, Rif'at. *Hasan al-Banna: mata, kayfa wa li-madha?*, Cairo, Maktabat Madbuli, 1977.

—*Safha min tarikh Jama'at al-Ikhwan al-Muslimin*, Cairo, Sharikat al-'Amal lil-Taba'a wa al-Nashr, 1990.

Shalabi, Ra'uf. *Shaykh Hasan al-Banna wa madrasatuhi "al-Ikhwan al-Muslimun"*, Cairo, Dar al-Ansar, 1978.

Shu'ayr, Muhammad Fathi 'Ali. *Wasa'il al-i'lam al-matbu'a fi da'wat al-Ikhwan al-Muslimin*, Jeddah, Dar al-Mujtama' lil-Nashr wa al-Tawzi', 1985.

Tal'at, Khayri. *Al-Ightiyalat wa'l-'unf al-siyasi fi Misr 1882–1952*, vol. 1, Minya, Dar Hira', 1991.

al-'Ubaydi, 'Awni Jaddu'. *Safahat min hayat al-Hajj 'Abd al-Latif Abu Qurah, mu'assis al-Ikhwan al-Muslimin fi'l-Urdun*, Amman, Markaz Dirasat wa'l-Abhath wa'l-'Amal al-Siyasi, 1992.

al-'Uwaysi, 'Abd al-Fattah. *Tasawwur al-Ikhwan al-Muslimin lil-qadiyya al-filastiniyya*, Cairo, Dar al-Tawzi' wa al-Nashr al-Islamiyya, 1989.

Wizarat al-Maliyyah/Maslahat al-Misaha. *Al-Dalil al-jughrafi*, Cairo, Matba'at al-Amiriyya, 1941.

Zaki, Muhammad Shawqi. *Al-Ikhwan al-Muslimun wa'l-mujtama' al-misri*, 2nd edn, Cairo, Maktabat al-Wahba, 1980.

Published Sources in European Languages

Primary Sources

Five Tracts of Hasan al-Banna (a selection from the *majmu'at rasa'il al-Imam al-Shahid Hasan al-Banna*, translated and annotated by Charles Wendell), Berkeley, CA, University of California Press, 1978.

Six Tracts of Hasan al-Banna (a selection from the *majmu'at rasa'il al-Imam al-Shahid Hasan al-Banna*), Kuwait City, IIFSO, n.d.

Heyworth-Dunne, J. *Religious and Political Trends in Modern Egypt*, privately published, 1950.

Mohi El-Din, Khaled. *Memories of a Revolution: Egypt 1952*, Cairo, AUC Press, 1995.

Sadat, Anwar. *Revolt on the Nile* (a translation of Sadat's memoirs *safahat majhula* (1954) by Thomas Graham), London, Allan Wingate, 1957.

al-Samman, Muhammad Abdullah. 'The principles of Islamic government', *Die Welt des Islams*, vol. 5 (1958), pp. 245–53.

Secondary Sources

Abaza, Mona and Georg Stauth. 'Occidental reason, orientalism, Islamic fundamentalism: a critique', *International Sociology*, vol. 3 (1988), pp. 343–64.

Abdalla, Ahmad. *The Student Movement and National Politics in Egypt*, London, Al-Saqi Books, 1985.

Abdel Nasser, Hoda Gamal. *Britain and the Egyptian Nationalist Movement 1936–1952*, Reading, Ithaca Press, 1994.

al-Abdin, A. Z. 'The political thought of Hasan al-Banna', *Hamdard Islamicus Pakistan*, vol. 11 (1988), pp. 55–70.

Adams, Charles C. *Islam and Modernism in Egypt*, London, Oxford University Press, 1933.

Alexander, Mark. 'Left and right in Egypt', *Twentieth Century*, vol. 151 (1952), pp. 119–28.

Ali, Abdallah Yousuf. *The Glorious Kur'an*, Beirut, Dar al-Fikr, n.d.

Aly, Abd al-Monein Said and Manfred Wenner. 'Modern Islamic reform movements: the Muslim Brotherhood in contemporary Egypt', *Middle East Journal*, vol. 36 (1982), pp. 336–61.

Ansari, Hamid. *The Stalled Society*, Cairo, AUC Press, 1986.

Ansari, Zafar Ishaq. 'Contemporary Islam and nationalism: a case study of Egypt', *Die Welt des Islams*, vol. 7 (1961), pp. 3–38.

Arsenian, S. 'Wartime propaganda in the Middle East', *The Middle East Journal*, vol. 1 (1948), pp. 417–29.

El-Awaisi, Abd Al-Fattah. 'The conceptual approach of the Egyptian Muslim Brothers towards the Palestine question 1928–1949', *Journal of Islamic Studies*, vol. 2, no. 2 (1991), pp. 225–44.

Azzam, Maha. 'The use of discourse in understanding Islamic-oriented protest groups in Egypt 1971–1981', *British Society for Middle Eastern Studies Bulletin*, vol. 13, no. 2 (1987), pp. 150–8.

Baer, Gabriel. 'Egyptian attitudes towards land reform 1922–1952' in Walter Z. Laqueur (ed.), *The Middle East in Transition*, New York, Praeger, 1958.

—'The dissolution of the Egyptian village community', *Die Welt des Islams*, vol. 6 (1959–61), pp. 56–70.

—*Studies in Social History of Modern Egypt*, Chicago, University of Chicago Press, 1969.

Baldick, Julian. *Mystical Islam: An Introduction to Sufism*, London, I. B. Tauris, 1989.

Beinin, Joel. 'Islam, Marxism and the Shubra al-Khayma textile workers: Muslim Brothers and Communists in the Egyptian trade union movement' in E. Burke and I. Lapidus (eds.), *Islam, Politics and Social Movements*, Berkeley, CA, University of California Press, 1988.

Beinin, Joel and Zakariyya Lockman. *Workers on the Nile: Nationalism, Communism, Islam and the Egyptian Working Class 1882–1954*, London, I. B. Tauris, 1988.

Bello, Ilysa Ade. 'The Society of the Moslem Brethren: an ideological study', *al-Ittihad*, vol. 17 (1980), pp. 45–56.

Bensaid, Said. 'Al-watan and al-umma in contemporary Arab use' in Ghassan Salamé (ed.), *The Foundation of the Arab State*, London, Croom Helm, 1987.

Berque, Jacques. *Egypt: Imperialism and Revolution* (translated by Jean Stewart), London, Praeger, 1972.

Bertier, Francis. 'L'Idéologie politique des Frères Musulmans', *Orient*, vol. 8 (1958), pp. 43–57.

Binder, Leonard. *In a Moment of Enthusiasm: Political Power and the Second Stratum in Egypt*, Chicago, University of Chicago Press, 1978.

Botman, Selma. *Egypt from Independence to Revolution 1919–1952*, New York, Syracuse University Press, 1991.

Brown, Nathan. *Peasant Politics in Modern Egypt: The Struggle against the State*, New Haven, Yale University Press, 1990.

—'Peasants and notables in Egyptian politics', *Middle Eastern Studies*, vol. 26 (1990), pp. 145–60.

Burgat, François and William Dowell. *The Islamic Movement in North Africa*, Texas, University of Austin, 1993.

Cantwell Smith, Wilfred. *Islam in the Modern History*, Princeton, N.J., Princeton University Press, 1957.

Carré, Olivier and Gérard Michaud. *Les Frères Musulmans 1928–1982*, Paris, Editions Gallimard, 1983.

Carter, Barbara. 'On spreading the Gospel to Egyptians sitting in darkness: the political problem of missionaries in Egypt in the 1930s', *Middle Eastern Studies*, vol. 20 (1984), pp. 18–36.

—*The Copts in Egyptian Politics 1919–1952*, London, Croom Helm, 1985.

Cohen, Amnon. 'The beginnings of Egypt's involvement in the Palestinian question: some European perspectives', *Asian and African Studies*, vol. 16 (1982), pp. 137–45.

Cooper, Artemis. *Cairo in the War 1939–1945*, London, Hamish Hamilton, 1989.

Crecelius, Daniel. 'Non-ideological responses of the Egyptian ulama to modernization' in Nikkie Keddie (ed.), *Scholars, Saints, and Sufis*, Berkeley, CA, University of California Press, 1972.

Dann, Uriel (ed.). *The Great Powers in the Middle East 1919–1939*, New York, Holmes and Meier, 1988.

Davis, Eric. 'Ideology, social classes and Islamic radicalism in modern Egypt' in S. Arjomand (ed.), *From Nationalism to Revolutionary Islam*, London and Albany, Macmillan and State University of New York Press, 1983.

—'The concept of revival and the study of Islam and politics' in Barbara Stowasser (ed.), *The Islamic Impulse*, London, Croom Helm, 1987.

Dawn, C. Ernest. 'The formation of pan-Arab ideology in the interwar years', *IJMES*, vol. 20 (1988), pp. 67–91.

Deeb, Marius. 'Labour and politics in Egypt 1919–1939', *IJMES*, vol. 10 (1979), pp. 187–203.

—*Party Politics in Egypt: The Wafd and its Rivals 1919–1939*, London, Ithaca Press, 1979.

Denoeux, Guilain. *Urban Unrest in the Middle East: A Comparative Study of Informal Networks in Egypt, Iran and Lebanon*, Albany, State University of New York Press, 1993.

Donohue, John J., and John L. Esposito. *Islam in Transition: Muslim Perspectives*, New York, Oxford University Press, 1982.

Duran, Khalid. *Islam und Politischer Extremismus*, Hamburg, Deutsches Orient Institut, 1985.

Elpeleg, Zvi. *The Grand Mufti Haj Amin al-Hussaini: The Founder of the Palestinian National Movement*, London, Frank Cass, 1993.

Enayat, Hamid. *Modern Islamic Political Thought*, London, Macmillian, 1982.

Eppler, John. *Operation Condor: Rommel's Spy*, London, Futura Publications, 1977.

Esposito, John. *Islam: The Straight Path*, New York, Oxford University Press, 1988.

Gaffney, Patrick D. 'The local preacher and Islamic resurgence in Upper Egypt: an anthropological perspective' in Richard T. Antoun (ed.), *Religious Resurgence: Contemporary Cases in Islam, Christianity and Judaism*, New York, Syracuse University Press, 1987.

Gallagher, Nancy Elizabeth. *Egypt's Other Wars: Epidemics and the Politics of Public Health*, Cairo, AUC Press, 1993.

Gellner, Ernest. *Postmodernism, Reason and Religion*, London, Routledge, 1992.

Gershoni, Israel. 'Arabization of Islam: the Egyptian Salafiyya and the rise of Arabism in pre-revolutionary Egypt', *Asian and African Studies*, vol. 13 (1979), pp. 22–57.

—'The emergence of pan-nationalism in Egypt: pan-Islamism and pan-Arabism in the 1930s', *Asian and African Studies*, vol. 16 (1982), pp. 59–94.

—'The Muslim Brothers and the Arab revolt in Palestine 1936–1939', *Middle Eastern Studies*, vol. 22 (1986), pp. 367–97.

—'Rejecting the West: the image of the West in the teaching of the Muslim Brothers 1928–1929' in Uriel Dann (ed.), *The Great Powers in the Middle East 1919–1939*, New York, Holmes and Meier, 1988.

Gilsenan, Michael. *Saint and Sufi in Modern Egypt*, Oxford, Clarendon Press, 1973.

—*Recognizing Islam: Religion and Society in the Middle East*, London, I. B. Tauris, 1992.

Goldberg, Ellis. 'Bases of traditional reaction: a look at the Muslim Brothers', *Mediterranean Peoples*, vol. 14 (1981), pp. 79–96.

—'Muslim union politics in Egypt: two cases' in E. Burke and I. Lapidus (eds.), *Islam, Politics and Social Movements*, Berkeley, CA, University of California Press, 1988.

—'Smashing idols and the State: the Protestant ethic and Egyptian Sunni radicalism', *Comparative Study of Society and History*, vol. 33 (1991), pp. 3–35.

Goldschmidt, Arthur. 'The National Party from spotlight to shadow', *Journal of Asian and African Studies*, vol. 16 (1982), pp. 11–30.

—*Modern Egypt: The Formation of a Nation-State*, Cairo, AUC Press, 1988.

Haim, Sylvia. 'The principles of Islamic government', *Die Welt des Islams*, vol. 5 (1958), pp. 245–53.

Halpern, Manfred. *The Politics of Social Change in the Middle East and North Africa*, Princeton, N.J., Princeton University Press, 1963.

Harris, Christina Phelps. *Nationalism and Revolution in Egypt: The Role of the Muslim Brotherhood*, Stanford, CA, Hoover Institution Press, 1964.

Hillgruber, Andreas. 'The Third Reich and the Near and Middle East 1933–1939' in Uriel Dann (ed.), *The Great Powers in the Middle East 1919–1939*, New York, Holmes and Meier, 1988.

Hirszowicz, Lukasz. *The Third Reich and the Arab East*, London, Routledge and Kegan Paul, 1966.

Hjärpe, Jan. *Politisk Islam*, Stockholm, Skeab, 1980.

Hourani, Albert. *Arabic Thought in the Liberal Age 1798–1939*, London, Oxford University Press, 1962.

al-Husayni, Ishaq Musa. *The Moslem Brethren: The Greatest of Modern Islamic Movements*, Beirut, Khayat's College Book Cooperative, 1956.

Hussain, Asaf. *Islamic Movements in Egypt, Pakistan and Iran: An Annotated Bibliography*, London, Mansell, 1983.

Ismael, Tareq Y., and Jacqueline S. Ismael. *Government and Politics in Islam*, London, Frances Pinter, 1985.

Issawi, Charles. *Egypt: An Economic and Social Analysis*, London, Oxford University Press, 1947.

Jankowski, James P. 'The Egyptian Blue Shirts and the Egyptian Wafd, 1935–1938', *Middle Eastern Studies*, vol. 6 (1970), pp. 77–95.

—*Egypt's Young Rebels: "Young Egypt" 1933–1952*, Stanford, CA, Hoover Institution Press, 1975.

—'Egyptian responses to the Palestinian problem in the interwar period', *IJMES*, vol. 12 (1980), pp. 1–38.

—'The government of Egypt and the Palestine question 1936–1939', *Middle Eastern Studies*, vol. 17 (1981), pp. 427–53.

Jansen, Johannes J. G. 'Hasan al-Banna's earliest pamphlet', *Die Welt des Islams*, vol. 32 (1992), pp. 254–8.

de Jong, Fred. 'Aspects of the political involvement of Sufi orders in twentieth-century Egypt 1907–1970: an exploratory stock-taking' in Gabriel R. Warburg and Uri M. Kupferschmidt (eds.), *Islam, Nationalism and Radicalism in Egypt and the Sudan*, New York, Praeger, 1983.

Kampffmeyer, G. 'Egypt and Western Asia' in H. A. R. Gibb (ed.), *Whither Islam*, London, Victor Gollancz, 1932.

Kaplinski, Zvi. 'The Muslim Brotherhood', *Middle Eastern Affairs*, vol. 5 (1954), pp. 377–85.

Khadduri, Majid. 'Aziz Ali al-Masri and the Arab nationalist movement', *Middle Eastern Affairs*, vol. 17 (1965), pp. 140–63.

Koshelev, V. S. 'Iz istorii tainykh antibritanskikh organizatisii v Egipte', *Narody Azii i Afriki*, no. 1 (1980), pp. 111–19.

Kotob, Sana Abed. 'The accommodationists speak: goals and strategies of the Muslim Brotherhood of Egypt', *IJMES*, vol. 27 (1995), pp. 321–39.

Krämer, Gudrun. 'History and legitimacy: the use of history in contemporary Egyptian party politics' (paper presented at the Dutch Institute in Cairo), 1987.

—*The Jews in Modern Egypt 1914–1952*, Seattle, University of Washington Press, 1989.

Kupferschmidt, Uri. 'The Muslim Brothers and the Egyptian village', *Asian and African Studies*, vol. 16 (1982), pp. 157–70.

—'Reformist and militant Islam in urban and rural Egypt', *Middle Eastern Studies*, vol. 22 (1986), pp. 403–18.

Laban, Abdel Moneim. 'Der islamische Revivalismus: Ablauf der Bewegung der Moslem-Brüder', *Die Dritte Welt*, vol. 6, no. 3–4 (1978), pp. 446–71.

Lawrence, Bruce. 'Muslim fundamentalist movements: reflections toward a new approach' in Barbara Freyer Stowasser (ed.), *The Islamic Impulse*, London, Croom Helm, 1987.

Lia, Brynjar. 'Imposing on the past the order of the present: a critical analysis of Hasan al-Banna's autobiography *Mudhakkirat al-da'wa wa al-da'iyah*' (paper presented at the British Society for Middle Eastern Studies (BRISMES) 1995 Annual Conference).

—'The use of history in Egyptian party politics', *Midtøsten Forum*, vol. 2 (1995), pp. 38–43.

de Luca, Anthony R. '"Der Grossmufti" in Berlin: the politics of collaboration', *IJMES*, vol. 10 (1979), pp. 125–38.

Malik, Hafeez. 'Islamic political parties and mass politicization', *Islam and the Modern Age*, vol. 3 (1972), pp. 26–64.

Marsot, Afaf Lutfi al-Sayyid. *Egypt's Liberal Experiment 1922–1936*, Berkeley, CA, University of California Press, 1977.

Marston, Ella. 'Fascist tendencies in pre-war Arab politics', *The Middle East Forum*, vol. 25 (1959), pp. 19–34.

Mayer, T. 'The military force of Islam: the Society of Muslim Brethren and the Palestine question, 1945–1948' in E. Kedourie and S. G. Haim (eds.), *Zionism and Arabism in Palestine and Israel*, London, Frank Cass, 1982.

Miloslavsky, G. 'Assotsiatsiya Brat'ev-Musulman v Egipte', *Strany Blizhnego i Srednego Vostoka* (1972), pp. 97–110.

Mitchell, Richard P. *The Society of the Muslim Brothers*, London, Oxford University Press, 1969.

Mousalli, Ahmad S. 'Hasan al-Banna's Islamist discourse on constitutional rule and Islamist state', *Journal of Islamic Studies*, vol. 4 (1993), pp. 161–74.

Nicosia, Francis R. J. 'Arab nationalism and National Socialist Germany: ideological and strategic incompatibility', *IJMES*, vol. 12 (1980), pp. 351–72.

Rodinson, Maxime. *Marxism and the Muslim World*, London, Zed Publications, 1979.

Rosenthal, Franz. 'The Muslim Brethren in Egypt', *The Moslem World*, vol. 37 (1947), pp. 278–91.

Sabit, Adel. *A King Betrayed: The Ill-Fated Reign of King Farouk of Egypt*, London, Quartet Books, 1989.

Safran, Nadav. *Egypt in Search of Political Community*, Cambridge, MA, Harvard University Press, 1961.

Sansom, A. *I Spied Spies*, Harrap, London, 1965.

Smith, Charles. 'The crises of orientation: the shift of Egyptian intellectuals to Islamic subjects in the 1930s', *IJMES*, vol. 4 (1973), pp. 382–410.

Tignor, Robert L. *State, Private Enterprise and Economic Change in Egypt, 1918–1952*, Princeton, N.J., Princeton University Press, 1984.

Tripp, Charles (ed.). *Contemporary Egypt through Egyptian Eyes: Essays in Honour of P. J. Vatikiotis*, London, Routledge, 1993.

Utvik, Bjørn Olav. 'Islamism: digesting modernity the Islamic way', *Forum for Development Studies*, vol. 2 (1993).

—'Filling the vacant throne of Nasser: the economic discourse of Egypt's Islamist opposition', *Arab Studies Quarterly*, vol. 17 (1995), pp. 29–54.

Vatikiotis, P. J. *The Modern History of Egypt*, London, Weidenfeld and Nicholson, 1969.

—*Nasser and his Generation*, London, Croom Helm, 1978.

Warberg, Lasse A. 'De islamske fatwaer – noen rettslige momenter', *Midtøsten Forum*, vol. 2 (1994), pp. 54–7.

Warburg, Gabriel R. and Uri M. Kupferschmidt (eds.), *Islam, Nationalism and Radicalism in Egypt and the Sudan*, New York, Praeger, 1983.

Weber, Max. *The Theory of Social and Economic Organisation*, New York, The Free Press, 1966.

—'Legitimacy, politics and the State' in William Connolly (ed.), *Legitimacy and the State*, Oxford, Basil Blackwell, 1984.

Wild, Stefan. 'National Socialism in the Arab Near East between 1933–1938', *Die Welt des Islams*, vol. 25 (1985), pp. 147–70.

Winder, R. Bayly. 'Islam as the state religion: a Muslim Brotherhood view on Syria', *The Muslim World*, vol. 44 (1954), pp. 215–26.

Wynn, C. Wilton. 'The latest revival of Islamic nationalism', *The Moslem World*, vol. 38 (1948), pp. 11–16.

Youssef, Hasan. 'The democratic experience in Egypt, 1932–1952' in Ali Hillal Dessouki (ed.), *Democracy in Egypt: Cairo Papers in Social Science*, Cairo, AUC Press, 1978.

Zaalouk, Malak. *Power, Class and Foreign Capital in Egypt: The Rise of the New Bourgeoisie*, London, Zed Books, 1989.

Zubaida, Sami. *Islam, the People and the State: Essays on Political Ideas and Movements in the Middle East*, London, I. B. Tauris, 1993.

Index

Society of the Renaissance of Islam
(Jam'iyyat Nahdat al-Islam)
46n.29
Society of Supporters of Muhammad's
Tradition (Jam'iyyat Ansar
al-Sunna al-Muhammadiyya)
142
Special Apparatus (military wing of the
Society of Muslim Brothers)
6, 162, 177–81, 256, 270–1,
277n.121, 285
Spencer, Herbert   78
sports   170, 244
Stack, Sir Lee   177
Stellbogen, Wilhelm   179, 180
student movement of the Society of
Muslim Brothers   162, 163–4,
181–6, 196n.96, 224–7
Sudan   155
Suez, Rover Scout camp in
193n.26
Suez Canal Company   41, 261
Sufism   25–6, 37, 38, 45n.17, 54,
59–60, 114–19, 174, 286
al-Sukkari, Ahmad Effendi   48n.56,
206, 261–2
branches of the Society of Muslim
Brothers and   42, 43
education and   68, 138
formation of the Society of Muslim
Brothers and   35
internment of   181, 222, 263,
264, 265
Sulayman, Muhammad Effendi   40
Sultan, Hajj Muhammad   22
Summer Team for Preaching and
Guidance   164–5, 166
Syria   154, 155, 156, 158n.36

Tahir, Muhammad Ali   179
Tall Bani Tamim, Society of Muslim
Brothers branch in   121–2n.8
Tanta
Religious Institute in   267

Society of Muslim Brothers branch
in   121n.5
Tantawi, Shaykh Jawhari   97,
123n.29
taxation   210, 213
Taymur Pasha, Ahmad   29, 47n.32
Teachers' Syndicate   212, 229n.48
al-Tha'libi, Abd al-Aziz   237
al-Tiftazani, al-Sayyid   116
al-Tilmisani, Umar   5, 222
al-Tir, Shaykh Mustafa   145n.14
Tripp, Charles   5, 276n.99
Tukh, Society of Muslim Brothers
branch in   122n.17

al-'Uluwwiya, Society of Muslim
Brothers branch in   122n.8
Umar Tusun, Prince   29, 137, 138,
238
Union for Economic, Political and
Islamic Studies   185–6
urban areas, migration to   74
al-Urfi, Shaykh   23
Uthman, Abu Zayd   221

Wafd Party   189, 201, 203–4, 209,
216
as government   6–7, 249, 258,
268, 269
military wing   177
Muhammad's Youth and   248
Palestinian Revolt and   237
Society of Muslim Brothers' alliance
with   11, 221–2, 223, 249,
268, 269
socio-economic characteristics of
9, 189, 201
youth movement   132, 168,
181–2
Wajdi Bey, Farid   29, 30, 47n.34
al-Wasita, Society of Muslim Brothers
branch in   122n.19
Weber, Max   114–15
welfare societies   29–30, 54–60